The Five Pillars of Happiness

Your new life step by step

Dave Robson

29.5.2012.

To Claire,

Hope you get a lot out of this. Enjoy...

All the best,

Dave Robson.

Wizard Publishing

First published in Great Britain by Wizard Publishing in 2010

ISBN 9780955021039

Typeset by Hope Services (Abingdon) Ltd.
Printed in Great Britain by CLE Print Ltd. St Ives. Cambridgeshire

The publishers are grateful to:
Barbara James for editing and proofreading.
Paul Dunning for cover design.

Published By:

Wizard Publishing
(An imprint of Gilbert Massara Publishing)

www.wizardpublishing.co.uk

Contents

The Roof
Happiness

About the Author

Dave's philosophy in a nutshell: *'The answer's yes, now what's the problem?'*

In 1982, facing imminent divorce, homelessness and the inevitable collapse of every other aspect of his life, Dave realised he had to reinvent himself.

He spent many years practicing different meditations, experiencing therapies, groups and workshops; much of it under the guidance of the late Indian Guru, *Osho*. Finally Dave's life began to look up.

Living true to yourself is Dave's basic tenet. He received his certificate in Life Coaching from *The Coaching Academy* in 2004. As a highly experienced life coach, Dave pioneers meditation as a powerful coaching tool; a process through which his clients have achieved spectacular results. He has collected tools, techniques and wisdom from over 40 years on his path of personal development, the most powerful of which he shares in these pages.

Dave runs a fortnightly meditation group and also produces *Namaste*, his free monthly e-newsletter for people who want to live more consciously. Recently he founded the *Pen and Ink Club*, an informal writers' group as well as maintaining his lively Blog site and Twitter following. Further details of these can be found via the web addresses in the bibliography. Dave's other passions include sailing and woodturning.

List of exercises

An asterisk (*) indicates there is a form you can download for the exercise.
Please visit: www.thefivepillarsofhappiness.com

Acknowledgements

I am eternally grateful to the many people who have inspired my life and thereby the material in this book. I only have room to name a precious few of them:

To the memory of my grandparents, ***Emanuel and Harriet***, who taught me absolute integrity

To my late father ***Joe,*** who taught me that love is always the answer

To my beloved mother ***Charlotte,*** who instilled in me the spirit of freedom and rebellion, and the urge always to think for myself

To my wonderful partner ***Rachella,*** who understands everything and stands by me through thick and thin

To my fantastic brother ***Jeremy,*** a shining role model of following your creative passion, come what may

To my beloved son ***Daniel,*** a wonderful example of choosing you own path and going for it, whatever the cost

To our absolutely adored and recently deceased golden Labrador ***Chutzpa,*** for a never ending demonstration of unconditional love, acceptance and for giving us all a shining example of how a life should be lived

To my beloved late teacher ***Osho,*** who gave me the courage to believe in myself

To all my courageous ***clients,*** for being such brilliant teachers

To my publisher ***Gilbert*** for believing in me enough to put his time and money where my beliefs are

And lastly to ***Existence,*** for giving me a sense of wonder, and the qualities of humility, perseverance, determination and grit

Dave Robson
London, July 2010

How this book works

This book is designed to propel you into a hands-on, practical process that will enable you to create the life you want, step-by-step. I have used the metaphor of building a house with five pillars to represent the building that is your new life, and the process of building it. The book is divided into three parts. The first part symbolises ***The Foundation,*** the second part represents ***The Five Pillars*** and ***The Roof,*** while the third part takes you ***Beyond Goals*** to a whole new dimension.

At times it's a bit like a jigsaw puzzle with each chapter providing new pieces – you may only begin to get a sensible picture once you have got a fair number of the pieces. To follow the building process through from start to finish will take some persistence on your part but the rewards will be well worthwhile, for when you take a thorough, holistic, step-by-step approach starting from square one, as we do in this book, the life you learn to build will endure.

In the first part we lay a solid foundation by explaining the basic principles and many of the key concepts upon which this process rests. It contains many powerful tools and exercises that will prove invaluable as you get underway with the exciting adventure of building your new life *exactly* as you want it to be. They will support and guide you all the way on your journey and help you develop the attitude you need for success.

In the second part we begin building the five pillars one at a time, each one adding an essential dimension to the new life you are creating. Finally, with a sense of completion, the roof, our crowning glory, is fitted and your new life is up and running.

Many readers will be happy to stop there, but for those who are interested in some additional commentary to add yet a deeper perspective to your inspiring new life, the third part takes you beyond goals on a further journey into the spiritual realms of true meaning and purpose.

The journey towards our goals can be just as fascinating and important as the goals themselves, and in many ways sometimes the journey is the goal. For that reason, I hope you don't forget to enjoy your journey ...

The Five Pillars of Happiness

The model gives you an overview of a methodical, step-by-step process in which you build yourself a harmonious, balanced, productive, joyful, peaceful and fulfilling life in which you are tuned into your flow. You will start by building a firm foundation, and then, one by one, the five pillars are added.

Finally, the roof virtually fits itself as an integrated, sustainable structure emerges.

We all of us already have within ourselves everything we need to be happy, fulfilled, creative and at peace. The paradox is you don't have to achieve anything,

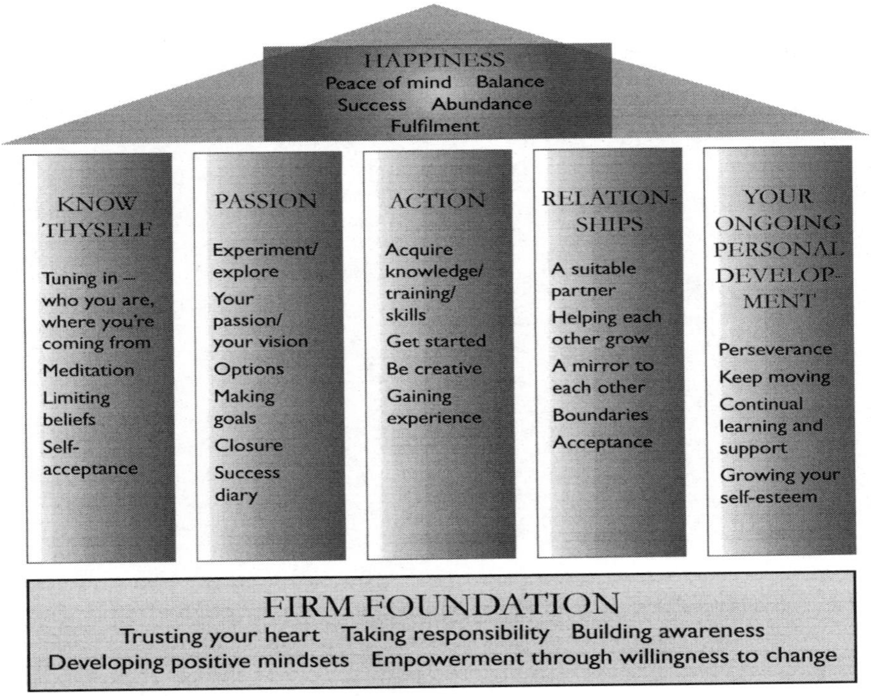

HAPPINESS
Peace of mind Balance
Success Abundance
Fulfilment

KNOW THYSELF
Tuning in — who you are, where you're coming from
Meditation
Limiting beliefs
Self-acceptance

PASSION
Experiment/explore
Your passion/your vision
Options
Making goals
Closure
Success diary

ACTION
Acquire knowledge/training/skills
Get started
Be creative
Gaining experience

RELATIONSHIPS
A suitable partner
Helping each other grow
A mirror to each other
Boundaries
Acceptance

YOUR ONGOING PERSONAL DEVELOPMENT
Perseverance
Keep moving
Continual learning and support
Growing your self-esteem

FIRM FOUNDATION
Trusting your heart Taking responsibility Building awareness
Developing positive mindsets Empowerment through willingness to change

it's simply a question of allowing yourself to come to your natural balance, because there are no other resources you need. You have everything already within yourself.

The work in this book will help you shift your perceptions so you can bring out, organise and focus your innate gifts and resources and thereby awaken the lion within.

When you do that there is no limit to what you can achieve.

Introduction

Happiness is not an accident…

Happiness is not an accident, it's something we can consciously choose. To be more accurate, it's a series of positive choices that continue for as long as we wish to remain happy. When I say 'positive' I mean choices that align with our core values and beliefs. In other words, you are being absolutely true to yourself and conducting your life only in ways that have real meaning for you.

Here's an example of what I mean. One of my clients is passionate about nature conservation and saving endangered species but he was doing a job he hated and it began making him ill. Eventually he found the courage to give up his job as a financial advisor and created a charity devoted to conserving endangered animals. He now does the work he loves passionately and, even though he works longer hours, every one of those working hours seems worthwhile to him.

What I am talking about is in essence a spiritual journey but with very tangible, physical manifestations and applications in real life. It doesn't matter what your goals or aspirations are, nor what obstacles might appear in your way. The aim of this book is to help you navigate your way through them until you get to live the life you want.

Imagine springing out of bed on a Monday morning and actually feeling excited about the day ahead – or even better, feeling excited about the whole of your life ahead! That kind of fulfilment happens every day for the person I mentioned above, and it can happen for you too when *your* life takes on meaning and purpose.

When you live every day in harmony with your purpose you might think you have died and gone to heaven. You haven't – on the contrary, ***YOU'VE BECOME FULLY ALIVE!***

The first thing we need to understand when trying to make our lives the best they can be is that all our experiences are the results of our own actions, choices or beliefs, they are our *interpretations* of what happens to us. To put it another way, everything we encounter in the world around us is a direct reflection of whatever we are carrying inside. So the first step is to accept and take responsibility for that. The only alternative is to remain one of life's many victims, and that's not an appealing prospect.

So why is it we so often sabotage ourselves? It can only be due to a lack of awareness. In other words, all too often we don't actually notice what we are doing, thinking, feeling or believing. We act on autopilot, taking our beliefs for granted, assuming them to be true without question. This is the heart of the matter. It is the choices we make that we are not aware of which often sabotage our best endeavours, no matter how hard we might work at creating what we want.

That is why happiness begins with stopping and listening very carefully to what's going on inside. If you don't like your life and you want it to be different, obviously you have to make changes. But herein lies a danger because all too often we rush into formulating hasty, ill thought out goals that come from our conditioning or our egos, and not from our hearts. If you do that, you may be happy for a short while, but that happiness won't be sustainable.

First golden rule

Here's my first golden rule: *if you want to be sure the changes you are making are right for you, you first need to get to know yourself inside out.*

Developing a happy life is like building a house. This book aims to give you the tools, know-how, skills, materials, understanding and even the blueprint you need, then it's down to you to customise the design and get on with the building. The concept of the five pillars will give you a firm framework with plenty of guidance and support so the building process can be an enjoyable and fascinating one. However, the proof of the pudding is in the eating, as they say, which means the result is every bit as important as the journey.

The following two exercises are designed to kick-start your journey, to get you in the mood and start you flying straight away. If you're really, really serious about finding happiness, I highly recommend you don't just read the exercises in this book – get a pad and a pen and *do them all.* They are all tried and tested many times over and I promise you they will benefit you enormously, either straight away or in the long run.

Exercise 1: Are you ready?

(If you don't want to write in this book, you can download and print the exercise from www.thefivepillarsofhappiness.com)

Are you ready?

Before you embark on your new life quest I want you to take a piece of paper and put the date at the top. Then write down the following four questions and answer them. Alternatively, download and print the page below, which has the questions already on it, from our website. Don't forget to fill in the date. Be totally honest and write each answer as spontaneously as possible. Don't think about any of the questions for more than 30 seconds:

- Will you do whatever it takes to deal with your issues and start to succeed?
- Are you ready to formulate meaningful goals that come from your heart?
- Would you relish a new start on a radically different path to achievement?
- Do you love practical results with tangible benefits?

Now imagine a scale of 1 to 10 for each question, where 1 is very low and 10 very high. Where on that scale do you see your answer? For example, if your answer to the first question is 'I think I probably will do what it takes, but I'm feeling a bit wobbly about it,' you might give yourself a score of let's say 5 or 6. Write the score out of 10 next to each question. Then add up the total, which will be something out of 40, and write it at the side.

Now ask yourself another question:

- What would have to happen, or what would I have to do, for me to nudge this score up a little bit higher?

Write down your answers and put the paper in a safe place for reference later.

By pondering the last question you automatically start to develop an attitude for success, and by writing down the question and the answer you greatly reinforce its effect. This will be a recurring theme – instead of berating yourself because your situation is not as good as you would like, simply focus on how to improve it. It's a neat trick of the mind, very subtle and very powerful. If you remember to keep applying this principle in all situations, you'll be amazed at how differently you start to feel in a remarkably short time.

The reason for dating the exercise is so that you can do it regularly at, say, two monthly intervals and compare the results to see if there has been any change.

There is no right or wrong, only the truth about how you feel matters, so don't judge yourself harshly or beat yourself up if you get a low score. Also always remember it doesn't matter what others think – you are doing this for you.

Exercise 2: The meaning of happiness

(If you don't want to write in this book, you can download and print the exercise from www.thefivepillarsofhappiness.com)

THE MEANING OF HAPPINESS

There's one more vital question to ponder as you embark on your journey of self-discovery:

- What exactly does happiness mean to you?

Only by answering that question can you begin to know what elements you need to assemble to start building your foundation. What does your happy life look like and what does it contain? Only your heart knows the answers. They are to be found only through deep introspection, witnessing and visualisation. The following chapters will show you many ways you can conduct that inner search.

Commitment

Finally, a few words about commitment. I get awfully fed up with books (or coaches) that promise quick fixes. This process takes as long as it takes and each person has his or her own chosen speed. There can be no right and wrong timescale and no self-judgement. That is not meant as an excuse for dallying or doing nothing. The only thing that matters is your commitment and the love in your heart.

If you want your life to have meaning and purpose, fulfilment, balance and happiness, you need to be sure your goals are sincerely conceived in your heart. This is important because fulfilment comes from one place and one place only – your heart. This also means making the shift from spectator to participant.

At first this prospect might seem scary or uncomfortable, but it's exciting too. You will learn to identify and drop lifelong sabotaging behaviour and begin to trust your innate wisdom to guide you into new ways that support your aspirations. It may sound like a paradox, but by relinquishing hard and fast control, you end up completely in control, but in a relaxed and stress-free way, as I hope you will see.

In this book we analyse in depth what sabotages our happiness and come up with feasible strategies to stop ourselves doing that. However, strategies alone change nothing. The only way your life changes can come about is through your action, so I suggest at the outset you start to cultivate a 'can do' attitude. Forgive me if as times my manner seems a little harsh and uncompromising but it's important I continually thrust responsibility for your life onto you, the reader, because this is not a rehearsal, and no-one can do this for you. Take heart, this is your chance to shine!

Come on! There is much to take on board and much to do, so let's get cracking …

Summary

- Happiness is not an accident, it's something we can consciously choose
- When you live every day in harmony, *you've come fully alive!*
- Our experiences are the results of our own actions, choices or beliefs, they are our *interpretations* of what happens to us
- Much of the time we act on autopilot, taking our beliefs for granted and assuming them to be true. This leads to us making choices we are not aware of that can sabotage our best endeavours
- Happiness begins with stopping and listening carefully to what's going on inside
- The process takes as long as it takes and each person has his or her own chosen speed. There's no right and wrong timescale and no self-judgement. The only thing that matters is your commitment and the love in your heart
- It doesn't matter what other people might think – you are doing this for you
- You need to be sure your goals are sincerely conceived in your heart
- Fulfilment comes from one place and one place only – your heart
- It is necessary for you to make the shift from spectator to participant
- The only way your life changes can happen is through your action, so cultivate a 'can do' attitude right from the start

First golden rule

- If you want to be sure the changes you are making are right for you, you first need to get to know yourself inside out.

Exercises to find out where you are at

Exercise 1: Are you ready
Exercise 2: The meaning of happiness?

PART ONE

We begin with a discussion to help us understand why building a foundation of personal awareness is essential, and the importance of trusting your heart if you are going to feel truly integrated and balanced in all aspects of your self, no matter what direction you take in your life. Other crucial issues that come under the microscope in this part include being true to yourself, and making a positive mindset your new habit.

These underlying principles apply to every aspect of your life and will stand you in good stead whatever your goals or aspirations might be.

1

Trusting Your Heart

Who looks outside dreams, who looks inside wakes
C.G. Jung

The heart/mind balance

Too much thinking is an absolute killer. Too much thinking leads to what coaches call *analysis paralysis.*

Excessive thinking sabotages your authenticity, your spontaneity, your ability to take action, your creativity, your *joie de vivre* and your sense of purpose. It suppresses your spirit and keeps you in a state of confusion and unable to function effectively – in short it destroys everything that leads to a joyful, spontaneous and happy existence on this beautiful planet of ours.

The only things that too much thinking nurtures are procrastination, indecision, self-doubt, fear, feelings of failure, low self-esteem, negativity and depression. So if over-thinking is your pattern, might I first suggest you reduce your thinking and start *feeling* and *acting* instead.

The fact that you are reading this book suggests you have had enough of self-sabotage in your life and you are coming to a point where you would like to learn to focus on the positive and start to enjoy your life. That's where I can help, but first we must understand the basic principles at work here.

I am not saying there is anything wrong with proper use of thinking, the mind, the intellect or our mental powers. What's important is to recognise that *your mind is a powerful tool to be used as and when appropriate.* Like all powerful tools it can hurt you, even destroy you, if it's allowed to take over, but in skilled hands it can be used to build something beautiful. Most of us feel insecure, hence the unconscious obsession by our minds of wanting to be in control, and that can be a problem because some of the mind's programming or conditioning produces unconscious negative, sabotaging behaviour. That's why it is essential for you to become its master and to relegate your mind to its rightful role of your obedient servant, a situation in which it can support you excellently and prove itself immensely valuable.

Your mind is so indescribably powerful it can and will manifest anything. Therefore, rather than leaving things to chance, it's almost certainly going to need retraining so it produces the effect you want. Imagine you are a builder. When you master the techniques for using the correctly adjusted tools at the right time there's no limit to what you can accomplish, but a chainsaw in untutored hands can chop your leg off.

The conditioning, or programming, of your unconscious mind begins at birth or earlier, perhaps even at the moment of conception. In simple terms, when a child is born, the unconscious part of its mind is like a blank slate. Nothing is written on it, except some inherited basic instinctive behavioural commands. For example, when perceiving danger or experiencing fear, you are already pre-programmed to prepare to fight or run away. The unconscious can also be likened to a sponge because it soaks up any input that comes its way indiscriminately.

That's the problem. The unconscious mind cannot make value judgements, meaning it can't tell between right or wrong, positive or negative, supportive or counter-productive. In effect, it just accepts all the material that comes in and makes beliefs out of it. For example, imagine you are a schoolchild whose father, meaning well but not realising the damage he might be doing, tells you to work harder, or you have a teacher who says you could do better at maths. You might well grow up believing 'I'm lazy' and 'I'm no good at maths,' either or both of which could be blatantly untrue.

The reason why this matters is because beliefs like this limit you and make you feel bad about yourself unjustifiably, and that obviously makes it much harder to enjoy life and achieve what you want. Even worse, such beliefs might screen from you the very things you most want without you realising it.

That's what I mean when often I talk about distinguishing between your own inner voice, which comes from your very essence, and the voices of your conditioning. The latter – the voices of your conditioning – are entirely constructed by your unconscious mind from outside input mingled with your interpretations, which in turn may derive from earlier input. To go back to the example above, in your heart you might love maths, and you might be as happy as a sand boy with a career as a mathematician, scientist, engineer or accountant. However, if you believe you're not good at maths you are likely to avoid these paths and pursue instead something you are not so good at. The net result is you avoid something you might love in favour of something you don't love. Crazy or what?

When we begin to understand the mechanics of this game so many of us play unconsciously, it comes as no surprise that under such circumstances inner conflict is inevitable and happiness and fulfilment virtually impossible.

The only way to successfully counter this mind-dominated tendency to act from your conditioning is to become aware of it. When that happens you will begin to realise that these conditioned beliefs actually have nothing to do with you. *They are not part of the real you.* To use our hypothetical maths example just one more time, if you consciously stop and listen you will hear your heart telling you to get involved in the world of mathematics in some way, and that *is* coming from the real you.

This is a vital concept to understand and take on board if you are serious about wanting to set yourself free, by which I mean *free to be who you are.*

It is because in many cases our unconscious minds are so heavily conditioned with negative beliefs coloured by our negative perceptions, leading to neurotic, self-sabotaging behaviour, that this reprogramming of the unconscious needs to take place. We do ourselves an injustice if we blame ourselves, however, for this situation is inevitable. We've all had a version of this problem at one time or another, it's part of the human condition.

Much of the work in this book is about identifying what needs changing and doing the associated reprogramming. It is necessary because *everything that happens to us and all that we manifest depends entirely on our mindset or perceptions.* When we change our mindset our whole outlook, experience and behaviour changes. As Aldous Huxley said: *'experience is not what happens to us, but how we interpret what happens to us.'*

In the Western world much emphasis is placed upon the virtue of developing our minds, with the result that most of us are mentally far too over-stimulated. Our education system heavily emphasises cerebral development and as a result we learn to rely on our minds to solve our problems, even to work out how we feel! But often solutions have nothing to do with our minds, so it is little wonder so many of us feel confused and frustrated.

Your heart, on the other hand, seems to be either a much underrated and underused tool, or it is completely mis-used and misunderstood. At the very least the efficacy of your heart as a powerful tool in its own right is widely underrated. Sometimes our heart and mind come into conflict and there can be an almighty internal power struggle which only serves to stoke up the inner conflict many people in this situation experience. We can learn which one to listen to at any given moment, and we can teach the mind and heart to work together in a harmonious state of balance.

In my experience that's the only answer to this tumultuous state of affairs. We must work to find a balance between heart and mind, to hone both of them so they become keen instruments we can use appropriately. Then we can take a step back so we can keep everything in perspective. In this way we can always trust our judgement to select the right mix of tools for any situation while heart and mind work as a team.

To be able to do this, first we must embark on an inner journey to find out who we really are.

Your inner journey

If you are with me so far a multitude of questions now arise, such as just how do we conduct this inner journey to find out who we really are, and why do we need to know who we are anyway?

There are many ways of conducting the journey within and another of this book's primary aims is to provide some answers to that question. One powerful way is via meditation, but more about that later. The inner journey is such an immense undertaking the only way to approach it without feeling overwhelmed is to take it one step at a time. First I want to explain in a little more depth why we should take this inner journey. There are some basic principles for us to bear in mind:

Principle number 1: *Your inner voice, which metaphorically speaking is the mouthpiece of your heart, is the greatest, the most dependable, the most trustworthy friend and* *guide you will ever have. It will never let you down or lead you astray, it always knows the truth about what the real you needs. When you learn to go inside and tune in to that still, small voice and trust it's guidance through thick and thin, the doors to your creativity are flung open and your life can really start to take off. Following the calling of your heart fills you with the courage you need to find and follow your true path, whatever the cost. In this respect your own heart is your ultimate Life Coach and finding the courage to trust and follow it's guidance without question is the journey.*

As many of us have already found out, the journey within has its joys and its pitfalls. It's not something to embark upon lightly and it's not for the chicken-hearted. But what does that mean with regard to our daily lives? What are the full implications and why do we need to make this inward journey?

It's very simple. It's because *everything we need is within.* We need only to understand how to perceive and access it, and it all comes from our heart. You may not believe me at this stage, in fact you may be totally out of touch with what I am saying and you may even vehemently deny it. Deep down inside, however, you know the following must be true: *whether we begin by looking on the outside or by looking on the inside doesn't matter, because sooner or later, if we want to set ourselves free, the journey within has to commence.* It is inevitable because only your heart, your inner voice, knows who you are and what you need. Therefore, if you want fulfilment, balance and happiness, what your heart is whispering to you needs to become your number one avenue of enquiry.

'Hang on a minute,' I hear you exclaim. 'First you say everything is dictated by your mindset and now you're saying it all comes from your heart. What on earth are you talking about?'

Well, in the words of countless Jewish sages throughout the ages, 'you're right, but also I'm right too!' Let me try to explain this conundrum: if we can enable our minds to step aside and let our hearts speak, we will be easily able to understand what we need and want. Of course the process of communicating the messages your heart sends out has to be facilitated through your mind, but the messages must be allowed to come through pure and unadulterated. We don't want your mind to re-interpret them and colour them with its conditioning. That's what the concept of the mind being a faithful servant is about. It must become a conduit or channel that carries the messages from your heart. I call this quality of heart-driven guidance when objectively conveyed by the intellect *emotional intelligence.*

Self-sabotaging behaviour patterns

Let me conjure up an imaginary situation of the sort that often happens in real life. Imagine you are a young man and you see a beautiful woman at a party. First your heart takes a leap as you recognise a powerful attraction, but then immediately your mind jumps in, saying, 'Hmmm, she looks terrific, I wonder if I can sum up the courage to talk to her … oooh she might be married … oooh she wouldn't want to speak to me anyway … oooh she might think I'm too eager …' etc. None of this is in the least bit helpful and of course, it's pure fabrication. Your mind has immediately taken over and created imaginary obstacles, fears and assumptions that now stand in the way of your heart's intention. You have, in effect, created problems out of nothing.

It is hugely significant that your heart took a leap as you instinctively recognised the attraction. That should speak volumes to you, but did you consciously notice it or did you quickly, unconsciously, dismiss it or stuff it down? Your heart spoke loud and clear but did you listen? In a case like this, which would you say is better to listen to, your mind or your heart? What you have allowed your fearful mind to do is to make it far more difficult for you to approach the woman.

You will never know if she's married, available, wanting to speak to you or thinking you're too eager unless you find the courage to approach her, and courage comes from your heart. Perhaps last time you spoke to a woman you were rejected, so you unconsciously fear it's certain to happen again. *But you don't know if this is true until you put it to the test.* In this kind of situation, if you listen to what your mind is telling you, you are immediately sunk without trace because your mind typically produces fear and insecurity – the exact opposite of courage. However, if you allow yourself to be guided by your heart, many possibilities can open up.

It's vital to develop the habit of being alert to these signals or they are immediately lost. That's why it's important to build your conscious awareness.

Your inner journey will enable you to begin to see the self-sabotaging patterns of behaviour created by your unconscious mind by bringing conscious awareness to your unconscious habits. It's like shining a light into a darkened room. With awareness you can see scenarios like this as soon as they start developing, and then you can consciously choose to switch to more constructive behaviour instead.

So what's the alternative to this inner journey? As we saw in the introduction, the only alternative is to bumble on in a state of unconsciousness and incomprehension, suffering as Shakespeare says 'the slings and arrows of outrageous fortune.' In such a frame of mind, life happens to you while you lurch from one crisis to the next, or you carry on in a state of boredom, despair and mediocrity doing and being something that will never properly fit with who you are. In life we have two choices. We can be either a participant or a spectator. You can make things happen or you can remain a victim. Which will you choose?

An essential ingredient for forging the life you want is to be proactive. That means you have to take initiatives. You have to make things happen. But first it's vital to understand yourself. What makes you tick? What exactly do you want? What do you need to change? You may not know the answers at the beginning, but you can certainly make a start and gradually increase your self-understanding as you go along.

What we have discussed so far is important because it explains why what we *think* we want and need is not always the same as what we *really* want and need. Furthermore, it matters that whatever we do is congruent with our core beliefs and values. If not, no matter how brilliantly we achieve our goals, we merely set ourselves up for more conflict, anxiety, stress and guilt.

My antennae really come out on stalks when I hear someone say, 'life's so hard,' or 'life's a bitch,' as if 'life' has a mind of its own and is out to get you. Life, or existence, doesn't 'do' anything, it just 'is.' Life is not something out there that you can touch, see, hear, smell or taste, it's a quality within you. We choose how we shape it, but our conditioning colours our view if we let it. Blaming 'life' for negative outcomes that you have manifested is a supreme abdication of personal responsibility and that's a cop out. And in this book, cop out's are not an option!

'How do I know whether to believe you?' someone asked me once.

What or whom you believe is up to you. I just tell it like it is. I've been there myself, on the negative side, blaming life and other people for my misfortunes. Then, fortunately for me, when I decided I had suffered enough and became thoroughly fed up with seeing myself as one of life's victims, I decided to join the side of the people who were enjoying life. Gradually I learned to trust my heart and to take personal responsibility for everything that happened to me. Also, in my work as a Life Coach, I have seen my clients going through a similar process many, many times. When you learn to trust your heart you are then in a position to ask yourself, 'does this have the ring of truth?' Yes or no, you know you can believe the answer. None of this is rocket science – it's obvious when you learn not to think to destruction.

Have you ever wondered why every person on this planet has a different life story? You might try to put yours down to circumstances, but it has been demonstrated time and time again that *we make our circumstances and we can change our circumstances.* The first part of that message always applies, whether you like it, or know it, or not. The second part only works if we take personal responsibility for making the changes we require.

Here's another crucial principle:

> **Principle number 2:** *By raising our level of conscious awareness, we empower ourselves to actually change our behaviour despite the conditioned messages in our unconscious minds, if we are completely willing and committed to making those changes. That's because it is absolutely possible to create a positive, supportive mindset based on new, positive conditioning – conditioning that we consciously choose – that assures us of a full and balanced life.*

Facilitating the above is, in a nutshell, the reason for taking your inner journey.

I once had a client who was seriously depressed and angry. Whenever I confronted him with a view to working through his angst to free himself of it he became acutely defensive and said:

'Hey, just a minute Dave, can't you see it's not my fault that I'm like this? Don't you think I have every right to feel like this?'

'Yes, of course I can see it,' I replied. 'It's not your fault. So now what are we going to do …? We're stuck. Of course you have every right to remain a helpless victim for the rest of your life and spend every waking hour licking your wounds, if that's what you want to do.'

'But I don't want to be like this,' he wailed. 'Aha,' I replied, 'as soon as you realise that *and mean it,* you have a fighting chance. That's a great first step, but now you must go further or you're stuck at step one.'

Imagine if you were addicted to smoking and you claimed it was not your fault and you wanted to give it up. Would you expect me or someone else to give up smoking for you? Can you give up smoking by proxy? There is only one way to give up smoking and that is to *decide* you really want to give up smoking, and then stop doing it. I emphasise the word 'decide' to highlight the fact that your stopping smoking is within your power and no-one else's. The same principle applies to all our issues, challenges and desires – you have to take personal responsibility for every change or achievement you want in your life, or it simply isn't going to happen. You don't necessarily have to do it alone – for example you could consult a hypnotherapist to help you stop smoking, The point is you have to acknowledge you have a problem, take responsibility for finding appropriate help, and use it for a positive outcome.

So here's the $64,000 question: *if you don't like the state you're in, what are* ***you*** *going to do about it?*

As Dr. Phil McGraw points out in his book, *Life Strategies*, 'people do what works and it's a good idea to identify the payoffs that drive your behaviour and that of others.' He also says, 'the behaviour you choose creates the results you get.' Right on brother! Absolutely true!

From the above we can deduce that if you don't like the results you are getting and you don't understand why you are getting them, the behaviour that created them is unconsciously driven. That means you are going to have to find out what you are doing unconsciously to sabotage yourself and *change your thinking and your behaviour.* Incidentally, this also implies that when we engage in self-sabotaging behaviour it's for a 'good reason'. There's always a payoff if we did but realise it.

In the case of the client I mentioned earlier, it became clear after much probing that deep in his heart he didn't really want to change. For him, the prospect of letting go of blame was far too scary, though of course he would never admit that openly. The payoff was having a golden excuse for abdicating any responsibility for his situation.

He unconsciously believed it allowed him to remain the same without feeling too badly about himself. It was as if clinging to his anger and helplessness was a sort of comfort zone from which he was reluctant to emerge. In fact I distinctly had the feeling he came to see me so he could say to himself he'd tried everything, even Life Coaching, and it hadn't worked. Now he could blame me and Life Coaching for not 'fixing' his alleged misfortunes and his depression.

The prospect of taking a stand must have been too scary and too painful I suppose. All the above behaviour, and the payoff, was, of course, unconsciously motivated. He did not consciously realise the game he was playing, even though I clearly mirrored it back to him.

By maintaining his helplessness he could feel vindicated in remaining welded to his depression. It was a brilliant unconscious strategy if ever I saw one, and powerfully self-sabotaging. Unfortunately he used the strategy to make quite sure he remained stuck for good – unconsciously of course. Needless to say no amount of Life Coaching, therapy or anything else would ever make any difference unless he declared himself ready to step up, look at himself in the mirror and make some real changes.

So although there's a perceived payoff, it's not real because the price of remaining in your so-called comfort zone in a case like this means being caught forever in pain and anxiety. If you are unaware you don't realise this and remain in a state of bewilderment. Only by raising your awareness can you cotton on to what's really happening and elect to do something different that supports you.

When you read about such behaviour it seems ridiculous, but many people behave like that or in equally self-defeating ways all the time. More often than not they are completely mystified as to why their lives don't work as they would wish. If you see yourself in any of the cases I describe, I hope you will begin to understand just how destructive it can be to remain unconscious and unaware.

Consider for a moment this insightful comment from Albert Einstein: 'we cannot solve our problems with the same thinking we used when we created them'.

Please note Einstein says *we* created them (our problems) with *our* thinking. Our problems did not arise out of nowhere and they we not thrust upon us. He also implies *we* can solve them by changing *our* thinking. This is a vitally important principle for all of us who strive for emotional and psychological liberation, and it's very empowering. *If we have problems, we must take responsibility for the fact that we created them ourselves. Then we are empowered to un-create them by discovering what we were thinking, and then changing our thinking.*

Many people take refuge in the known and the familiar and find comfort in beliefs, no matter how apparently bizarre, that confirm their negative self-image. This is because challenging your self-image can make you feel intolerably insecure – or at least, that's the fear. You fear you won't know who you are any more. This can have destructive consequences. For example, if you believe you are not worthy of love, you are very unlikely to attract someone who will love you, and if someone tries to get close you will unconsciously push them away so you can feel vindicated in believing you are not worthy. There's a perverse sense of security to be had from that, but of course it keeps you lonely. As is so often the case, the payoff has a price. With awareness you can ask yourself, 'is it worth it?'

Another client was convinced he was a useless salesman, despite on the surface wanting to be successful. The results he got, to the chagrin of his manager, were zero sales and this served to confirm his belief that as a salesman he was a failure. On one level this enabled him to rest in his comfort zone, but it was short-lived for soon he was sacked. So then he adopted a substitute comfort zone by playing the unfortunate, hapless victim. By sacking him, his boss had 'proven' my client's belief that he was an inept salesman. This made him even better able to play the game called 'poor me,' a commonly deployed unconscious strategy to ensure people would feel sorry for him and say it was not his fault because he 'couldn't help it.'

Again and again he was able to confirm his negative beliefs about himself and have the perfect excuse to avoid taking responsibility for changing anything. Seeing himself as victimised allowed him to feel vindicated and gave him a quasi sense of identity so he didn't feel quite so insecure. I use the word 'quasi' because if he had been honest with himself, deep down in his heart of hearts, this man knew he was evading an uncomfortable truth.

He would have been true to himself and everyone around him had he admitted the simple truth – he was not remotely interested in being a salesman and the idea of success in that field left him cold. Not only that, but the idea of trying to sell to someone simply terrified him, so he avoided even trying. To recap, all this was happening on an unconscious level, which is why he was mystified as to why he always felt undermined and could never seem to get motivated. He would have been better off either to acknowledge his fear and then try selling, or get another job that didn't involve selling. But then he might have been successful, and he would have had to change his self-image. He would no longer have any credibility as a victim.

Only by waking up and witnessing his patterns of self-sabotaging behaviour could this man have any hope of creating a fulfilling life.

All of which leads us neatly to one last important principle:

> **Principle number 3:** *Blaming others or even yourself never gets you anywhere. Blaming is a device politicians and others use for avoiding personal responsibility. Only when you start to take personal responsibility for your life and everything in it (without beating yourself up) does positive change become a possibility.*

Regularly during the course of one-to-one coaching sessions with clients, similar unconsciously held negative beliefs emerge. In every case they are guaranteed to ruin a person's life. Some common examples are, 'I'm not worthy,' 'I'm not good enough,' 'I'm a failure,' 'I'm unlovable,' and so on in various versions. Negative self-beliefs are very common and I repeat, if you hold on to them they will ruin your life unless you wise up to what's happening and do something about it.

Returning to our salesman for one final moment, it is also important to realise that his problems had nothing to do with his job but with the fact that he did not want to change his negative perceptions of himself, a prospect far too scary. He had a vested interest – fear – in remaining stuck. But what was he afraid of? After considerable probing he finally realised he found comfort in the known and the familiar role he had created for himself, however unpleasant. It was like an old pair of slippers. He feared if he started making changes and coming alive now, he might not know who he was any more.

It's very easy to unwittingly set yourself up for failure if you are not aware of what's going on inside. Unconscious behaviour of that sort tends to ruin your life if you carry on with it. They say the truth hurts but in my experience the pain of facing the truth

is short-lived, whereas the effects of unconscious sabotaging behaviour hurt far more and for the whole of your life. We fear what we expect will be painful, and that's why it requires courage to unearth and face the truth about ourselves and make the changes we want. That's what Susan Jeffers meant when she coined her famous phrase, '*Feel the fear and do it anyway*'.

Here's an ironic truth that might be helpful: when you realise the deleterious effect your unconscious behaviour is having on your life, you can benefit from this discovery by understanding, by deduction, that you are on the wrong path. Strange though it may seem, it is not always apparent to an unaware person when they are on the wrong path, or that they could create a more fruitful and enjoyable one. You can use the gradual awakening of your awareness as your cue to re-invigorate your inner search for your right path. More about 'your path' later.

Quite often I will ask clients, when they finally begin to realise what's stopping them, 'are you going to let a little bit of fear stand in the way of making your dreams come true?'

It's not only fear. If you want to be genuinely happy, fulfilled and stress-free, any kind of repressed feelings are bad news because, although you might think you have them under control, they will always come back and bite you when you're not looking. Anger is a classic example of an emotion which, when deeply suppressed, can lead to depression, violence, addictions and all sorts of sabotaging behaviours. Far better to go inside and uncover the feelings, however scary, and let them be expressed. Let them have their moment. Then it becomes possible for them to pass so they evaporate out of your system leaving you free and unburdened. More about expressing emotions safely and effectively in later chapters.

If only our misguided salesman could have found the courage to embark on his inner journey, he might have understood what he was doing to himself. He could have gathered more insight into the conflict between his heart and his unconscious mind, a battle that was constantly being played out in his uncomprehending conscious mind. All he seemed to know of it was turmoil and torment though he never really understood why, or what he could do about it. Saddest of all, he was unable to see he was the author of his own misfortunes, yet armed with awareness he could have written himself a happy ending.

Your maximum creative flow

This seems like the perfect moment to introduce my concept of your *maximum creative flow*. How do you know when you are in your *maximum creative flow?*

It's one of those things where, if you have to ask, you're not in it. It is like a love affair, when you're in it you can't mistake it. When you become so absorbed in the moment you are in, when whatever you are doing or being comes straight from your heart and your self-doubt and other mental sabotaging processes set themselves aside, everything just flows and seems to happen easily. In that moment you are functioning from your heart and everything you create seems to flow through you as if you are merely a conduit, a vessel for giving birth, as if the finished object has nothing to do with you. It's as if it has come from a higher place. It has come unimpeded from your heart via your creative imagination, a state in which you are at your most creative. That's being in your *maximum creative flow.*

A great example of this is the renaissance artist Michelangelo who said he never sculpted anything but was able to see the figure in the lump of marble and his job was merely to release it by chipping away the extraneous material. It was as if the figure created itself and he was merely the facilitator. As he chipped and chiselled away, his creativity flowed through him as if he were a conduit, and the sculpture would appear.

This never happens when you try to do something you hate, you don't feel drawn to or you don't have a talent for. For example, if you find yourself doing a job just for the money but you couldn't really care less about it, there is no way you can flow. At best your day will be boring, at worst, a nightmare – either way it's pointless. On the other hand, let's say you are someone who feels compelled to be an actor and you are trying to make a name and establish a career merely because you love acting and the theatre. Even at the start of your career, when poverty is your constant companion, there will be moments when you are on that stage when the past and future disappear, you are in the moment and everything comes easily. In a case like that, assuming you have the talent and you are creatively expressing a burning desire in your heart, you experience the profound satisfaction that only comes when you flow.

Whether or not you become rich and famous is irrelevant. When you are in your flow, your life has meaning and you feel fulfilled. You are fulfilling your life's purpose by expressing your passion to the full. You have become utterly creative and your life is worthwhile because of what that means to you. A situation like this is the exact opposite of our unwilling salesman who, by refusing to change, refuses to flow.

The Indian mystic Osho puts this very poetically:

'It is only in the moments of deep creativity that the ego disappears, time disappears, space disappears. And it is only in the moments of total absorption in a creative act that one merges into the whole. It is ecstatic to be creative.

What you create does not matter, the product is not important but the act of creation is. It is not a question of whether you become a Picasso or you remain an unknown painter. It does not matter whether you create great sculpture or you are just a poor potter; it doesn't matter at all. When I am saying be creative my whole emphasis is on the very act of creativity, not on what it produces.'

Because most of us have become so dependent of figuring everything out mentally and have cut ourselves off from the whisperings of our hearts, it is common for many of us to be unaware of our passions or callings. Occasionally I get a client sitting in front of me claiming he has no passions, talents or even interests. I just don't believe it. *Each person has a unique contribution to make even though they might not know it.* It might be ever so humble, like sweeping the streets, but if you have it in your heart to give your neighbourhood clean streets you'll be amazed how happy and flowing you can be if you let yourself do it.

Only by finding your unique gift can you hope to flow. If you still insist you don't know what your gift is, then your inner journey is even more essential. This journey within is a gift to you, a portal into understanding your mysterious inner workings.

If you are feeling lost, dazed, confused or overwhelmed by too many choices, your inner journey can help you rediscover your passions, talent, calling, vocation, gift, aptitude, call it what you will, and any one of these is your surefire route to your creativity. If you stop, listen and witness the clues that come from within, you let your heart make the choices for you.

This is why it is not always a good idea to set goals right at the start of the coaching process. Better to get a thorough knowledge and understanding of yourself first. Otherwise it's very easy to rush off and achieve the 'wrong' goals. Wrong goals are those which do not accord with your passions and core values but with your conditioning or your ego and therefore they do not allow you to flow. Such achievements never lead to long-term happiness, peace, balance or fulfilment. For many people it is first necessary to discover the goals that are right for them, so it pays to pause awhile and listen intently to your inner voice.

Here's a great tip – when things aren't going quite how you want and you can't figure out why, look to your mindset and ask yourself, 'is there flow in my life?' If the answer is 'no' then you know for sure you need to take a look inside and ask your heart for guidance.

I realise you may feel overwhelmed with information overload right now but please do not despair. Soon I hope my step-by-step approach will enable you to start seeing a way though this process to a happier and more fulfilling life.

Summary

- Too much thinking leads to *analysis paralysis*
- Your mind is a powerful tool to be used appropriately, but first it almost certainly needs reprogramming
- Your mind is so powerful it can and will manifest anything
- When we change our mindset our whole outlook changes
- The unconscious is like a sponge, it soaks up any input that comes its way
- Your conditioned beliefs have nothing to do with the real you. Learn to identify your self-limiting beliefs so they can no longer hold you back
- Learn to distinguish the voice of your heart from the voices of your conditioning
- Your own heart is your ultimate Life Coach
- Everything we need is within and it all comes from your heart
- We create our circumstances and we can change our circumstances
- If you don't like the state you're in, what are *you* going to do about it?
- The behaviour and beliefs you choose create the results you get. Wake up and notice what you are choosing and believing
- It's very easy to unwittingly set yourself up for 'failure' if you are not aware of what's going on inside
- Each person has a unique contribution to make
- Your inner journey can help you rediscover your passions, talent, calling, gift or vocation
- For many people it is first necessary to discover what's right for them before they start setting goals
- If there is no flow in your life, you know you need to look inside to hear the guidance of your heart

Fundamental principles

1 *Your inner voice, the mouthpiece of your heart, is the greatest, the most dependable, the most trustworthy friend and guide you will ever have. Your heart is your ultimate Life Coach.*

2 *By raising our level of conscious awareness, we empower ourselves to overwrite the conditioned messages in our unconscious minds, making it possible to create a positive, supportive mindset that assures us of a full and balanced life.*

3 *Blaming others or even yourself never gets you anywhere. Only when you start to take personal responsibility for your life and everything in it (without beating yourself up) does positive change become a possibility.*

2

Building Your Self-awareness

Don't ask what the world needs, ask what makes you come alive, and do that. Because the world needs people who have come alive

Harold Whitman

To briefly recap, the essential key to success with any kind of personal development work, goal achievement, psychotherapeutic or spiritual healing process, is the understanding that increasing your personal awareness has to be your top priority and number one commitment. This is especially true if happiness, fulfilment and a sense of meaning and purpose are ultimately your most important goals. There are many reasons for this and they will become apparent as this book unfolds.

There are lots of ways of achieving this heightened personal awareness, and this chapter describes some of them.

You are not your story

For centuries mystics and enlightened masters have been using the device of insisting their students ask themselves time and time again the key question, *'who am I?'* Today this question is just as essential as it ever was for the many of us who have simply lost touch with who we *really* are. It's important to note this distinction: who we *really* are is not necessarily the same as who we *think* we are or who we *think* we *want to be.*

Many of us have also lost touch with what we *really* need and want. Again this is not necessarily the same as what we *think* we need and want, or *think* we *ought* to need and want.

Only when you fully experience who you really are and give yourself permission to be your authentic self, can you properly relax and flow. The act of allowing yourself to be who you really are, and to be seen as being that person, is a gesture of trust in yourself. It's important to understand that if you don't have that trust it can be developed, as you will see later. For the moment, let's just be clear about the rules of the game, for an unambiguous understanding of these basic principles is vital to building a solid foundation for your new life.

When we were babies we knew exactly who we were and what we wanted and were not afraid to be our authentic selves. When a baby is tired, hungry or in need of a nappy change, he or she cries, anywhere and in any situation, loud and long and without inhibition, and it's amazing how most mothers know what the problem is by recognising intuitively the exact nature of the crying. However, as we grow older we learn 'good behaviour' or behaviour designed to facilitate tactical survival and we forget the art of direct communication.

If you cannot put your hand on your heart and say, in all sincerity, that you know who you are, how on earth are you going to create meaningful goals for yourself? Goals that, when achieved, will bring you the happiness, fulfilment, balance, peace of mind and the freedom that you crave? And how can you flow creatively unless you know the true nature of the creative streak you have inside that longs to be expressed?

Unless you know the essence of the real you, how can your life be anything other than a series of unconscious reactions to your conditioning, your self-beliefs (limiting or otherwise) and your perceptions? Many of these, especially the negative ones, almost certainly have nothing to do with the real you.

This is the primary reason why building your self-awareness is so important. Without awareness you blunder on unconsciously trundling out the same old habitual, obsessive and sabotaging behaviour, based on the same old conditioned beliefs, and your life becomes a succession of knee-jerk reactions. When you become fully aware of what you do you empower yourself to make new choices, and the possibility arises of changing the behaviour, beliefs and decisions you don't want any more. You can take a step back to get a better perspective. You are now empowered to see just how counter-productive your conditioned behaviour and beliefs can be if they remain unchallenged, and how they can ruin your life. Once you are able to see them objectively for what they really are, it becomes possible to let them go.

In the previous chapter we noted that your conditioned beliefs have nothing to do with the real you. Now here's another aspect of this – *you are not your story*. Let me explain by sharing something I witnessed once:

it happened when I went to a gathering with Catherine Ingram, an 'awakened' spiritual teacher from the USA, and at first I was shocked.

A man near the front of the room, no doubt hoping for some sympathetic feedback from Catherine, was pouring his heart out describing his tragic life story which, he implied, was at the root of his unhappiness. Catherine cut him off suddenly, saying, *'I'm not interested in your story'* as if to demand to know what was really going on with this person on a deeper level. At the time it seemed a bit brutal but later I realised exactly why she did that. Everyone has a story, but if we allow ourselves to identify with ours, to adopt it, to indulge in it, to analyse its minutiae, to continually regurgitate it, to let it define our present and future behaviour, to believe it is responsible for how we are now, we almost guarantee that nothing will ever change. We will remain stuck in victim mode indefinitely.

Don't most of us have a tendency to do just that? We say, 'it's not my fault I'm like this, someone else is to blame.' It's as if we wear our misery like a worn-out but much loved old coat. Well that's OK if you don't want to change, grow, heal, and get over being stuck in the pain of the past. However, if you want to start enjoying a fruitful life, sooner or later you have to drop the habit of using your story to define who you are and move into the world of current reality. That, among other things, entails finding out who you *really* are – not in the past, not sometime in the future, not somewhere else, but *right here, right now.*

Unfortunately, many people fear that if they were to find their real self, the person they would discover might be perceived as unacceptable, not only to others and the world at large, but also to themselves. Because this is potentially so frightening, these same people adopt a strategy of denial that never really works. They tend to run away from self-discovery, hoping they can hide in the past or in a world of fantasy and delusion. This pattern almost always operates on an unconscious level, therefore only by developing an awareness of what they do can they choose to make changes.

What then is reality? According to many masters and mystics there is no reality, there is only our perception, and after much reflection and life experience I am inclined to agree with them. The good news is, we choose our perceptions (for example, is the glass half empty or half full?) Once you really get that message you can choose happiness, fulfilment, fun, beauty, love, acceptance, excitement, or whatever. You can stop blaming, change the record and start to re-engineer your life. In that sense *you can actually choose and manifest whatever reality you want.*

Prem Rawat, the Indian 'man of peace', put it another way when he said: 'people say to me we need more peace in our world. I say no, *you* need more peace in *your* world.'

No doubt Catherine Ingram's abruptness was intended as a wake up call to those in the room that day because none of us has any time to waste. *If you want to become a fully integrated person, you need above all a strong sense of who you really are.* Your story is incidental.

'Who am I?' is a powerful question you can ask yourself to propel you on your inner journey to find the true, original, pure and unadulterated 'you', not the 'you' that is a product of your conditioning. Be assured, no matter how lost, buried or hidden you might fear it is, the 'original you' is still in there, deep inside.

Of course the 'who am I?' question cannot be answered in words, but the individual asking the question can experience a powerful sense of 'Self'. The answer resides within your heart so, as we discussed earlier, listening to your heart is the thing to do if you want that answer. This is so important I want to reiterate – *it is essential to know the 'real you' and to make that 'real you' conscious, because only the 'real you' knows what you need and want. Only by bringing the 'real you' back out into the light can it sparkle again like it used to when you were a tiny child.*

It follows that once you begin to experience who you really are, that is the perfect time for deciding on more serious goals. This way you can create heartfelt goals as opposed to ego-driven goals, goals which are entirely in tune with your core values, ethics and beliefs. *These are the only goals which, when achieved, will give you lasting fulfilment.*

If you are someone who has lost touch with your inner voice and don't know who you are any more, you are going to need powerful tools to facilitate this inner journey. The following exercise is one such powerful tool.

Exercise 3: Tell me who you are?

TELL ME WHO YOU ARE?

Find a close friend or confidante to work with and sit down together in private, in a quiet room or in a peaceful corner of your local park or woods. One of you elects to be person A, the other is person B. Sit on chairs, cross legged on the ground or on cushions, facing each other very closely.

Person A says to person B: *'Tell me who you are?'* and then sits in silence while person B responds. Person B is given exactly five minutes to speak while person A keeps track of the time. Then it's the other person's turn and person B asks person A the same question. Person A then gets exactly five minutes, timed by person B, in which to speak while person B sits in silence.

Then you swap again and have two more turns each, so each person gets to speak for three turns of five minutes each within the space of half an hour. At that point you both take a break and resume later with further half hour sessions if you wish.

It's very important that the person listening remains silent and, if possible, impassive, without verbal reactions or visually expressed judgements. The exercise can be even more powerful if you refrain from discussing it afterwards. I have known may people do this exercise and they all tell me how valuable it is to feel listened to at a deep level and without judgement, and indeed what a rare phenomenon that is. So if you are the person listening, remember this is your gift to your partner so concentrate intently and *let your listening be total and unconditional.*

At first the person invited to talk will probably start with fairly superficial observations such as a physical description, for example, *'my name's Dave, I live in London, I'm a Life Coach and I'm five foot eight.'* Soon the speaker will run out of these rather obvious characteristics, which amount essentially to a description of his or her *persona* or outer appearance, and will be obliged to start digging more deeply for answers. So the next phase might sound like this – *'I love travelling in warm countries and meeting new people, I'm very keen on Thai food and I love my car'.* So in this hypothetical example Dave is now beginning to talk about his feelings and is no longer just giving a physical description.

Eventually, perhaps by his third invitation to speak, Dave will have to start looking even more deeply within for answers and may start talking about his passions and what really makes him tick. He might even start to mention pet hates, things that make him angry, things that make him sad or happy, things that get him excited and things he certainly does not want in his life, for example *'I absolutely adore sailing, and writing is one of my greatest passions. Yes, that's it, I love writing. I hate politics, religion and committees. I don't like being told what to do, I'd much rather find out for myself, even if it's slow and painful.'*

Can you see how this exercise powerfully moves both participants to focus more and more deeply into the core essence of who they really are, what they really want to do, be and achieve? It's well worth investing the time in doing it.

Just one final reminder – don't fall into the trap of analysing. Just tell it like it is and accept whatever emerges.

At this point I want to recount a sailing story that serves as a perfect metaphor to illustrate this point. One late afternoon in September some years ago as the sun was setting and casting pastel colours all around the beautiful Hampshire countryside, I sailed into the Lymington River and tied up at Lymington Town Quay. Minutes later I was standing in front of the bar in the riverside pub gazing at a cool lager before me in pleasant anticipation of its restorative and recuperative powers. Then my gaze fell upon a man sitting on a stool next to me sipping a pint, and I started talking to him. It turned out he was an officer in the Royal Navy and part of his job was to take young raw recruits on adventurous and challenging sailing trips on large yachts, especially on transatlantic crossings.

'So why,' I asked him, though I already knew the answer full well, 'does the Royal Navy spend taxpayers' money sending young lads off on sailing holidays when we all know that naval ships are propelled by engines these days, and not sails?' He answered me with three words, three words that rang through my brain, three words that have stayed with me ever since, three words that explained everything. 'Sailing changes people' he said. And indeed it does. But why? And in what way?

Well for a start when you go ocean sailing you have to become far more self-sufficient than most of us would ever dream of on land. Also, there will be many times when you are called upon to dig deep inside yourself to find inner resources you never knew you had, physically, mentally, emotionally and spiritually. Many times you will be a long way out of your comfort zone, maybe for prolonged periods, and you will have to embrace the unknown and the unexpected on a regular basis, and deal with every fear that arises.

Even when things are going well, on a three to six week passage you are going to have extended periods of intense aloneness, even on a fully-crewed boat, and that's the real challenge. You are going to get to know yourself far better than you could ever imagine. Will you like what you see? For most novice sailors their biggest fear, though they might not know it, is not the relentless sea, storms, darkness, whales, physical exertion, uncomfortable conditions, minimalist food, sea sickness, or other perceived dangers; it's that they might not like what they see of themselves in moments of aloneness.

When you are out on that big wide ocean, issues of self-acceptance, self-esteem, self-belief and self-confidence are going to confront you and there will be no choice but to allow them to be processed through your heart and mind. At home, most people are in the habit of putting enormous efforts into avoiding or suppressing these issues. In truth, sailing doesn't change people, instead it helps them reveal who they really are, to discover the stuff they are made of. The persona dissolves while the real person comes through so it appears the person has changed, but in fact they have reverted to being their authentic self.

This is a powerful phenomenon and that's why it takes a certain type of person to go sailing or do any other activity that incorporates serious personal development. Here's the real challenge and it's not the wind and the waves: *If you are going to make it a positive experience, you are going to have to raise your conscious awareness about what you do, think and feel, and like it or not, you will soon begin to know precisely who you are. When that happens, you will start to feel more comfortable with yourself.*

Now to travellers on the path of personal development who want to achieve a perfect balance between mind, body, spirit and emotions, this matter is of great interest because getting to know who you are is the essential starting place in feeling more relaxed and confident and really coming alive.

Of course you don't have to go sailing to experience this. You could go mountaineering or travelling alone, or whatever. There is another powerful way to experience your authentic self that is accessible to everyone and its called *meditation*. When you meditate, especially in silence and with no distractions, your inner journey invites you to make a start. You have no choice but to face whatever comes up because there is nowhere to go, nothing to do and nothing to distract you. If you persevere, after a while the initial turmoil in your mind begins to settle down and you start to get brief instances of stillness through which you can begin to glimpse who you really are.

All of the above summarises why, in my estimation, it is probably fruitless, perhaps even counter-productive, to start setting goals until you begin to know who you are and learn to listen to yourself. And that's why I approach Life Coaching as a long-term process. (Chapter

5 is devoted to the subject of meditation and gives details of the simple method I have developed.)

Exercise 4: Trespasso

TRESPASSO

Another powerful tool for allowing the 'real you' to be revealed is called *Trespasso*, from the Spanish word meaning 'an exchange.' The exercise was devised and developed in the 1960s by the Bolivian born Oscar Ichazo, a personal development pioneer who started experimenting with this at the awareness camps he organised in Arica, Chile. He subsequently went on to form The Arica Foundation in 1968, now headquartered in Connecticut, USA.

As in the previous exercise, Trespasso is done with a willing partner and you sit face to face closely in front of each other. Then both parties simply sit in silence gazing into their partner's *left* eye while at the same time reciting internally and silently the mantra *'holy love'* over and over again. It is important to emphasise that each partner looks into the other person's *left* eye, not both eyes and not the right eye, and that the mantra is recited internally, not spoken aloud.

Most people report that the effect, after a minute or two, can be described as metaphorically looking directly into the other person's heart and soul. Each participant seems to see right through their partner's persona to directly what is underneath. It could be beauty, tranquillity, a loving nature or whatever, but all to often what we see in the other is a lot of pain. If that's what is really there under the person's persona, so be it.

More important, the person on the receiving end of your gaze is allowing themselves to be truly seen, maybe for the first time since they were a baby. This seems to be the visual equivalent of being truly heard as in the previous exercise. They are being received with unconditional acceptance by you, and at the same time you are receiving the same phenomenon from them. It truly is a heart to heart exchange and the effect can be profoundly healing.

Sometimes when doing this exercise one partner finds it very difficult to accept the other person's gaze. Allowing themselves to be truly seen and revealed is simply too painful and frightening. If that happens to you or your partner, don't worry about it, don't brand yourself 'a failure,' simply observe and learn from the experience how strongly defended you are and how powerfully you cling to your persona so you can hide behind it. It's an important learning.

Having done the above two exercises, *Tell me who you are?* and *Trespasso,* for perhaps the first time in your adult life you have been both heard and seen unconditionally by another. Could these perhaps be the first two steps towards loving and accepting yourself unconditionally? Don't take my word for it, try the two exercises and see what happens. If you approach everything in life as if it were an experiment, you will always learn something at the very least, and that will help you grow your awareness, insight and understanding.

Balance and your maximum creative flow

We make a mistake if we take ourselves too seriously, for then we run the risk of becoming obsessional. Balance in all things is what I aim for. The reason I stress balance is because I spent much of my early life missing my flow and as a consequence existing in a state of disharmony and imbalance. The resulting turmoil, struggle, conflict, stress and anxiety this created, troubled me greatly for many years.

Obsessional behaviour is the exact opposite of balanced behaviour and very often when a person gives up one type of obsessional behaviour they swing to the other extreme and pursue the opposite obsessional behaviour. This is especially common when dealing with addictions but is by no means exclusive to them. Going to an opposite extreme simply replaces one stress-creating situation with another. It's not until the person comes back towards the middle and finds the exact point where they feel balanced that they can relax, gain a calming perspective and get on with being who they are.

Not only that, but self-acceptance depends on finding that inner balance in all aspects of your life, because to accept yourself unconditionally, you have to feel comfortable and at home with yourself. You can't do that when you are obsessing and getting stressed and anxious.

Achieving balance, by the way, does not mean becoming boring, dull or sedentary. On the contrary, if you are a dynamic person, your dynamism will shine out unhindered and hit its target far more often and far more effectively, producing stress-free, satisfying results. In short, your energy will be far more efficiently targeted so you can develop spectacular results, perhaps even miraculous. Moreover, if you are someone who has always been thwarted despite your sincerest efforts, arriving at a place of balance will help you ignite your dynamism and rediscover your enthusiasm.

Perhaps the most powerful tool for achieving this balance is developing the art of witnessing, a subject discussed in detail in Chapter 5 which focuses on meditation.

My ultimate goal has always been peace of mind, balance and a life of fulfilment, and that's why I was drawn towards making a long inner journey in a quest to find out who I was and what made me tick. You could describe it as the ultimate spiritual journey to discover and express my higher self, which may be how it turned out, but that's far too pretentious and contrived a description for someone who was stumbling blindly like I was.

In truth, I had no idea where I was going or how long it would take. I didn't consciously know why I was doing it, or even how to go about it. Somehow I just knew I had to travel within to find the answers I was seeking. I finally discovered that this state of balance and absence of inner conflict in which I find myself most of the time nowadays is actually very ordinary and simple. It's the exact opposite of contrived, pretentious, pompous or clever. That's why it feels so relaxing. With self-acceptance the need to pretend and to maintain a defensive persona no longer arises.

Things get done more easily now and life *flows* like a river because I do what I love doing. There is now very little 'pushing' of the river, and the doings of day-to-day life feel like the most normal and natural thing in the world.

Renowned social entrepreneur and wealth consultant Roger Hamilton describes this as 'the way of least resistance', which it is, though I prefer to describe it as the path of *maximum creative flow*. Why miss out the all-important creative element, and why not make it an active state? This is a state in which whatever you want from deep in your heart comes to you easily.

There are two ways of achieving goals. One is to use up all your energy chasing after them, like most of us do especially in our early working years. That's fine when you are young and bristling with energy, ambition and ego, for being stressed is just part of the game and you feel driven to 'prove' yourself. However, most people find this kind of frenetic activity ultimately unsustainable and it doesn't usually bring much long lasting joy, often only ego gratification, failure, or burnout.

The other way, which is far more subtle and genuinely exciting, is to get into your *maximum creative flow* and allow your goals to come to you. That way you can relax and rejoice as you give and receive full-heartedly in this bountiful world of ours. It's obviously a far more satisfying state of affairs.

Take the example of business mogul Sir Alan Sugar. If you watch his antics you will notice that Sir Alan, although he might express anger momentarily, rarely seems to get stressed or flustered. On the contrary, he appears to be totally comfortable to be seen to be exactly who he is, completely in his flow and hugely enjoying the power games he plays with big business. If you want to flow in the world of big business, Sir Alan might be a good role model for you.

They say that we end up teaching the very thing we most need to learn, and I'm sure that's why I took up Life Coaching. I love showing people how they can find the courage to be propelled by their flow and replace hard work with creative enterprise which is exhilarating, vital, more fascinating and easier to achieve as each day unfolds. That's not to say we can drop all responsibility for making things happen – far from it, when we are in our flow we become more proactive than ever.

Many years ago a friend offered to pay me to take him out on my boat for a few days to teach him sailing. We agreed the amount and off we went. When the trip was almost over he pulled out his chequebook and started writing.

'It doesn't feel right taking your money because I haven't done anything except enjoy myself,' I said to him.

'Nonsense,' was his immediate rejoinder. 'Not only have you done everything you said you would do, but you've gone out of your way to teach me as much as possible, to make sure I enjoyed myself and to look after me beautifully in every way.'

'But that's no more than any skipper worth his salt would do for any friend or crew member,' I replied.

'Stop arguing,' he replied. 'We have an agreement and now it's my turn to stick to my side of the bargain. In fact, not only am I writing you a cheque, but I'm going to make it out for more than we agreed because I enjoyed myself so much. I'll be very offended if you refuse.'

'OK, thank you very much,' I finally agreed meekly.

It was obvious this was a powerful gesture coming from someone I knew to be extremely hard up and possibly one of the most frugal people I have ever known. I had simply shared what I love doing and somehow I had touched his heart simply by doing my own thing.

The really strong lesson I got from this incident was a sudden realisation of how, somewhere along the line, I had picked up the notion that 'work' equals something arduous, unenjoyable, energy draining, serious, non-creative and joyless. To put it another way, unconsciously I believed that an activity that raises my spirit and makes my heart sing can't be defined as 'work' for it does not have sufficient gravitas.

My reward for facilitating so much pleasure for my friend was not only money but a strong wake-up call that led me to completely re-evaluate the attitude, mindset and limiting beliefs regarding work that I now realised I had unconsciously adopted. Of course teaching sailing can be hard work, but for me it comes naturally. There is no resistance, only flow when I'm out on the high seas, so while it is tiring it is also energising. Channelling your energy into work that comes from your heart is a joyful way to go and it certainly leads to sleeping well at night, insomniacs please note.

I hope this anecdote illustrates what I mean about not trying to control outcomes. We want to get paid for our work because we have to eat and support ourselves and our families, so to that extent we engineer a controlled outcome. However, by offering work based only on what comes from your heart, once you have established the deal you can just focus on doing what you want to do, what you love doing and what you are good at to the best of your ability. And very often unpredictable additional rewards will come flooding in.

'Be realistic, plan for a miracle,' said Osho, the Indian mystic I went to see in 1982. He also said, 'relax and let god possess you.' How right he was! This is all about letting go of trying to control every outcome while instead allowing a profound spontaneity to take over. Trying to be in control in the sense of expecting and insisting on a particular result is so exhausting and anxiety provoking. Letting go lets you find and enter your flow and opens the doors to your inner creative powerhouse.

We were all put on this planet for a higher purpose, by which I mean we are here to rise above the mundane and the mediocre, to express, manifest and develop our innate talents, gifts, vocations, aptitudes or callings. We each have something unique to contribute and finding and delivering our contribution, day after day, is the key to a life of fulfilment, meaning and purpose, and a heart that sings. When you start to act out your purpose you are propelled into your flow, and finding that purpose is another reason for enquiring within.

So take courage, *Feel the Fear and Do It Anyway,* to quote Susan Jeffers' famous book title. Finding your flow means giving unstintingly from your heart. This in effect entails expressing your true self irrespective of the consequences and no matter what others might think.

Exercise 5: Your spontaneous self

YOUR SPONTANEOUS SELF

Try this experiment. Just for one hour instead of trying to be in control let your spontaneous self have full reign. See if you can make peace with yourself, for this experiment only works with self-acceptance. If you feel you can't yet be spontaneous, don't beat yourself up about it. Simply acknowledge the fact that you cannot yet trust sufficiently to know that the real undefended you will be OK out there in the world. It's still work in progress. Give yourself credit for trying and at the same time promise yourself you will continue the work you are doing on yourself until one day you will suddenly realise you're being spontaneous – you're doing it!

As your personal development process progresses hand-in-hand with your inner journey, try this again from time to time and ask yourself if you notice any change.

A sage somewhere sometime pointed out there are no pre-drawn paths and there's nowhere to go. There is only the path you make for yourself as you travel along it. By the same token, when you voyage in your flow there are no charts. You don't need them. This is the journey within and your heart, as expressed by your inner voice, is your trusted guide, companion and mentor. If you tune in it will always show you the way.

New clients are often surprised when I suggest to them that the first challenge is to find out who you are. Of course a few people already know who they are, or think they do, in which case I would encourage them to continue going inside as deeply as possible because this is a journey without end. In almost every case, the goals that really matter come later, for as I explained earlier, it's important to get to know yourself inside out before you can begin to understand which goals are right for you.

'Everything in your mind, body and emotions is striving for balance,' explains inspirational researcher, speaker and author Dr. John Demartini.

However, out of fear or for other reasons we often become addicted to one side or another – for example, happiness *or* sadness, pleasure *or* pain. For optimum growth we need balance, and that means challenge. In other words we must accept what's real, a balance of happiness *and* sadness, pleasure *and* pain, and so forth. Only love leads you to that acceptance and balance, which is why Demartini adds, *'all my suffering is designed to wake me up to love.'*

For years I have been explaining to my clients that we create all our problems, anguish, turmoil, pain and suffering by insisting on clinging to our resistance, our refusal to accept what is. In other words, if you can see and accept the world as what you actually see in front of you with your own eyes, rather than how you would like it to be, hey, all of a sudden, where did all my problems go? But that requires trust, supreme awareness and maybe also deep insight. So let me give you another fundamental question to leave ringing in your ears:

> *Do you have the courage, can you find the love in your heart, to trust and accept everything just as it is? That includes yourself, your partner, your children, your parents, your friends, your relatives, your colleagues, your customers, your suppliers, your boss, your teachers and role models, your authority figures, your bus driver, your postman, your local shopkeepers, your neighbours, your guru, the dog that bit you, the bank manager who refused your loan, the person who was rude to you, even your enemies. Can you see that* ***no matter what they have done or not done, and even if you don't condone their behaviour, they have value and are worthy of love, just as you are****?*

That folks, is the ultimate challenge for most of us travelling on this path towards personal transformation! Can you accept the seemingly unacceptable?

Why does it matter how you feel about others? I am hoping that by the time you've finished reading this book you'll find yourself enjoying a state of acceptance of every thing and every being in your world more than you were able to before. Then you'll understand exactly why it's important. You can never be happy for long when you are suffering inner conflict, and that's what you get if you continue to resist acceptance.

Participant or spectator?

Finally one more non-scientific exercise, this time designed to help you see some of your innate personality traits and then to decide if a process of personal development is for you. It's supposed to set you thinking in a not too serious way and it's called *Participant or spectator?* But first a few more words of explanation to set this in context.

What I ask of you, my readers, is a big ask, for undoubtedly my approach is not for the chicken-hearted. It comes from many, many years on my own path of self-discovery and personal development, and my lifelong observation of human behaviour. As you know, my style offers an in-depth approach that starts with building a firm foundation for yourself and your life. It appeals especially to those who have already tried everything else and virtually given up in despair.

Imagine you are a radio

To understand more clearly what I am driving at, imagine your heart and mind are a radio. Unless you are accurately tuned in to the channel of your choice you won't hear your favourite music. You'll only hear noise, or nothing, or worst of all, music you don't like.

Now ask yourself about your life. Do you love the music you are hearing, or would you rather change channels? Remember:

- If you want your life to have *meaning* and *purpose* it's essential to understand exactly *who you are* and be tuned in precisely to your inner voice, the voice of your heart. Then the goals you set and achieve are congruent with your core values, beliefs and talents, and enable you to express your passionate and creative self to the full.
- When you also cultivate a self-supportive, proactive mindset you create your very own *paradigm shift* which enables even seemingly impossible things to happen, and brings about whatever changes you want.

However, before embarking on any journey of personal development it's a good idea first to be honest with yourself and decide, do you want to be a *participant* or a *spectator* in life?

This is important, because participants choose their radio stations and do their own tuning. If you don't feel ready to step up to the many challenges you will encounter as a participant, better to be honest now and accept yourself as you are. If you are not sure but suspect you might want something more, for your life to be the best it can be, then by all means try the simple two minute exercise below. It's been designed specifically to help you evaluate where you are on the scale between participant and spectator. From that you will be able to judge more accurately where you *really* want to be and then in which direction to go.

As usual this is an experiment and there are no right or wrong answers. Only the truth is of interest, so try to answer as honestly as you can.

Exercise 6: Participant or spectator?

PARTICIPANT OR SPECTATOR?

Where do you feature in life's rich tapestry?

Do you realise you have a limitless power inside of you which is almost certainly nowhere near its amazing potential? You can achieve the sense of meaning and purpose you desire, but only if you seize the initiative and start to orchestrate your own life. This two minute exercise will help you see where you are with this. Answer the questions honestly, spontaneously and from your heart. In other words, don't think about the questions or your answers until afterwards and please don't take this too seriously.

(If you don't want to write in this book, you can download and print the exercise from www.thefivepillarsofhappiness.com)

	Yes	No
• Do you catch critical moments of opportunity?		
• Do you make things happen?		
• When the game begins, are you in the ball park?		
• When the game begins do you know the rules, have you developed the skills, do you have the right equipment and are you itching to play?		
• Would you prefer to get paid to play than pay to watch?		
• Do you like to tune your own radio rather than have someone else tune it for you?		

If you have 5 or 6 Yes's you are a participant, congratulations! If you have 3 or 4 you are getting there, so once again, congratulations! If you have 2 or less but you would rather score higher, now you know which way to go, so congratulations to you too. If you have no interest in participation and are perfectly happy to spectate, terrific, no worries – you can relax!

Inspiration

Finally, a few words for extra inspiration from Osho:

> *'Your daily life is your temple, and your religion. Act in awareness, act consciously, and many things will start changing.'*

Summary

- The most important question you can ask is '*who am I?*' A highly developed sense of Self is the best way to ensure your goals are congruent with your core values and beliefs
- Heightening your self-awareness gives perspective and insight into your sabotaging patterns and empowers you to challenge the mindsets that create them
- When you cultivate a supportive, proactive mindset, it enables even seemingly impossible things to happen
- If you want your life to have *meaning* and *purpose* it's essential to understand exactly *who you are* and be tuned in to your inner voice, the voice of your heart
- When you begin to understand who you are, you empower yourself to start formulating goals that are congruent with your core values, beliefs and talents. Only goals that come from your heart can be like that
- You are not your story
- The 'conditioned you' is not the 'real you'
- There are two ways of achieving goals: one is to use all your energy chasing after them; the other is to enter your *maximum creative flow* and let them come naturally and spontaneously to you
- When you allow yourself to be who you really are, you can relax and flow creatively. Letting go of your persona frees up your energy so you can put your attention into finding and entering your flow
- When you succeed in finding your flow and the courage to jump in you will be able to express your innate creative qualities joyfully, and more fully, each day
- Channelling your energy into activity that comes from your heart is a joyful way to go and it leads to sleeping well at night

- Meditation helps you to raise your awareness and find your own place of balance
- A key question to find out what's going on in your heart is, 'how do I *feel* about this?' It is not 'what do I *think* about it?'
- If you approach everything in life as if it were an experiment, you will always learn something new and valuable that will help you grow
- We end up teaching what we most need to learn ourselves
- The acceptance of 'what is' must surely be the ultimate challenge for anyone yearning for personal transformation. In that sense, you choose your own reality

Exercises for discovering and revealing your inner self

Exercise 3: Tell me who you are?
Exercise 4: Trespasso
Exercise 5: Your spontaneous self
Exercise 6: Participant or spectator?

3

The Behaviour of the Impeccable Warrior

This above all: to thine own self be true, and it must follow, as the night the day, Thou canst not then be false to any man

William Shakespeare, *Hamlet*

The concept of the Impeccable Warrior and his associated behaviour is something I learned some thirty-five years ago from the books of Carlos Castaneda, a Californian sociology student who went to learn the secrets of the Yaqui Indians of New Mexico.

There his teacher, Don Juan, versed him in his secret knowledge of shamanic sorcery, which included a teaching about the behaviour of the Impeccable Warrior. I found this a great and inspiring metaphor for how to live your life and I've never forgotten it. The Impeccable Warrior became my imaginary role model.

In essence the teaching shows how the Warrior's behaviour is Impeccable because he always acts with absolute integrity, that is, in accordance with his core beliefs and values *and* his gut feelings, instincts, intuition and hunches. He never abandons his values and he never succumbs to the temptation to adopt anyone else's. Above all, he is always true to himself. That way he never has anything to reproach himself for, *whatever happens.*

Before we develop this further, let's try to understand some of the implications of what this might mean and why it's relevant. Let's imagine, as a hypothetical example, you are a young person about to leave school and apply for university. You feel strongly you want to be a vet, but your father is very keen for you to become a solicitor, as he believes you will have greater security, higher pay, fewer unsociable hours and higher status, and you'll be better able to support a family.

If you 'give in' and take the 'sensible' route by taking up law, you are compromising yourself immediately because your heart is telling you to go to veterinary college, if you would only admit it. By accepting second best your chances of enduring happiness and fulfilment are greatly reduced and very likely you will always have regrets even if you become highly successful as a solicitor. This runs directly contrary to the behaviour of the Impeccable Warrior and ultimately is almost certain to affect your self-esteem and self-belief detrimentally. You have acted in accordance with someone else's values instead of maintaining your integrity.

Sometimes, as in this case, you may fear that the way of your heart is too risky. After all there are never any guarantees of success and if you do become successful, it will have to be entirely by your own efforts and you may doubt your own ability or motivation. Your father is no doubt well intentioned and maybe he has a point? It's also easy to give in to self-doubt, that little voice from your conditioning that tells you, 'you might not be good enough, you might fail' if you insist on following your chosen route while ignoring the more experienced person's advice and so it's perfectly understandable if you accept that. Maybe you don't want to come out of your comfort zone, and why should you?

The gaping flaw in this argument is that as time goes by you will see that the so-called 'comfort zone' you have opted for is anything but comfortable. That is why the Impeccable Warrior, faced with this sort of dilemma, will always insist on following his heart above all else by doing the vet training first. To him there is no dilemma. If later on it turns out he hates the veterinary business, he can then train to be a solicitor, or anything else to which his heart directs him. By approaching it that way round he puts his truth to the test, makes appropriate adjustments and has no cause to beat himself up or regret anything.

The Impeccable Warrior is acutely aware that his conditioning has nothing to do with who he really is. This is plain and simple old-fashioned common sense – you wouldn't be drawn to being a vet if you didn't have an aptitude for it and a love of animals. In such a case your chances of success in the veterinary field are far higher than they would be if you pursued the law, an area that leaves you cold, because you will have natural motivation and you won't have to contrive it. Yes, of course you will have to work hard for a number of years to get qualified, and there will be times when you have an off day, in which case take a break. Don't forget you are looking for balance, so don't work so hard it becomes obsessional.

Bear in mind what you are aiming for, while at the same time allow yourself to enjoy your journey. The knowledge and skills you'll need will come naturally to you and there will be little resistance to studying because you are fascinated and you love what you do. Ultimately, your hard work will bring you fulfilment.

You can combine the Impeccable Warrior approach with the heightened awareness we discussed in the previous chapter. If you find you are giving yourself a hard time or branding yourself a failure because that's what you used to do before you changed your behaviour, you begin to see yourself doing it and can ask yourself, 'is this justified?' The person who studied to be a vet can answer, 'no, I have behaved with integrity. I have been true to myself, therefore I no longer have grounds for judging myself harshly. It's just an old habit and I'm stopping it right now.'

The Impeccable Warrior knows it's never a good idea to act on anyone else's advice. By all means listen to other people's feedback, points of view and their experiences, as long as it's someone who knows what they are talking about, but above all listen to your own guidance, the voice of your heart, and then *make up your own mind.* Likewise, the Impeccable Warrior will always seek the very best teacher available if he needs more knowledge and understanding, he will only listen to people who he respects and feels talk from experience, and even then, *he will still listen to his heart and make up his own mind.* That's the heart and mind working in harmony, the perfect heart/mind balance.

You may have noticed that teachers, gurus and coaches who are worth their salt never give advice, but encourage their students to take responsibility for finding their own answers. Your answers are the only valid ones for only they contain the truth about what is right for you.

Feeling guilty is another classic example of an old habit that lots of us carry around for no good reason. If your behaviour in any situation has been impeccable, why should you feel guilty? It's nonsense. Warrior behaviour gives you a model for guidance and inspiration, while your growing awareness enables you to see what you do and to make new decisions where appropriate.

Don't take my word for it. Try behaving impeccably for a few days and you'll be amazed how great you start to feel about yourself.

How do I know what my heart is saying?

Good question. My method, which I touched upon in the previous chapter, depends on the understanding that certain things cannot be worked out in the mind. Ask yourself, 'how do I *feel* about xyz?' not 'what do I *think* about xyz?'

Going back to our example, first ask yourself, 'how do I feel about becoming a vet? Can I imagine myself doing it? How would it feel to save the life of an animal? How would it feel if an animal dies despite my best efforts? Could I cope with that?'

Then ask yourself, 'how do I feel about becoming a solicitor? Can I imagine myself doing it? How would it feel to save a client from jail? How would it feel if I failed to save someone from jail? Could I cope with that?'

If you are honest with yourself, the answer will be pretty self-evident. It is most important not to intellectualise or analyse any of this. There is no right or wrong reasoned answer and no judgement either way. The only thing that matters is discovering your truth, how you actually *feel,* and acting accordingly.

Exercise 7: The scale of impeccability

(If you don't want to write in this book, you can download and print the exercise from www.thefivepillarsofhappiness.com)

At this point you may be wondering where exactly you stand on the *scale of impeccability,* in which case the following exercise might shed some light for you. Get a pen and answer the following questions as frankly and spontaneously as you can. *Try not to think too much – a gut reaction is best.* Remember you might as well be totally honest because if you are not, the only person you are deceiving is yourself, and then you render the exercise pointless.

THE SCALE OF IMPECCABILITY

Find out where you stand

Answer the following simple questions with a simple spontaneous Yes or No to see where you stand on the *scale of impeccability*:

	Yes	No
• Are you completely honest in every situation at all times?		
• Do you love what you do and do what you love?		
• Do you always let people know how you feel?		

	Yes	No
• Do you avoid being economical with the truth?		
• Do you always treat you spouse/partner with respect?		
• Do you always act in accordance with your core beliefs and values?		
• Do you always treat others with respect?		
• Do you take the time and trouble to maximise your talents?		
• Do you have a group of close friends with whom you feel a strong affinity?		
• Do you refrain from gossiping about people behind their backs?		

You might be tempted to answer the first question, say, with something along the lines of *'well sometimes yes, sometimes no, it's not so simple, it's not fair to insist on yes or no, it depends…'*

Impeccability knows no half measures or compromise. This is a self-esteem issue which is why there is no room for discussion. 'Maybes' in this context are simply attempts to justify or rationalise away the times when you are not being totally honest. Of course we all make mistakes occasionally, but if we act against our gut feelings or our core beliefs and values, even occasionally, we are not behaving with integrity. In short, anything other than an unequivocal 'yes' can only be construed as a 'no'.

So count up your Yes's and don't be surprised if you get 10 No's. If that happens, or if the No's are in the majority, you'll know this issue needs your serious and urgent attention.

Taking personal responsibility

Often when someone achieves something great in their life the people they come into contact with, instead of feeling inspired to make their own lives wonderful, put down the person's achievement to good luck, fate, the stars and planets or other phenomena that are out of our control.

While I am the first to acknowledge there is more going on in existence than we can possibly know about and that supernatural or astral forces may well have an influence, I usually feel quite angry when I hear someone say to another person, 'ooh, you're so lucky.' It is as if the other person's life is purely the result of luck, a happy accident, and that their own life will never be OK because they never get lucky.

This is a gross abdication of personal responsibility. If you want to change your life you can, and in a sense you can create your own luck, *if you work at it and take full responsibility for making it happen.*

Do you think Sir Alan Sugar was born rich? I don't think so. He started as a barrow boy in the East End of London, and so did Jack Cohen, founder of Tesco, now the largest retail business in the UK. Richard Branson started his first business, Virgin Records, when he was still in school. These are just three examples of people who nurtured a vision and took personal responsibility for making that vision real.

Of course you don't have to go to such extreme material accomplishment to be happy and successful – it all depends on what your vision is and how you define success. The Impeccable Warrior takes note of his or her personal vision, whatever it might be, and takes action to make it happen. He does not wait passively to get lucky, he creates opportunities for himself.

All this begins with tuning into your heart and following its guidance. It takes courage and integrity, which is why I use the word, 'Warrior'.

Here's an example from my own life. Several people have said to me over the years, 'you're so lucky you've got a boat and you know how to sail'. They switch on a sort of faraway, wistful look as if they wish they could do something similar but they believe it's obvious that they can't. Well of course, holding a belief like that guarantees they never will.

'No, actually luck has very little to do with it,' I tell them. This is how it works: *when you decide to follow your heart and thereby get into your flow, the necessary opportunities always present themselves if you are sufficiently awake to see and seize them.* I made a choice. Something inside told me to learn sailing and my heart told me to manifest a boat.

To start with I sold everything I owned that I did not need or really want, while at the same time I worked hard and long to save up, working my way through a succession of mostly second-hand boats from tiny to a reasonable size. Over a number of years I did virtually every Royal Yachting Association (RYA) sail training course and exam there is to do in the UK. I also put in many miles of practise in any vessel I could get my hands on with any skipper kind enough to take me out on his boat, or in my own boat, until I mastered it. I made it happen.

Of course all this took years of perseverance, but anyone with enthusiasm and an aptitude for sailing can do likewise. The same principle applies in any field of endeavour.

When I was young I had a belief that sailing, especially yachting, was 'only for rich people,' and it was only when I began to develop a vision of how I could make a start and get it to happen that I began to make progress with this goal. The vision grew so strong it eventually overpowered the belief that was holding me back.

I'm just an ordinary bloke and I'm perfectly happy with that. All of us are ordinary, but we have the potential to live lives that are extra-ordinary. The principle here is perfectly obvious to the Impeccable Warrior. You choose what you want, make it your number one priority and do what is necessary to make it happen. If you need knowledge, get knowledge; if you need experience, get experience; if you need money, get money. The only qualities you need for success are self-belief, determination, honesty and perseverance – and of course, the ability to be silent and listen to your heart at regular intervals. These are the skills of the Impeccable Warrior and *you can develop them all and use them gainfully if you choose goals that are relevant to your talent, and you want the achievement in question with all your heart.*

There have been times when I saw dolphins and, yes, you could say that was lucky, though I believe it has more to do with putting myself in the right place at the right time. Going sailing was something I decided to do and the dolphins were an added bonus. When you find your passion and follow it, magical things happen all the time.

You may have inner critics; you may have a powerful inner saboteur; you may be riven with self-doubt, fear and low self-esteem; you may have financial, physical, psychological or emotional issues. Are you going to let those stop you? Certainly not! Once you get the bit between your teeth, there'll be no stopping you if you are following your heart.

So drop the ego, stop *thinking* about it, just listen to your inner voice and take action.

Come on, you can say *'YES'* to life. You can make your own luck if you choose to, and you can make your dreams come true. Just discover what you want to do, believe in yourself – and get on with it!

What it means to tell the truth

Talking glibly about telling the truth is easy enough. What does it really mean to tell the truth, and what are the ramifications?

Every time we tell someone the truth we take a risk. The other person might not want to hear it and may have a hostile reaction. We might not want to face it either. Another possibility is that we may hesitate to state our truths today because we fear we might change our minds tomorrow.

Sometimes we fear the truth might make another person angry, sad or cold. They might cut off from us, we might be shouted at, cried on, or never be forgiven. We might even lose our relationship. We ourselves might fear being reminded by the truth that we feel angry, sad, afraid or heartbroken and therefore be tempted to espouse a strategy of denial. Of course, there is also the possibility that both parties in a relationship might be happy or relieved in the long term by facing the truth, but the probability of this outcome is often obscured by fear of the short-term possible consequences.

There are thousands of possible scenarios, but whichever way you look at it, and most of the people I have spoken to agree, when you have to express an unpalatable truth, *fear* is the predominant feeling. Whether we will face our fear and deliver our truth anyway is an issue that we often shirk. To the Impeccable Warrior there is no issue for he knows he has to face his fear, deal with it and tell it like it is, *whatever the outcome.* It's the only way he can behave with integrity.

We sometimes fail to appreciate that avoiding the truth carries even greater risks to our self-esteem. Integrity is not a game we can play with ourselves. We cannot say one thing and mean another because it seems expedient, and seriously expect to feel good about ourselves. It simply doesn't work like that.

By taking an honest approach to life and the myriad issues that constantly come to confront us, we may be pilloried for being too forthright, tactless and heartless. The judgements of others may rain down on our heads, but as long as we act with awareness and sensitivity, our self-esteem remains intact. There is no need to be tactless, abrasive, aggressive or rude. When we treat people with the respect they deserve, truth can always be declared sensitively.

It is also noticeable that when we take that approach, other people of integrity, though they might disagree with us, intuitively treat us with respect. In time, those who are more grudging and unaware will feel obliged to respect us too, even though they might resent it. Either way, what is of far the greatest importance is that by sticking to our truths, we respect ourselves, no matter what happens. The reactions of others are for them.

Our fear of speaking and living in truth is based entirely on fantasy, for we do not know how another will react. Even if our fear is based on past experience with that same person, it is not safe to assume an adverse reaction from them will necessarily be repeated, unless unconsciously we set it up that way.

The point behind this is that another person's reaction to anything is their business, not ours. Of course, awareness will guide us towards being compassionate, and common sense may lead us into sensitively waiting for a suitable moment. However, the truth is inescapable and if only for the sake of our integrity and that of anyone else affected, it has to be told sooner or later, preferably sooner.

So if the reactions of others are their business, not ours, why does it matter to us how other people react? Most of us have a neurotic belief system, implanted by our conditioning and our interpretation of past experience, which makes us automatically fear that another person's reaction to an 'unpalatable' truth will make us feel guilty, angry, resentful, rejected, sad or hurt in some way. We perceive these feelings as too difficult to live with and we would rather avoid them. So we cling to the forlorn hope that by avoiding truths and potential confrontations, we can avoid having those feelings.

However, because of the way we are, when we avoid the truth we suffer other unpleasant feelings, for deep inside it is impossible for us to fool our hearts and our inner voices that a situation feels OK when it doesn't.

An examination of this whole area reveals what a potential minefield we create if we try to follow a strategy of avoidance. To base what we say and do on another person's possible reaction is clearly not a viable way carry on, for among other things we simply give away our power, while perhaps also disempowering the other person. It's ridiculous to adjust our behaviour for fear of a possible reaction that has not happened yet, or to try to manipulate a situation to produce a desirable but inauthentic reaction.

Moreover, because our conditioning interacts with the conditioning of the people with whom we relate on many subtle and not so subtle levels, when two parties avoid the truth they merely collude with each other in a spiralling entanglement of fiction and fantasy which ultimately does no-one any good. When we behave like that in any kind of relationship, both partners help each other suppress the truth in an effort to avoid so called unpleasant feelings, thus rendering any attempt at a heart-to-heart connection meaningless.

There is an insidious element of emotional blackmail here too, sometimes with compound deception and self-deception on both sides, which can become immensely complicated and is usually largely unconscious. For example, one partner might feel afraid to say something to the other for she may shout at him, in which case he will feel rejected and hurt, and she might cry, in which case he may feel guilty as well. So either he says nothing or he offers a watered down, more 'palatable' version of the truth, or he lies, and the goal of avoiding the pain is temporarily achieved by both parties.

'So what?' you might say. We could live reasonably enough in this way, I suppose. But if we do, we will never reach our full potential for joy, happiness and fulfilment in our lives and relationships. If that matters to you, then this issue really is important. Do you want to go through life relating only on a superficial, insincere level? Millions do, but I certainly don't!

To put this in perspective, everyone I have ever met suffers from this problem to a greater or lesser extent, so let us not judge ourselves or each other too harshly if we are not at all times perfect in our sincerity.

A much better strategy, and one that works, is to observe our own behaviour in detail, take note of how it works, and simply decide to change the bits we don't like. It is important to understand that the way to modify our habits to our satisfaction is not by using repression or 'will power', but through awareness. With awareness, changes for the better happen automatically and spontaneously. The Impeccable Warrior goes out of his way to cultivate his personal conscious awareness.

When you follow a path of integrity, despite whatever fears you may have beforehand, you will soon find they are replaced with elation, freedom, balance, satisfaction and higher self-esteem, self-worth and self-belief. Living in truth is not just a matter of how we conduct our relationships, it has to become a lifestyle. We need to find the courage to live consistently in accordance with the guidance of our inner voices and the feelings in our hearts.

Many heart-rending and soul-searching decisions become necessary for most of us at various times in our lives. Here are some real-life examples of people I have met over the years: leaving the religion of his birth; dropping a well paid but highly stressful job as a jet-setting executive for the tranquillity of becoming a rural village postman; getting divorced; having an abortion; leaving the city to live in a commune; selling up to live in the countryside; going to live in another country. People do all sorts of things like this because living in truth is a prerequisite to making their dreams come true and fulfilling their human potential as individuals. This often requires starting their lives all over again from scratch.

We can never run away from ourselves, no matter how far we may travel. But we can change our behaviour so we delight in living with ourselves. We can change the record and dance to a different tune any time we so choose.

Living in truth is what is meant by Impeccable behaviour and is the only way to deal cleanly with life situations. Don't confuse it with seeking perfection, which is an impossible achievement because we are perfect already. Aiming for perfection is an ego-driven goal, and it has nothing to do with conducting our lives with sincerity.

Putting up a façade

Being unwilling to let ourselves be revealed for who we really are is another way in which we can be dishonest, because then we are showing the world our *persona*, or false self, while trying to pass it off as real.

This is a very common defence mechanism with people who are not at all happy with how their life is right now, or who they think they are. These are not pleasant truths to acknowledge and ones most of us will gladly hide from if we can get away with it. The problem is, when someone can only relate to another through a façade, he or she will find it well nigh impossible to have a deep, sincere and heartfelt relationship.

Clearly such a person has not, for whatever reason, discovered *who they really are and started to act accordingly*, or they would not feel a need to hide. Perhaps they believe they are their persona? Now there's something huge to think about ...

Whatever the truth of the matter, once you understand the situation, the only remedy is to make that voyage of self-discovery and to start living your truth, even if at first you are terrified.

Danger of attack

Of course there will be those so-called friends who will feel challenged when you start stating your truth, and their reaction might be to attack you, even if they don't realise they are doing it. You are standing out from the crowd, and this immediately makes you a vulnerable target for nervous 'snipers' who perceive you as a threat to their delicate egos as they strive to maintain their status quo. If they are not progressing, it's understandable that your growth and development makes them feel insecure.

Our very real fear is that because of our new-found Impeccable behaviour, we might get our heads blown off by such insecure people, metaphorically speaking, and indeed there is every chance that this may happen.

In my experience, snipers rarely feel good about themselves and what they are doing. They are driven by their own repressed anger and their erroneous, and usually unconscious belief, that if they destroy our sense of empowerment by intimidating us,

they will then feel less disempowered as a result. It's a balance of negatives and it never works. People who live in such unconsciousness usually don't have the faintest idea why their lives remain dysfunctional, and joy eludes them to the end.

This knowledge may seem to be of little comfort to us as we lie wounded and bleeding, as it were. However, once we cotton on and understand that people sometimes try to put us down or destroy us in an attempt to mask from themselves their own painful feelings, their 'bullets' seem to loose their effectiveness and the attacks begin to feel irrelevant. If our old friends can't cope with the changes we are going through we must respect their right not to change, while respecting our own desire to grow. Perhaps the best course is to compassionately let them go, while acquiring a new circle of friends who are moving along paths parallel to our own.

In relationships we need people who can mirror us, and as our needs change sometimes we need to change mirrors.

By adhering carefully to our truths and keeping clearly to our paths we empower and balance ourselves, and this empowerment and balance enable us to keep our heads intact and bullet free. We are starting to believe in ourselves, and we can simply deflect the flak by staying centred. Compassion cannot exist where there is fear. With understanding – of ourselves and of others – and a sense of knowing who we really are, we feel less threatened so we begin to find room in our hearts for compassion instead of fear. Awareness, not covert defensive behaviour, nor even aggressive behaviour, becomes our shield.

The good news is, though at first we might fear attack, when we begin living our truth we will notice that we quickly start to attract, as well as to radiate, far more positive than negative feedback. If we are lucky, some of the people who feel anger towards us might begin to understand this and realise they are, in effect, being presented with the possibility of taking responsibility for their anger by ceasing the attack and taking a look inside. They can ask themselves, 'what is really going on in here?' But whether or not they learn from this incident is entirely up to them.

Does this mean there is no value in expressing anger? Of course not. If we are boiling over, or even if we are only lightly simmering, we hurt ourselves unless we let our anger out. Later we will discuss ways of doing this safely without dumping or hurting anyone, but for the moment it's important to realise that expressing anger is only the beginning of a process, another layer that must be peeled from the onion. It is another gateway, another invitation to enquire within.

Conventional wisdom says, 'attack is the best form of defence.' Contemporary wisdom says, 'a man who is open has nothing to fear.' Every time we reflect inwardly after expressing anger, we will almost certainly discover we have some very painful feelings to experience and express which until now we have skilfully avoided looking at. They need a voice.

For those of us who have been brought up to avoid inward enquiry and intense emotional self-expression, it can be very difficult indeed, not to say frightening, to get really angry and convey our feelings someone, or to deliver any bad news that we fear will be negatively received or might hurt another person's feelings. But by avoiding, we are being true neither to our feelings, nor to the other person's. Once again we are reminded that behaving with integrity (that is, adhering to the truth) is the only way to proceed through life with our heads held high.

Experience has proven to me time and time again that avoiding is *always* counter-productive and where others are concerned it inevitably leads to bad feeling on both sides in the end. The Impeccable Warrior knows how to deal with situations in which the truth needs to be told because he knows himself inside out and he's always true to himself. His way is simply to acknowledge he has deep-seated fears and he allows himself to experience those scary feelings, which many try to suppress for years. He tells it like it is, straight from his heart, because he knows no other path.

He also knows those feelings will pass without damaging him, even if it takes time. Thus he empowers himself to deal with any situation in which the truth is required.

He is in the habit of listening to his inner voice and checks himself out carefully at regular intervals by asking himself how he *feels,* he knows in his heart that what he is doing is right for him and therefore he is being true to himself.

'What about Martin Luther King?' somebody said to me once. 'He lived his truth and was literally gunned down for speaking from his heart.'

Yes, it's true and it's very sad. But how could he have behaved differently? King believed he was put here to speak out and lead his black brothers in their fight for justice. Could you imagine a man like him hushing up because he feared the possible consequences of his actions? His behaviour was Impeccable, but had he behaved in any other way, could he have lived with himself? I doubt it. His passion was such that he could never have kept quiet, *no matter what.* He died with his integrity intact.

Of course, that does not in any way exonerate the man who shot him. It simply means that the assassin did not have sufficient conscious awareness to behave Impeccably.

Maybe you believe he too was following his heart and acting out his beliefs, but my gut feeling and experience tells me that when you follow your heart you will realise you can never solve your problems by proffering violence, either to yourself or to anyone else. Moreover, blaming someone else because you feel badly never works and is usually counter-productive and deeply sabotaging. All the murderer succeeding in doing was making Martin Luther King an even greater icon and adding considerable impetus to the liberation movement.

One of my clients confronted me angrily once saying, 'It's all very well doing what's right for you, but what about what's right for the other person? How do you know you are doing what's right for them, or don't you care about them?'

Of course you have no idea what might be right for someone else and it would be presumptuous, even arrogant, to try to act in someone else's best interest unless they told you specifically what that is. That's what delineates the Impeccable Warrior from a 'do-gooder', pleaser, avoider or busybody. The Impeccable Warrior, by simply behaving with integrity, extends an implied invitation to the other person to behave likewise, if he or she so wishes.

I reiterate, while you are pursuing a path of personal development and transformation, *other people's behaviour is none of your business.* The Impeccable Warrior is not in the business of solving other people's problems for them or removing their pain. He is a light unto himself, a role model and a shining example for those who have eyes and ears to understand. He is a walking lesson in how to feel good about yourself.

Consider the other side of the coin for a moment. If you are suffering unhappiness and depression and you feel like a victim with low self-esteem, what could possibly be the reason? A good place to start is by scrutinising your behaviour. Are you economical with the truth, do you avoid and evade issues, do you keep your feelings bottled up? If you suspect that maybe, just maybe, something of that nature could apply to you, try following a path of Impeccability for a few days and see how you feel then.

The blame culture

Some of my closer friends know, when they are feeling mischievous, that the best way to wind me up is to engage in the blame culture. If there's one plague the Western world suffers from, the blame culture is it! Here's how it works. You do something wrong, you look for someone to blame. You pass the buck. You do not admit responsibility, you do not own your embarrassing mistake and learn something from the pain you feel, you don't even acknowledge the pain. You blame someone else. Politicians are very adept at doing this, and it's the height of dishonesty. It's always the fault of the previous Government when our economy goes into recession. Some data is mislaid, someone must be blamed. A burglary is committed, a road accident occurs, someone loses a sale – there has to be a scapegoat.

When I left college and got my very first job at the age of seventeen, it was in a world famous advertising agency in the heart of London's

West End. Here I learned that the blame game was a matter of survival. The prevailing culture was that no matter how brilliant you might be, you were 'as good as your last cock-up.' A mistake here could easily cost the company £3 to £4 million, a huge amount of money in 1967, and you could be sure that someone's head would roll. My colleagues advised me, 'you must protect your backside and when something goes wrong, pass the buck immediately.'

Not surprisingly this and similar experiences marked for me the start of a long slide into a deep depression as it became clear to me that success in this field requires you to sell your soul. I was working with the elite alright – these were some of the lowest self-esteem, most lacking in self-respect, most deeply unconscious denial artists the City of London could muster! I soon began to understand that I would never enjoy a glittering career in this field of endeavour. It was a strong and painful lesson, but one that has stood me in good stead, for nothing is wasted and everything you do comes back to serve you beautifully in the end.

In the context of building a happy and fulfilling life, blaming others achieves nothing, and avoiding personal responsibility helps us not a jot. Indeed we lose valuable potential learning opportunities. In a place like an advertising agency you might save your job and you might even keep the client, but it would always be at the expense of your integrity. If you don't mind living in a state of unconsciousness and personal disharmony, then by all means be my guest. No need to change a thing!

On a personal level, how do we feel when refuse to take responsibility for our pain and anger by blaming others? Lousy. It's the perfect recipe for low self-esteem, depression and feeling out of balance. The Impeccable Warrior never fears making a mistake. Although he tries not to, if he does, he understands what he needs to learn and moves on to bigger and better mistakes. He tries not to make the same mistake twice but if he does, well it just proves he's human and he needs to pay more attention to what he's doing.

Nobody ever learns anything if they don't make the odd blunder! In fact I'd even go so far as to say that a person who doesn't come a cropper from time to time is not challenging himself enough.

Blaming someone else for our pain is another brilliant avoidance technique and it always proves utterly fruitless.

Telling the truth means having the guts to go totally with your inner voice, no matter how frightening. This may be a new and unfamiliar way of behaving to you, but ultimately the effect is like an emotional and spiritual spring cleaning, an unburdening and a powerful feeling of freedom, release and empowerment. Quite simply you become a fully functioning human being.

Those I know who have adopted this way of being find their lives work much more along the lines they want, and with far less effort. In fact the only real effort in this strategy is in maintaining your awareness.

Denying your feelings

There are many ways of being dishonest without realising it and one way is denying how you feel. When you feel hurt or angry you can take it on the chin like the civilised, repressed and politely conditioned human beings that most of us are, but this self-effacing strategy is nothing other than disempowering. You will be the loser because you have to walk around with a burden of unexpressed emotion, and until that emotion is given expression, the underlying feeling of malaise cannot be resolved. Behaving in a 'civilised', 'grown-up', calm or composed manner when you actually feel emotional or volatile is a classic vehicle of self-deception.

More often than not this tendency to cut off from our feelings is unconscious, hence the urgent need for more awareness of what's really going on. Open up, look more deeply inside. I have never met anyone who is genuinely totally devoid of anger, sadness and pain, not even those who claim to be enlightened, but all the time I meet plenty of folks who are cut off from those feelings. So express your anger, but remember it is yours so don't blame and don't dump it. And for heaven's sake be careful, *don't hurt anybody, including yourself.* That will not help at all. Never forget whatever happens as a result of your thoughts and actions is your personal responsibility. Later we will discuss safe ways of expressing anger.

A state of acceptance of all our feelings is the goal. Living in truth includes acknowledging present moment reality while making no attempt to change, bend, alter or manipulate it. It's a practice of embracing what is. This is the one and only recipe for a healthy, genuine and happy life as far as I am aware.

Some people find it hard to cry, others find it easy. Some find it hard to laugh. Whatever your particular situation, for the sake of your own mental health and in the interests of learning to love life, not only is it necessary to get in contact with *all* your feelings, but you must also communicate them. To go deeper, we must be prepared to reveal who we are, warts and all, and share our true selves.

Just think about it. The possibility of letting go of the kind of control that guarantees you remain in a state of anxiety only arises when we truly and completely trust and believe in ourselves. That means we know we will survive emotionally *whatever happens* because we have a happy relationship with ourselves. We become self-sufficient and we do not depend on the actions of others for our wellbeing. Therefore we are independent, and in our relationships we become inter-dependent rather than co-dependent. (Chapter 26 discusses co-dependency and relationships in more detail.)

The only person who can let us down is ourselves. However, the act of becoming an Impeccable Warrior implies we will never do that because, by definition, we know and *accept* exactly who we are unconditionally. That means we can trust ourselves to be utterly dependable in looking after ourselves because the best interests of our hearts are being Impeccably looked after in our own safe and trustworthy hands.

So now we have another building block for the foundation of our new life, let's just recap a moment. We need to get to know ourselves inside out so we can find out exactly who we are and what we *really* need and want. We need to raise our awareness so we know exactly how we feel and why we feel the way we do, and then we adopt the behaviour of the Impeccable Warrior so we can always be trusted to be true to ourselves. By doing those things we begin to learn the art of tuning in to be guided on our paths by our inner voices and the bidding of our hearts.

As long as we continue to be guided by our hearts, how can we go wrong?

Take heart

At this stage you may be feeling disheartened because you still might have no clue as to how to tune in to your heart. That's fine, for the first part of this book attempts nothing more than an explanation and preliminary exploration of basic principles. 'How to do it' comes later. First we must examine every detail thoroughly because they really matter. I assure you your patience will be rewarded in the long run.

What I describe is not merely a matter of theory or intellectual argument. When we experience on a deep level the Impeccability concept I have outlined, a profound realisation dawns that we are no longer dependent on the actions or reactions of others. We discover it's not actually that hard to stand on our own two feet and when we begin to follow our individual true paths, we soon find ourselves unconditionally loving, accepting and trusting ourselves. It happens automatically as sure as night follows day and with it comes a deep knowing that we will always be alright, come what may.

When we arrive in that condition, we are easily able to have fruitful relationships with other like-minded folk. This is a very balanced, relaxing, liberating and energising state of being, and most people find that at this point, their creativity begins to flower.

If you find yourself in a position where you feel stuck and your creative flow dries up, as yourself, 'do I feel in balance?' Almost certainly the answer will be 'no', in which case the first place to look is to your Impeccability. Here's how it works: *when you feel good about yourself your creativity flows, but you can't feel good about yourself if your behaviour is less than Impeccable.*

Ask yourself self-monitoring questions along the lines of, 'Am I doing what I love?' 'Am I being true to myself?' 'Am I opting for second best?'

Once you get your head around this new mindset and start to make it a habit – your new default setting if you like – you simply continue unhesitatingly to follow your unique path. You say and do what you really feel and what comes naturally, not merely what you think, nor what you think you ought to say, feel, do or think. In such a happy circumstance we set ourselves free to embark on our inner journeys towards the fulfilment that most of us crave deep down.

So where does this leave us in relation to the 'real' world? I often get questions such as, 'will I feel fulfilled … if I make a lot of money,' or '… if I get married and have babies,' or '… if I forge a brilliant career,' or '… if I become an artist,' or '… if I travel around the world' etc.

The only possible answer is 'how on earth do you expect me to know what's right for you? Only you know the answer.' It depends upon what is in your heart. For you, the most important thing might be to fly round the world in a hot air balloon, or it might be to become a Buddhist monk sitting in silence at the feet of a master for twenty or thirty years. One of the great joys of life is that we are all different and we each have something unique to give and to be given. For actress

Joanna Lumley it was seeing the Aurora Borealis, and once she had seen it she said she could 'die happy.'

That is the whole purpose of finding your path and journeying on it, to live your life according to whatever you find in your heart. It could be many things or one particular thing, and all we can know in advance is that when we live in this way our creativity will flourish and our hearts will sing. There is no intellectual process that I know of for working out answers to finding your path, but your heart knows exactly where and what it is.

Here's the key

Find the courage to start believing in yourself and your instincts one hundred per cent, and back your gut feelings to the hilt. Soon you will know your answer.

I speak from experience for I tried the route of no awareness and it didn't work for me. Indeed it merely deepened my depression and gave me a nasty hangover. It is in the inner realms, I eventually discovered, that real and lasting happiness lies. This is why I say to you, man or woman, be a spiritual Warrior. Have a love affair with yourself and life, but not in a narcissistic way, and allow everything to slot into place.

This book is about making our lives exciting, happy, fulfilling, dynamic, creative, fantastic, powerful, effective, filled with awe and wonder, miraculous, abundant, effective, heavenly and whatever else we want. Our efforts have to begin with an ongoing commitment to telling the truth and living in truth, whatever the cost.

There is no time like the present! As you sit reading this why not join me right now in making that commitment to yourself – now and for the rest of our lives? I invite you to get a pen and paper and write down the following powerful affirmation:

'COME WHAT MAY I FOLLOW A PATH OF IMPECCABLE TRUTH AND INTEGRITY'

Let that be your mantra from now on.

I don't know what I want to do

Yes you do!

Sometimes a client tells me, 'I don't know what I want to do; I don't know who I am; I don't have any passions, talents, calling, vocation or anything to get enthusiastic about; and I'm confused by such a dazzling array of choices.'

I don't believe a word of it, except the bit about being confused by too many choices. If this is you, you are not looking in your heart for answers, you are looking in your mind. In a case like this no amount of knowledge or thinking will illuminate you or make the truth less scary. As I said at the beginning, too much thinking will paralyse you, it will kill your passions and leave you feeling bored, listless, depressed, confused and fearful. You are cutting yourself off from your feelings and there are many possible reasons for that which we don't need to go into right now. This is why I repeat, believing you don't know what you want is a cop-out. You may not realise you know, but deep down inside you do.

I once had a friend in London who was a disciple of a guru who lived in India. One day my friend wrote to his beloved master with the question, 'master, what should I do with my life?' Two or three weeks later an answer appeared through my friend's letterbox. The letter said simply, 'whatever you like.' Beautiful! The guru had put the responsibility for answering the question squarely back where it belonged, right into my friend's lap!

You can make this as easy or as difficult for yourself as you want. Just bear in mind that *all the suffering and resistance in the world will not answer the question,* nor will it earn you any spiritual brownie points, for there is no virtue in suffering or beating yourself up. *The only thing that will cast light on your question is to look into your heart* using some of the techniques we have described already, and some that will be explained as you read on.

Unfinished business

Finally, the Impeccable Warrior makes a point of dealing with unfinished business. That way he gets closure and is able to move on. Trying to ignore unfinished business is like leaving a sword of Damocles hanging over your head and your senses of self-acceptance and self-esteem cannot flourish unfettered when something is making you feel guilty, sad, angry or nervous. There will always be something nagging away at you, draining your energy and enthusiasm and stopping you from entering wholeheartedly into the next phase of your life. It may take a while, but it has to be dealt with so you can make a clean break.

Here's an obvious example: most married couples who separate will sooner or later want to divorce. Apart from the legal implications, this is a highly symbolic way of dealing with unfinished business for both parties so they can move on. Even though it can be emotionally fraught and very traumatic, a divorce is an essential part of undergoing and completing the healing process of a broken marriage and is usually deemed necessary even if the two people concerned don't want to remarry. Most people find it very hard to have a serious relationship with a new person, or even to build a new life on their own, while they are still married to someone else.

The same principle applies to all relationships in life, as well as to our jobs and other issues. Here's another example: an elderly client lost her husband and could not seem to find a new direction in her life even after going though the ordeal of her husband's funeral and a year of mourning, both of which are ways of getting closure. There was one more thing she had to do. She sold her large house in London and bought the cottage of her dreams by the seaside in Sussex. Eventually she found happiness again, but not until the unfinished business of her London house had been dealt with.

The behaviour of the Impeccable Warrior in all its many aspects holds the secret to developing solid self-esteem, as well as winning the love and friendship of others who also behave with integrity.

Summary

- The behaviour of the Impeccable Warrior decrees that you always act with integrity, according to your core beliefs and values *and* your gut feelings, instincts and intuition. Never abandon them and never adopt anyone else's, and always trust your first impressions. That way you never have anything to reproach yourself for, *whatever happens*
- Listen to other people's feedback and experiences, but above all listen to your own guidance, the voice of your heart, and then *make up your own mind*
- When self-doubt creeps in, remember always to go with the feeling in your heart. If you are not sure what your heart is telling you, ask yourself, 'how do I *feel* about xyz?' not 'what do I *think* about xyz'
- The Impeccable Warrior trusts what his heart tells him and acts accordingly

- To maintain high self-esteem, you need to be authentic at all times, especially towards yourself. The Impeccable Warrior has no skeletons in the cupboard – nothing to hide, feel ashamed of or guilty about
- If you want to change your life for the better you can, *if you work at it.* The Impeccable Warrior takes note of his vision and takes action to make it happen. He does not wait to get lucky, he creates opportunities for himself
- Apart from the appropriate talent, which you already have, the qualities you need for success are self-belief, determination, honesty and perseverance – and the ability to listen to your heart at regular intervals
- When you follow a path of integrity, you will find your fears are replaced with elation, freedom, balance and satisfaction, as well as higher self-esteem, self-worth and self-belief
- When you decide to follow your heart and get into your flow, the necessary opportunities present themselves if you are awake to see and seize them
- All of us are ordinary, but we have the potential to live lives that are extraordinary
- Blaming others achieves nothing and is a brilliant avoidance technique; it's the perfect recipe for low self-esteem, depression and feeling out of balance
- Avoiding personal responsibility does not help us; indeed we lose valuable potential learning opportunities if we do that
- Avoiding is *always* counter-productive and where others are concerned it inevitably leads to bad feeling on both sides
- If old friends can't cope with the changes you are going through, respect their right not to change, while also respecting your own need to move on
- Compassionately let them go and acquire new friends who are moving along paths parallel to your own
- When the Impeccable Warrior has deep-seated fears he acknowledges them and allows himself to experience those feelings. Then he does what he feels to do or tells it like it is, straight from his heart, because he knows no other path

- The Impeccable Warrior, by behaving with integrity, extends an implied invitation to others to behave likewise, if they so wish. He is a role model for those who have eyes and ears to understand and is a shining example of how to feel good about yourself
- Other people's behaviour is none of your business
- A person who doesn't make the odd blunder from time to time is probably not challenging himself enough
- Nothing is wasted and everything you do will serve you in the end
- Telling the truth means having the guts to go totally with your inner voice, no matter how frightening. Quite simply you become a fully functioning human being. The only real effort in this strategy is in maintaining your awareness
- Never forget whatever happens as a result of your thoughts and actions is your personal responsibility, so be careful what you think and do
- A state of acceptance of all our feelings is the goal. It's a matter of embracing 'what is'
- When we begin to follow our individual true paths, we soon find ourselves unconditionally loving, accepting and trusting ourselves. With it comes a deep knowing that we will always be alright, come what may
- The purpose of finding your path and journeying on it is to live your life according to whatever you find in your heart. This way your creativity flourishes and your heart sings
- Your heart always knows exactly where and what your path is
- The only way to cast light on the question of what to do with your life is to look into your heart
- Unfinished business is an energy drain and detrimental to your feeling of integrity. If something remains unresolved, get it sorted and move on!
- The behaviour of the Impeccable Warrior holds the secret to developing solid self-esteem, as well as winning the love and friendship of others who also behave with integrity

Self-assessment exercise

Exercise 7: The scale of impeccability

Questions to propel you on your path

- Try following a path of impeccability for a few days by asking yourself, as each situation in your day unfolds, 'how do I *feel* about that?' and then acting accordingly in every case
- If you find yourself in a position where you feel stuck and your creative flow dries up, as yourself, 'do I feel in balance?' Almost certainly the answer will be 'no' in which case the first place to look is to your Impeccability. Great follow-up questions to ask yourself include:

  Am I doing what I love?
  Am I being true to myself?
  Am I opting for second best?

* Make this commitment to yourself now and for the rest of your life. Get a pen and paper and write down the following powerful affirmation and let it be your mantra from now on:

'COME WHAT MAY I FOLLOW A PATH OF IMPECCABLE TRUTH AND INTEGRITY'

4

Developing a Positive Mindset

The mind is the master-weaver, both of the inner garment of character and the outer garment of circumstance

James Allen

So far we have emphasised the heart and its workings. Now it's time to put the workings of our minds under the microscope, for there are some further basic principles we need to understand in building our foundation.

We have seen how choosing, creating and visualising appropriate goals is largely a matter for the heart, but of course the mind must have some say in the matter too.

It's common knowledge that the two hemispheres of the brain are responsible for different types of thinking. The two halves and the two types of thinking are referred to as right brain and left brain. When we experience a passionate urge to do something, let's say to play football, we talk metaphorically of that passion coming from our heart. However, in reality this is probably more accurately defined as the processes of the creative, intuitive, holistic, imaginative side of our minds in action; in other words our right brain, which drives us to pursue the activity as creatively as we can. At the same time the execution and practice of the game is the business of our left brain. This is the intellectual, logical, analytical side; the side that wants to grapple with the theory, technique, strategy and the logistics by which the game is played at a high level.

Of course, the David Beckhams of this world probably don't realise consciously what they are doing in the heat of the moment, but in essence when they perform at their peak they have developed the ability to create a perfect balance between right brain and left brain functioning. When occasionally they go out of balance, they experience that as an off day when nothing flows, they score few goals and everything seems like hard work rather than a joy. When they get the balance right again, they are unstoppable.

All the top sports performers who consistently turn in quality performances over a period of years do this. Just watching Roger Federer playing tennis or Tiger Woods playing golf when they are on a roll is a perfect lesson in developing unswerving, laser-like focus and keeping balanced.

If we want to perform at our peak we must develop a right brain/left brain balance. Many find this especially difficult because usually one side of the brain is more highly developed than the other, and each side of the brain grows more powerful the more it is stimulated, like a muscle that grows stronger when it is exercised.

For the sake of simplicity I describe the interaction of the two hemispheres of the human brain as the heart/mind balance, this being a metaphor that most people can relate to, or I refer to the heart and mind being in or out of balance. But if you prefer to think of the term 'heart' as your right brain in this context, that's fine. I'm not a scientist so I'm going to stick to my metaphor of the heart/mind balance because that has obvious and clear meaning for me and hopefully you can empathise with it too. The term, I believe, also conveys the appropriate kind of symbolic image. When we do what we *love,* it *feels* as if it comes from our *heart.*

In the main, our education system puts far more emphasis on left brain activities, and as we grow up most of us get into the habit of taking a left brain or intellectual approach to solving our problems, and that's where we often come unstuck. Not only that, but the whispering voices of our hearts (or right brains) hardly get a look-in at most schools, and that is why so many of us grow up losing the ability we all had as babies to intuitively tune in to what's going on deep inside.

Whichever way you look at it, and even if the above was not true for you, both heart and mind are involved in any kind of personal development, transformational or consciousness-raising process, and the secret of getting a happy result depends on getting them in balance. *Much emphasis these days is placed on the so-called work/life balance, but of far greater importance is the heart/mind balance.* Why? If you can achieve a good heart/mind balance you have the potential to crack virtually all your problems. Immediately you start to feel less stressed, anxiety begins to melt away and you are able to flow. You feel better about yourself and therefore better able to allow everything else to fall into place sooner or later, including the work/life balance. Just how you can achieve that balance is something we will discuss later.

First, let's look at some general aspects of the mind in greater detail. It has become abundantly clear to me that our minds can create literally anything our hearts desire, and if we are not careful, even things we don't desire – things we dread. To put it simply, *your mind will manifest more of whatever is your dominant thought.* Another way of putting it is that *your mind creates whatever you expect.* It is vitally important to understand this because in many cases our dominant thoughts and expectations are unconscious – yet another very strong reason to raise our conscious awareness as much as possible.

Only too often a person will have a goal and they do all the right things in stating and expressing it, they do affirmations for years and they tell themselves they believe in it wholeheartedly and they even take action, yet they fail to achieve it and cannot understand why. In almost every case it's because they don't realise they have a dominant thought or expectation running directly contrary to their stated goal, so the goal is thereby sabotaged every time. This unconscious belief, which is another way of describing it, overrides all thoughts of the goal precisely because it is more dominant in your mind than your belief in your ability to achieve the goal. Even though it might be unconscious, the sabotaging belief still dominates.

Let's take a hypothetical example: you have a goal to become a highly successful entrepreneur with millions in the bank. You phrase the goal correctly (Chapter 17 is all about powerful ways of setting goals), you do all the right things yet you remain in poverty. After some digging we uncover some negative messages playing over and over again in your unconscious mind along the lines of 'I'm a failure,' 'everything I touch turns to dust,' 'I can't be trusted,' 'I'm not worthy,' 'I can't do this,' etc.

Am I ringing any bells here? Does any of this start to sound familiar? Despite your noble and most energetic intentions, your dominant thoughts and expectations in this fictitious example, though you don't realise it, are of failure. So guess what? Failure is what you create. Only by uncovering and acknowledging those unconscious, sabotaging thoughts or beliefs do you stand any chance of creating anything in his life other than failure. In the immortal and much quoted words of

Henry Ford, 'whether you believe you can or whether you believe you can't, you're right!'

And so we return to square one: *if you want to make meaningful goals and achieve them, the first step is to get to know yourself inside out, and every effort must be made to raise your level of conscious awareness.*

More or less all the current personal development gurus say that what you think and believe shapes your life and determines your experiences, but they don't always explain why. I hope the above explanation sheds some light on this because an understanding of this is pivotal to your journey. The author Aldous Huxley described this very well when he explained, 'experience is not what happens to a man; it is what a man does with what happens to him.'

Self-limiting beliefs and conditioning

If you take on board the idea that what you think and believe shapes how you experience the things that happen to you, you will realise that within your personal and unique random mix of unconscious beliefs, there are some that support you and help you make progress while others sabotage or limit you. It is these self-limiting beliefs, or as Christopher Howard calls them *limiting decisions,* that stop you from achieving your most deeply felt goals and dreams. Therefore it is very important to start to identify them and to become consciously aware of them, so you can choose to replace them with new, constructive beliefs or decisions that supercharge your efforts to get yourself into your flow and achieve what you want.

Imagine your mind is a computer hard disk and processing unit. The results produced by the computer are entirely dependent on the programming on the hard disk. If some of that programming is incorrect, corrupted or in some way mistaken, then no amount of keyboard or other input will produce the desired result. Clearly the faulty programming must be identified, eliminated and replaced with new programming that performs constructively.

When you switch on your PC or laptop at the start of a work day, it automatically activates certain settings (known as default settings), which you can change or control if you want to. These settings are designed to make the computer automatically respond consistently in ways you choose when executing certain tasks. You might not be aware of them, but they are there to help you get the result you want with minimum stress.

If you think of a computer's default settings as comparable to a person's unconscious response patterns and self-beliefs, what you are trying to achieve in your own mind is a reprogramming of your unconscious to new, supportive default settings (beliefs and behaviours). Then when you wake up in the morning and start functioning, exactly like your computer when it is switched on, you automatically start behaving in ways that support your every effort while you hardly have to think about it.

I have heard it said that training the mind in this way is 'like brainwashing'. It is a bit like brainwashing, but there is nothing to fear because *you* are controlling the brainwashing and *you* decide what you want and don't want in your unconscious mind. Harkening back to our Roger Federer analogy, he has programmed his mind and body to produce, for example, the killer cross-court backhand in response to his opponent hitting a shot to a certain position on the court. There is no time during a match for Federer to debate in his mind how to respond or to weigh up the options, for too much thinking and analysis would obviously be a disaster. It's largely a conditioned response learned from endless repetition, and it's automatic. Clearly Federer is a man who can rely on his 'default settings' to support him, but only because he has trained them that way.

Mary (not her real name) came to see me for Life Coaching sessions and proceeded to tell me at great length and with a fiery passion what she wanted to achieve. Then in the next ten minutes gave me at least twelve reasons why her goals were 'impossible pipe dreams.' She had in effect conceded her power to her self-limiting beliefs, which as far as she was concerned, were the gospel, the unshakeable truth about her.

These are just some of the reasons she presented as proof that her goals were impossible: 'life has not been kind;' 'people think I am cold;' 'if I had lots of money I would … but I don't have lots of money;' 'I'm not the sort of woman men want;' 'I'm too insecure;' 'I'm not resourceful;' 'I'm not interesting;' I was made to feel unimportant;' 'I feel like a second class passenger;' 'I'm very scared of anger, you must never lose your temper;' 'if I can't live in … maybe I can visit …'

At this point you might be forgiven for thinking that this woman was a lost cause, uncoachable and impossible to help. However, the fact that she had beaten a path to my door, after first trying hypnosis and other psychotherapeutic disciplines, indicated a certain undefeated spirit and a determination to find out what to change and how in spite of her fears. I admired her courage and I knew that it could pull her through the deep dark tunnel she was in, into a sunnier, happier situation, if she could persevere.

That's the key, *courage.* As well as persistence, determination, and grit. Qualities that can be summarised by the old fashioned word, *gumption.* If you want to identify and modify those self-limiting beliefs you can do it, but it takes *gumption.* So gird up your loins, make the decision to do it and get ready to make your life better ....

If you are now thinking, 'I haven't got gumption. I'm not that type,' understand that that in itself is a self-limiting belief and you can modify or transcend it. *If you look in your heart you will find the courage you need.* You might not believe me at this stage, but I hope you will by the time you have read some more of this book and put some of my suggestions into practise. It might seem scary at first, but you'll get over it if you keep focused on what you want to achieve.

So how exactly do we start to make ourselves aware of our self-limiting beliefs? Try this simple exercise. It's called *'what do I believe about myself?'*

Exercise 8: What do I believe about myself?

WHAT DO I BELIEVE ABOUT MYSELF?

Take a blank sheet of paper and a pen and put your name and today's date at the top.

Write down the question and then ask it to yourself, over and over again, ***'what do I believe about myself?'***

Now simply write down the answer you get after each time you ask yourself the question in the form of a list of your beliefs about yourself, whatever they are. Try to be as spontaneous and honest as you can – do not spend lots of time thinking about it. As usual, gut reaction is what we want. As an example I quote the first three of many beliefs from the list of one of my clients:

- *Money is hard to come by*
- *Life is hard*
- *Nobody loves me*

When you have done that, its time to do the other side of the exercise, which is to ask the question, *'what do I <u>want</u> to believe about myself?'*

Exercise 9: What do I *want* to believe about myself?

WHAT DO I *WANT* TO BELIEVE ABOUT MYSELF?

Take another blank sheet of paper and a pen and once again put your name and today's date at the top. Write down the question then ask it to yourself over and over again, **'what do I *want* to believe about myself?'** Again, write a list but this time of beliefs you *want* to have about yourself, but *in the present tense*, as if you already hold those beliefs. Don't be deterred by thinking it's impossible. Just be sincere and spontaneous.

As an example, here are the first three items from the same person's list:

- Money flows to me easily
- I love my life and everything in it
- People find me loveable

The purpose of this exercise is to first find out those unconscious beliefs you have that limit you and secondly, to identify a more positive set of beliefs that will support you. In this way you can identify which beliefs you wish to modify, and in what way, so you begin to develop thoughts and beliefs that will support you in creating the life you want. The reason for putting a date at the top is so that you can do both exercises again at, say, three monthly intervals and compare the results to evaluate your progress.

Attitude, attitude, attitude

This is all about commitment. Probably the most important thing to take on board if you want to change your life and you are still wondering how, as Louise Hay points out in her numerous and excellent published works, is embracing a *willingness to change.* If you are ready in your heart, if you can no longer put up with the way your life's been up to now, if you resolve to face your fears – the very moment you get serious and make the decision you are willing to change *and really mean it,* that is the pivotal moment when the change you are yearning for becomes inevitable. As sure as night follows day it will happen. It may take a while, and you may have to re-affirm your commitment many times, but sooner or later change will occur.

A negative, cynical, pessimistic, non-believing attitude will not do, for under such circumstances all the goal-setting techniques in the world will not help you turn your life around. If you are looking for a root and branch transformation, you have to cultivate a completely positive attitude. That's what makes Tiger Woods and Roger Federer stand on the shoulders of giants and makes them winners time after time.

Exactly this same principle applies to you and me. If I wanted to sail around the world single-handed (and let me assure you I most certainly don't) I know I could do it and so could you. However we will only achieve it if we develop the necessary commitment, if we sincerely want it with all our hearts, and we are prepared to devote ourselves to the task. You just have to make the *decision* and *be willing* to do whatever it takes – in accordance with your core values and beliefs, of course.

This is the way the Impeccable Warrior deals with situations like this: he asks himself, 'do I really and truly want this goal enough to put everything else aside and devote all my energy to making it come true?' If the answer is an unequivocal 'yes,' he'll go for it; if not, he'll drop the idea like a hot potato. This way of monitoring yourself by asking yourself how you *feel* almost always gives a very clear-cut 'yes' or 'no' answer, if you are honest about it. Don't forget, anything other than an unhesitating 'yes' is, in fact, a 'no.'

There is a caveat to that. If you do get a half-hearted 'yes' and you're still not sure, ask yourself why you are hesitating. It might be fear or lack of self-belief which could be overcome with a little more digging, a tad more courage. Bear in mind *you don't have to know at this stage how your goal will be achieved or your issue resolved,* you are just preparing a foundation for further work, like fertilising a seedbed in preparation for planting.

Most people are simply not interested in extreme achievements like those of the iconic sports personalities mentioned above, and that's fair enough. Most of us want a happy and fulfilled life, and what *you* want in *your* life is the only thing that matters. The illustrations and analogies above are merely to demonstrate the awesome power of your mind and to help you start believing that you can organise your thoughts in such a way that you end your inner chaos and live a life of flow, creativity and achievement.

This is why I insist my clients thoroughly scrutinise their goals and test them out with incisive self-questioning. This is important in finding out if the goals you have stated are your true goals. Are they realistic? I will ask someone, for example, 'are you sure you want to be a millionaire, or would you rather go fishing?' In other words, it's a nice idea but are you really committed to it? If not it's a fantasy and should be acknowledged as such.

We see many millionaires on our televisions, and we hear through the media about the latest characters who top the annual rich list. The cult of the entrepreneur is being greatly encouraged for it makes compelling television, but it is obvious that the truly successful ones devote almost every waking moment to building their businesses and investments. When they are not actually doing it, they are thinking about it. They virtually eat and breathe money, finance and investment.

Be honest with yourself. Do you have that kind of commitment and, most important, does it come naturally to you? If so, you too can succeed at making money. If not, it's surely a far better strategy to find out where your natural talents lie and what you do feel committed to and be successful at that.

Dealing with addictions

Incidentally, this same principle can be applied if your issue hinges on giving up an addiction. This could include smoking, alcoholism, drugs, gambling and even co-dependency. It can also be useful in getting over illnesses. An attitude of positivity and commitment is essential to success.

There is no doubt in my mind that no amount of detoxing and rehab will help you kick your alcohol or drug habit unless you dedicate yourself to achieving that goal. *With the correct mindset anything is possible.*

In the case of an addiction, build your awareness as much as you can so you fully notice the day when you reach the end of your tether and decide with all your heart that you must do something about this. That is the time to seek out all the support you can get from the professionals. They will then be able to help you build a can-do attitude and start believing in yourself, even if you falter from time to time. Then, and only then, do you stand a chance of success. (More about getting over addictions in Chapter 26.)

With a determined mindset, when you falter, when the inevitable self-doubt creeps in, when you fall off the wagon, you do not give up and you do not beat yourself up fruitlessly. Instead you take stock, give yourself a brief time to recover your focus, and start again. If you can maintain a compassionate attitude towards yourself in which you fully credit yourself for every tiny increment of progress and also commend yourself for your considerable courage, you will get there in the end.

On a slightly less serious note but nonetheless remarkable, I remember when I was about eight years old deciding to get over the hayfever I suffered every spring and summer. It was driving me crazy, I was sneezing all the time, suffering a sore nose and feeling wretched. What's more, the antihistamines which my father prescribed me (he was a doctor) made me feel drowsy, so I felt like a zombie and I didn't like it one bit. One day in a fit of pique I threw away the tablets and resolved to focus instead on something positive I was interested in, making model airplanes probably. I simply decided I didn't want hayfever and I would not have it any longer. Sure enough, in a very short time there was no more hayfever and there never has been to this day, some fifty-three years later.

The human immune system is a miraculous and powerful healing and defence mechanism, but sometimes it needs a little help. Developing a positive and determined mindset helps it enormously. I have even seen people get over seasickness by simply deciding sincerely to get over it. If you want to read a great, true and touching story about using the power of the mind and the emotions help a person's immune system to get over cancer, read Brandon Bays' seminal work, *The Journey*.

At this point someone usually says to me, 'that's all very well, but I bet your mind can't heal a broken leg for you.' Well as a matter of fact, a positive attitude will greatly assist and accelerate the healing process in a case like that too. I actually saw my partner's son do exactly that. He healed the leg he broke while skiing in a much faster time than the doctors had predicted through his determination, tenacity and focus. These kinds of personally witnessed experiences are why I feel it's absolutely reasonable to believe that a positive attitude, in the form of *deciding* to affect a healing, is an essential aid to our immune systems, and without it we struggle.

Don't put the cart before the horse

As I said earlier, sometimes a person will tell me that they have no talent, calling or passion and there's nothing they feel drawn to. On further investigation this usually translates as, 'well actually I'd love to be an artist (or whatever) but I could never make a living doing that,' at which point I usually start tearing my hair out.

In the beginning of this process I am not interested in how you will earn your living. I just want to know what you love doing, what you are naturally good at and what you feel drawn to. The implication of financial insecurity is really scary for many people and they will go to the most incredible lengths to avoid giving a straight answer to this very simple question once they bring an element of money into the equation. If you feel unable to give a straight answer, then once again we are talking about avoidance, a refusal to acknowledge what's really going on inside, and in many cases a cutting off from your emotional side. What reason could there be for this behaviour other than fear? If, for example, you want to be an artist, admit it and say 'I want to be an artist.' One step at a time. I repeat, never mind about earning a living for the moment.

It's only a question. I'm not suggesting you immediately quit your day job to become a starving artist in a garret. I realise there is no virtue in poverty and the fear of financial insecurity is very real and understandable. Or could it be that you perceive it as too painful to acknowledge the truth about what you love doing because that would make your present work in doing something else even more unbearable?

If the latter is the case, then the real issue is still being avoided. Whatever the reason, if you persist in avoiding your real issue, you will never resolve it. It will always nag away at you on the quiet until one day you can no longer ignore it. I am hoping you are now at that point. It's a sad, unfortunate fact that many of us will take action for change only when we reach the end of our tether, when we feel totally boxed into a corner, when we are desperate, or when we feel we cannot put up with our suffering any longer.

If that's how you want it to be, then so be it. But it doesn't have to be like that. Instead of waiting for your nervous breakdown you can act now! You just have to be willing and committed. Wake up and smell the coffee!

Here's an important lesson I learned from Robert Kiyosaki's book, *Rich Dad, Poor Dad,* which talks about a new perspective on wealth. If you say, 'I can't afford it,' you immediately shut down all possibilities for your mind to find a way of affording whatever 'it' might be. However, if you ask yourself, 'how can I afford it?' you actually invite your mind to search creatively for ways and possibilities you might not have previously thought of to be able to afford it. You automatically open the doors to your creative powerhouse so that ideas can start to flow.

It was Einstein who pointed out that our imaginations are far more important than our knowledge, and that's how scientists put people on the moon. Someone, or a group of people, had a vision and then they set about discovering how to make it possible. Just because something has never been done before doesn't mean it's impossible, it means nobody thought about it seriously.

The same principle applies to everything in your life. If you say I can't afford to follow my dream because I couldn't earn a living doing that, you are using money as an excuse for avoiding the real issue, which involves taking that scary leap in the dark and embracing the unknown. Why not start doing what you love, money or no money, even if it's only part- time or in free time moments, and *see what happens?* Don't forget life is an experiment.

When you start to follow your path, all sorts of things start to happen. Let the money follow, *if it will.* Of course there's nothing to stop you from giving it a helping hand. Maybe it turns out you are happy pursuing your passion in your leisure time while you do something else you love to make a living. If you worry about earning money before you start following your passions you are putting the cart before the horse. Your vision might include an obvious path for making money, or it might not. That may emerge later, but that doesn't make your vision or your path any less valid.

As you already know, one of my great passions is sailing and over the years I have done almost every Royal Yachting Association course there is to do in the UK up to the level of professional yachting instructor, but no sooner did I get my instructor's ticket than I decided I did not want to be a professional yachtsman. Nevertheless, having that qualification has given me a great deal of satisfaction and I feel I stand among my peer group as a competent skipper who could, in theory, sail anywhere where there is water. The point is that while I was following this process I didn't know what I wanted from it or what the outcome would be. I just knew I wanted to do it. I earn my living by following other passions, namely coaching, writing, and teaching meditation. That's the perfect balance for me.

I recount these stories not to blow my own trumpet but to illustrate the power of your mind to manifest anything you want it to. Be aware, sometimes your mind needs carefully directing, focusing and opening up, or it might thwart your efforts through sabotage from unconscious negative beliefs.

Avoid negative input

One final warning before we put this chapter to bed. *It is very important to be discriminating about what input we allow into our delicate psyches.*

When a new client comes to see me and says they feel depressed, almost always my first suggestion is to stop reading newspapers. That's not to say you need to be ignorant of what is going on in the world, but there are other ways of finding out. Unfortunately, all the mainstream newspapers seem to fill their pages with the most negative possible spin in the belief that, for some bizarre reason, it's what their readers want and they will sell more papers if they do that.

If you are prone to depression, some of the information, or should I say misinformation, you read in the papers will register in your unconscious mind even if you don't believe it consciously and before you know it you feel even worse, perhaps even suicidal. Even if you are a born optimist it's much harder to focus on anything positive when you fill your mind with negative input.

Many people, when they begin an inner journey or a path of personal development, find they seem to shed many former friends and colleagues and acquire new ones. This is exactly as it should be, for when you are trying to grow and learn new things it's important to start to associate with others who might have something to teach you or who are seeking similar knowledge. It's very helpful to have people to whom you can relate and who inspire you, rather than negative people who don't want to change and who try to drag you down. Remember, *whenever a choice arises, always choose something positive.*

Also remember, you can learn anything if your heart is in it and you dedicate yourself. It might be necessary to find a teacher or mentor (in which case get the very best one you can find), it might be necessary to study and read, to go to seminars or do a college course, maybe even go to university. Do whatever it takes to achieve the life you want. I want you to understand here and now, *you can do it if you develop a positive mindset.* If you believe you have to be someone special then you haven't noticed that you *are* someone special. You *are* the living miracle known as a *human being* and you embody all the secrets of creation, no less.

Here in a nutshell is how it works: *if you let go of your self-limiting beliefs and replace your negative mindsets with positive ones, a whole host of possibilities and opportunities come naturally within your grasp.*

Summary

- If you want to perform at your peak you must develop a balance between your right and left brain activity
- A good heart/mind balance enables you to crack virtually all your problems. You feel less stressed, anxiety melts away and you are able to flow, allowing everything to fall into place, including your work/life balance
- Your mind will manifest your dominant thoughts and your strongest expectations. What you think, believe and expect shapes your life and determines your experiences
- 'You can't solve your problems using the same thinking you used when you created them.' Albert Einstein
- 'Whether you believe you can or whether you believe you can't, you're right.' Henry Ford
- *If you want to make meaningful goals and achieve them, the first step is to get to know yourself inside out, and every effort must be made to raise your level of conscious awareness.* In other words, you need to find out what's going in your heart and in your mind.
- Self-limiting beliefs stop you from achieving your most deeply-felt goals and dreams. It is important to identify them, to become consciously aware of them, so you can choose to replace them with new, constructive beliefs that help you get you into your flow and achieve what you want
- You are trying reprogramme your unconscious to new, supportive default settings, so that when you wake up in the morning you automatically start behaving in ways that support your every effort while hardly thinking about it
- If you look into your heart you will find the courage you need to make the changes you desire
- If you are ready in your heart and resolved to face your fears, *you are willing to change.* That is the moment when the change you are yearning for becomes inevitable. *With the correct mindset anything is possible*

- You don't have to know at this stage how your goal will be achieved or your issue resolved. You are preparing a solid foundation for further work
- Are you sure you want to be a millionaire, or would you rather go fishing? It's a nice idea but are you really committed to it? If not, it's a fantasy
- Developing a positive and determined mindset helps your immune system
- What do you love doing, what you are naturally good at and what you feel drawn to?
- You don't have to keep on suffering. Instead of waiting for your nervous breakdown you can act now! You just have to be willing and committed
- Our imaginations are far more important than our knowledge. That's how scientists put people on the moon. Someone, or a group of people, had a vision and then set about discovering how to make it possible. The same principle applies to everything in your life
- When you start to follow your path, all sorts of things start to happen
- If you worry about earning money before you start following your passions you are putting the cart before the horse
- *It is very important to be discriminating about what input we allow into our delicate psyches.* If you are feeling depressed, stop reading newspapers, watching horror films and hanging out with negative, narcissistic, egotistical people. Even if you are a born optimist it's much harder to focus on anything positive when you fill your mind with negative input
- *Whenever a choice arises, always choose something positive*
- You can learn anything if your heart is in it and you dedicate yourself
- If you believe you have to be someone special to get the life of your dreams then you haven't noticed you *are* someone special. You *are* the living miracle know as a *human being* and you embody all the secrets of creation, no less
- *When you let go of your self-limiting beliefs and replace your negative mindsets with positive ones, a whole host of possibilities and opportunities come naturally within your grasp*

Exercises to test your beliefs

Exercise 8: What do I believe about myself?
Exercise 9: What do I *want* to believe about myself?

PART TWO

The Five Pillars

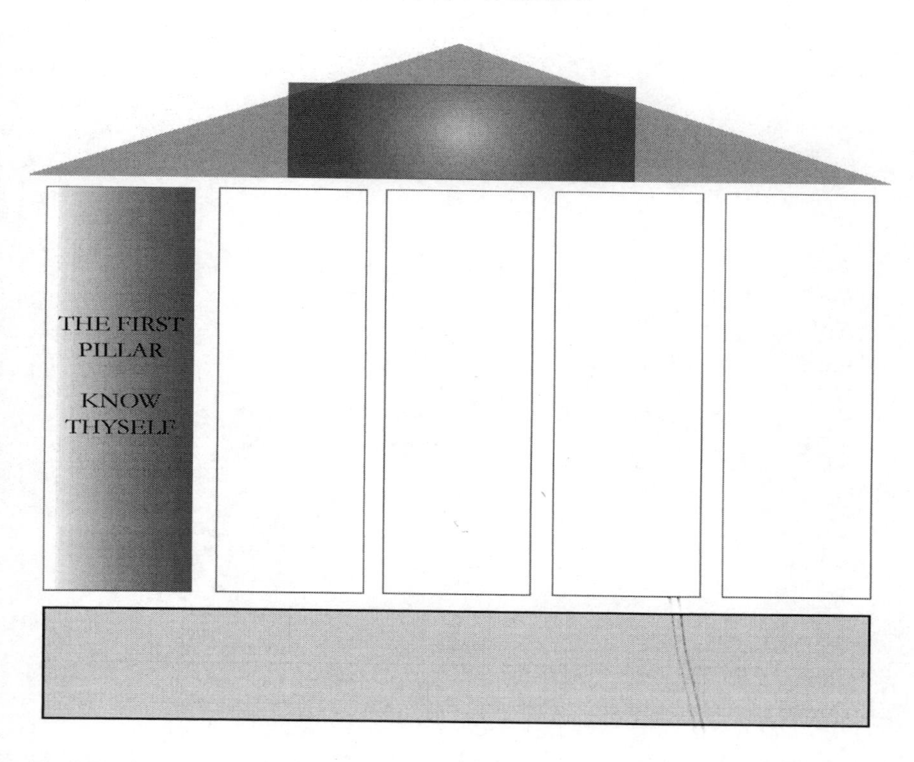

Tools, tools, tools! It's amazing what you can build when you have a bagful of tools! The first pillar we are going to build is the one called **Know Thyself.** *It's about getting to know yourself inside out. By the time we have finished building it you will have a fine collection of powerful, tried and tested tools, and some deeply insightful questions to ask yourself, all specifically designed to help you deepen your self-knowledge.*

We begin with the most powerful tool of all, meditation.

5

Tuning In

Self-awareness is key, and it grows quietly and without fanfare. It is a powerful force that moves mountains through its subtlety … things change far more deeply when the change is subtle

Ingrid Bacci, *The Joy of Effortless Living*

This chapter, which is about meditation and the art of witnessing, is arguably the most important chapter in this book and if you only ever read one chapter, I urge you to make sure it's this one, because then you will be sure to get something immensely valuable. *Meditation will take you far, far beyond ordinary goals, to a place of balance, peace and profound fulfillment.*

Meditation is the greatest gift you can give yourself because through the benefits of meditation you can get your life absolutely in balance, and then everything and anything becomes possible. That's why, in these days of stress and hurry, the internet, networking and passive wealth creation opportunities, I offer you meditation.

The art of witnessing

As you have no doubt noticed, meditation is a major hobby horse of mine, I simply love it! Why is it so important? There are many reasons which I will describe as we go along, but suffice to say that *meditation is the most potent, powerful tool for transformation I have ever found after over forty years on the path of personal development and personal transformation.* I use it for myself and, among other things, as a coaching tool with my clients. It's the most powerful tool in my tool bag actually – yet very few Life Coaches seem to use it and I believe they're missing a trick, and unfortunately so are their clients.

There are probably more methods of meditating than ways an Italian chef has of making pasta dishes, and I have tried quite a few over the years. The meditation method I offer here is specifically designed for increasing your self-awareness and is the result of cherry picking the best bits from the various methods I have come across over the years.

Some people exhibit strong resistance when I describe this meditation, but I assure you, if you avoid mediation you are missing out big time and making the creation of your new life far more difficult and much slower than it need be. I try never to give advice, but this is the one exception. I have never known anyone come to any harm from meditating and I strongly recommend it to anyone and everyone. As usual, don't take my word for it, try it yourself and see what happens. You may believe it's hard to do, but once you get used to it you'll see it's as easy as falling off a log! That's because you don't have to do anything, master any skills or put on a performance. This meditation is really about *non-doing*.

Lots of people have their favourite meditation methods and are reluctant to change. I am not asking you to give up your present practice if it works for you, I am simply saying *try this one too.* Make a commitment to yourself to do this regularly and *see what happens.* If you can manage twenty minutes twice a week to start with, that's great. Repetition is important, so little and often seems to work better than long periods once in a while. If you are really enthusiastic, an hour every day is fantastic, but most important is to make your commitment realistic and achievable and don't overdo it so it becomes drudgery.

If you have a tendency to put things off or leave it until it's too late, create a written schedule for your day in which your meditation practice has a clearly defined place. As you will see later, writing things down greatly enhances your chances of turning your intentions into deeds and then results. If you miss a day, please don't beat yourself up about it. Just note your omission and return to your schedule. At the same time, don't let that be an excuse for avoidance.

Exercise 10: Silent meditation

SILENT MEDITATION

The following notes describe my very simple meditation technique, which is specifically designed to be easy to do. You can do it for as long as you like – even five minutes twice a week is better than nothing, though about an hour every day seems to be ideal. Most people choose to meditate first thing in the morning, but that's optional.

Please note: *whatever your religious persuasion, if any, there should be no conflict between your religion and this meditation because meditation is non-religious.*

Sit up either in a straight-backed chair, on the floor or on cushions, with your back straight but not tense. Take a few deep breaths and you will find your breathing easily supports your upper body without creating tension. Avoid slouching, reclining or lying down unless you have to. Close your eyes and take a few deep breaths. You are going to sit in silence for the length of time you have allocated so turn off your mobile, switch on your answer machine and put out your 'do not disturb' sign.

During your meditation, almost certainly many thoughts and feelings will come into your mind.

The trick is ***not*** *to try to stop those thoughts and feelings, judge them, suppress them, hang on to them, control them or get involved with them. Instead simply observe them objectively as if they were someone else's. Take a step back, detach yourself, become an impartial witness, and allow your thoughts and feelings to come and go at will.* ***Wait to see what comes clear to you in the fullness of time without trying to control the outcome or work anything out.***

There is a knack to witnessing in complete objectivity and it may take you a while to get the hang of it. Don't give up – persevere.

During the meditation you may notice you have lost your witnessing quality and gone off on a tangent with some thought or another. When you become aware of that, simply stop, bring yourself back and start again. Don't worry about it or judge yourself harshly. In the early days you may have to do that 100 times in fifteen minutes. No matter, just start again.

Many people mistakenly assume that when doing this meditation they are required to still the mind, but most of us cannot do that. It is impossible because as we saw in the previous chapter we have been educated to vastly develop our minds to the maximum, and we're trained to stimulate our minds and to solve our problems by intellectual analysis. *Don't even bother to try to still your mind, because you'll be wasting your time.* Just be *a witness* – even if you are witnessing chaos and turmoil. Eventually, if you keep doing this every day or whenever you can, moments of stillness will spontaneously occur. At first it may be for only a millisecond, but that glimpse could be just enough, if you are alert and aware, to begin a transformation.

So please begin, and remember, *allow whatever thoughts and feelings arise and be a witness. Don't interfere. Don't judge.* This meditation is about allowing yourself to do absolutely nothing. No work is involved, it is an experience of no-effort. If you find yourself making an effort, you've missed the point. Try again.

The art of witnessing is also an experiment in letting go of control. Many people find this prospect potentially frightening because of course no-one knows what might happen, but unless you are willing to experience whatever your unconscious mind reveals, you will never be able to clear the way for your heart to reveal itself. So be of good courage and almost certainly you'll find in retrospect that the letting-go experience wasn't so scary after all – on the contrary, it was fascinating and insightful.

VERY IMPORTANT: You will notice there is no mantra, no candles, no incense, no music, no watching the breath and no other devices for your mind to focus on. This is where this particular meditation differs radically from most others. *The whole point is to let your mind be unfocused* so you can find out what's really hidden in your unconscious mind that wants to arise and reveal itself, warts and all.

Raising awareness

The single most important benefit of the silent mediation I described above is the effect of enhancing your conscious awareness. You are trying to discover what's actually going on in your unconscious mind so you can identify the unconscious messages that control your behaviour patterns.

As soon as we are born, and all the time we are growing towards adulthood, we all receive conditioning in the form of messages, overt or covert, from our role models, authority figures, people around us including other children, and the environment in which we live. These lodge in our unconscious minds and each of us interprets them in our own personal way. To take an extreme example, a boy who sees his father treating his mother with drunken violent abuse is himself likely, in adulthood, to deal with relationship problems violently and perhaps drunkenly, without even thinking about it. This is simply because that is what he learned by example from his dominant male role model. It's an unconscious response and unless he raises his conscious awareness, it may never occur to him that there might be another, more harmonious way.

Likewise a girl observing her mother being subjected to such behaviour might automatically assume that it's normal or even tolerable for men to get drunk and lash out at women, and that females are supposed to be subservient and not make their men angry. She may even think such behaviour is her mother's fault and she deserved it.

There is also a very strong likelihood – and this is the really scary bit – that she will unconsciously attract into her life the very kind of men who behave like this towards her. This is why dysfunctional patterns of behaviour tend to be repeated through generation after generation. The only remedy is increased awareness and understanding. If she understands what she does she can modify her beliefs, choose different behaviour and most important, teach her children differently.

In the case of the boy, unless he finds out what is driving his father's drunken behaviour and does something about changing it in himself, he will never understand why as an adult he's always in trouble, why he lashes out only to regret it later, and why he is constantly labeled as 'wrong'. Meditation can help him discover what his unconscious drivers are.

It is very common for messages that condition our unconscious minds to develop and become fixed as unconscious self-limiting beliefs. Imagine a tape-loop playing non-stop in the back of your mind that's saying to you, for example, 'I'm not good enough,' 'I'll never be successful,' or 'nobody loves me.' Under such circumstances it's going to be really difficult to achieve anything positive or to feel loved. That is why we need to discover and address these messages and make them conscious.

What's the point? As soon as you make those beliefs conscious, *they start to loose their power to dominate and ruin your life.* Awareness, as we have already seen, gives you choices. As soon as you *recognise* your old pattern riding over the hill to sabotage you, you can choose different behaviour. You can literally talk to your saboteur as if he were a separate entity and say, 'go away, I'm not listening to you any more.' (Chapter 8 discusses this in more detail.)

Conditioning can also be self-created, from our own interpretation of our experiences, as well as from outside input, and these interpretations also help form self-limiting beliefs. Questions arise such as: 'Why on earth did I do that again?' 'Why do I never get what I want?' 'Why do people always seem to get angry with me?' Only by getting to know ourselves inside out can we hope to gain insight and understanding into our situation. Meditation helps us in that endeavour.

As Dr. Phil McGraw points out in his book, *Life Strategies*, 'people do what works' and it's a good idea to 'identify the payoffs that drive your behaviour and that of others.' He also says, 'the behaviour you choose creates the results you get.' Your choices are very often unconscious of course and it can be quite a revelation when you fully assimilate this. The problem arises for some people when they realise they want different results, but much probing to get at the truth reveals that deep in their hearts they are reluctant to change, even though they might think they ought to. The simple reason is that the prospect of change is perceived as far too scary. In other words they want change but they fear it, so they lapse back into unawareness.

Others run into problems because the need to change simply hasn't dawned, which is another form of unconsciousness.

Many are the times when I see someone suddenly understand that they alone are responsible for their life situation. No amount of blaming others, or citing unfortunate circumstances, can enable them to wriggle out of this new reality that is suddenly staring them in the face – that *they* are the cause of their problems.

It is not unknown for someone to come to me for Life Coaching even though they have no serious intention of changing anything. This behaviour is almost certainly unconscious – the person doesn't do it on purpose, indeed he doesn't even realise he's doing it – but it gives him a golden excuse to say to himself, 'look, I've tried everything, even Life Coaching, and it didn't work.' Thus he gives himself license to remain stuck in the familiar pattern he knows so well while blaming me for not fixing his woes.

This is a great illustration of just how brilliant and inventive the unconscious mind can be in its subterfuge. By employing this strategy the person concerned never has to face the feelings of fear and insecurity he might experience if he strayed out of his comfort zone by confronting his issues. This way he feels vindicated in avoiding taking responsibility as usual, and strange as it may seem, that's the payoff. A very sophisticated unconscious strategy if ever I saw one, and powerfully self-sabotaging. He made quite sure he remained stuck and a victim for good. No amount of Life Coaching will ever make any difference unless he declares himself sincerely and consciously ready to change.

When you read about it in a book like this it seems crazy, but many people behave like that or in equivalent self-defeating ways all the time, and more often than not they are completely mystified as to why their lives don't work as they would wish. If you are baffled about an issue in your life, especially if it recurs, ask yourself, 'am I taking responsibility for my life and everything in it? Have I yet realised I am the architect of my own fortunes or misfortunes? Could this situation be of my own making?' Remember, be careful not to slip into beating yourself up for not being good or perfect enough (more on that in Chapter 8).

Many people take refuge in the known and the familiar and they take comfort in beliefs, no matter how bizarre, that confirm their self-image. For example, if you believe you are not worthy, you are very likely to pursue behaviour unconsciously that corroborates your belief that you are not worthy. There's a perverse sense of security to be had from that.

It's very easy to unwittingly set yourself up for failure if you are not aware of what's going on inside. Unconscious behaviour of that sort tends to ruin your life. They say the truth hurts but in my experience the pain of facing the truth is short-lived, whereas the effects of unconscious sabotaging behaviour hurt far more and for the long term. You might try to rationalise it away, saying to yourself, *'it's not so bad. I can live with it.'* You might even believe that's normal, but if you really let your feelings in, you will realise you are hurting. You may fear the pain you anticipate, so courage is required if you are to unearth and face the truth about yourself and make the changes you want to make. That, I am sure, is what Susan Jeffers was getting at in *Feel The Fear And Do It Anyway*.

Quite often I will say to a client, when he finally begin to realise it's fear that's stopping him, *'surely you're not going to let a little bit of fear stand in the way of making your dreams come true – or are you?'*

But it's not only fear. If you want to be genuinely happy, fulfilled and stress-free, any kind of repressed feelings are bad news because, although you might think you have them safely packed away in a little box with a tight fitting lid, they will come back and bite you when you're not looking. Anger is a classic example of an emotion which, when deeply repressed, can lead to depression, introversion, sarcasm, temper tantrums, violence, addictions, self-harming, anorexia, suicide and all sorts of sabotaging behaviour. Far better to go inside and discover the anger, however scary, and let it be expressed in a safe and supportive environment. Let it have its moment. Then it becomes possible for the anger to pass so it evaporates out of your system leaving you free and unburdened.

In later chapters we will discuss how to deal with anger and other strong emotions safely. I chose anger as an example of a suppressed emotion in this chapter to emphasise the need to discover and acknowledge whatever unexpressed emotions we have.

Getting in tune

Because many of us have become dependent on figuring everything out mentally and have cut ourselves off from the whisperings of our heart, it is common for us to be unaware of what it is trying to tell us. Meditation can help you tune in.

If you are feeling lost, dazed, confused or overwhelmed by too many choices, it's almost certain you are trying to work out an answer by thinking. Silent meditation, in which all thinking is removed, can help you regain the balance between mind, body, spirit and soul, or if you prefer, your inner and your outer worlds. Meditation helps you retrain your mind so it resumes it's intended role of faithful servant.

Your inner journey is all about helping you rediscover and reconnect with your passions, talents, calling, vocation, call it what you will, and opening up to your creativity. Meditation, in effect, lets your heart tell you what choices it wants you to make. This is why it is not always a good idea to set goals right at the start of your coaching process. It is very easy to rush off and achieve the 'wrong' goals, that is goals that your mind has cooked up based on your conditioned beliefs, rather than what your heart desires. These 'wrong' goals do not allow you to flow and therefore never lead to lasting happiness, peace, balance and fulfillment. For many people it is first necessary to discover the goals that are right for them.

So if there is no flow in your life, you know for sure you've got work to do! The first step is to start meditating.

Meditation does not rely on fossil fuels nor on technology, and neither does it produce carbon emissions. Moreover, unlike a lot of our modern technology, it relieves stress and it's free! Research cites many benefits for meditation. Have a look at this I found on the web recently:

> *'Meditation stimulates positive changes in mental, emotional and spiritual health … People who meditate every day are many times happier than those who don't. They're*

also healthier and live longer. And their sense of well-being is much higher than that of non-meditators.'

'Meditators' minds are also sharper, and their problem-solving abilities are better. That's one reason why many high-powered executives and even CEOs of Fortune 500 companies meditate.'

'Meditators make a lot more pleasurable brain chemicals pretty much all the time, and have dramatically better mental health. They have less anxiety, anger, depression and fear, and they have better human relationships, more friends, and feel much more fulfilled in their lives.'

(This information comes from the website of the Centrepointe Institute in America www.centrepointe.com)

A few words about freedom

What exactly do I mean when I talk about setting yourself free? I'm talking about freedom from being driven by unconscious, neurotic and self-sabotaging behaviour patterns; freedom from anxiety and fear-driven responses; freedom from low self-esteem and low self-worth; freedom to be confidently proactive; freedom to trust, love and accept yourself and others unconditionally; and the freedom to believe in yourself, to make your own choices and live your own life in your own way. These are the ultimate freedoms that no one can take away from you once you have found them, and you find them by getting to know who you really are and accepting and loving yourself unconditionally. Not the conditioned you but the *real* you.

Here's the key: *the real you is always unconditionally acceptable and lovable. Therefore, have the courage to reveal the real you and be yourself.*

Now, bearing in mind the above, if I hear you say, 'but when you get to know me you'll realise I'm a horrible person,' I will know straight away I'm not hearing from the *real* you. All I can suggest is more meditation, more awareness and more courage to see beyond the negative programming, the self-limiting beliefs, and the denial you have allowed into your vulnerable psyche. Be kind to yourself. Discover the miraculous product of creation that you are. Are you a special case? Why should you be any the less miraculous a being than the rest of us?

I am aware that faultless self-love is an idyllic scenario and I honestly believe it's one that is achievable. But this is the real world. It is true to say we each have the necessary ingredients within our own beings to experience balance and therefore peace in our lives, and so it follows in theory we simply need to allow those qualities to surface and activate themselves. However, we must also acknowledge that many people in their daily lives experience nothing but conflict, confusion, anguish and turmoil – all the ingredients of stress – to a larger or lesser degree. Feeling continually stressed is a most unpleasant experience and it's no way to live your life.

'OK, so how can mediation help me to find this freedom, and anyway, what on earth has all this to do with personal development and the Five Pillars of Happiness?' you may ask.

It has everything to do with it. To recap, if you can develop the art of listening to your inner voice, the voice of your heart, it will always guide you with integrity. All you need is the courage to follow its guidance without question. To tune in and hear that still small voice, it is necessary at regular intervals to be still and silent, and listen with all your attention. Silent meditation is a powerfully effective way of doing that.

Don't be tempted to take short cuts. Creating a happy life that remains happy to the end of your days is a long-term process. That's why, unless you are someone who knows yourself inside out already, self-exploration has to come first, goals can come later. The best possible situation is when your goals seem to emerge by themselves and become self-evident. Then you know you are onto something.

There are exceptions, of course. For example if you happen to be born as Mozart, your path ahead is screamingly obvious from the age of about three. If you were born as Vincent Van Gogh, you wouldn't need a personal development book or a Life Coach to help you discover you should take up painting. However, let us not forget that these two characters, and many more astoundingly creative figures I could mention, lived wildly dysfunctional lives by anybody's standards and suffered greatly as a result. It is my gut feeling that almost certainly they would have enjoyed their lives more, and without detriment to their respective talents, had they stopped occasionally for a spot of silent meditation.

In short, meditation helps things fall into balance naturally, so you can more easily see the bigger picture, get a truer perspective and allow your next steps, even your goals, to emerge. It's a very non-forcing approach and it can quite literally produce profound transformation in a person's life.

Finally, I want to share with you the exact unsolicited words a client said to me recently, because this woman really understood how her meditation practise was supporting her: 'I am really into meditation now, Dave. It helps me so much. It really is a part of my life now. I just love it and I really look forward to doing it. And it's really helping me through some very hard times at the moment.'

And on her way out of the door after a meeting of my fortnightly north London meditation group, one participant said 'thank you Dave, that was exactly what I needed.'

I reckon those two people say it all.

Summary

- Meditation will take you far, far beyond ordinary goals, to a place of balance, peace and profound fulfillment
- If you avoid mediation you make the creation of your new life far more difficult and slower than it need be
- Practice the art of witnessing. Don't try to still your mind because you'll be wasting your time. Just be a witness, even if you are witnessing chaos and turmoil
- This meditation is about allowing yourself to do absolutely nothing. It's about non-doing. No work is involved; it is an experience of no-effort. If you find yourself making an effort, you've missed the point. Try again
- The art of witnessing is also an experiment in letting go of control, but that's not as scary as you might think. Let your mind be totally 'unfocused'
- The single most important benefit of the silent mediation is in enhancing your conscious awareness
- As soon as you become conscious of your conditioned self-limiting beliefs, they loose their power to dominate and ruin your life. Awareness gives you choices and silent meditation gives you that awareness
- Repressed feelings are bad news because, although you might think you have them under control, they will come back and bite you when you're not looking. Anger is a classic example
- If you are feeling lost, confused or overwhelmed by too many choices, it's almost certain you are trying to work out an answer by

thinking. In silent meditation all thinking is removed. This can help you regain balance and perspective

- To tune in and hear the still small voice of your heart, it is necessary at regular intervals to be still and silent, and listen with all your attention. Silent meditation is a powerfully effective way of doing that
- Meditation helps things fall into balance naturally, so you can see the bigger picture, get a truer perspective and allow your next steps and goals to emerge
- Try it for yourself and see what happens
- The *real* you is always unconditionally acceptable. Have the courage to reveal the *real* you and be yourself

Exercises

Exercise 10: Silent meditation

Questions to ask yourself

If you are baffled about a recurring issue in your life, ask yourself the following questions:

- Am I taking responsibility for my life and everything in it?
- Have I yet realised I am the architect of my own fortunes or misfortunes?
- Could this situation be of my own making?

6

What Does Your Life Look Like Right Now?

With the right programmes in place, doing the right thing is easy; with the wrong programmes running your mind, it's virtually impossible.

Paul McKenna

Wheel of Life

This is a brilliant diagnostic tool used by coaches the world over in one form or another for enabling their clients to see instantly where their life is at right now. It gives you an instant visual check on which areas of your life need work and which don't, and helps you quickly evaluate which are the most and least urgent. It is also very useful for measuring progress and change.

What a lot of people don't realise, however, is that it can also be used to focus in closely on specific areas – wheels within wheels as it were – and this makes it very helpful in gaining deep insight and understanding of those more elusive issues.

Here's how it works:

Exercise 11: Wheel of Life

WHEEL OF LIFE

(If you don't want to write in this book, you can download and print the exercise from www.thefivepillarsofhappiness.com)

The diagram or template below represents a wheel – the wheel of your life. It's divided into twelve equal segments. Each segment has a label and represents an area of your life. If you don't agree with one of the labels you are perfectly at liberty to change it or delete it and the segment. You can also introduce new labelled segments to the wheel.

Now imagine each section divided across by ten equal divisions numbered with invisible numbers from 0 in the middle to 10 on the circumference (see example on page xxx).

Before you start this exercise it is important to write the date on it so you can do it again at regular two or three monthly intervals and compare the result with previous efforts to assess your progress. You can make several photocopies of the template (Template 1) in this book for future use, or as stated above you can download copies as you need them in PDF format free from our website, www.thefivepillarsofhappiness.com

On the next page you will find another template entitled ***Wheel of Life Shortlist*** (Template 2). You will also need photocopies or downloaded PDF copies of this, also available free from the above website. Use of both templates is explained below.

Template 1

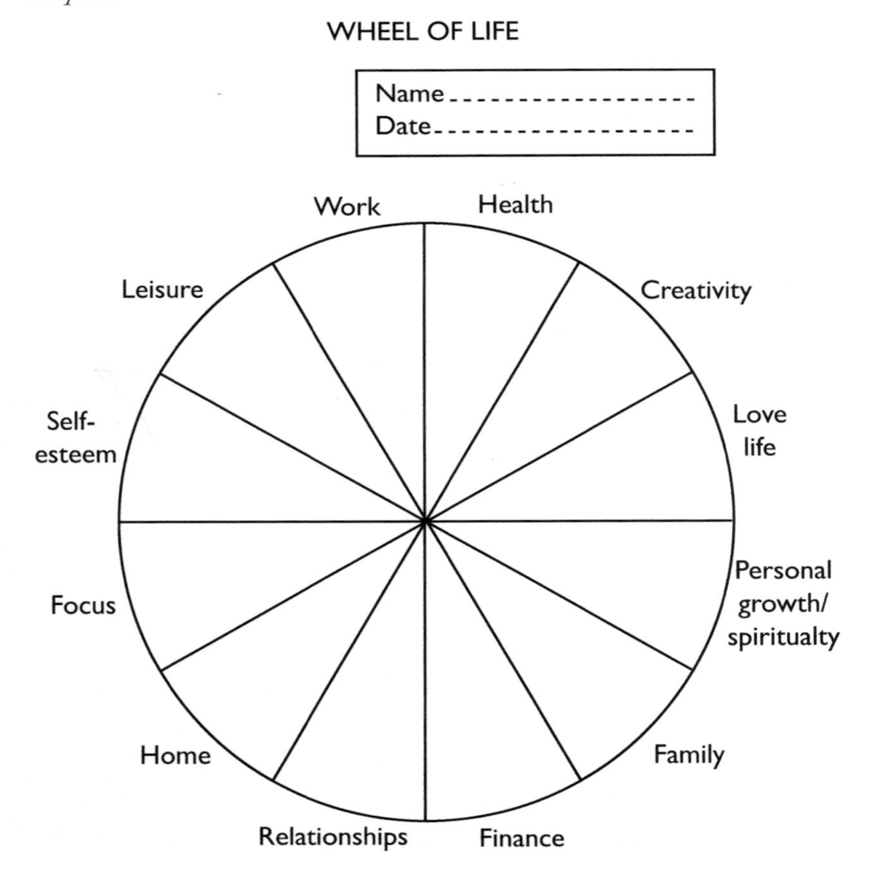

Template 2 **WHEEL OF LIFE SHORTLIST**

Name ....
Date ....

Areas that need enhancement

1) ______________________
2) ______________________
3) ______________________

Three possible actions for ….............

1)
2)
3)

Three possible actions for ….............

1)
2)
3)

Three possible actions for ….............

1)
2)
3)

Shortlist of chosen actions Start date of action

1)
2)
3)

Motivation for chosen actions (score out of 10) – what would have to happen?

1) _____ ______________________________
2) _____ ______________________________
3) _____ ______________________________

Wheel of Life – Instructions

1) Fill in your name and the date.

2) Go round the circle (Template 1) with a pen or pencil and consider each segment in turn, asking yourself how you *feel* (not what you *think*) about the subject represented by that segment *at this moment*, and give it a score from 0–10, where 0 is low and 10 is high. Try to think as little as possible and put down spontaneous scores and answers that come from your intuitive gut feelings. Don't edit or censor your responses.

Now draw a line at the relevant point across the segment in question. For example, if you decided your finances were in a reasonable state but not brilliant and you felt a score of 5 would be about right, draw a line across the *Finance* segment about half way up, because 5 is approximately at the half way point. Do the same with every segment in the wheel and don't feel badly if they vary wildly in their scores. That's not unusual.

3) Now look at each segment in turn, especially the low scoring ones, and decide which ones you wish rated higher. The wheel highlights areas that require attention but bear in mind that if a sector gets a low score, that does not necessarily mean you want to attend to it right now, or ever. It may not be the right time for it to take priority, but at the same time be careful you are not avoiding. By the same token, don't just assume because a segment gets a high score that no further work is needed and you can sit on your laurels. Attention, awareness and action might be required to keep the score high. It is important to interpret what your wheel is showing you with a liberal application of common sense.

4) Using a copy of your ***Wheel of Life Shortlist*** template (Template 2), fill in your name and the date once again. Then, while referring to your ***Wheel of Life*** (Template 1), create a short list of the three most important areas of your life that you feel need enhancement and write down three possible actions you could take *for each one* that could improve matters. Review the options you have just created and choose which ones you feel you want to action. Write these actions down in order of priority in the space provided to be developed later into goals, and add a dateline for actioning each one. The template and the example below will guide you through the procedure.

5) Again using the same template (Template 2), examine your motivation for each of your chosen actions and score out of 10.

6) Finally ask yourself, 'what could I do, or what would have to happen, to raise the level of my motivation?' and write down the answers at the bottom of the template.

Example

The following is an example based on a fictitious person. Their scores are:

Health	7
Creativity	8
Love Life	6
Personal growth/spirituality	4
Family	9
Finance	1
Relationships	7
Home	7
Focus	9
Self-esteem	6
Leisure	2
Work	8

Template 1

WHEEL OF LIFE

Name *Bill Jones*
Date *27th October 2010*

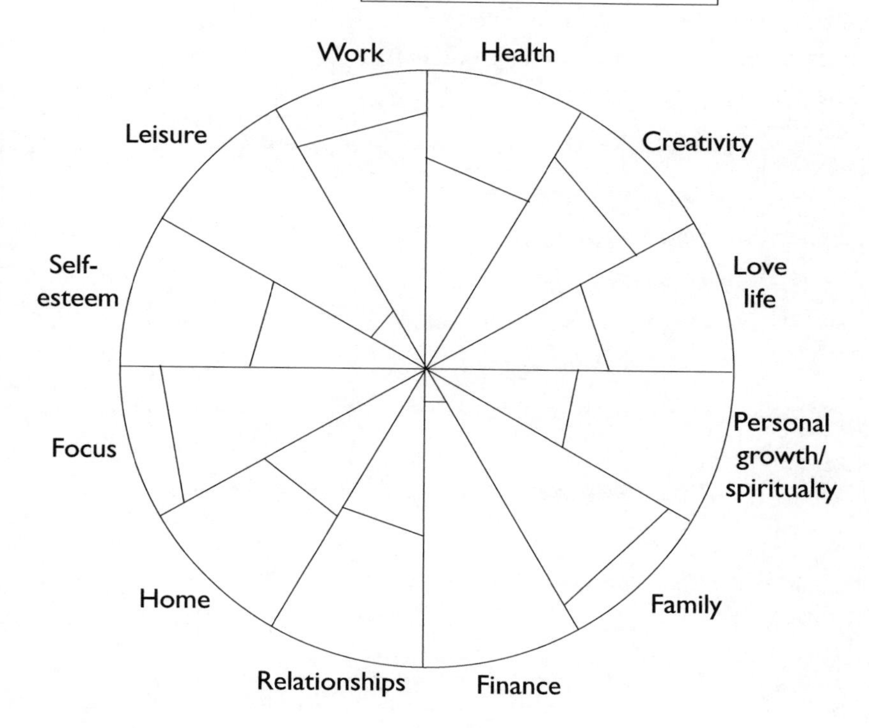

Template 2 WHEEL OF LIFE SHORTLIST

Name Bill Jones
Date 27th October 2010

Areas that I wish to enhance

1) Leisure
2) Personal growth/spirituality
3) Finance

Three possible actions for Leisure

1) Play more tennis
2) More time hanging out with friends
3) Learn a language

Three possible actions for Personal growth/spirituality

1) Do 1/2 hour morning meditation Monday, Wednesday & Friday weekly
2) Read Feel the Fear & Do It Anyway
3) Go to a Mind, Body, Spirit Festival

Three possible actions for Finance

1) Find out what to do to become self-employed
2) Learn/ study business, investments and entrepreneurialism
3) Develop/ advertise the service I offer/ start networking

Shortlist of chosen actions	Start date of action
1) Learn a language	28th. October 2010
2) Read Feel the Fear & Do It Anyway	28th. October 2010
3) Develop/ advertise the service I offer	4th. November 2010

Motivation for chosen actions (score out of 10) – what would have to happen?

1) 6/10 Change self-limiting belief 'I'm no good at languages'
2) 8/10 Buy the book
3) 6/10 Acknowledge fear of failure and make a start

The power of writing

Would you not agree, after going through the above exercise, that the state of every part of your life at this moment has become very clear to you, as have the strengths and weaknesses of its various areas? Most important, by going through the exercise as honestly and spontaneously as possible, you make it much easier to identify intelligent yet heartfelt action points. The *Wheel of Life* is not only great for developing insight and understanding, but also facilitates the heart/mind balance to give you some *real* answers. It also provides you with an accurate baseline in creating an action plan for yourself.

All life coaches will tell you a goal that is written down stands a far greater chance of being achieved, but the two main reasons are rarely explained. Firstly, writing helps to imprint the learning you get from any exercise more firmly into your mind simply because the act of writing requires you to think about, and concentrate on, the words you are writing, and their meanings. Secondly, while your attention is taken up with writing you are focussed entirely on what you are writing and its meaning. You are not thinking negative or irrelevant thoughts because you can only think actively about one thing at a time.

The simplest way to avoid thinking negative thoughts is to focus on something positive, and writing makes you concentrate on the matter in hand and puts you automatically in the present moment. These two benefits greatly reinforce the creation of the new habit you are trying to cultivate, which is to find out what you want to change so that you focus only on the positive steps that are going to get you to where you want to be. For that reason, you will find many more exercises in this book that emphasise writing.

Some people learn more easily by visual means, and for them – indeed for most of us – the power of visualisation cannot be overstated. For that reason visualisation exercises will also be described as we go along. The *Wheel of Life* has something of the written and the visual, for the wheel is designed to give you a visual impression of your life at a glance.

Exercise 12: Wheels within wheels

WHEELS WITHIN WHEELS

Now let's get into more detail. The ***Wheel of Life*** concept can be further developed or focused down by taking just one segment out of the wheel above and making another wheel out of that. For example, Bill scored 6 in the sector labelled '*Love Life*'. From that he might conclude, '*well my love life is quite good and my relationship's OK, but I'd love to get it up to 8 or even 10. How do I do that?*'

If no possible actions or options come to mind Bill can analyse further by making a wheel about his love life. He could call it, for example, The ***Wheel of Love***, and he can label the segments however you want. It might look something like this:

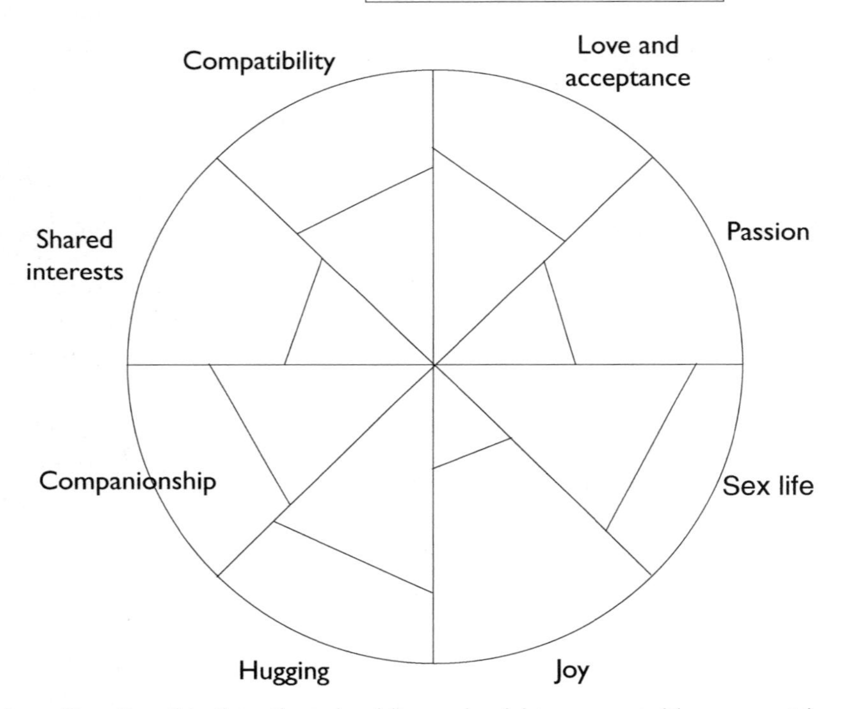

You will notice this time the wheel has only eight segments. You can put in as many or as few as you wish.

From his Wheel of Love, Bill might deduce that he has quite a lot of sex and he does hug quite a lot, but in the passion department things are a bit lacking. By implication, this could call into question the quality or satisfaction element of his sex life, or it could mean the quality is high but the frequency is low. This implies that the score could be a bit suspect because the question asks how he feels about his sex life. Re-examination might be called for to check that this answer is an honest one. Compatibility could also be an issue because if that's not fairly high in any relationship it calls into question the quality of the love and acceptance.

Bill can, of course, then do the second part of the exercise using Template 2 as applied to this new wheel. This will help decide on further action points pertaining to this particular issue, but first it might be more interesting to gain further insight into the quality of the sex, the compatibility and the love and acceptance segments. So he could now do three further wheels, called, let's say, the ***Wheel of Sex***, the ***Wheel of Compatibility*** and the ***Wheel of Love and Acceptance*** respectively. If he wants to be really thorough he could do a Template 2 exercise for each of these new wheels.

It depends how far Bill wants to go with this.

Using the *Wheel of Life* in this way offers a valuable tool or method to gain deep insight into the issues in different areas of your life, and of course you can go on focussing down and down if you have the patience. *Don't get too bogged down in doing endless exercises while neglecting to take action.* This is a diagnostic guidance technique designed to highlight where action needs to be taken, but with no action comes no results and no change. It's also for monitoring progress when you do the exercise at regular intervals and similarly, if there is no action there is no progress.

Soon we will discuss how to use the information gleaned from this and other exercises in the creation of goals, but first we are going to move on to the next powerful tool for helping to change your mindset, the Success Diary.

Summary

- The *Wheel of Life* gives you an instant visual check on which areas of your life need work and which don't, and helps you quickly evaluate which are the most and least urgent
- It is also very useful for measuring progress and change
- The same technique can also be adapted to focus in closely on specific areas – wheels within wheels
- You are perfectly free to change or delete any segment label or the segment itself. You can also introduce new labelled segments

- Don't forget to enter your name and the date
- A low scoring sector doesn't necessarily mean you want to attend to it now. It may not be the right time, but be careful you are not avoiding
- Don't assume because a segment gets a high score that no further work is needed. Use common sense when interpreting your results
- Ask yourself, 'what could I do, or what would have to happen, to raise the level of my motivation?'
- Think as little as possible and put down spontaneous scores and answers that come from your intuitive gut feelings. Don't edit or censor your responses
- By going through this exercise you make it easier to identify intelligent yet heartfelt action points
- The *Wheel of Life* is not only great for developing insight and understanding, but done in the way I describe it also very much facilitates the heart/mind balance to give you some *real* answers
- A goal that is written down stands a far greater chance of being achieved
- Writing helps to imprint the learning you get from any exercise more firmly into your mind because writing makes you think about, and concentrate on, the words you are writing, and their meanings
- While your attention is taken up with writing you are focussed entirely on what you are writing and its meaning, so negativity cannot arise
- The *Wheel of Life* concept can be focused down by taking just one segment from your original wheel and making another wheel of that
- Don't get bogged down in doing endless exercises – with no action comes no results, no change and no progress

Diagnostic exercises

Exercise 11: Wheel of Life
Exercise 12: Wheels within wheels

7

Success Diary

Total belief in yourself results in complete power of manifestation

Brian Mayne

So far in building our first pillar we have seen how you can use *meditation* as a powerful tool for discovering what's going on in your unconscious mind and tuning in to hear what your heart is trying to tell you. We have also discussed the *Wheel of Life*, which can give deep insights into how the various parts of your life are working. Now we come to your *Success Diary*, yet another amazing tool you can use in helping build your new life of freedom and achievement. *Your Success Diary is specifically designed to help you build a positive mindset and to start to experience yourself as a successful 'can-do' person.*

I choose the word 'success' deliberately, and when I introduce it to people either during a one-to-one coaching session, or as a group, there's always a good proportion of those who shudder at the very mention of the word. It's as if the notion of perceiving themselves as 'successful' somehow goes against the grain. Maybe it sounds like boasting – it doesn't seem very British and perhaps some people believe it's not cool to be successful. But lets face it, nobody wants to be unsuccessful! In truth, feeling sheepish about being successful is false modesty. 'It serves nobody for you to play small,' as Nelson Mandela pointed out (he was actually quoting Marianne Williamson).

If that person suffering discomfort describes you, then I deliberately use the *'S'* word to press your buttons. This is because I want you to look at this, not because I'm a smart Alec, but because I want you to get over your embarrassment and start to function properly. I am not suggesting you go around bragging, aggrandising your ego and boring the pants off the people you meet. I just want you, like a well-maintained engine, to function efficiently on all four cylinders so you can be happy doing what you are supposed to do – which is being successful.

Lets make no bones about it, I want success for myself, but also for every single person who takes the trouble to read this book.

A *Success Diary* is a must for anyone who even faintly perceives themselves as a failure, a non-achiever, not worthy, a misfit, unlovable, incapable, incompetent, not talented, unimpassioned or depressed, and it's almost certainly a great idea for everyone else too. It's especially great for people who love writing but even if you don't it's still worth doing.

The meaning of success

Our vitally important first question in this context has to be, 'what does success mean to you?'

Success, like so many things in life, is relative. It means different things to different people, so it's up to you to decide what success looks like for you. Let's take a couple of hypothetical examples: two people might say they want more money and one will feel happy, successful and fulfilled when he has added £500 to his bank account, whereas the other person may feel successful when he makes £100,000. It's important to be honest with yourself about exactly what you want and how much of it because you want to feel good about your success. It's also a good idea to take into account the baseline from which you start so you can measure your success as it grows.

To someone receiving unemployment benefit, getting a modestly paid job is a success; while for a high-flying entrepreneur, doing a deal to net £3 million is a success. For someone who is depressed and unable to function, just getting out of bed in the morning might be a success. For someone who is constipated, going to the toilet can be a major success. The principle applies on all levels and in all areas of our lives.

For me, an important ingredient in any success is the feeling that whatever I have achieved has come from my heart and is therefore saturated with meaning and purpose. When my partner and I jointly bought our boat, having worked hard to raise the money, I was blown away with the success. Yet when I go sailing I see many far more expensive and prestigious yachts around us all the time. I don't care that my boat is over thirty years old. She's a quality boat, she's looked after us in many a gale and mountainous sea and in return I make it my business to keep her seaworthy and well maintained. I'm totally in love with my boat for she enables me to express my passion for being at sea. It's not the status, or lack of it, that interests me, it's what going sailing does for me as a person.

That's not to say that my success is better or more worthy than anyone else's success, nor is it inferior. Each person must make an honest assessment of this for themselves. If status is very important to you, admit it and go for it.

Here again we see the importance of settling on the right goals. I remember vividly when I was working as a carpenter many years ago, I set a goal of wanting more customers, and in a very short time I achieved it. The problem, I soon realised, was that I became so busy my feet hardly ever touched the ground, with the result that though I earned more money I became exhausted, stressed and had little leisure time. In the end I got ill and had to give up work for three months, which financially set me right back to square one.

Eventually the penny dropped. I did not really want more customers or more work – I already had as much as I could comfortably handle. What I really wanted was more money, but I made the classic mistake of believing that to make more money I needed to do more work. So although I had achieved my goal, I had succeeded only in hurting myself, and that was not the kind of success I wanted.

So when I resumed work I put my prices up with the result that some of my extra customers went to someone cheaper, which was fair enough, while those who recognised the value of the work I was doing gave me more work, so the whole thing balanced itself up nicely and I ended up with about the same amount of work as I had in the first place but more money was coming in.

It was a win/win situation – the customers who went elsewhere were happy to get their job done more cheaply, my existing customers felt good about recognising my true worth, and I was happy because I was no longer under-selling myself and I received the money I felt in my heart that I deserved. I had believed in myself and had the courage of my convictions, so my self-esteem was enhanced too. Of course I realised I had to fulfill my side of the bargain and make sure my work was excellent, but it was no problem because I felt reinvigorated to do my absolute best for my loyal customers, and new ones too, so they benefited by feeling beautifully looked after. That's what I call success.

Being successful at someone else's expense is a hollow and short-lived victory. Win/lose never really works for me and the Impeccable Warrior would never countenance such a state of affairs. Win/win always works for all concerned, which is why I always market my services in that manner. When coaching someone I often stop and ask myself, 'what could I do to add value to that person's coaching experience?' When I come up with an answer, I consider that a successful result, especially if my client experiences a lightbulb moment, and it ensures I continue to enjoy my work. It also results in lots of referrals, which can't be bad, and that provides even more material for my *Success Diary*.

How it works

You go into your local newsagent and buy yourself a book containing blank pages. This is your personal *Success Diary* so write your name on it in big letters above the words SUCCESS DIARY. It can be expensive and ornate, it can be cheap and humble. All that matters is that you get a book with blank pages.

From then on, anytime you do something even remotely successful you write it in your *Success Diary*. It's a good idea to go well over the top with plenty of hyperbole and wild exaggeration in describing how fantastic the success is, why it's so significant, what a great advance you have made, and so on. Bear in mind this is not an official historical document and it's for your eyes only, therefore you can write anything you like in it, however personal, without embarrassment or inhibition.

The reason for the exaggeration is simply that it helps very much in reinforcing the new message you are wishing to implant into your unconscious mind. It makes the process an even stronger tool for reprogramming deeply ingrained mindsets and self-limiting beliefs. It also gives you a chance to express yourself at length, so you uncover even more of what's in your heart.

It's worth emphasizing again that there is amazing power in writing things down. Primarily, writing up your *Success Diary* causes you to focus your attention on your successful endeavours, which in itself is bound to help you manifest further successes. It helps you create a new habit of thinking about success, because while you are doing that you can't think about failure. If you don't believe me, try laughing and crying at the same time. You'll see it's impossible.

Most importantly, you will start to think not just of success, but of yourself and success inextricably associated with each other. You will develop an invisible aura or atmosphere of success around you and gradually you will find yourself attracting success more easily.

This is a powerful auto-suggestion technique. What you are doing in essence is strongly planting positive dominant thoughts into your mind. Remember we discussed how your mind tends to manifest more of whatever your dominant thought is? Well this puts you in control. At last you are choosing the messages you want to plant in both your conscious and subconscious minds. By carefully choosing positive input, you are making positive outcomes far more likely. This is especially powerful because those messages are based on your experience, so you know they are true, and you have chosen them.

Some people like to update their diaries first thing in the morning or in the evening, others do it every two or three days, and some have a mammoth session once a week. I also know one or two people who do it once a month. Whatever works for you is great as long as you do it, you put everything in it, and don't let it lapse.

You will also find, when one day a few months later you get a wobbly moment of self-doubt, that with your new awareness you can ask yourself, 'am I justified in feeling doubtful about my ability to be successful, or is it just my old habit trying to reassert itself?' If you are still in doubt you now have a growing body of physical evidence that you can re-read to remind yourself, 'hey, I can be successful! I am already successful! I have always been successful!' It cannot be denied, it's there in black and white in your *Success Diary* so you can stop beating yourself up. And don't forget, when you send your saboteur packing like that, of course you have another success to record!

Your awareness will grow in leaps and bounds. You will see your saboteur approaching at a hundred paces and simply tell him or her to get lost. Success breeds success and before you know it you will have grown personally and expanded your comfort zone beyond recognition. If you keep at it, eventually success will become your new default setting and I assure you, you will be a much happier bunny as a result.

One hundred things in a day

Finally to wrap up this chapter, consider this: let's say you do one hundred things in a day and ninety-nine of them go really well but one goes pear-shaped. Which is the one you will focus on? The one that didn't work out as you wanted, of course! It's natural, it's human nature. Most of us want to be perfect, we don't like admitting to mistakes or having to repeat something that went wrong.

When you stop to think about it, it's crazy to think, feel and behave like that because we totally ignore or take for granted the ninety-nine things we did that went right. Instead of giving ourselves credit for them and enjoying the success and raised self-esteem that will automatically accrue, we choose to put ourselves down, to belittle ourselves, to 'play small.' This serves no one and is most emphatically not the behaviour of the Impeccable Warrior!

Mistakes are how we learn. Getting things wrong occasionally is a necessary part of growing and understanding, and that's why I believe it's far more constructive to regard everything in your life as an experiment, for then you cannot fail to learn something. The concept of failure cannot even arise because whatever happens in an experiment, you learn something if you have an open mind. You might not get the result you wanted, but that shows you either that the action you initiated needs to be different, or you need to drop your attachment to your required outcome and accept reality for what it is. Then you have no conflict.

Incidentally, you are almost certainly more successful on a regular basis than you realise. For example, if you forget the idea of failure but say to yourself instead, 'wow, I really didn't expect or want that result, but I learned something,' that in itself is a success. You've turned your mindset around from negative, focusing on failure, to positive by realizing you have learned something. Dropping a preconceived idea in favour of accepting 'what is' constitutes another success for similar reasons. All these changes of perception need to go into your *Success Diary*.

Occasionally someone tells me they have never succeeded at anything in their life so they have nothing to put in their diary. If that's how you feel about yourself, I ask you to consider this. Look at a toddler trying to learn to walk. Many, many times they will totter to their feet and try to stagger a couple of paces before falling over. Most children fall over literally hundreds of times before they master the skill of walking. They do not give up or berate themselves, they simply try again and again till they get it. Each time they fall they learn a little more of the balance and co-ordination required to succeed in the task of walking.

Most adults take walking for granted but if you can walk you have mastered a complex set of skills requiring considerable learning, so by definition just by being able to walk, or breath, or talk, or digest your food, you are a highly successful person. You have mastered the basic skills needed for survival, so at the very least you can put those things in your diary to start with.

Once you get the ball rolling, you will realise many other accomplishments that deserve writing up. How many times does a child get back on his bicycle before he masters the art of balance? How many successful decisions and gear changes does a person have to make to drive a car safely from A to B?

Have I convinced you yet that you are already a miraculous and highly successful being? If not, maintaining your *Success Diary* eventually will. My point is, no matter how badly you might feel about yourself or your ability to be successful, you are already far more successful that you can ever imagine – so give yourself due credit. If you persist in punishing yourself and refusing to acknowledge this point, you are being disingenuous.

Over the years my own *Success Diaries* have helped me move from deep depression to achieving my highest goals, so I know first-hand this device works. Write anything and everything you can think of that could even vaguely be described as successful in your *Success Diary* and you will immensely enhance your powers of achievement. You will start to believe in yourself and your self-esteem will grow. Furthermore, you will enjoy the writing process more and more as your creative and imaginative process of self-expression starts to flow and gathers momentum. How can it be otherwise?

Summary

- The *Success Diary* is specifically designed to help you build a positive mindset and to start to experience yourself as a successful 'can-do' person

- I want you to get over your embarrassment and start to function properly so you can be happy doing what you are supposed to do – which is being successful
- The *Success Diary* is a must for anyone who even faintly perceives themselves as a failure, a misfit, unlovable, incapable, incompetent, not talented or impassioned, or depressed. It's almost certainly a great idea for everyone else too
- It's important to be honest with yourself about what you want and how much of it, because you want to feel good about your success
- For me an important ingredient in any success is the feeling that whatever I achieve comes from my heart and therefore has meaning and purpose
- Being successful at someone else's expense is a hollow and short-lived victory. Win/lose never works and the Impeccable Warrior would never countenance such A state of affairs. Win/win always works for all concerned
- Anytime you do something even remotely successful, write it in your *Success Diary* and always keep your diary up to date
- Exaggerate when describing how fantastic your success is, say why it's so significant, what a great advance you have made, and so on. This enhances the strength of the new message of success you are implanting into your conscious and unconscious minds
- There is immense power in writing things down. You will start to think not just of success, but of yourself and success inextricably linked. You will develop an aura of success around you and you will find yourself attracting success more easily
- Your *Success Diary* is a powerful auto-suggestion technique. What you are doing in essence is strongly planting positive dominant thoughts into your mind
- Your *Success Diary* puts you in control. At last you are choosing the messages you want to plant in both your conscious and subconscious minds. By carefully choosing positive input, you are making positive outcomes far more likely
- This is especially powerful because those messages are based on your experience, so you know they are true

- When you maintain a *Success Diary* the evidence of your success is there in black and white *so you can stop beating yourself up*
- Success breeds success and you will grow personally and expand your comfort zone beyond recognition. Success will become your new default setting
- Mistakes are how we learn. Getting things wrong occasionally is a necessary part of growing and understanding
- You are almost certainly more successful on a regular basis than you realise
- Just by being able to walk, breathe, talk, or digest your food, you are a highly successful person. You have mastered the basic survival skills
- Write everything you can think of that could even vaguely be described as successful in your *Success Diary* and you will enhance you powers of achievement, start to believe in yourself and your self-esteem will grow

Questions to ask yourself

- What does success mean to me?
- Am I justified in feeling doubtful about my ability to succeed, or is it just my old habit trying to reassert itself?

8

What Stops You?

In life, we don't get what we want; we get what we expect
Christopher Howard

Sooner or later nearly every one of us runs into a roadblock, something in our mind that stops us dead in our tracks, kills our motivation, fills us with fear and panic and freezes us into a paralysis. When that happens, taking action is out of the question and our progress and growth grind to a halt.

What it is that stops you can be very perplexing and elusive to figure out because more often than not the reason is unconscious. Of course, you need an answer, or at least a solution, if you are to overcome or bypass your block and resume progress towards your intended goal. The good news is that once you have discovered the nature of the blockage you are halfway towards understanding what to do about it. It follows, therefore, that the all-important first step is to develop more awareness around what's really going on deep inside you.

Sometimes all you need is a lightbulb moment, a little feedback or some reassurance, at other times a tool or technique accompanied by appropriate action gets you moving again. More often than not, time spent meditating in silence will precipitate the necessary vision. This chapter contains more powerful insights, tools and tips aimed at giving you enough understanding to crack the problem and resume your progress.

Why you need to unearth your self-limiting beliefs

As we have seen already, every one of us is subject to conditioning in many different forms and unfortunately some of it is bound to be negative. Even our own interpretations of the experiences we have, or that we witness, can result in negative conditioning. This is almost certainly top of the list of factors that can stop you or make any achievement far more difficult than it needs be, and as it usually operates at an unconscious level you might not realise what is happening or why. This leaves you puzzled and perplexed as to why your life is such an uphill struggle while the personal development gurus keep telling us life should be a flow. As long as you remain baffled, you cannot hope to change anything.

Can you remember a situation in which you had a terrific idea, you started to feel enthusiastic and upbeat about it and were about to take action. However, then a little voice piped up in the recesses of your mind saying, 'I can't do it,' or 'it's bound to end in failure,' or even worse, 'it's not even worth trying,' or 'if I try I'm bound to lose money.'

This little voice is what I call *the voice of your conditioning*. I used to hear mine time and time again whenever I had an ambitious idea or even when I wanted to do something ever so slightly unconventional or risky, and it took me years to realise this voice had nothing to do with me. This is such an important point and I want to repeat it, only this time with a little more precision, *the voice of my conditioning has nothing to do with the* ***real*** *me.*

The conditioned me

This is a little complicated and I don't mean to patronise or bore you by repeating myself, but the details and implications of this concept are so important they are worth reiterating and spelling out as simply and clearly as possible, so please bear with me while I do my best to clarify my meaning.

In the previous paragraph I referred to a *real* me, and that implies there is also another kind of me. Well there is, in my imagination of course, there is the *conditioned* me.

The conditioned me is the part of me who listens to and automatically believes these unconscious messages and lets my behaviour be dictated by them. Let's take a fictitious example. I get an idea to start a new business, but while I'm researching my market and putting together my business plan, a little voice creeps in and says, 'is this really such a great idea? I might lose all my money. I'm not very good at making money.'

If you continue to walk around with the self-limiting belief, 'I am not very good at making money,' it's obvious you will never make any because, as we said before, your mind will create the subject of its dominant thoughts. But you might not realise you have this belief. Something is stopping you from starting your new business, you're not quite sure what it is, and it's guaranteeing your continued poverty. Of course there is always the possibility you will lose money when you start a business, especially if you carry limiting beliefs like that. However, that is not the issue in this context. What really matters in a case like this is that *you cut yourself off from any possibility of creating anything worthwhile, be it wealth or anything else, while your self-limiting beliefs remain unconscious.*

Perhaps even more problematical than not starting the business is a situation where you feel discouraged but try to soldier on anyway. The business plan never quite gets finished and the business is launched half-heartedly in a confused and uncertain way. This obviously militates strongly against any chance of success, but lots of people do this sort of thing and the root cause is always a lack of awareness, for this ensures their limiting beliefs remain undetected. They can't understand why their initial enthusiasm has drained away.

By contrast I met one aspiring entrepreneur who told me he made it part of his pre-launch business plan to go for sessions in psycho-therapy and Life Coaching so he could discover what his unconscious self-limiting beliefs were. He made it his business to find out what was going on deep inside himself before launching his business on a shoe-string budget. As a result, after a few years, he became an extremely wealthy man and, more importantly, a happy and fulfilled person.

This person made a highly intelligent use of the tools and resources I have described in earlier chapters, and others we have not yet discussed. After first acknowledging the potential shortcomings in his attitude to himself in business he took appropriate action to empower himself and build his self-belief *before* he started working towards his business goals, and as a result got there quickly and with relatively little stress.

Now for the next piece of this particular jigsaw. What exactly did I mean when I said earlier that *the voice of my conditioning is nothing to do with the real me?* How can I dissociate myself from my conditioning?

The art of witnessing, which we discussed in Chapter 5, is very helpful for developing the knack of seeing that your conditioning is nothing other than input received from the outside. You weren't born with it. You weren't born with anything. This is how the story often goes: your teacher says to you when you are five years old, 'you must try harder,' and you, the child, take in a message that you interpret as, 'I'm not good enough'. The unconscious mind at that age is struggling to make sense of the world and can often extrapolate further to create additional messages such as: 'I'm not worthy;' 'I must be punished;' 'Nobody could ever possibly love me;' 'When things go wrong it's my fault, I don't deserve to be loved (or to be successful);' etc.

As an adult, if you develop sufficient awareness to consciously notice you still have these messages circulating in your mind, you will realise their origins. You can say to yourself, 'hey wait a minute; these are just judgements I developed and laid on myself out of something said to me by that teacher in school. I wasn't born with them, therefore they do not reflect who I am'. You have realised those negative beliefs are not justified and that in turn gives you the potential to drop them, or replace them with the stronger belief that you are absolutely OK exactly exactly as you are.

Let me just say that one more time because so many people refuse to let it in, preferring just to brush it aside, but it's absolutely pivotal: *you are absolutely OK exactly as you are!*

Of course I don't expect you to take my word for it, and even if you believed I might be right you're not going to change your habitual ways of thinking overnight. No-one said this would be easy. But if you can find sufficient faith to practise and master the tools in this book, you will find out for yourself. They are designed to help you do the work of changing your self-limiting beliefs.

Brandon Bays describes our very human situation beautifully in *The Journey*. In that book she explains (I paraphrase) that deep inside at the centre of our being, each of us is a diamond-like essence that sparkles and causes our inner light to shine forth (you need only look at a newborn or very young baby and you'll see exactly what she means). As we progress through life we accumulate all sorts of conditioning that piles up like layers of detritus, a sort of outer skin which obscures the diamond, shutting off its light and hence its ability to sparkle.

So what do we do? Typically we polish up the surface of the outer layer of the façade we have developed to make it look as acceptable as we can, and we present that to the world as if it were our real self. We tend to keep all the layers of debris in place out of fear, so it becomes a defensive barrier. We become afraid of being seen for who we really are, sometimes even by ourselves. We keep our authentic self hidden by this mask, or *persona*. That persona (or false self, or adapted self, as some psychologists describe it) is what I describe as the *conditioned* you. The *real* you is the diamond.

Now here's the good news. Despite being obscured, the diamond is still there and is capable of sparkling again if only the light can get to it. That is the essence of the work in this book – to help you peel away the layers of your conditioning so the light can get to the diamond again, and the resulting sparkle can shine forth. Whether you realise it or not, that diamond, which I repeat is none other than the authentic you, is still intact and yearning to shine and sparkle like it did when you were a baby.

It's a bit like asking your persona to step aside to reveal the real you, hence the well worn but nonetheless apposite advice we hear so often to *'get out of our own way.'*

Meet your saboteur

The voices of your conditioning, coming as they do from outside sources, are a bit like a person sitting on your shoulder telling you what to do, even when it's against your own best interests. Hence I call that imaginary person your saboteur.

The metaphor of the saboteur is used by many coaches and therapists, and it will help you to embed this concept if you visualise your saboteur as a real person, autonomous and separate from yourself. When you set out to achieve something and self-doubt starts creeping in, or you start feeling guilty, you can bet your life your saboteur is approaching. However, with raised awareness you can see your saboteur coming at a hundred paces and you now have the option of saying to him, as it were, 'aha, I see my saboteur is approaching. That's all you are, a saboteur bent on destruction. Go away; I'm not listening to you any more.' It really is as simple as that.

This once again takes us back to the concept of the Impeccable Warrior, for he will have no truck with his saboteur. The Impeccable Warrior seeks every opportunity to raise his awareness and is therefore well equipped to recognise and see off his saboteur. As we saw earlier, the Impeccable Warrior always behaves with integrity and absolutely in tune with his core values and beliefs, and so never has any reason to reproach himself. For example, when the Impeccable Warrior starts feeling guilty about something, he can see immediately his saboteur is trying to hold sway and he sends him packing at once. He knows perfectly well in his heart of hearts he has nothing to feel guilty about because his behaviour has been impeccable, he has done what he absolutely believes is right, so he simply won't countenance erroneous feelings of guilt.

Defence mechanisms

Many of your conditioned beliefs can make you feel afraid or insecure, and this is our prime motivation for creating our defence mechanisms. For example, your lover rejects you and you feel hurt so you withdraw into your shell. Nobody likes being hurt and it's quite possible you will avoid exposing your real self ever again for fear of further rejection. Instead you present your persona or false self, or you hide away, because you feel less exposed to any perceived risk. You might even get angry, vindictive or violent in your efforts to defend your real self from being exposed and made vulnerable.

Whatever your response, it is prompted by a fear of being hurt again and is also a reaction to having been hurt already, and is therefore an attempt to defend yourself. Unfortunately, your defence mechanism, acting like a wall, also stops the shining rays of your diamond from being visible and that's hugely detrimental if you unconsciously yearn to express your real self but are too afraid. One ramification of this in practical terms, to follow this example further, is that by being defensive you are almost guaranteeing further rejection because you make it very hard for someone to love and accept you unconditionally. They can't reach you – the *real* you, that is.

For those reasons, in most cases, your defence mechanism is counterproductive and is therefore another manifestation of your saboteur. Most potential lovers want the real you, not the persona, even if they don't consciously realise it, as is often the case.

When you were a developing child you needed these defences for your mental and emotional survival. They served a valuable purpose because you were vulnerable and powerless. But now you are an adult capable of looking after yourself and standing up for yourself (or learning to do so), and these mental constructs get in the way of your ongoing development and growth. Hence the clearing work must commence in earnest.

For many of us the problem starts right here, for our defence mechanisms function on an unconscious level much of the time. For that reason you will almost certainly be unaware of why you are feeling an inner conflict – your real self wants to get out but it feels too scared so your defences stop it, much to your continued puzzlement.

So why do I go into such details in a book about happiness and achievement? It is because any or all of the matters we have discussed in this chapter could be part of what is stopping you from being happy and achieving what you want. Only by making them conscious do you stand any chance of changing them. We all really do need to take this on board.

Are you a control freak?

Trying to control outcomes to excess is another certain recipe for creating lots of stress in your life. Basically you are resisting change and the unknown, which means you are putting up a fear barrier against reality. All this resistance can certainly stop you from achieving a creative, flowing life of abundance, even if it's only through exhaustion. If you are a control freak, instead of putting your energy into following your path to your goal, you squander it on trying to maintain the status quo or attempting to bend reality to fit your fantasy.

That's quite a statement to assimilate, so let's look at a real life example from one of my clients. Francis (not her real name) was onto her third marriage and things weren't going too well. To me and most casual observers it was obvious that she and her husband were completely incompatible – indeed they were polar opposites. He was defended to the hilt, a cold fish who had difficulty expressing himself and rarely seemed able to access his emotions, while she was a red-hot full blooded, passionate woman who was over-emotional to the point of hysteria. Clearly neither party would ever be able to get their needs met by the other, yet they managed to sustain an uneasy relationship for some seventeen years.

The first time John (not his real name) announced he was going to leave Francis she became completely hysterical and then depressed and did everything in her power to manipulate John to try to make him stay. He left for a week or two but eventually was persuaded by Francis' continued hysterical behaviour, not so subtle manipulation and guilt trips, to come back home.

Francis then went from control freak to pleaser. She tried everything she could think of to please John so he would love her again and stay home. But the truth, which was obvious to everyone else who knew the couple, was that he simply did not love her any more. Indeed I doubted if he ever had. She also oscillated between love and hate and when she started talking about him she would get very angry.

All the while she was dragging him off to couples counselling once a week, which of course was of no avail, while she flitted from one psychotherapist to another. Several times I suggested she might have some issues to address with her therapist but every time she ended up blaming John and feeling worthless. In one breath she convinced herself she was a 'bad person' and 'to blame' for her situation, and the next minute she blamed John.

Eventually after a few months he left her for good. She was very upset and her doctor recommended her to a psychiatrist who referred her to a private mental hospital and gave her anti-depressants. Then, after a few days her leg swelled up and she was diagnosed with a thrombosis and transferred to a regular hospital for treatment.

After some days she calmed down and began to accept reality instead of trying to control it. John simply did not love her and there was nothing anyone could do about it. Trying to control him and then trying to please him had only caused her more suffering and finally made her physically ill. Her extreme co-dependency had made her panic and fear for her very survival, but eventually she had been forced into giving up trying to control and as she lay recovering she discovered, to her surprise, that she could and did survive.

Eventually she was able to see that she was actually better off on her own instead of continually putting herself up for more suffering by trying to make a non-sustainable relationship work.

Nobody ever really achieves anything of merit when they try to be in control to such an extreme. Of course we sometimes try to influence events to work out in our favour if we can, but in a situation like this where it's clearly impossible, it's almost certainly best to let go of control and instead follow a path of acceptance.

You could argue that Frances was following her heart, but in fact she was pursuing a path of extreme co-dependency, a powerful defence mechanism brought about by the immensely complicated conditioning she developed during her childhood. Only by building supreme awareness of what she was doing to herself via her powerful saboteur could she hope to emerge from the self-destructive journey she had unconsciously chosen. If you see yourself in this story, I can only suggest you seek the assistance of an experienced psychotherapist, for it will be very difficult to climb out of this on your own. Psychotherapy is another great tool you can use in your quest to address your issues.

Letting go

Time and time again I have seen it demonstrated in real-life scenarios: *if you do what your heart guides you to do and follow the way of the Impeccable Warrior, things always turn out for the best. If you think they don't, it's only your judgement, your viewpoint or your attachment to a different outcome that makes it a problem.*

Of course I don't expect you to believe that just because I say so, so why not put it to the test. Next time a challenging situation occurs, take responsibility by doing whatever you *reasonably* can to get the outcome you want and then find the courage to let go. You may or may not get what you originally wanted, but what you get might be better and just what you need. Let me know what happens.

By way of further illustration, let me tell you of a true story that happened to me. In 1982, I was beginning to see that my own three-year marriage was becoming untenable. At the same time I was seriously searching for purpose, meaning, fulfilment, balance and peace of mind in my life. I wanted to understand why I felt the way I did and where I was coming from. I had totally lost touch with who I really was. It was a very scary, depressing and painful time.

Then I discovered Osho, the Indian guru formerly known as Bhagwan Shree Rajneesh, who had just moved his ashram from India to Oregon in the USA. To cut a long story short I went to Oregon to visit the ashram and while there I took *sannyas,* which means I became a disciple or *Sannyasin.* This was not as easy as it sounds and it took a great deal of soul searching. In the end I decided to go for it, mainly because I knew I would be given a new name and this would enable me, symbolically, to start my life all over again. That's exactly what I wanted

– a rebirth. I was profoundly unhappy with being me, Dave Robson, and I loved the idea of getting a new life and starting again at the age of thirty-three.

At the same time I was terrified because somehow I knew my whole life and everything in it would be turned upside down whether I liked it or not and there would be nothing I could do to stop it or determine the outcome. To resist or try to control would be futile for the process was too big and awesomely powerful. I had let the genie out of the bottle and now the only option was to go with the inevitable flow, whatever that might mean.

It was around that time I heard Osho say, 'life should be a flow from the known towards the unknown.' I was in no doubt it would be that all right. The prospect of the unknown was what made everything so terrifying. At the same time it all seemed incredibly exciting and I really wanted it. I was on fire! I knew my life was a shambles and needed urgent remedial work, whatever form it might take. I also had a strong feeling that Osho had something important and significant to share and I wanted a piece of it.

Sometimes the initial stages of a healing process are more painful than the original injury. That's when I also heard Osho say, *'if the gold wants to be purified it must go through fire. Love is fire.'* I desperately wanted to be 'purified,' by which I mean I simply wanted to resolve my issues, which seemed mountainous, to get my life sorted out so I could be happy, and if I had to go through fire to achieve that, so be it.

Three weeks after arriving in America I returned home and to cut a long story short, six months later I found myself separated from my wife, three year-old son and my home, and living in a rented communal house in north London with a group of other Osho *Sannyasins*. Shortly after this my freelance public relations, advertising and journalism business collapsed leaving me with heavy debts, and that's when I took up carpentry for a living. Life started to look up immediately because I had let go of two things that had been bringing me way down – my marriage and my business – and tumbled into the unknown. These were the two things I was most afraid to let go of, but as luck would have it and to my great surprise not only did I survive, I started feeling a whole lot happier. Around that time I also took up sailing and that was a real call from the heart, which is why I describe my relationship with my boat and the sea as a love affair.

Of course it was not the end of my problems but it was a fantastic new beginning and it enabled me to draw a line under my disasters and start from scratch to build a far more enjoyable and fulfilling life. I was also able to build a good relationship with my son, who continued to live with his mother, and gradually I got my debts paid off.

This also enabled me to see that when I was forced to let go and went where my heart directed me, everything turned out much for the better, whereas before I let go my life was a total nightmare. I realise this is only anecdotal evidence, but it's good enough for me.

To summarise, what had been stopping me was fear of the unknown, fear of letting go of control, a whole host of limiting beliefs, and my defence mechanisms. Once I was forced to let go of all those my life took off in a new and much happier direction.

Finally let me emphasise the phrase *'I went where my heart directed me.'* Things will always turn out for the best *if you go where your heart is guiding you.* This is as I have already stressed many times, a compelling reason to meditate in silence, so you can hear the voice of your heart and distinguish it from the voices of your conditioning. Remember, *if you want to know what's really going on inside, sooner or later you must be still and listen.*

Exercise 13: What do you believe about yourself now?

WHAT DO YOU BELIEVE ABOUT YOURSELF NOW?

Now we've come a bit further it's a good time to revisit the exercise, *What do you believe about yourself?* but this time we're going to go a little deeper and into more detail. It's a simple and effective exercise and as we have already seen, it will help you become more aware of the inner workings of your mind. Incidentally, you can repeat any or all of the exercises in this book whenever you like – indeed it's important that you do so to measure your progress at regular intervals. For that reason, always put the date at the top of every exercise you do.

Here's what you do:

Get a blank sheet of paper and write the heading at the top **WHAT I BELIEVE ABOUT MYSELF.** Write your name and the date at the top.

Now with as little thinking as possible write down all the things you believe about yourself, positive and negative, that immediately come to mind. Try to be as spontaneous as possible and be scrupulously honest with yourself. Don't censor your comments.

When you have finished, highlight or circle the negative beliefs that clearly sabotage you and then list them out separately on another sheet.

Now you have made yourself aware of your self-limiting beliefs. The next stage is to understand and accept that this is how you feel and ask yourself if each one of them is justified. It's crucial to remember that even if you decide a belief is *not* justified, it is important to accept that you have that belief and you do feel that way about yourself. *How you feel is how you feel. It can't be right or wrong. There can be no argument or judgement about that.*

You can also ask trusted and loyal friends for feedback, saying, for example, 'do you think I'm unlovable?'

Keep your list of self-limiting beliefs pinned-up somewhere where you will see it often, perhaps on the door of your fridge or wardrobe, and soon you will begin to realise what absurd fabrications they are. When you want to do something and a voice in your head says *'I can't,'* you will instantly realise that voice is one of your old friends, a self-limiting belief. Ask yourself if you really *want* to do that thing you were about to do. If you do, with your new found awareness, the self-limiting belief will no longer be able to stop you no matter how loudly it shouts its messages of certain failure.

As your self-knowledge grows, you courage will grow with it and your self-limiting beliefs will start to lose their power over you and you can let them go. When your stubborn saboteur tries to reappear, you will see him coming and tell him in no uncertain terms where to go!

Can you allow yourself to fail?

This is a curious story that speaks volumes about another tendency many of us have that can stop us taking any action or achieving anything, namely the quest for perfection.

I went to a *Satsang* once in London with a modern enlightened master named Satyananda (website: www.satyananda.org) originally from Uruguay. *Satsang* is a Sanskrit word meaning *'a meeting in truth.'* In India it's been a tradition for centuries for disciples to gather in the presence of their master to sit in silent meditation and then to ask questions and listen to answers or a discourse from their beloved guru. Osho described it as 'a heart to heart communion between a master and his disciples.'

In the 1960s, when young travellers from the Western world were discovering the wisdom of the Eastern religions and philosophies, it was necessary to go to India or somewhere in that part of the world to be present at such a gathering. Nowadays many Westerners have themselves become enlightened and feel it is their role to become teachers of consciousness (the word *guru,* incidentally, is also a Sanskrit word, meaning *a teacher*). Such people frequently jet around the major population centres of the world holding *Satsang.* Certainly London, where I live, is blessed with periodic visits from such teachers, and these are events not to be missed.

So back to Satyananda! He came across as a very laid back individual and most entertaining, leaving long silent spaces between his phrases and sentences. More to the point, he had a lot of very interesting things to say. When questions from the floor were invited, someone in the audience piped up with a long-winded story of how he had failed to live up to his own expectations of himself and how this was causing him much grief and sorrow. *Satyananda's* reply was simply to enquire of this man if he ever allowed himself to fail.

This idea aroused my interest for although I had never thought of it in quite this way, I knew what he meant immediately. Allowing oneself to fail is the exact opposite of being a control freak. So many times over the years I had seen myself and others tie ourselves up in tangles of frustration because we were striving for perfection, when in many cases perfection had been entirely unnecessary. Here's the distinction – *perfection may seem desirable but usually it's unnecessary, and pursuing it at any cost can lead to a lot of superfluous stress and frustration.*

Let me explain. When I got my first tiny yacht she was very much second-hand and in need of repainting. She would spend winters ashore in a yacht club yard in Bembridge, Isle of Wight and, come the springtime and the new sailing season, I would go over to stay on the island for a couple of weeks to make her ready for sea.

At the time I bought her I was completely inexperienced in yacht ownership and the ways of the sea, for my previous two boats had been sailing dinghies which I had sailed on a lake. This new boat, a wooden vessel which I named *Om Shanti*, was my pride and joy and I wanted her preparation to be perfect so everyone would see she was the most beautiful boat in the Solent! In my determination I completely ignored the fact that this would only be achievable if I spent the entire spring and summer in the boatyard painting, varnishing and repairing – an entirely unrealistic proposition.

That first springtime I spent two weeks slaving over the boat and by the end she looked much improved but still every bit a second-hand very old boat, and a long way from being the most beautiful in the Solent. However, she was launched eventually and she sailed really well, so I was happy. At the start of the following season I had a long talk with myself, asking myself, 'did I want a boat to go sailing, or to spend hours, days, weeks painting and varnishing?' The answer came at once, loud and clear, it was the former. The experience had taught me very clearly that I love sailing and I hate painting and varnishing. So during my second springtime maintenance season I focused the overwhelming majority of my time on the island doing only what was necessary to preserve the timber and make sure the boat was seaworthy, and I spent only a few hours on cosmetic jobs. The upshot was that during that spring, summer and autumn I spent a lot more time sailing and a lot less time on maintenance, and that's exactly what I wanted.

So although you could say I 'failed' in my original goal of making her the most beautiful, I soon realised it was an impractical, impossible goal. I settled instead for achieving another goal that was actually more important to me, to master the arts of sailing, navigation, seamanship and boathandling. If I had refused to 'fail' and insisted instead on trying to be in control of my original intention, what would I have achieved? A lot of backbreaking, frustrating work, and for what? For nothing! She would always be an elderly, second-hand, tiny yacht, but nonetheless worthy of respect for who or what she was. So why try to hide that?

That was yet another occasion when I learned it really is a good idea to check with yourself at regular intervals that the priorities you have chosen are right for you, and that the goals you try to achieve are fully aligned with them.

When the quest for perfection gets out of control and becomes obsessive, quite often you achieve nothing of consequence, or if you do, the cost is so high it wasn't worth it. Of course you may only see this in retrospect but you can see it at the time if you keep a firm perspective. If you are brutally honest with yourself, you will admit that all too often what you have achieved when striving for perfection is insignificant in the great scheme of things especially when you consider the price in time lost, jangled nerves, stress, anxiety, perhaps frayed relationships and maybe even a heart attack.

Many times I have seen people with high temperatures struggling into their office because they didn't want to 'let down their colleagues'; or for fear they would be discovered to be not so indispensable as they would have liked; or to score brownie points with the boss for this feat of martyrdom; or simply from the fear of feeling a failure. What is the point when your body is telling you to stay in bed? Will the company crash around your ears? Will the earth stop turning? If either of those things happen it's highly unlikely to be because of anything you did or didn't do!

When you take Satyananda's advice, which does seem so appealing when you stop to think about it, and allow yourself to be less than perfect when appropriate, you instantly cut a whole chunk of stress out of your life in one fell swoop. Also, in the case of surrendering to an illness, you will probably help your body to right itself far more quickly. Then you can return to work in a suitable state to enjoy what you do and contribute something of value. Undoubtedly the solutions to many of our 'problems' are simple and easy if we would only get out of our own way and allow ourselves to follow an easier route.

This does not mean you give yourself permission to apply shoddy standards of behaviour and performance. What it means is you aim high and do your absolute best, as befits the behaviour of the Impeccable Warrior. If your result is of a good enough standard, even if its not perfect, you are satisfied and move on. If not, you do it again. That is what I call finding a balance, a middle way, as opposed to the way of the obsessive, and it's definitely a way to a happy and healthy life.

What you emphatically do not do, and we'll discuss this in detail in a minute, is beat yourself up for not being perfect. Better to congratulate yourself for being human.

While it is probably inborn into person's nature to strive for perfection, to push boundaries of knowledge and experience and to seek ever greater challenges, the pursuit of perfection in situations where it is unnecessary is driven by yet more conditioned or learned behaviour. It is another manifestation of your saboteur. Perhaps it comes from an early childhood perception that you will only be accepted, loved and approved of if you turn in perfect results or exemplary behaviour every time. Whatever the reason, when it becomes obsessive it can be counter-productive. Even worse, the fear of failing to attain perfection can stop you from ever getting started on a goal, especially if at the beginning the goal seems highly ambitious.

What is the antidote to this syndrome? As usual, super-awareness is the key. If you catch yourself striving and getting stressed out, ask yourself, 'what does this mean to me? Is it really worth all this effort? Do I simply need more knowledge and experience? Am I flowing with this, or pushing the river? Should I put up with a modest result, try again, or allow myself to fail and do something else?'

We have to apply common sense here. Sometimes it's worth making an effort, to try again and do better, sometimes it isn't. There will be other times when you might conclude that you are simply not cut out for the goal in hand, or not sufficiently motivated to crack its associated problems. I'm like that with motor mechanics. I can turn my hand to most things, but when it comes to working with objects made of metal, like engines, I leave it to the experts. When it comes to making sure your vehicle is roadworthy, obviously a reliable and high standard is necessary because your life and those of others depend on you having properly functioning brakes. In my younger days I tried in vain to master automotive engineering so I could fix my motorbike, but in the end I concluded my heart wasn't in it and it just wasn't me so I found a mechanic to whom the job was second nature. He achieved perfection, or pretty close to it, naturally and without striving.

Listen to your heart, problem solved, no stress, win/win all round! Simple!

How to stop beating yourself up

Many of us have what I call a *mea culpa* tendency, otherwise known as a habit of beating yourself up. This where you tell yourself off or generally feel guilty for doing something 'wrong', 'unsuccessful' or for making an honest mistake. This really is a one way street to nowhere. As we have seen already, apportioning blame gets nobody anywhere. Blaming yourself leads only to low self-esteem, low self-belief, under-achieving and perhaps even depression, as well as lots of negativity. It also has the effect of pushing your goals further away.

If you do something whose outcome is, *in your judgement, 'wrong'* or not good enough then simply do it again until you get it *'right'*. If you can't do it, learn what you need to learn and get the practise you need, or delegate the task to someone else who is good at it. Instead of blaming yourself, give yourself credit for at least giving it your best shot and focus on your next task.

If it's a relationship and you are doing something *'wrong'* that hurts the other person, let's say you weren't quite honest, all you can do is apologise and ask their forgiveness. Next time you will be more careful. Don't fall for the temptation of beating yourself up though because, as I said, that path is barren and fruitless.

If you are *'unsuccessful'* in something you try to do or be the same applies, but with the added caveat not to forget that life is an experiment and getting an unwanted result teaches you something new. If you are regularly updating your *Success Diary* you will also be well aware that your many *'successes'* far outweigh your *'failures'* and give yourself full credit for those.

Making an honest mistake simply means you are human. The most important thing to do next is to admit you are mistaken, in public if necessary and with an apology if appropriate, and put right your mistake if it is within your power to do so. If it isn't, then admit that and hand the task over to someone who knows how to do it – after first checking with yourself that it's not just a self-limiting belief that's stopping you from doing it correctly. If our politicians behaved more like that, perhaps we would have more respect for them and admire their honesty, even if we disagree with their political viewpoint.

I am assuming that by now you have adopted the behaviour of the Impeccable Warrior and that you are doing your very best to behave with integrity in accordance with your core values and ethics. If that is the case, you know you never have grounds to reproach yourself. Therefore, because you are also developing your awareness through meditation and other means, you will notice when the temptation to beat yourself up arises. Ask yourself if you are justified in giving yourself a hard time. Is it just another version of your saboteur? If you have done your reasonable best you will see the futility of what you are doing to yourself and then it becomes relatively easy to stop doing it.

Putting yourself down is simply a bad habit and like all habits, with sufficient awareness and impeccable behaviour, you can get over it. If you are going to be a happy person who achieves what you want in your life, you need to develop a new habit of treating yourself with respect.

To sum up, if you have a goal and something is stopping you from taking that first step, it's a fair bet that fear in one form or another is the culprit. Perhaps you lack confidence or you don't really believe you can do it. Whatever the case, it's essential to build your awareness, to focus on the positive and develop your perception of yourself as a successful person.

Summary

- Once you have discovered the nature of your block you are halfway towards understanding what to do about it
- The voice of your conditioning has nothing to do with the *real* you
- You cut yourself off from creating anything worthwhile while your self-limiting beliefs remain unconscious
- Whether you realise it or not, the diamond which is the authentic you is yearning to shine and sparkle
- The Impeccable Warrior knows he has nothing to feel guilty about because his behaviour has been impeccable, so he simply won't countenance feelings of guilt and sends his saboteur packing
- When you behave defensively you almost guarantee rejection because you make it hard for anyone to get through to you and love and accept you unconditionally
- If you do what your heart guides you to do, things always turn out for the best
- If you want to know what's really going on inside, you must be still and listen
- How you feel is how you feel. It can't be right or wrong
- Perfection is often desirable but unnecessary, and pursuing it can lead to stress and frustration
- When the quest for perfection gets out of control and becomes obsessive you may find your achievement amounts to nothing of consequence despite its perfection
- Allowing yourself to fail does not mean you give yourself permission to apply shoddy standards of behaviour and performance. Neither do you use it as a pretext for beating yourself up for not being perfect. Better to congratulate yourself for being human
- Super-awareness is the key. If you catch yourself striving and getting stressed out, ask yourself: 'What does this mean to me? Is it really worth all this effort? Do I simply need more knowledge and

experience? Am I flowing with this, or pushing the river? Should I try again, or allow myself to fail and do something else?'

- Beating yourself up is a one way street to nowhere. Blaming yourself leads only to low self-esteem and lots of negativity
- If you want to be a happy person who achieves their goals, it's essential to develop a habit of treating yourself with respect and stop putting yourself down

Exercise to unearth your self-limiting beliefs

Exercise 13: What do you believe about yourself now?

9

Count Your Blessings

Let the loves and the gratitudes run your life, not the fears and anxieties

John Demartini

I never realised, when I was a small kid, the significance of the little phrase my parents used to say to me, 'count your blessings,' for only in recent years have I fully understood the importance of gratitude.

In accordance with the principle we discussed earlier that your dominant thought determines what you create, focusing on your state of abundance, which is what you do when you experience gratitude, will help you create more abundance. However, there's much more to it than that. Gratitude can lead you beyond your normal anxious state of turmoil to a whole new level of acceptance and relaxation, and also to feelings of greater enjoyment and celebration in your life.

Let's start at the beginning. When I wrote this chapter the world seemed to be entering a period of economic gloom with many people losing their jobs, and just about everyone is feeling a financial squeeze. At times like that it's even easier than usual to slip into a feeling of lack or deprivation, which in turn can lead to stress, anxiety, anger and panic. Let's not forget, however, that the Western world is probably still more wealthy than it has ever been. Also most of us are, if we did but notice it, overflowing with abundance, or at least potentially so. Not necessarily with money, but with abundance.

These are still hazardous times, for we are in great danger of setting ourselves up for monumental self-sabotage if we allow ourselves to get swept up in a collective panic spurred on by continuous media frenzy. We need to watch ourselves like hawks, especially when we start hunting for someone to blame. *The strategy of scapegoating is not in the least bit helpful.* When you blame others you avoid taking personal responsibility for your situation, and that renders you powerless. That's why so many people have lost faith in our politicians, they like to play the blame game, and nothing could be more uninspiring than that.

Moreover, blaming ensures you remain stuck in a state of anxiety, panic, fear or anger, and then it becomes much harder to function creatively and enthusiastically while adapting to new circumstances, which in effect is what you are doing if you are making major changes to your life and mindset.

I am always telling clients, 'now is the perfect time to re-invent yourself,' and it's true. Whenever *'now'* occurs, that moment is always the perfect time to do anything. *'Now'* is always the time for creative solutions. I call it the Darwin principle – *the species that can best and most quickly adapt to environmental changes are the ones that survive and thrive.*

So let's immediately drop any ideas of blaming, panicking or dwelling on what we have lost or never had. Let's move out of victim mode and instead start to focus on our abundance while asking ourselves how we can create more of it. This is a far more fruitful avenue on which to put our attention.

The Gratitude Diary

Exactly how do we create more abundance? Enter stage left yet another simple but effective tool I can offer to keep us on an even keel as we navigate through life's challenges, the *Gratitude Diary.*

It is founded on a similar principle to the *Success Diary*, which encourages your mind to focus only on success, thereby manifesting more success, only in this case by focusing on what makes you feel abundant and your gratitude for that, you create more abundance. As with the *Success Diary*, you call into your local newsagent and buy a notebook with blank pages in it. On the front cover you write your name and the words GRATITUDE DIARY, then you open the book at the beginning, put the date at the top and start writing.

Once you get started you'll be amazed how quickly the words begin to flow. Simply write as much as you like about anything you feel grateful for; don't forget to explain why you feel the gratitude and what the significance is. Next day you get your *Gratitude Diary* out and start again, writing as much or as little as you like.

In the early stages most likely you will be writing obvious, maybe superficial entries. They are nonetheless important, for example, 'I'm so grateful I've got the best partner in the world. She means everything to me.' Or, 'I'm so grateful for my car – I love the way its sits on the motorway solid as a rock at 90 and doesn't deviate an inch. It gives me so much confidence.' Or, 'My dog's terrific and I love the way she makes sure I get plenty of exercise.'

In later sessions, as the days go by, and you exhaust the more obvious things, you will find yourself digging deeper, writing things such as, 'I'm really grateful for the way I handled our disagreement yesterday. Only a year ago I would have flown off the handle, but this time I really listened and I'm sure we resolved something.' Or, 'My boss really appreciates me – he must do or I wouldn't have been promoted and given a pay rise. I'm really grateful he noticed me and did something about it.'

Can you see where we are going with this and how it's going to build your self-esteem? Can you feel yourself beginning to drop any tendency to put yourself down or think little of yourself and instead starting to feel good about yourself?

You could adopt a programme of writing up your *Success Diary* and your *Gratitude Diary* on alternate days, while also meditating three or four times a week. Imagine how powerful that would be in developing more success, abundance, clarity and insight as well as greater balance, higher self-esteem and a more creative view of your life. You'd be so busy focusing on positives there would be no time or space for anxiety or negativity to arise.

You'll notice I keep suggesting exercises that involve lots of writing. That's because writing makes you concentrate, develop your thoughts and express your feelings, while keeping you focused on the positive subject you are writing about. The act of writing by hand, as opposed to word processing, even more strongly reinforces the new messages you are trying to imprint into your unconscious mind – messages of success, abundance, self-belief and so on.

Repetition is also crucial when trying to develop new habits, hence meditating and using your other tools regularly and often is crucial.

If you are an arty type of person, you can embellish your diaries with drawings or paintings. This is a great idea, because the unconscious mind understands thoughts, feelings and concepts in symbolic form. But don't neglect to do the writing as well. I know this is all very labour-intensive and time consuming, but it will bear fruit and prove worthwhile in the end.

'OK,' I hear you say, 'my wife left me, I lost my job, the bank is foreclosing on my house, my dog bit the postman and he's suing me, and I drove my car into a brick wall. What have I got to be grateful for?'

Well you're still alive aren't you?

But seriously, you hated the job so now you have nothing to lose in going for a career change; your wife never loved you so now the way is open for you to meet someone who does; and when you crashed your car you walked away unscathed. All reasons to be grateful.

Remember we saw in an earlier chapter how you can ensure your mind fixes only on positive thoughts by focusing on something positive? It follows, therefore, that when you write about all the things in your life you feel grateful for, you automatically rule out feelings of lack and deprivation, and by so doing you very much diminish your opportunity for experiencing panic and anxiety. They simply cannot arise because you are not creating those thoughts. You are busy creating positive thoughts instead.

Once you calm down and start thinking positively, the possibility opens up of thinking creatively and evolving strategies to get you out of your difficulties. This in turn creates more gratitude, and so you carry on feeling better and more empowered each time you write up your *Gratitude Diary*.

Of course, the *Gratitude Diary* is just as effective in times of economic boom and collective optimism. Any time you feel a lack, or your self-esteem or self-worth takes a dive, get the diary out and start writing. Better still, don't wait till you're feeling down, keep your diaries going on a regular basis. They will greatly assist and empower your inner journey.

Summary

- Focusing on your state of abundance, which is what you do when you experience gratitude, helps you create more abundance
- Gratitude can lead you beyond your normal anxious state of turmoil to a new level of acceptance and relaxation, and to feelings of greater enjoyment and celebration in your life
- *The strategy of scapegoating is not in the least bit helpful.* When you blame others you avoid taking personal responsibility for your situation, and that renders you powerless

- When you are in a state of anxiety, panic, fear or anger, it is much harder to function creatively and enthusiastically while adapting to new circumstances
- The *Gratitude Diary* works by getting you to focus on what makes you feel abundant and your gratitude for that. Thus you create more abundance
- Imagine how powerful it would be if you were to adopt a programme of writing up your *Success Diary* and your *Gratitude Diary* on alternate days, while also meditating three or four times a week
- When you write about all the things in your life you feel grateful for, you automatically rule out feelings of lack and deprivation, and you diminish your opportunity for experiencing panic and anxiety
- Once you start thinking positively, the possibility opens up of thinking creatively and evolving strategies to get you out of your difficulties. This in turn creates more gratitude
- Don't wait till you're feeling down, keep your diaries going on a regular basis. They will greatly assist and empower your inner journey

10

You Gotta Have Chutzpah!

Who dares wins

The SAS – Special Air Service

So far in this book we've had several Sanskrit words. Now we've got a Yiddish word to get our heads around. It's not so much a word, more a mindset, and its essence encapsulates the secret ingredient of success and achievement more than any other concept. That's why *chutzpah* has a whole chapter to itself.

I've searched high and low but, as yet, have never found a satisfactory definition in English for *chutzpah*. According to Wikipedia, the online encyclopedia, '*in Yiddish and English, chutzpah has developed ambivalent and even positive connotations. Chutzpah can be used to express admiration for non-conformist but gutsy audacity.*' While this is true, that definition falls woefully short.

Just that one word *chutzpah* conveys an ethos, an atmosphere, an attitude, an approach to life, perhaps even a philosophy. Sometimes it is mistaken for arrogance and that's because *chutzpah* is an attitude. Someone who overdoes their *chutzpah* or uses it inappropriately is indeed in danger of falling into the trap of being arrogant and as a consequence of suffering an adverse reaction from others. The reason it is so useful as a basis for action is that when used correctly it gets spectacular results. Virtually all movers and shakers, the people who make a difference in this world, have *chutzpah*. You can have it too. Some people have it naturally but if you don't, you can develop an attitude of *chutzpah*.

The SAS (Special Air Service), the renowned crack commando unit in the British army, have a motto, 'who dares wins.' That's *chutzpah*. When you have *chutzpah* you believe in yourself so much that you dare to go all out for what you want. You risk sticking your neck all the way out, if necessary far beyond the place where most people who are content to underachieve draw a line and give up. You will think nothing of boldly doing whatever it takes, even when others tell you your ideas are doomed to failure.

If you have passion and a vision and your creativity is working overtime, add *chutzpah* to the mix and you become an unstoppable force for achievement. Even if it means going against the trend and especially conventional wisdom, you carry on undeterred. The person with *chutzpah* displays the ultimate proactive attitude.

Of course, with *chutzpah* you don't take stupid risks just for the sake of it. *Chutzpah* only works for your benefit if you have a heartfelt, passionate vision of how you can make something work by taking action that might be controversial; or if you have the unshakable conviction, based on solid self-belief, that the answers you need will reveal themselves if you take *appropriate* action, even though others might not appreciate that at the time.

If you don't have that self-belief, you can still employ *chutzpah* beneficially by *acting as if you do* until you start believing in yourself.

The Impeccable Warrior plays an essential part in this of course, because you still want your behavior to accord with your values, ethics and whatever is important to you. With *chutzpah* you are sufficiently cheeky, audacious and outrageous to push yourself right to the limits of what others find acceptable. That might be a long way outside of your comfort zone, but in true warrior style, if you sincerely believe in what you are doing you will never have grounds to reproach yourself whatever the outcome, for you will have left no stone unturned.

The best way for me to demonstrate the full extent of what *chutzpah* implies is to give a couple of vivid examples.

Towards the end of World War Two, British Prime Minister Winston Churchill, together with his generals, strategic advisors and of course US General Eisenhower, planned the invasion of Normandy in a bid to liberate Europe from Hitler for once and for all. It was an audacious plan and highly risky, but also it was highly imaginative in its conception and execution. It required tremendous nerve to initiate because it was hazardous in terms of strategy and would be costly in terms of lives. If the plan went wrong, the consequences for the Allies would have been unthinkable, for it might have spelled the end of a free and democratic Europe. Even worse, a lot of men would have died in vain.

The operation began with an air assault in which British, Canadian and American troops were landed behind enemy lines. However, the main thrust came from the sea, with considerable diversionary operations going on to distract the German Navy and shore defences. One essential element in the plan involved the subtle dissemination of misinformation to trick the German High Command into believing the invasion would come in the Calais region, the nearest point in France to Britain. The hope was that the bulk of Hitler's defensive forces would be in the wrong location, giving the Allies more time and, with luck, the element of surprise.

Here's the really amazing part of this story. During the preparatory phase, the Allies assembled in the English Channel the largest fleet of warships ever seen. The fleet included ships to bombard the French coast from offshore to 'soften up' the German defences and give cover across the inshore stretch to the beaches, enabling hundreds of landing craft full of assault troops to make a dash to the shore. They even assembled groups of mulberries to tow across the Channel; these structures had been built in secret locations in England and were used to create temporary harbours for landing supplies and munitions to support the invasion. Meanwhile other troops landed silently behind enemy lines in gliders to help clear a way for the columns of soldiers as they advanced from the coast. Was this plan audacious or what?

All this was going on virtually under Hitler's nose and although his reconnaissance planes and spy network accumulated many clues about what was about to happen, Hitler refused to believe it was possible. He seemed convinced the alleged plan to invade Normandy was a deception, a decoy plan to wrong-foot him. Somehow Hitler had assured himself that the invasion, when it came, would take place further north-east, even though apparently some of his High Command tried to tell him it would be in Normandy.

This is a grossly simplified description of the plan to illustrate my point, and we all know how the story ends. What makes it so fascinating is that the outcome hinged entirely on human psychology. Hitler seemed to be deeply in denial about what his intelligence reports were trying to tell him. Perhaps he felt invincible, and very likely he didn't believe the Allies would have the sheer *chutzpah* to attempt such an operation. This was one of the widest parts of the English Channel and the Allies would be sitting ducks for the German air force and land defences; also the coastline of exposed beaches backed by cliffs was difficult terrain for invading troops because of the lack of cover.

Churchill and the Allies knew full well it would not be easy but realised that only a daring and imaginative plan stood an earthly chance of success. This is a classic example of the creative and audacious use of *chutzpah* and, although there was sadly a huge cost in terms of human lives, ultimately it succeeded. Only a highly original group of thinkers who believed in themselves to the full could have pulled it off.

What's really sad is that humans still don't seem to have learned that war is always a bad idea and one, ironically, that the Impeccable Warrior would never condone except in an extreme case of self-defence.

Let's look at a totally different story as another demonstration of *chutzpah*. This one began in 1984 when Michael Buerk, the well-known BBC television and radio presenter, was working as a foreign correspondent in Africa. He and cameraman Mohammed Amin filmed and broadcasted reports on the famine taking place in Ethiopia, bringing the plight of millions of starving people to British screens, probably for the first time ever.

One person who watched the TV reports with mounting, jaw-dropping horror was the singer Bob Geldof, who felt himself stung into taking action. He realised it was useless waiting for the world's political leaders to do anything but he also understood the effectiveness of people power. He set about persuading, bullying and cajoling a host of famous pop stars into coming together and giving their time for free to create an ad hoc band called *Band Aid*. They made a Christmas record to raise money to relieve the starvation in Ethiopia, which became a number one best-selling hit and raised millions.

That wasn't enough for the audacious and angry Geldof and he then set about organising a massive concert, entitled *Live Aid*, undoubtedly the largest and most ambitious television event ever known at the time. It took place simultaneously in London's Wembley Stadium, and in the JFK Stadium in Philadelphia. Geldof pulled no punches in using the concert to persuade millions of people to part with their money to help the starving in Africa.

I have read many reports of the outrageous lengths to which Geldof went in persuading a long list of megastars to give their time and music for free in aid of this cause. The details vary, but what is clear is that the list of names, which reads like an encyclopaedia of British and

American popular music of the 1980s, was assembled almost entirely because of Geldof's *chutzpah*. This was no easy matter and either Geldof had phenomenal self-belief, or he acted as if he had. It seemed his *chutzpah* new no bounds. I'm sure many of the artists he galvanised were lovely people and only too happy to help out, but we are also talking about some giant egos here, busy people used to earning huge sums who might have needed some considerable persuasion. It must have cost some of the artists a lot of money to alter their schedules, cancel travel plans and in some cases, get out of long standing contracts to perform elsewhere on that day.

Moreover, there was no way Geldof was going to hide his anger from the world for letting these people in Ethiopia die – on the contrary, he went to great lengths to communicate his anger to the fullest, and it was infectious. It was as if he was speaking for the entire world TV audience. His incredible achievement undoubtedly shifted the perspective of many in the wealthy Western world while raising many millions for Ethiopia. It was also a win/win situation for millions of people around the world who were able to enjoy a fantastic TV concert.

These true stories and many others like them mean that when someone tells me they can't make a difference, I don't believe them. Each one of us, even the most humble, can make a difference. What's more, people will secretly admire you for your *chutzpah*. If you have a vision and the *chutzpah* to do whatever it takes to make it happen, a mouse can move a mountain.

By the same token, if you have a dream, a burning ambition, a goal, a passion, a calling – whatever – you can make it happen, especially if you've got plenty of *chutzpah*. So please let's be serious – if you feel too shy to stick your hand up and be counted, get over it. Act as if, and develop the art of *chutzpah*. It's perhaps the most powerful life skill there is and it will always help you to break through.

Summary

- Used correctly as a basis for action, *chutzpah* gets spectacular results, and virtually all the people who make a difference in this world, have *chutzpah*
- You can have *chutzpah* too. Some people have it naturally but if you don't, you can develop an attitude of *chutzpah*

- If you have passion and a vision and your creativity is working overtime, add *chutzpah* to the mix and you become an unstoppable force for achievement
- Even when you use *chutzpah,* because you still stick to your core values and beliefs, in true warrior style you will never have grounds to reproach yourself whatever your outcome
- Each one of us, even the most humble, can make a difference
- If you have a vision, a dream, a burning ambition, a goal, a passion, a calling – whatever – you can make it happen, especially if you've got plenty of *chutzpah*
- If you feel too shy to stick your hand up and be counted, get over it. Act as if, and develop the art of *chutzpah*
- *Chutzpah* is perhaps the most powerful life skill there is and it will always help you to break through

11

Go Deeply Into Your Resistance

We cannot solve our problems with the same thinking we used when we created them
Albert Einstein

Ever had that grungy Monday morning feeling when you know you've got important things to do but all you can say to yourself is, 'can't be bothered!' That's resistance.

Ever found yourself doing every chore under the sun instead of the one you really want or need to be doing? That's resistance too.

Resistance comes in all forms, shapes and sizes and it's the kiss of death to any kind of motivation or noteworthy achievement. But instead of fighting it, you can turn it greatly to your advantage if you take the trouble to understand the nature of resistance, how it works, its many guises and why it can actually be your best friend, not your enemy. In fact I consider that to be a vital part of anyone's personal development programme.

'Oh good heavens, now Dave's completely lost the plot,' I hear you say. Not so, not at all so. It took me many years to realise this but finally I got it – you can use your resistance like a great big signpost. It can show you where your attention can best be focused to get you unblocked and back on the road to progress in no time at all. Resistance is a giant clue that works every time. In short, *your resistance shows you where you are blocking yourself.*

Always remember there are those who get on with their lives and there are those who make plans to get on with their lives. Make your choice – *in which camp are you going to pitch your tent?* Procrastination is just a habit and another form of resistance, and if you want to be happy you must figure out what you need to do to drop it and get on with your life. Resistance itself can show you the way.

Why we have resistance

The most common cause of resistance is fear, especially fear of failure or fear of being hurt. Consciously or unconsciously we perceive it thus: if we put our heart and soul into trying to be successful in something we dream about and we fail, then our hopes and dreams will be dashed forever and we will feel hurt, disappointed, frustrated and maybe even angry. We don't want to experience all those feelings so we find all sorts of excuses to put off taking even the first step.

If your resistance is really clever, you might take the first step towards doing something meaningful and then stop at that, saying to yourself it's not your fault you were thwarted because you gave it your best shot. You made a start and nothing happened, which proves it can never work and therefore you are justified in giving up and staying stuck. This is a very tenuous attempted rationalisation, a strategy some people adopt to try to fool themselves into feeling vindicated in their refusal to take further action. It's your saboteur in yet another guise. The reason you gave up is fear, plain and simple.

Like resistance, fear also comes in all shapes and sizes and the possibility also exists that what you fear is success, bizarre though it might seem. If you are successful you may have to surrender your victim status for ever. You might have to live up to a whole lot of new expectations of yourself and operate on a much higher level or, even worse, you might be successful for a while and *then* fail. Then you'd really feel like an idiot!

Whatever your fear, if your unconscious perceives further action as too risky it will try to find ways of rationalising everything away so you feel alright. But you don't really feel alright, not deep down inside. The problem is, if you allow yourself to acknowledge that truth you won't be able to live with yourself until you do something about it. So it's in your interest for it (and you) to remain unconscious, except that in reality it isn't at all in your interest, if you get my meaning. Your mind is attempting to deceive you through denial, in other words, a refusal to accept your truth.

This kind of unconscious behaviour tends to go in patterns and is deeply sabotaging. The same patterns repeat themselves, sometimes in different forms, time and time again. However we can, with awareness, recognise the behaviour when it starts happening and choose to act differently. Now that would be in our best interests.

Many people I come across have huge resistance to doing the method I teach of silent meditation for that very reason, though they may not realise it at the time. Unconsciously they have a vested interest in remaining unconscious because somewhere they sense a 'danger' that meditation will wake them up to the truth about what's really going on, and that's just too scary to allow. Once I ever so gently point that out and get them to admit it, they gradually start to meditate and soon find themselves feeling better. Why? Because they are gaining understanding, they are developing insight, they are growing their awareness so they feel empowered. Soon they begin to realise there's not really much to be afraid of after all.

This needs to be emphasised because it's important to get this. If you are stumped by the question, 'how do I overcome my resistance?, start by noticing it. Make yourself as aware of it as you possibly can be every time it arises. Keep using at least some of the methods or tools for raising awareness we have described already, especially meditation. Continue their practice on a regular basis.

Drop your attachments

The Buddha teaches that our propensity to want to hold on to our attachments brings us untold misery, and if we want release from that unhappiness, all we have to do is to let go.

Unfortunately this valuable teaching seems to be widely misunderstood, but in its correct interpretation it makes a lot of sense and we can use this as another powerful tool. Many people assume he is talking about letting go of our material possessions, things we buy or acquire as life goes by, which may be appropriate to your situation but not necessarily. They dismiss the teaching because they don't want to kiss goodbye to their hard-earned money, their fast car or their beautiful house to live the life of the ascetic wandering around with a begging bowl. I don't blame them. I wouldn't want to do that either. I don't imagine living a hand-to-mouth existence would do an awful lot for my self-esteem! I see no virtue in poverty or austerity.

Where the Buddha's advice can be most usefully applied is in dropping our attachments to our neurotic unconscious behaviour patterns, our desire to control, our refusal to embrace change, and of course to our resistance.

There is nothing wrong with possessions per se as long as we realise they are merely items and nothing to do with who we really are. If we depend on our possessions for our sense of wellbeing or validation, then we're potentially in trouble. If we believe they make us better or more important people, we've got a problem. If your sense of well-being is dependent on any source outside of yourself, how are you ever going to experience true peace of mind, happiness and fulfilment, for all those things are temporary? If those are your beliefs, they are in direct conflict with goals of true happiness and you are almost certainly heading for a painful wake-up call.

As we have already discussed at length, we tend to repeat sabotaging behaviour and it blocks our attempts at happiness every time. By being defensive and sticking to our resistance we avoid building our conscious awareness and, oh boy, do we suffer as a consequence!

Letting go is a bit like saying 'relax, chill out,' but before we can do it we have to notice we are tense, stressed, anxious, fearful, resistant, obstinate, conceited, egotistical, controlling and stuck. Letting go simply means *stop pushing the river and go with the flow.* When you push the river you merely exhaust yourself – you go nowhere fast, your efforts bear little fruit and the whole thing is pointless and painful. There is no meaning, purpose or fulfilment in a life that goes nowhere.

Exercise 14: Accepting the outcome

ACCEPTING THE OUTCOME

Why not try this strategy instead? Rather than insisting on particular outcomes, do whatever you feel to do from your heart. Do not do what you think you ought to do, nor what your conditioning tells you to do, nor what your habitual behaviour pushes you to do. Then see what happens *and accept the outcome*. It's an experiment. Then instead of getting stressed you will learn something. Why not try it and see how you feel?

How do you know what your heart is telling you to do? Meditate, be still and silent for a while and listen. Be a witness. If you do that without making judgements or trying to suppress or modify whatever comes up, it won't be long before guidance, perhaps explicit or maybe in the form of a clue, is forthcoming.

If you feel you can't accept the outcome you now know you have to change your actions. In such a case there is no need to be afraid of change – it may be just what is needed. You may have to creatively explore many avenues, do some research, acquire new knowledge, skills and experience, or you may simply need to change your attitude. Once you realise this, if you feel resistance building up, you will be aware of it and push through it more easily by taking appropriate action.

Have you ever had that feeling of trying as hard as you can to make something work, yet no matter how hard you try, you just can't manage it. Finally you give up in a fit of frustration, rolling your eyes to heaven and yelling, 'that's it! I give up!' For a few seconds you are flushed with anger and frustration but an instant later a rushing feeling of relief and release courses through your whole body. You might not admit it or even notice it, or if you do you may shut the feeling off in an instant, but that moment of letting go is highly significant.

This is the whole point of going deeply into your resistance. If you resist as much as you can there will come a time when you just can't stand it any more. You will have built your awareness of your resistance to fever pitch and you will simply have to let go. *That's your moment of liberation.*

The acceptance of what is

The only way each of us we will find fulfilment is by following our unique path. That means being 100 per cent unconditionally who we are, for when we discover our unique self, our path is revealed. Sometimes it works the other way round – when we stumble upon our path we start to develop a stronger sense of who we are. Either way, knowing who we are and finding our true paths go hand in hand. We each acquire the required self-knowledge by stopping, being still and silent for a moment and listening carefully to our inner voice, the true voice of our innermost heart and soul, the inner wisdom we each have that always knows what we need. Then we act without hesitation in accordance with its guidance.

When we experience resistance we can be sure we are not properly tuned in and are not listening; or if we do hear, we are not acting in accordance with the guidance we are given. To be able to hear that small voice we must lapse into silence and stillness, a state of surrender. That can seem really scary because it implies giving up control and accepting whatever arises from within. But there is no other way.

In any life situation we are presented with two possible courses of action, resistance or acceptance. This is important because whichever of these two paths we choose to follow, the choice is ours and we are always free to make it – as long as we are aware we have that choice!

If we choose the path of resistance, the going will be tough. We will be constantly thwarted and life will be an uphill struggle in which we always end up trying to push the river against its natural direction of flow. If, by contrast, we drop our resistance and instead choose a path of acceptance, everything flows effortlessly and obstacles are easily surmounted, bypassed or turned to our advantage as more and more doors are opened to us.

Of course we cannot become sincerely accepting if we do not really feel it, but what we can do is *accept our resistance* and then move straight on past it. That is the simple secret, the trick that can end our conflict and take the stress out of living, by simply putting us in control of our lives.

If you want a strategy to make it easier to do that, you can accept your resistance and then *act as if* there is no resistance and carry on. It's another version of feeling the fear and doing it anyway.

With awareness our choices are revealed to us, which, as I repeat ad infinitum, is why cultivating awareness is crucial to making our lives work. If the truth be known there is nothing to fear. This happens to be an excellent state of affairs because invariably when we follow our flow we start to feel fulfilled, happy, less stressed and so on.

It is by hanging on to our resistance at all costs that we actually create our own problems. It might seem ridiculously simple, but when we accept who we are and go where our inner voice is guiding us, our problems melt away.

Changing your mindset will inevitably result in the need to make some radical life changes and that can seem a very frightening prospect. So courage is needed for you are going to have to embrace the unknown and the unfamiliar and come out of your comfort zone. Going into the unknown on a whim is stupid; following your inner guidance, maybe one step at a time, with eyes wide open and constantly monitoring yourself, is the only viable path towards a happy and fulfilling life.

Dealing with insecurity

When it comes to acceptance, especially self-acceptance, it pays to know yourself and what you are like in detail, so you can act accordingly. For example, if you are a very cautious person then proceed cautiously. If you try to be over ambitious or reckless you will be acting out of character and that can result in severely denting your confidence. When that happens people often grind to a halt because everything seems too overwhelming and scary. Better to accept that you feel more comfortable when you act cautiously. Slow progress is far better than no progress.

Let's take a real life example. I have a client who does not want to be named and she had been pursuing a high-powered and highly stressful sales job before being made redundant. She was happy with the redundancy because she hated the job, which made her feel depressed, and it gave her the push she needed to quit. Now she was faced with what to do next. She was determined to change to a career path in which she could flourish. Our conversation went roughly as follows:

> *Dave:* 'You say you are artistic and you love painting and decorating, yet you are looking at office jobs. How does that make sense?'
> *Client:* 'I understand admin and sales. I could easily get a job in admin. I don't have the knowledge I need to be a high-quality up-market decorator.'
> *Dave:* 'Are you telling me that in a city like London in the twenty-first century you can't acquire knowledge of how to do sophisticated painting and decorating?'
> *Client:* 'I'd have to do a training course.'
> *Dave:* 'Exactly.'
> *Client:* 'But I have to earn money. I can't go back to being a full time student again at my age. I'm almost fifty.'

Sooner or later just about every person I coach about starting a new career path brings up the issue of money, or lack of it, as an allegedly insurmountable obstacle. If I say 'you are using money as an excuse,' I am presented with more resistance. Age is another resistance strategy. Nowadays lots of people take up new careers when they reach retirement age. Our deep sense of insecurity keeps us trapped if we allow it to. Our conversation continued:

Dave: 'Who said it had to be full-time? What about studying part-time and working part-time? Could that work for you?'
Client: 'Then I'd have to be frugal and live on a much smaller budget that what I've become used to.'
Dave: 'This is true.'
Client: 'I couldn't cope with that. I'd feel desperately insecure.'
Dave: 'Do you *really* want to be happy?'

So here's the bottom line – *nobody said it was going to be easy.* You may have to make some radical changes and that might seem scary but if that's what it takes, so be it. Living on a small amount of money might seem scary too. The question is, *will you pay the price in order to get happiness in the long-term?* Each person will answer that differently for it depends how much you want the end benefit. Some people want a cast iron guarantee that they will receive the benefit, but of course it depends entirely on you making it happen.

Ask yourself honestly, *how highly motivated am I?* If by now you have started to develop the habit of focusing on the positive perhaps you will accept you are going to experience fear and then get on with it. You might also decide to accept the risk, knowing that whatever happens, as long as your behaviour is impeccable, that is to say you always give 100 per cent, you will never have anything to reproach yourself for. *You will always learn something, whatever happens.*

You might even realise, if that is your attitude, that in reality there is no risk, only a learning and growth opportunity. In this case the person concerned had already been made redundant, so she's not putting her livelihood at risk.

The best way to deal with the insecurity is to work out a strategy in which the goal is achieved one step at a time, moving at a pace that stretches you but doesn't put you off by frightening you to death. Each of us has our own speed and we must respect that as long as we make sure progress continues. For a client, the beauty of working with a coach is that they are always in the driving seat and they receive support and feedback every step of the way. This builds confidence and self-belief and ensures they keep going right to the end.

My 'let's get on with it' approach with the above client might seem crude, brutal and heartless but it's not. I only confront people who I care about. In this case, we both knew perfectly well she wanted to be challenged and gently pushed, otherwise she would not have come to see me. She wanted support and guidance in finding the courage to face her truth and work out a practical solution so she could make the changes she wanted.

After a while she and I together worked out a strategy and it helped her push through her resistance bit by bit. First she got an undemanding manual job which ensured she didn't get stressed and gave her just enough income to survive. Then she enrolled on a part-time course to learn the subtle arts and skills of high quality painting and decorating because she wanted to market herself as an up-market specialist, for which she seemed especially talented.

At the same time, friends and relations started inviting her to paint their bathrooms and hallways and even though she didn't ask for money, they were so delighted with the results they insisted on paying her. She also started redecorating her own house. She also invested in some high quality brushes and other relevant tools, and started building her experience. She had the courage of her convictions. She invested time, money and belief in herself and gradually it began to pay off handsomely.

Experience is an essential factor in starting a new career and it can't be taught. The only way to acquire experience is to go out and do whatever it is. To many of us, that prospect engenders enough fear to stop us in our tracks. So start small. Take on a small project first, then gradually progress to more sophisticated challenges and push yourself through your resistance as your confidence builds.

When you feel afraid, acknowledge the fear. Don't be in denial or the fear will always lurk in the background ready to destroy your growing self-confidence. When you admit to it, you will unfreeze, start taking action and the fear will pass. When you make the inevitable mistakes that we all make, learn from them. Never be afraid of making mistakes. Instead welcome them as valuable learning opportunities.

After a couple of years my client started getting the kind of commissions she wanted and she gave up her part-time job. With hardly a wobble she found she was self-employed, something that had hitherto filled her with tremendous fear and resistance, but she finally saw that it put her in a strong position and gave her the freedom she wanted. She was able to put her own unique stamp on every job and as a result she built a reputation, and referrals started flooding in. She practically glided into her new profession. She entered her *maximum creative flow* and needless to say no longer felt insecure about money. Even more important, her depression was left way behind.

When contemplating my path there is one important thing I have learned, that if I remain sufficiently aware, each day I can turn from creating a path of resistance towards treading a path of acceptance. There are no pre-laid paths, of course, only the path we create as we walk along. Even with so-called well-defined career paths, each person's journey is unique and that's why each person needs a tailor-made approach.

Defence mechanisms

Several times I have mentioned the term *'defence mechanism.'* It's just another form of resistance or trying to retain control. When you feel attacked verbally or physically you become defensive to protect yourself from being hurt, physically or emotionally.

If you really are under attack then raising your defence mechanism is probably a good idea. The downside is that it's very difficult, or even impossible, for a defended person to fully function on an emotional level, because when we cut off from one emotion, in this case fear, we cut off from all of them. This resistance to being seen as who you are is counter-productive in the extreme, especially if you are trying to conduct a relationship which includes some degree of intimacy, or even just a friendship or business relationship.

Once again we come back to awareness, and I know we've already covered this point but it's so important it will do no harm to remind ourselves of it in the context of resistance – first we need to notice when we are being defensive and secondly we need to consciously decide whether it's in our best interest to open up or remain defended. If you feel good about yourself there is little risk in being open, but there is no doubt there will always be someone who wants to transgress your boundaries or behave insensitively towards you. In such cases it's important to remember that other people's behaviour is their responsibility, not yours, and it's always up to you to evaluate the degree of truth in any situation. The Impeccable Warrior is far more likely to feel comfortable about being in a state of openness because he doesn't need the approval of others. He is his own person.

If someone shouts at you and starts blaming you for something, your natural human reaction will almost certainly be to become defensive.

When that happens, any resolution to the conflict between the two of you is virtually out of the question. You can learn something from that, which is if you want to sort out a conflict with someone, don't blame and don't be aggressive. Just say how you feel. By doing that, you make it possible for the other person to open up and say how they feel.

When two people understand a little more about where the other is coming from, it is far more likely they will be able to reach an accommodation. However, if you cling to your resistance you make resolution of your issues impossible.

Finally ...

Don't be afraid of your resistance or regard it as a problem or even as the enemy. Go deeply into it so it can become a part of your guidance system.

Summary

- Your resistance shows you where you are blocking yourself
- The most common cause of resistance is fear, especially fear of failure, though you may also fear success
- If you want overcome your resistance, start with noticing it. Make yourself as aware of it as you possibly can every time it arises
- Letting go is a bit like saying 'relax, chill out.' It actually means *stop pushing the river and go with the flow*
- Why go deeply into your resistance? If you resist as much as you can there will come a time when you just can't stand it any more. You will have built your awareness of your resistance to fever pitch and you will simply have to let it go. *That's your moment of liberation*
- When we experience resistance we are not properly tuned in and are not listening; or if we do hear, we are not acting in accordance with the guidance we are given
- In any life situation we are presented with two possible courses of action, resistance or acceptance. The choice is ours and we are always free to make it – as long as we are aware we have that choice!
- If we choose the path of resistance, the going will be tough. If we drop our resistance and choose a path of acceptance, everything flows effortlessly

- When we accept who we are and go where our inner voice is guiding us, our problems melt away
- We might not be able to drop it, but we can *accept our resistance* and then move straight on past it. That is the simple secret, the trick that can end our conflict and stress, by simply putting us in control of our lives
- Following your inner guidance one step at a time, constantly monitoring yourself, is the only viable path towards a happy and fulfilling life
- If you are a cautious person then proceed cautiously. If you try to be over-ambitious or reckless you will be acting out of character and that can severely dent your confidence. Slow progress is far better than no progress
- Living on a small amount of money might seem scary, but the question is, *will you pay the price to get happiness in the long-term?*
- Some people want cast iron guarantees that they will receive the benefit, but that depends entirely on you making it happen. Ask yourself honestly, *how highly motivated am I?*
- You might decide to accept the risk, knowing that whatever happens, as long as your behaviour is impeccable, you will never have anything to reproach yourself for. You will always learn something, *whatever happens*
- You might even realise, if that is your attitude, that in reality there is no risk –only a learning and growth opportunity
- The best way to deal with insecurity is to devise a strategy in which the goal is achieved one step at a time, moving at a pace that stretches you but doesn't scare you too much
- Each of us has our own speed and we must respect that as long as our progress continues
- If you remain aware, each day you can turn from creating a path of resistance towards treading a path of acceptance
- Each person's journey is unique and that's why each person needs a tailor-made approach
- Your defence mechanism is another form of resistance, or way of trying to stay in control. If you remain permanently defensive the whole of your emotional side is insulated and you will feel isolated

- Awareness is the antidote. First we need to notice when we are being defensive and secondly we need to consciously decide whether it's in our best interest to open up or remain defended
- The Impeccable Warrior is more likely to feel comfortable about remaining in a state of openness because he doesn't need the approval of others. He is his own person
- If you want to resolve a conflict with someone, don't blame and don't be aggressive. Just say how you feel
- Don't be afraid of your resistance, or regard it as a problem or as the enemy. Go deeply into it so it can become a part of your guidance system

Exercise in acceptance

Exercise 14: Accepting the outcome

12

Go Deeply Into Your 'Negative' Emotions

A controlled man is a dead man, and whether you are controlled by yourself or by others does not make much difference

Osho

You may have notice in this chapter heading that the word *negative* is surrounded by inverted commas. That's because I don't really believe there are negative emotions, nor *positive* ones either. Emotions in my opinion are neither negative nor positive, they are what they are, they are exactly as they should be, and they need not garner our judgements. In the same way that life is neither good nor bad, it just *is*. Each of our emotions serves a specific purpose and if we want to benefit from that, our best option is to accept them exactly as they are.

Actually that's our only option, for the only other option is denial, and you must surely know by now my views about denial. It simply is not a viable option if you wish to live a meaningful life as a full-blooded human being.

This may sound like semantics, but it's important to understand this. It's easy to label anger, for example, as *negative,* but there are times when anger is positively helpful in expressing yourself and in making your feelings clear to others. At other times, in a different context or when used in an inappropriate way, it can be destructive.

If someone threatens you with a knife you might feel afraid and run away. Your fear has served you well because it spurred you to action which potentially saved your life or probable injury, so why should fear be judged as negative, as is so often the case?

The reason why this matters is because it's easy to fall into the trap of criticising ourselves and others for being angry, sad, afraid, perhaps even happy, but we only succeed in putting ourselves and others down when we censure our feelings or theirs. Sometimes we even apologise for how we feel on the basis that we perceive our emotional state as unacceptable, or we fear others will do so.

If we feel angry and as a result we hurt someone, that is something for which to apologise, but it's the action, not the feeling, that is inappropriate and merits the apology. Better to try to understand our emotional states and accept them for what they are, for then they will support us in every respect. It's when feelings go unacknowledged and unexpressed that they cause inappropriate actions which get us into trouble. Once again we see the need for awareness to make sure we notice how we feel, and learn appropriate ways to let our emotions have their voice.

We need lots and lots of awareness around this: on our propensity to judge our emotions; on our habit of judging others for their emotional states; and on our tendency to repress our emotional sides. If you don't express how you feel on a regular basis, either you're like a volcano waiting to erupt, or you'll dive into a deep depression. Either way, you are not treating yourself or the people around you with the respect that's due, and that is not the way of the Impeccable Warrior.

There is one other trap I must warn you about, for just about everyone falls into this one – now that you have read the foregoing passage, don't be tempted to judge yourself harshly for having judgements. If you discover that you have been judgemental, be kind to yourself and accept what you have done. Otherwise your self-esteem will take a dive. If you don't like what you did, notice that and decide not to do it again.

You may have to catch yourself many times before the habit is broken, but each time accept you are doing the best you can, give yourself credit for that and don't put yourself down. Remember the advice of Frank Sinatra when he sang, 'take a deep breath, pick yourself up, dust yourself off, and start all over again.'

In the next chapter we will discuss some powerful methods for dealing with unexpressed emotions.

Understanding fear, pain and anger

Have you ever had the feeling that you just want to cringe when you meet somebody at a party who is so nice, so perfect, so relaxed, so charming, so diplomatic and so even-tempered you know they just want to please everyone. Then they give you their window smile and a powerfully nauseous feeling creeps over you! People like that come across as unreal, disingenuous and insincere, probably because they are. They are showing us their façade or false persona and almost certainly they don't realise it because they are deeply unconscious. I suppose we can try to be compassionate and say, as Jesus so magnanimously put it, 'forgive them Lord, for they know not what they do.' But let us reiterate once and for all, *people pleasing is not viable behaviour,* and certainly well out of sync with the way of the Impeccable Warrior.

This kind of person, like the rest of us, wants above all to be loved and approved of. Ironically, people who behave like that, perhaps because they feel desperately insecure or they are working hard to repress a cauldron of anger, put people off and usually end up friendless. They perceive the idea of putting their genuine self on view as being too painful and/or scary. Almost certainly they suffer from low self-esteem, self-belief and self-worth, and *suffer* is the key word. Unconsciously they believe if people see who they really are and what they are really like, it will be impossible for anyone to love them.

The remedy? As we said at the very beginning of this book, 'to thine own self be true.' If you want to relate to real people on a heart to heart level, they will want the real deal from you, not just a cardboard cut-out. This is why it's important to go deeply into your emotional side. Get to know your anger, your fear, your pain, as well as your joy, bliss, happiness and so forth. Stop judging them and accept that they are part of the package that makes up you. Understand we humans are multi-dimensional and multi-faceted beings with depth, breadth, range and scope, and we are all the more fascinating for that.

It may seem scary to get to know your anger inside out, maybe you fear getting out of control and doing serious damage to someone or something. However, my knowledge and my experience tell me is it's actually far more dangerous to keep it bottled up inside. Let's take as a metaphor a pressure cooker sitting on a hob, bubbling away and building up pressure inside. That pressure represents your anger. Someone turns up the heat and the pressure builds. If you keep the valve closed and lid firmly shut, the inevitable consequence sooner or later will be the pressure cooker exploding. But if you open the valve, the pressure dissipates harmlessly.

Expressing your anger in a safe way is equivalent to opening your valve. You eliminate the possibility of an explosion and allow your anger to pass.

What is anger anyway? Anger is not actually a primary emotion, it's an aggressive defensive response. You will understand this clearly if you work through the layers of your emotional side, and you can do this through meditation, hypnosis and other introspection techniques. When you do, you will realise that there is something else underneath your anger.

One amazing process for penetrating your emotional layers and effecting deep healing to your emotional wounding is *The Journey*, mentioned in Chapter 4, a brilliant healing procedure devised and delivered by Brandon Bays. More about *The Journey* in the following chapter.

To cut to the chase, what you will find beneath your anger is fear, but even fear is not the very bottom layer. Look more deeply, keep on penetrating, and eventually you will find pain. Just about every ordinary mortal I have ever met, with the possible exception of a handful of enlightened beings, dislikes pain and has an emotional memory of it that produces fears of it happening again. When our fear is strong enough we will do anything to defend ourselves against the perceived risk of being hurt again. That's why some of us become habitually defensive, even when we are not under threat. The mere possibility of experiencing more pain prompts a defensive self-preservation reaction, known by psychologists as the *fight or flight* response.

If your mind decides on the *fight* option, your anger erupts and maybe you attack. If you don't fancy your chances you'll instinctively take the *flight* option and run away. What are you fighting about or running from? Under normal everyday circumstances *it's not your conscious, rational decision-making mind, but your unconscious fear of being hurt or wounded that's driving your behaviour.*

Obviously in a physical confrontation, such as when a tall twenty-stone angry man with muscles like Rambo threatens to beat you up in the street, it is entirely reasonable to adopt a defensive reaction, either fight or flight. But in this context we are talking about matters far more subtle than that. For example, imagine a man and a woman trying to have a relationship. One partner wants more intimacy and tries to advance, but the other partner fears getting emotionally hurt because he or she got hurt before and so steps back *in spite of the fact that unconsciously he or she also wants more intimacy.*

Let's just put that situation under the microscope for a moment, because it happens all the time and causes untold heartache. The partner who holds back is being offered what he or she always wanted – more intimacy, love and attention, but the obvious attraction of that is overwhelmed by a fear of being hurt, so that person withholds their love.

In the cold light of day when we examine rationally what is going on here we realise there is always a risk of getting hurt, but if you never take that risk you will certainly never get the love you want. Don't forget, just because you got hurt in the past does not necessarily mean you will get hurt again. If you evaluate the risk and weigh it up against the benefit, you might decide it's a risk worth taking after all.

In the earlier case of being threatened in the street, physical as well as emotional wounding is virtually inevitable if you rise to the threat, so flight would be perfectly reasonable. In the latter example, emotional wounding is by no means a foregone conclusion and emotional nourishment is a strong likelihood. It's not what's being offered that makes the person withdraw, it's a fear of something that might never materialise, and if you are reacting to something that hasn't yet happened that means you are living in a fantasy world. Wake up! Think twice, or you might miss out on your most cherished goal.

We may differ on this but in my view, to withdraw when your would-be partner comes closer because unconsciously you fear getting hurt, even though what you really want is more intimacy, is the height of self-sabotage. If it happens once and it's not your normal way, *maybe* you are justified, but if it's your pattern, though it's understandable, your defensive behaviour repeatedly destroys your chances of happiness. So take note – especially if it keeps happening every time you try to make a new relationship work.

To put this into perspective, the Impeccable Warrior wouldn't think twice about moving forward towards such a golden opportunity. Somebody with whom he is relating offers him what he wants. One quick thought is enough for him. He knows what he truly wants because he's regularly monitoring himself, he trusts his instincts and he goes with them. He also knows that whatever the outcome he will be alright, because he is his own person. Even if he is hurt, he knows he will soon recover. He likes to interact in an interdependent or synergistic way, but at the same time he is self-sufficient.

Here's the unvarnished truth – if you want to be a fully fledged participant in the game of life, to make your contribution and find your share of happiness and fulfilment, shrinking back will never do. Being miserly with your energy, refusing to take the brakes off and hiding behind a defensive veil will only result in meagre results. In the words of motivational speaker Christopher Howard, the best way forward is to *'step up and play all out.'*

This principle applies in all life situations, not only in physical matters but also in all sorts of psychological, spiritual, emotional scenarios, in your conversations and in your relationships. *It is crucial to understand that if your unconscious behaviour patterns are sabotaging your best efforts you will want to change them, and the only way to do that is to first become fully conscious of them.*

Let's take another hypothetical example, this time a typical domestic scenario. The two people above find the courage to enter into an intimate relationship and all is lovey-dovey for the first couple of weeks. Then one day she shouts at him because he left his dirty socks on the kitchen table. At this point an insecure person feels under attack and starts to behave defensively. However, an Impeccable Warrior, because of his heightened awareness and his sensitivity to his partner's feelings, understands that by expressing her anger she is merely opening the valve in her metaphorical pressure cooker. Instead of behaving defensively he might even find it within his heart to admit she might have a point, and remove the offending socks forthwith! A sincere person who believes in himself has no problem admitting when he is in the wrong.

Most importantly, because he has developed his witnessing skills he is immediately able to see the bigger picture, which is that she still loves him in spite of her irritation, and that's the only thing that really matters. He is not actually in danger of getting hurt *unless* he reacts defensively. With awareness, understanding, listening and a little vulnerability on his part, her anger passes and their loving relationship resumes.

Many people sit on their energy, which is a descriptive way of saying they are miserly in their willingness to engage with life in every aspect. They hold back, and often it's because of a refusal to believe in themselves. Such people do not believe they can, or even deserve to, achieve whatever they want. They don't even try for fear of the painful rejection or failure they feel sure they will experience. To make matters worse, they unconsciously repress those fears, not even realising they are there. Then they wonder why nothing ever changes in their lives.

Of course, nothing we want ever happens when we take no initiative and we refuse to make constructive changes, so the failure they fear is guaranteed. This in turn proves they were right – it is better to do nothing because failure is inevitable. Clinging to victimhood is apparently a much safer option. If this sounds like you, recognise the pattern and you start to unlock yourself.

Why go deeply into our emotions?

A person feels angry but does not express it. That anger has to go somewhere. So do sadness, happiness, grief and any other emotion that may arise. Emotions are pure energy and, like matter, they cannot be destroyed. They have to be expressed, and if we are not willing to express them, they will express themselves sooner or later by any means they can.

When a person's feelings are repressed, it is a recipe for illness, malaise, unhappiness, negativity, sadness, cynicism, bitterness and depression – perhaps even severe mental illness, violence and self-destructive behaviour. Either an explosion or an implosion is inevitable sooner or later. The energy that strives for release cannot get out and more energy is wasted keeping it in, so not much is left for creativity or joy.

On the other hand, if a person shouts his anger, cries his sadness or grief, laughs his happiness, in other words allows his emotions to express themselves, the pent-up energy is released and he becomes a healthy and vibrant conduit for those emotions. He opens himself like a channel so his energy flows harmlessly through him.

A repressed person cannot be fully creative, and certainly cannot experience the joyful release and empowerment that creative expression can confer on a person, because creativity is also an expression of emotional energy. It has to be allowed to flow through us. A creative block is nothing more than repressed emotions.

Being around a person who represses their anger is like standing next to a volcano. It makes us feel nervous because we are acutely aware that anything could spark off an eruption. If that person is not neurotically hyperactive and wired up, he is probably introverted, lifeless, bored and depressed. Nevertheless, he can still explode.

This analysis of our unconscious behaviour might seem unnecessary but actually it is of vital importance because it enables us to understand why the prospect of letting go can seem so frightening – to fully express ourselves we have to lose control. The important point to bear in mind is that we can keep things safe by applying our intelligence and sensitivity in choosing when to do that. We can only allow ourselves to let go if we trust the people around us, and more importantly, if we trust ourselves. That is the way it has to be. Understanding how this game works, in effect, puts us in control of when we can safely let go of control, if you see what I mean.

This confuses many people, so let's try to be absolutely clear. When I say we lose control what I mean is we let go of our veneer, our persona, the polite behaviour we adopt because we want approval, our defence mechanisms, our resistance, and let our *real* inner person shine forth without impediment. To put it simply, *we take control of our real lives when we allow our false selves to lose control of us.* That is the essence of it.

Being the Impeccable Warriors that we have chosen to become, we only do that in a safe place and at an appropriate time. A person who expresses his or her anger in an appropriate way and in a suitable environment, does not feel like a volcano waiting to erupt. He treats others with respect and finds a balance within himself that makes him a joy to be around. In every situation, awareness is always the key. Without awareness none of this is possible. That's why I continually reiterate, it is very important to do everything you can at every opportunity to build your awareness.

Falling is love is losing control. It is an entirely irrational act in which you allow your heart to express itself without hindrance from defence mechanisms. If you want to enjoy loving relationships your fear has to be set aside.

Opening up. Losing control. These words can strike fear in to the very cores of our beings. Because as babies and children we were innocent and in control neither of our lives nor our emotions, we were wide open to anything and everything. Powerful feelings bombarded us that were beyond our comprehension for we had never experienced anything like them before. We were overwhelmed, sometimes hurt and sometimes frightened. Most of us in our tender years responded by at least partially closing down to survive these painful feelings.

We learned to control our emotions, to get a grip and shoulder our onerous responsibilities, or we felt hysterical, panic-stricken or neurotic in some other way in our efforts to defend ourselves from the fear we experienced. That is how a person's false persona starts to develop. It starts as a protective shell. As adults we can get over this early conditioning. Try it and see for yourself. Notice when you are being controlling and decide to give it a rest. Once you get used to the idea of letting go you will discover that relinquishing control of your persona and letting yourself be real is relaxing, liberating, enlivening and exciting, and your creativity will flow unimpeded.

Obviously if it feels unsafe or inappropriate to let go in a given situation, don't. Never forget that your primary responsibility to yourself is always to safeguard your wellbeing and treat yourself with respect. Always find a safe, supportive environment when you want to let go. Ideally, our homes should represent such havens, but this is not always so. However, there are ways and places and we'll discuss a few in the next chapter.

Finally, cutting off, avoiding and denying puts the lid on all creative possibilities and robs us of the opportunity of realising our full human potential. If we want to be fully participating members of the human race, we must find the courage to seek deeply within to get in touch with the essence in each of us, and be guided by it.

In the next chapter I'll shed more light on this by telling you just a little of my own struggle with these problems, and how I learned to recover and deal with them with the assistance of some powerful tools, techniques and processes, some amazing teachers and, to put it bluntly, sheer tenacity.

Summary

- Our only viable option is to accept all of our emotions exactly as they are
- It's when feelings go unacknowledged and unexpressed that they cause inappropriate actions, which get us into trouble
- We need awareness to make sure we notice how we feel, and learn appropriate ways to let our emotions have their voice

- If you don't express how you feel on a regular basis you're a volcano waiting to erupt, or you may become depressed
- If you have been self-judgemental, be kind to yourself and accept what you've done. If you don't like what you did, notice it and consciously decide not to do it again
- If you want to relate to real people on a heart to heart level, they will want the real deal from you, not just a cardboard cut-out. This is why it's important to go deeply into your emotional side
- Stop judging your emotions and accept that humans are multi-dimensional and multi-faceted beings with depth, breadth, range and scope
- Expressing your anger in a safe way is equivalent to opening the valve of your metaphorical pressure cooker. You eliminate the possibility of an explosion and allow your anger to pass
- If you penetrate the layers of your emotional being, you will realise that there is something else underneath your anger. That something is fear, and beneath your fear you will find pain
- It's not your conscious, rational mind, but the unconscious fear of being hurt or wounded that's driving your behaviour when you behave defensively
- To withdraw when your partner comes closer, when what you really want is more intimacy, is the height of self-sabotage
- The Impeccable Warrior trusts his instincts and goes with them. He also knows that whatever the outcome he will be alright, because he is his own person
- Shrinking back will never do. Christopher Howard suggests we *'step up and play all out'*
- If you notice your unconscious behaviour patterns are sabotaging your best efforts, you will want to change them, and to do that you must first become conscious of them
- When you develop witnessing skills, you will have the awareness to be able to see the bigger picture – which is that you are not in danger of getting hurt *unless* you react defensively
- If you are sincere and believe in yourself, you will have no problem admitting when you are in the wrong

- Emotions are pure energy and they cannot be destroyed. They have to be expressed. If you are not willing to express them, they will express themselves sooner or later by any means they can
- When your feelings are repressed, it's a recipe for illness and sadness. The emotional energy that strives for release cannot get out and more energy is used keeping it in, so not much is left for creativity or joy
- When you allow your emotions to be expressed, the pent-up energy is released and you open like a channel so your energy flows harmlessly through you
- We can take control of our real lives when we allow our false selves to lose control of us, but we only do that in a safe place and at an appropriate time
- People who express their anger in an appropriate way and in a suitable environment treat themselves and others with respect, and find balance
- In every situation, awareness is always the key
- Your false persona starts to develop in childhood as a protective shell
- Once you get used to the idea of letting go you will discover that relinquishing control and letting yourself be real is relaxing, liberating, enlivening and exciting, and your creativity will flow unimpeded
- If it feels unsafe or inappropriate to let go in a given situation, don't. Always trust your instincts
- Cutting off, avoiding and denying puts the lid on all creative possibilities and robs us of the opportunity of realising our full human potential
- If we want to be fully participating members of the human race, we must find the courage to seek deeply within to get in touch with the essence in each of us, and be guided by it

13

Three Great Processes for Exploring and Expressing Your Emotional Side

The ripples of awakening, wholeness, caring and consciously responding to the needs of life will start from within our own hearts and move from there out into life

Brandon Bays

At last, as promised, this chapter and the next one describe three amazing and very different approaches to resolving unexpressed emotions. You can choose whichever one you feel drawn to and there is absolutely no reason why you shouldn't do all three. They are all very powerful. The first is a weekend seminar, the second takes an hour, the third is a two and half hour process. All represent excellent value for money and are available in many parts of the world. Of course there are many other methods or approaches, but I mention these because I have extensively road tested them myself, so I know just how powerful and effective they are if you jump in wholeheartedly.

So without further ado, here's the first one:

The Journey

I consider it my personal good fortune that there is a woman living on this planet called Brandon Bays. She's a very smartly attired short lady with fiercely piercing aquamarine eyes, long blond hair and a row of perfect pearly white teeth – just the kind of immaculate presentation you'd expect from a Californian. I interpret her appearance not so much as a persona trying to impress but as a mark of respect and high standards, for herself and for her audience, and it implies that what she will deliver will also be excellent – which it undoubtedly is.

I mention this because I have met many people, particularly English people, who are put off by the American, particularly the Californian, style of presentation, which can seem very full-on, in your face and perhaps even over the top. If that's how you feel about it, *get over it.* Don't shoot the messenger. This applies to any kind of personal development presentation, programme or seminar. It doesn't matter what you feel about the presenter or the presentation, don't miss getting the message, teaching or experience that's on offer, or you will be short changing yourself. *Getting the teaching, message or experience is all that matters.* You need it very much to support you on your journey of self-discovery.

The most important thing about Brandon Bays is that she's all heart and no bullshit. The second most important thing is that she has created *The Journey Intensive,* a weekend seminar in which you get to address all your issues on a deep level and clear them out. You can now participate in this workshop in many parts of the world.

Before you consider attending one of these weekends, it might be a good idea to read the book *The Journey* by Brandon Bays. Even if you decide this work is not for you it's a fascinating read and there's lots you can learn from it that will further your life journey.

The weekend is intensive and the size of the group quite large, but there are plenty of assistants who circulate during the exercises to provide individual support as necessary. However, if you prefer, you can book a private session to work one-to-one, as there are now some 1300 qualified Journeywork practitioners dotted around the globe. All the details you might need are on the website www.thejourney.com

The result is a very liberating and empowering release to put it mildly, and very cleansing. If you feel you and/or your life are all in a mess and you need healing, it's well worth checking this out. If it works for you like it worked for me, it will stand you in very good stead to restart your life and build it anew, exactly the way you want. You will acquire many tools and techniques during the weekend seminar, but perhaps the best thing I got from doing the seminar was letting go of my anxiety and experiencing instead a strange but welcome peacefulness stealing over me.

Before we go any further let's talk about money for a moment. To put it bluntly, I'm not writing this book to sell other people's books and seminars. My aim is to help my readers and provide them with the most effective, cost-efficient and powerful tools currently available, and this is one of them.

At the time of writing, the cost of the weekend workshop in London was in the region of £300. Some people consider this to be excessive but I look at it this way – if I can solve some of my major issues that have held me up or ruined my life for years simply by stumping up around £300 and then following a procedure that someone else has worked out for me, it's actually worth any amount of money. *This is because of what it will empower me to do and who it will empower me to be.* I get the benefit of a wise and experienced person's wisdom, I don't have to reinvent the wheel and I save a lot of time – perhaps years. It's a bargain. I don't underestimate the value of money and I know many of us find it hard to come by, but that's my view and I stand by it. If you have to sacrifice something else, so be it.

Don't ever let money be an excuse for stopping you reaching your goals. It is probably worth briefly repeating the lesson we mentioned in Chapter 4 from Robert Kiyosaki, author of the book *Rich Dad, Poor Dad,* who said, 'Instead of saying I can't afford it, ask yourself, *how* can I afford it'. As we noted in the earlier chapter, this opens up you creative thinking process and ideas will come as to how you can raise the money. The same technique can be applied to any goal that comes from your heart.

Allow me to quote a few phrases from *The Journey Intensive* website so you can begin to get a feel for whether this process might appeal to you:

> *'No matter what your issue is, no matter how deep, no matter how much you have struggled with it, the possibility exists for* YOU *to become absolutely free, whole and healed, ready to soar in true joy and freedom.'*
>
> *'[The Journey Intensive is] a simple, yet powerful step-by-step means to tap into your body's infinite wisdom and elicit its unlimited healing power to get to the root cause of any long-standing difficulty, fear, or block. In The Journey processes you are guided to uncover specific cell memories, resolve them completely and clear them out.'*
>
> *'At The Journey Intensive you will receive multiple Journey processes and also learn how to facilitate others so that you can share your experience with your family and friends. You'll leave the weekend with a set of practical, repeatable skills that you can continue using daily for creating true joy, happiness and freedom in all areas of your life.'*

As I write, at least ten years have elapsed since I participated in *The Journey Intensive,* and I still remember vividly the feeling of freedom and empowerment that filled me by the finish of the weekend. Since then I have been able to build on that experience through doing further Journey work and many other techniques.

In the last decade or more Brandon Bays has taken her work to many parts of the globe that urgently need healing, such as South Africa, where she discovered a raging thirst in people who wanted to live more consciously and get over their painful heritage and enmities. Many people at this time seem to be very open to the awakening she offers, not just middle-class white Westerners.

It seems important that I reiterate at this point that we must all take personal responsibility for our lives and everything in them, so please don't take my word for anything, always check it out for yourself. In this case its easy because Brandon's organisation now offers free introductory talks in various locations throughout the countries where Journey events are held, and once again, do refer to the website.

Osho Dynamic Meditation

If you thought meditation was sitting in silence all po-faced, think again.

Osho was an enlightened Indian master, or *guru,* who had an ashram for many years in Poona, and later in Oregon USA. Among his other many accomplishments, Osho developed some 108 methods of meditation, the vast majority of which are active. Many thousands of people have practised them over the thirty or forty years since he introduced them. Of those 108, *Osho Dynamic Meditation* is one of the most powerful.

From a Life Coaching or personal development point of view, *Osho Dynamic Meditation* is an excellent anger management tool. It is perhaps the best I've come across, because when you do this process you don't manage your anger in the sense of getting it under control and metaphorically stuffing it into a box where you can cope with it. Instead you express it along with your rage, sadness, joy, pain, fear and anything else that needs to be given a voice, at full volume, to music, and you get it out of your system in a safe and supportive environment.

Not only does the cathartic part of the procedure cleanse your heart and psyche, it also renders you fully alert, buzzing with aliveness and ready for the witnessing part that comes in the second half. According to Osho, when the first part is accomplished, the true meditation, the true silence, can begin. It's because of its incredible efficacy in helping you to clear out anger and other 'negative' emotions, *Dynamic,* as it is known, finds a place in this volume. The coaching journey, as I see it, is not just about achieving your goals, but also about empowering you to develop into a happy, whole, balanced and conscious human being – getting a life, as it were. Giving your emotional side full expression is a vital part of that process.

Before describing a little of how *Dynamic* works I should point out that there are many websites to visit for further details, and on some you will find a link to a video on YouTube where you can watch someone demonstrating the procedure. The official website is www.osho.com

Apart from the benefits I have already mentioned there are three great advantages with *Dynamic.* One is that you will find someone in virtually any part of the world who facilitates this meditation and can teach and support you as you get started. The second is that you can buy the CD of the music and do *Dynamic* at home noisily or silently, depending on your domestic circumstances, alone or with friends. That means, apart from an initial outlay for a CD, it can cost you nothing to do this, so money certainly can't be an excuse this time. Thirdly, the process takes only one hour, so lack of time can't be an excuse either.

Dynamic is a cathartic meditation, meaning that during the first three stages what you are doing is expressing all your pent up emotional energy as fully as possible. When you read the description that follows you may well think it sounds crazy, but I assure you, crazy is exactly what it isn't. I have used this method hundreds of times and I firmly believe it's one of the most wonderful discoveries I made that saved my sanity during the early 1980's – no exaggeration! For me it was essential.

Because of the importance of the cathartic aspect it's worth first reading a little of what Osho explains in his *Orange Book* about his concept before we get to the method. He said, *'Cathartic methods are modern inventions … In Buddha's time they were not needed because people were not so repressed. People were natural, people lived primitive lives – uncivilised, spontaneous lives … I am introducing cathartic methods, so that first what civilisation has done to you can be undone, so that you become primitive again. From that primitiveness, from primal innocence, insight becomes easily available.'*

The meditation is done with eyes closed, or even better, wearing a blindfold, and standing up.

Stage One is ten minutes long and is called *'chaotic breathing.'* The music begins with fast drumming and the idea is to breathe chaotically and fast through your nose, concentrating always on the exhalation.

The in-breath takes care of itself. You are instructed to use your whole body to push the air out, as if you were a bellows. *Don't forget to be a witness, even during the chaotic breathing.* Witnessing is an essential feature of all the meditations I mention in this book.

The music changes to herald **Stage Two**, also ten minutes long, which is known affectionately as the *'freak out'* or *'catharsis'* stage. Here you are invited to *'explode! Express everything that needs to be thrown out. Go totally mad. Scream, shout, cry, jump, shake, dance, sing, laugh, throw yourself around'* (but be careful not to hurt yourself or others if you are in a group). Three very important tips – hold nothing back, don't allow your mind to interfere, and stay alert – keep witnessing.

Stage Three also goes on for ten minutes and is the *'hoo'* stage. Again the music changes and you start to jump up and down with your arms raised yelling the mantra *'Hoo! Hoo! Hoo!'* as deeply as possible, *'allowing the sound to come from the bottom of your belly.'* Land flat on your feet and *'let the sound hammer deeply into your sex centre.'*

If you are still with me, give yourself a hearty pat on the back, for many a lesser mortal would have given up and thrown this book away by now! Doing *Dynamic* in a total way seems really difficult at first – shouting, screaming, yelling *'Hoo!'* and being a witness all at the same time, and probably your muscles will be screaming by now. But press on, for now we're getting to the good bit.

Stage Four, which takes fifteen minutes, is called *'stop!'* At the end of Stage Three a voice on the soundtrack yells *'STOP,'* at which point you freeze all movement no matter what position you find yourself in. Finally silence reigns and you are advised to *'stay completely still and silent, and be a witness to everything that is happening to you.'*

After what seems like an eternity the gentle start of the music heralding **Stage Five,** the last fifteen minute stage called *'celebration,'* pipes it's way into your consciousness and you know its plain sailing from now on. To me it always feels like an awakening. What sounds like a soulful, lonely flute summons the sunrise and is soon joined by a sitar in a soulful, sensitive call, reminiscent of the early morning call to prayer of the *Muezzin,* and then tabla and guitar join in. This is your invitation to *'celebrate through dance, to express your gratitude towards existence.'*

Fifteen minutes later, you're finished.

Wow! That's it! What more can I say. I'm not even going to attempt to describe the effect of this amazing one hour journey into your very centre. If you feel you can trust yourself enough to let go into it, give it a try and find out for yourself what happens. Like everything else in life, it's an experiment.

By the way, if you're not used to this sort of thing and you think it sounds completely mad, you ain't seen nothin' yet! Wait till you get to the next chapter. I promised you powerful tools and I try never to renege on a promise. This stuff really works.

Summary

- It's worth checking out *The Journey* because if it works for you like it worked for me, it will stand you in good stead to restart your life and build it anew
- The result by the end of the weekend seminar was, for me, a very liberating, empowering and cleansing release
- If you don't like working in a large group, you can book a private, one-to-one session with one of the 1300 qualified Journeywork practitioners dotted around the globe
- A seminar as powerful as *The Journey* is worth every penny because of what it will empower you to do and who it will empower you to be
- Don't ever let money be an excuse for stopping you reaching your goals. Remember the words of Robert Kiyosaki, author of *Rich Dad, Poor Dad,* who said, *'Instead of saying I can't afford it, ask yourself, how can I afford it.'* This opens up your creative thinking process
- *'[The Journey Intensive is] a simple, yet powerful step-by-step means to tap into your body's infinite wisdom and elicit its unlimited healing power to get to the root cause of any long-standing difficulty, fear, or block'*
- *'You will learn how to facilitate others so that you can share your experience with your family and friends. You'll leave the weekend with a set of practical, repeatable skills'*
- *Osho Dynamic Meditation* is an excellent anger management tool, perhaps the best I've come across, because you express your anger, rage, joy, sorrow and sadness at full volume to music, and get it out of your system
- *Dynamic* is a cathartic meditation, meaning that during the first three stages what you are expressing your pent-up emotional energy as fully as possible

- Witnessing is an essential feature of all the meditations I mention in this book
- Three very important tips when doing *Dynamic* – hold nothing back, don't allow your mind to interfere, and stay alert – keep witnessing

14

Aum Sweet Aum

Love and compassion are necessities, not luxuries. Without them humanity cannot survive

Dalai Lama

If you have read this far you will have noticed by now my distaste for compromise, especially with regard to matters of personal development and awareness. Half measures are of no interest because my time is too precious to waste, and so is yours. I am not impressed by extravagant claims or boasts, I am interested only in what works.

Why am I telling you this? Because when I first heard about the *Aum Meditation* (www.aumeditation.icom43.net/) some fifteen years ago it sounded crazy, totally insane and scary as hell, and absolutely, definitely, certainly, emphatically I was sure it was not for me. My resistance was massive.

The inevitable happened, of course, and I soon found myself doing it and, after getting over my initial shock, I actually began to enjoy it. It certainly didn't take long for me to see the incredible value of this process. It's especially valuable for those who find it hard to access or express their emotional side, and that was me. But not any more, thanks to this process. It also presents many physical challenges.

To quote briefly from the website: *'The Aum is a two and a half hour, twelve stage meditation and therapeutic process … unlike conventional therapy, the Aum is interpersonal, it can be deeply effective, experiential, and provide lasting results … the Aum team provides a safe and supportive space for you to explore these structures; you are encouraged – but never forced – to go beyond your limits.'*

In short, the *Aum Meditation* is a valuable and immensely powerful tool for reconnecting with your feelings. A safe and supportive environment is crucial if you are seriously preparing to come out of your comfort zone, which is, of course, the whole point of undergoing this journey.

My first experience with the *Aum Meditation* was in the mid 1990s at which time I was seeing a psychotherapist regularly for one-to-one sessions. I remember it vividly. Let me tell you how it happened. It's an amusing story, and terrifying at the same time!

Fast rewind to 1994, my psychotherapist's office ...

My jaw dropped open in horror as she intoned the words: 'I think you should do the Aum Mediation.' She sat back in her counselling room chair, self-consciously arranging, rearranging and rearranging again the pleats of her skirt. She knew she was suggesting something that would make me swallow hard. I did not know what the *Aum Meditation* was, but I could tell by the tone of her voice that I was not going to like it.

'What's the Aum Meditation?' I enquired meekly.

'It's a meditation technique devised by Veeresh,' she replied. The mere mention of that name was enough to send me into a cold sweat. I knew of Veeresh by his reputation, which precedes him by a very long way. Even if only one-tenth of the things I had heard about the man over the years were true, I knew I was in for a pretty scary baptism of fire. My resistance was palpable. Although, as I said, I was not even sure what the *Aum Meditation* was, this was soon to change, for after doing it several times in London I became very familiar with it and the wonderful healing, liberating and empowering effect it had on me. In truth, I was hooked after the first twenty minutes.

Swami Anand Veeresh originally came from the Philippines but grew up on the streets of New York. Originally named Denny Yuson, for fourteen long years he was a heroin addict until he ended up at Phoenix House, a drug rehabilitation centre in New York, where he was introduced to humanistic psychotherapy. After becoming deeply involved and inventing many powerful psychotherapeutic techniques of his own, Veeresh, who is now a long-standing disciple of Osho, set up a branch of Phoenix House in London.

In 1978 he founded the Rajneesh Humaniversity in Holland with Ma Samadhi-Mariet Wijnen, herself a veteran Osho disciple and therapist of some repute. Now renamed Osho Humaniversity, the establishment in Holland exists as a community in which all kinds of people in need of healing and nurture, and seeking increased awareness, arrive from the four corners of the Earth. They take part in groups, meditations, trainings and other programmes designed to help heal the damaged psyche and the wounded heart. The techniques used are intense and powerful and certainly not for the faint of heart. They focus mainly on human contact, emotional release, sexuality and meditation.

Although the Humaniversity and its work have their challenging aspects, there is no doubt in my mind that the place offers a very loving and supportive environment. It provides an ideal opportunity, if you are brave enough, to really look closely at what is going on inside yourself, with the benefit of expert guidance.

Veeresh operates according to the concept, 'love is always the answer.' This, I have discovered many times over, is the fundamental truth that lies beneath all worthwhile therapy and Life Coaching too, for only love can heal – nothing else can. It becomes even more potent when meditation is added.

Veeresh developed some meditation techniques of his own, which were endorsed by Osho before he died, and the *Aum* is one of them. Having benefited enormously from many of the meditations that Osho had created (for example, *Dynamic,* as described in the previous chapter), I saw every reason to trust Osho's recommendation. To quote from the Humaniversity literature, *'Veeresh is willing to explore anything and everything to get you to understand that life is beautiful and love is what we are here for. The time to go beyond your limits is now.'* I could not agree more. When I heard about all this, Veeresh seemed like a man after my own heart.

The suggestion by my therapist, herself a very powerful and effective practitioner, that I should do the *Aum Meditation* could not have come at a better time for me even though I was fearful, for I was feeling stuck and bored with what I interpreted as living too complacently within my limits. Once I agreed to myself to do the *Aum,* I became receptive to giving it a try.

It is clear to me, with the benefit of hindsight, that the *Aum Meditation* is in no way the cranky invention of a power crazy charlatan therapist, though many of Veeresh's critics would have you believe otherwise. The *Aum* is specifically designed to help you grow, heal and awaken, and it does exactly what it says on the tin if you participate wholeheartedly.

My belief in Veeresh's integrity unfortunately did little to mitigate my fear when I turned up for the first time at the appointed venue in London's King's Cross one Sunday morning, some two weeks after the aforementioned therapy session, for my initiation in the *Aum*

Meditation. I did not know then what to expect or what the effects might be. 'Now it is possible,' my therapist had informed me with a mischievous grin on her face, 'to do some of Veeresh's work here in London.' As I pushed open the door to the meditation space, I imagined my therapist rubbing her hands with glee. She had persuaded me. 'You'll love it' she had assured me. I had grunted sceptically. 'You mean I'll hate it, but it will do me good,' I replied ruefully.

I took off my shoes and walked into the room, warmly greeting one or two familiar faces and staring blankly at a host of unfamiliar ones. What would these people be like once we got underway? Perhaps if I put my glasses on I might recognise one or two more, I hoped in vain. Would these strangers give me a hard time? 'Why be so negative,' I asked myself? 'Because I'm scared witless, of course,' came the instantaneous answer from within. I changed slowly into my jogging pants.

The facilitator of this two and a half hour event was a tall, handsome, vigorous, charismatic man named Dhyano. He had recently qualified as a Humaniversity therapist – and that's no picnic either. He welcomed everybody and introduced the *Aum Meditation* as a happening in twelve stages, each accompanied by different music, some stages lasting for fifteen minutes and some only for ten. As he ran through the procedures for each stage, which were demonstrated by two willing volunteers who knew the ropes, he exhorted us to be 'as total as possible' to achieve the best results. Half-heartedness simply would not do. Then we began a warm-up, which consisted of dancing 'as totally as possible' to three or four funky disco numbers, which emanated from a small portable stereo. Finally, panting and sweating in the stuffy little hall, we were adjudged ready to begin.

Stage One: I hate you

We were herded unceremoniously into a small ring in the middle of the room, edged by foam mattresses to demarcate the boundary of the circle outside which we were not supposed to step. We were preparing for the first stage, known as *I hate you.*

We were instructed to each face a partner in the circle and make eye contact. When the music started, each had to yell at the top of his or her voice, 'I HATE YOU,' at their partner, that is, both partners were to shout at the same time. We were told it was very important *not* to take personally what was being yelled at us, indeed not even to listen to it, but to concentrate on our own shouting. 'Putting it out – that's what it's all about,' someone said.

After a minute or two, when we felt ready to do so, we moved on to another partner and did the same again. Then we moved to another partner, and another, while carrying on with the shouting non-stop. This continued for fifteen minutes, by the end of which time each person had connected with every other participant one at a time.

Meanwhile Dhyano and his three helpers would walk around the outside of the circle checking that the rules were being observed, encouraging those who were flagging and helping people who were getting stuck or seemed in danger of freaking out. Physical contact is prohibited in this first stage.

The instant the music began, the room exploded into bedlam. Suddenly some twenty people were all screaming 'I hate you' in each other's faces all at the same time, while Dhyano and his helpers moved around the perimeter of the circle urging us on. 'Keep going! Keep going! Don't stop!' he yelled in my ear as he saw me tiring after only the first two minutes. This was a very far cry from my upbringing, in which I was encouraged to be nice and polite to people.

I thought I surely had arrived at the very gates of hell, and probably Dhyano was Beelzebub incarnate. Next perhaps I would be roasted on a spit? Well, probably that would be less stressful. All I could feel was my enormous resistance and a strong urge to run away and hide.

'What the hell have I got myself into this time,' I wondered? 'Why am I here? What is the point of this? Yelling 'I hate you' at perfect strangers, and being yelled at in return. Not really my idea of fun.'

The point is, of course, that you are given the opportunity of really expressing all the anger, rage and pain you feel, unhindered by self-judgement and repression, or the judgement of others. The person you shout at acts as a mirror. In your mind's eye, they might represent your mother, father, lover, best friends, worst enemy, your boss, someone you encountered on the tube, someone who tried to rob you, or even your therapist or Life Coach – whoever you want to rail against. As the other person is shouting at you while you shout at them, you provide this service for each other. You have permission to be completely off the wall, outrageous and out of order, as long as you do not get physically violent or intimidate anyone. We had been warned repeatedly not to take any of this personally, easier said than done when you are not used to this kind of behaviour!

The first few times I did the *Aum,* I found *I hate you* very hard to do. It went right against the grain of everything I had ever been taught and it made my throat sore and my voice hoarse within minutes. It was a tremendous effort and keeping going felt like torture. Eventually, after four or five times of doing the *Aum*, I began to have a sort of break-through with *I hate you.* I began to look forward to it for I found that connecting with, and expressing, my anger in this way did have a curiously liberating, empowering and energising effect. Anger held inside not only masks our pain and probably other feelings too, it also poisons our inner being and dictates our unconscious behaviour in negative ways. Because of that, choices that should be ours are not at our disposal. Cathartic release, like I describe, can have an immensely cleansing effect.

Meanwhile, back to my initiation at the *Aum* .... By the time the first three minutes of that first stage was up my throat was on fire and I could hardly squeak, let alone shout. How did people manage to keep on shouting? Those who shouted loudest seemed to be coming from deep down in the gut. Try as I might, I could not seem to get the sound to come from my belly for there always seemed to be a constriction in my throat, not until months of perseverance had gone by. Then, one day it happened and, boy, did it feel good! What a tremendous release.

I was not even aware of feeling angry before entering into cathartic therapy techniques. Around this time I was becoming more and more aware, after many painful years of seeking to understand my inner workings, of my habit of cutting off from my emotions and turning the anger inwards in a kind of depression. Now at last during this first stage of the *Aum* I was delighted to notice that when I eventually started really getting into it, a feeling of aliveness I had not known since childhood was beginning to very gradually dissolve my depression. I understood after a while why Dhyano had insisted we keep going, and why, when I said I did not feel angry, I was advised to *act as if* I felt angry. It did not take long before pretending was replaced by genuine anger.

Stage Two: I love you

Stage Two, *I love you,* I found much easier, though paradoxically some people could not handle this at all and immediately burst into tears. I noticed that, with few exceptions, the most energetic *I hate you's* also seemed to be the most disabled *I love you's,* and vice versa.

We remained in the circle, though the boundary mattresses were removed so we were not so tightly packed, while the music changed to a soulful, mournful air. We were each to approach another person, look them in the eye and say 'I love you' to each other, before melting into a heartfelt hug with them. When both partners felt ready, they were to acknowledge each other and move on to new partners.

The contrast from the first stage was staggering and certainly served to heighten the already elevated emotional temperature for everyone. It was heartrending to see some people having difficulty with accepting and giving love and to see how they needed it so urgently. Once again we became mirrors for each other. Although, once again we were not supposed to take our partners statement personally, participants seemed to be crying out for, and lapping up, the emotional nourishment they were able to give each other as they let-go of their defences.

If Stage One was hell and Stage Two was heaven, the third stage, *Second wind,* surely was pure torture.

Stage Three: Second wind

In this stage we were on our own for the first time, though we could look, or make facial expressions, at each other for mutual encouragement. *Second wind,* basically a bio-energetics exercise, is simply running on the spot, picking your knees up as high as possible, while extending you arms straight up above your head, for ten long and excruciating minutes.

While this nightmare progressed, we were allowed, even encouraged, to make noises to express the pain that arrived within the first couple of minutes, and to move around the room, as long as we did not touch anyone else. The idea is to keep going and pass through the pain barrier and, in theory at least, into a whole new field of abundant, limitless energy that allegedly lies beyond.

It was obvious that most of my fellow participants also seemed less than keen on what they were being encouraged to do. Of course one or two athletic souls, seeming to take this in their strides, were all smiles.

In my own way, I must admit, I did experience more energy than before … eventually. However, by then my head was reeling and I was beginning to wonder if this was all some sort of weird hallucination.

During the preparation for the meditation, I had wondered with a kind of trepidation why Dhyano's helpers had placed several buckets and big rolls of tissues on the floor at intervals around the room. During *second wind,* I found out. The exercise was having its desired effect, throwing up because by sheer physical exhaustion (and clearly not an occurrence exclusive to me), helped many of us to let go of our little remaining reserve. Eventually I did find my second wind. So much so that by the time the fourth stage, *kundalini shaking,* began, I felt I was virtually jet-propelled.

Stage Four: Kundalini shaking

We were now required to stand with legs apart and knees slightly bent, letting our bodies begin to shake all over. As your knees are bent and your thigh and other leg muscles are supporting your whole weight, it is not long before you forget about *doing* the shaking and the shaking itself takes over. It is as if the shaking happens by itself. This is based on an ancient Yogic technique which Osho himself plagiarised to good effect in one of his better known meditations called *Osho Kundalini Meditation.*

Osho's comments on the subject of shaking, which I read many months later, are fascinating. He said, 'When I say shake I mean your solidity, your rock-like being should shake to the very foundations so that it becomes liquid, your body will follow …'

'Kundalini is not really meditation. It is just preparation. You are preparing your instrument. When it is ready, then you stand in silence, then meditation starts. Then you are utterly there. You have woken yourself up by jumping, by dancing, by breathing, by shouting – these are all devices to make you a little more alert than you ordinarily are. Once you are alert, then the waiting.'

'Waiting is meditation. Waiting with full awareness. And then it comes, it descends on you, it surrounds you, it plays around you, it dances around you, it cleanses you, it purifies you, it transforms you.'

A beautifully poetic description of *Kundalini Meditation* by the man himself. My only comment: I have done *Kundalini Meditation* many times and it is most enjoyable.

Stage Five: Catharsis

Back to the *Aum*. This, my first experience of Veeresh's inspired invention, already had me breathless and reeling and wondering what on earth was coming next when, lo and behold, the fifth stage began. *Catharsis,* or *'freak-out'* as it is more colloquially known, was something with which I was familiar from *Osho Dynamic Meditation.* I can't honestly say, hand on heart, that I enjoy 'catharting,' but I was at least used to it and I realise there is nothing to fear. It's a powerful process and I must, in the interests of fairness and honesty, acknowledge the immense clearing out and healing potential of a really good freak-out.

In this stage of the *Aum* you do not actually have to make a noise, indeed some people go though it in relative silence or in floods of tears. If you need to get something off your chest, however, *Catharsis* is another opportunity to kick up a row but this time on your own, without a partner. The beauty of the *Aum* was revealing itself to me gradually – for once in your life you are in a situation where no one judges your outrageous behaviour, or tells you to behave 'properly,' and most important, *you are not judging yourself.* In this stage you might want to have a good cry, stamp around, beat up a cushion, whatever comes up spontaneously, though again you must not touch anyone else in the room.

As a child I was brought up to close doors and switch off lights behind me, and to tread lightly when people were asleep. In my house the idea of shouting or getting angry with someone was definitely not on, so making a noise was certainly something I still needed to learn when I reached adult life. Now in this venue in King's Cross this Sunday morning, everything was different. I was in a safe environment where I was invited to do whatever I liked within the structure of the meditation. I could give vent to some of my childhood frustrations if they came up, and my present-day adult ones too. *What a gift a cathartic opportunity is, to be sure.*

By this time I was so blown apart that nearly all my inhibitions had flown out of the window.

Suddenly, I found my voice, what was left of it, and my anger too. Wow, it felt good. The power, the feeling of boundless energy flowing though me as if I were a conduit. I felt as if I was taking off. I took full advantage of the opportunity. At last I was enjoying this hugely.

There were times in my younger days when I was worried that if I let go of my self-control and allowed my behaviour to reflect how I really felt deep down, that I might, for want of a better word, go crazy. I also feared I might become so angry and out of order that I could kill someone, anyone who happened to cross my path at the time, just out of sheer livid, out-of-control anger. Who knows what might come up if we get totally out of control?

It was mainly through letting go, little by little, into exercises of *Catharsis* in situations where a structure was set up for safety and support, for example in organised sessions of *Osho Dynamic Meditation,* that I began to feel it might be OK to trust and let go gradually. It was something that felt impossibly scary at first. The *Aum* and structures like it are designed to allow you to emerge from your hiding place step-by-step to taste the waters of freedom in a supportive environment. I think of it as a way for the traumatised baby to be delivered safely.

As I said in an earlier chapter, now in the light of experience, it seems obvious that it is far more likely that a person, if they really are that wounded and frustrated, will suffer mental imbalance and become, homicidal or suicidal if they *do not* let go and express their anger and aggression in a safe environment. What is more likely, however, is that they will become ill and depressed. *Keeping emotions bottled up is a dangerous practice.*

Letting feelings out can also have its hazards if you are not used to it, which is why I keep stressing the safety and support element. We are dealing with the human psyche and if we try this alone and unsupported, and especially in a public place, we might find ourselves in the unpleasant position, when we start letting go, of not knowing how to look after ourselves when the craziness that most of us possess starts to really come out. We may also dump or inflict damage on some innocent bystander. Don't forget, it behoves us as Impeccable Warriors always to take responsibility for our thoughts, feelings and actions, even when letting go, which is why I stress that *going through Catharsis, at least in the beginning, is something that should only be done in an appropriate situation and in the presence of one or more trained facilitators.*

Osho, referring to the *Catharsis* stage in *Dynamic Meditation,* elaborates, 'someone has said the meditation we are doing here seems to be sheer madness. It is. And it is that way for a purpose. It is madness with a method; it is consciously chosen.'

'Remember, you cannot go mad voluntarily. Madness takes possession of you. Only then can you go mad. If you go mad voluntarily, that's a totally different thing. You are basically in control, and one who can control even his madness will never go mad.'

It sounds like one of those Zen Koans, such as *what is the sound of one hand clapping?* You lose control without losing control and you go mad without going mad! It's very subtle.

What Osho is saying is, if you consciously choose to do this crazy, cathartic meditation, you won't go crazy because the conscious decision to do it puts you in control. On the contrary, you can give voice to your inherent craziness instead of trying to contain it, so you no longer create the unnecessary fear, pain and conflict that can threaten your mental wellbeing.

Let's not get this out of perspective. All we are doing in this process is making a conscious decision to allow our feelings to express themselves. We simply open up, and whatever is inside comes out spontaneously. For once we do not stop it or judge it, or even make it happen. We stand aside, we get out of our own way, we take the brakes off, we allow our inner true selves to be expressed exactly as they are.

That is why a *Catharsis* stage is incorporated into the *Aum Meditation,* a process which is all about expressing every feeling we can possibly experience. This was my first time, but already I was beginning to see what a cleverly worked out, comprehensive, holistic clean-up programme the *Aum Meditation* is, and all distilled down to an intensive two and a half hour procedure.

Stage Six: Dancing

The sixth stage, what a relief, turned out to be *Dancing.* Though by now I was exhausted, I was sure this would be a breeze compared to what had gone before. The instructions were simple enough, simply express whatever comes up in the dance. Celebrate your aliveness, as the saying goes (and believe me, if you have come this far and you are still alive, you have something to celebrate)! 'Let the dancer disappear so only the dance remains,' we were instructed.

I cannot speak for anyone else, but by this time, assuming you have been 'as total as possible,' I would be surprised if you are not absolutely ready to let go, relax and let your dancing possess you. The music is slow, languid, sexy and emotional. For once we are not going at breakneck speed. The sound of heavy breathing and the smell of stale sweat filled the air as some twenty people let their dances possess them.

As in the *Kundalini shaking* and the *Catharsis* stages, each one of us was alone in our *Dancing*. I couldn't help but register that the dance and its aloneness was a perfect metaphor for life itself. There was a tangible air of relief in the room as most of us relaxed into our let-go's, for by now, I suspect, we were considerably happier in the knowledge that the most difficult and challenging stages were behind us, or so we fervently hoped.

But the *Aum* was not finished with us yet. As I was soon to discover, further big time confrontation awaited us.

Stage Seven: Crying

Stage Seven was a tricky one for many of us. We were each told to find a space on our own, sitting or lying on the floor or on a mattress and simply have a good *cry* for ten minutes.

There are a lot of people, not only men, who find it very difficult to cry. Typical conditioning for a most people, deeply ingrained during childhood, runs something like, 'big boys don't cry,' or 'hush now, there's a good girl.' The subliminal message being conveyed unconsciously is that crying is not good. Very young children often perceive the meaning in this message, also unconsciously of course, as a risk that parental love may be withdrawn if they continue to cry. This possibility is unconsciously interpreted by most babies as potentially life threatening and to be avoided at all costs. It's the existential fear that psychotherapists refer to, meaning you fear unconsciously that your very existence is under threat.

Parents please take note: I know as a parent myself who has made every mistake in the book, that you have the very best of intentions and you believe you soothe your babies by hushing them. But this is not always so, for many babies and children who are thus soothed unconsciously feel they have to repress their feelings and, as a result, they grow up in the habit of not expressing, and therefore not properly experiencing, their emotions. Unless physically in pain or discomfort or hungry, babies almost always stop crying when they receive what they want or need, even if it is only attention that is required. They don't need to be hushed up, they require their needs to be met.

Having said that, it is not humanly possible for a parent to 'do everything right,' so please don't beat yourself up if you are a parent who has made mistakes. We all make mistakes and we do the best we can with what we know and understand, and the state we are in, at any given time, so please give yourself credit for that.

There is a multitude of reasons why so many of us find it hard to cry, especially in public. Being sufficiently vulnerable is something most of us choose to avoid. Whatever the reason for the difficulty, here in the *Aum Meditation* is an opportunity to rectify the situation. If you cannot cry, I was advised, act or pretend and think of something sad. It really is surprising, if you persevere, how quickly real tears start to flow.

It is important, no matter what your age, that you are able to express *the entire range of your emotions* because unless you do, you cannot feel fully alive. Instead, you suffer from low self-esteem and feel disempowered, frustrated, angry or depressed and cannot relate to others successfully. It took me a long time to understand that feeling alive entails not only feeling joy and bliss, but everything else too, like anger, pain, grief and sadness.

As I explained in Chapter 12, what we strangely term the *'negative emotions'* are not in the least negative. They are necessary for feeling alive and they should be welcomed, for they have to be fully experienced. Imagine an internal combustion engine, like a typical small car engine, with four cylinders. It is possible for the car to move when the engine fires only on two or three of its cylinders, but to function optimally it needs to be carefully tuned so it fires consistently on all four cylinders. The tuning also needs readjusting at regular intervals so maximum performance is maintained.

When you have spent much of your life cut off from your emotional side and feeling like a zombie, or only half a person, as is often the case with someone who is depressed, as you begin to build your awareness just about any emotion is welcome because of the feeling of aliveness it brings with it. Some feelings, like jealousy or anger, are uncomfortable and hard to accept. However, when you find it difficult even to cry or shout, feeling anything is a major breakthrough. That's why I recommend the *Aum* to anyone who wants to reawaken their aliveness.

The purpose of encouraging grown adults to cry within a group, or even in individual therapeutic situations, is to enable those people to experience or re-experience the feelings of sadness, pain, grief, sorrow, mourning and anguish that so many try to cut off from, maybe for years. It is important to express them. There are no short cuts if you want to heal your emotional wounds and reach emotional maturity, we have to establish a new habit of allowing our emotions rather than denying them.

The idea of incorporating crying into a group meditation is nothing short of brilliant. The participant experiences the associated emotions in a spiritual context and with the full support and guidance of the group leader and assistants, as well as with the encouragement of the group. Thus it cannot fail to deeply touch that person's heart, for the structure of the meditation is designed to help facilitate access to such deeply buried feelings. There is no doubt those feelings are in there somewhere, for our memories never forget anything. No matter how deeply buried and difficult to access our memories are, the hard disk of the human biocomputer can never be erased.

Stage Eight: Laughing

Eventually it was time for the eighth stage, *Laughing*.

At this point I began to wonder if Veeresh was taking the mickey. After a great deal of effort I was just beginning to experience overwhelming sadness and now I was expected to laugh. Once again my resistance was almost tangible. I certainly did not feel like laughing. All I could think of was my anger towards Veeresh for playing with my emotions, as it seemed.

During the *Laughing* stage we were allowed to remain alone or to interact with others. We were encouraged to help each other laugh by tickling each other, pulling faces, making silly animal noises and so forth. At first attempting to laugh felt hollow and somehow I could not allow it to flow spontaneously. There was nothing to laugh about, or so it seemed. The very idea of laughing to order seemed preposterous.

Then I began to wonder, how had I become so serious, and why? I never used to be like this. After all, this whole situation was only a game. Life is only a game. For a while I became obsessed with the idea that seriousness had crept up on me surreptitiously over the years while I had not been looking. 'What is fun'? I asked myself.

There is nothing that works so well as a meditation for letting a person see themselves objectively. One of the things I saw so clearly during that *Laughing* stage was how even a mild depression, like mine was, can keep a person absolutely stuck. Without going into too much detail, I did have some illuminating revelations during this stage, for at last I was beginning to understand behaviour patterns that had been dogging me all my life and denying me my birthright, *my aliveness!* In this moment of awkwardness and embarrassment as I tried in vain to come up with a sincere laugh, I was given some strong clues about what to do to come alive and get healed.

Through meditation, time and again, I have been given glimpses into the workings of my unconscious mind which have invariably proven immensely valuable. I have also been allowed a clear hearing of my inner voice on many occasions, which always knows what to do and just needs me to pay attention.

A window into the unconscious is like a rugby player unexpectedly receiving the ball. In rugby, if the ball is passed to you, and it always happens in the twinkling of an eye, you immediately have to run with it. When you run, you have to overcome many obstacles. You might drop it or pass it and later receive it again. If you immediately run with it every time you are given it back, sooner or later you will score a try, or if you quickly pass it on, someone on your team will score.

In this analogy, the opposing team represents our defence mechanisms, our ego, our conditioning. In other words, all those learned behaviour patterns which drive us unconsciously towards self-sabotage and which will fight like crazy to get the ball back. But once the workings of an unconscious behaviour pattern are exposed, even if only for a few seconds, we have a chance to get a handle on it and change the pattern. Choice becomes an option.

Be careful, for it is not at all helpful to regard anything within yourself, even your conditioning or sabotaging behaviour, as 'the enemy' for you don't want to start a war in your mind. Simply noticing and accepting them is a far better strategy. Once you score a few metaphorical goals or tries, you start to take control of the game of life and your saboteurs are relegated to the second division.

And there the analogy ends, for the beauty in the game of conscious awareness is that in meditation, as in consciousness itself, there are no losers.

Stage Nine: Dance of the lovers

The ninth stage of the *Aum* is for many people the most confrontative of all, the *Dance of the lovers,* for here, I was soon to discover, we were to put our feelings about our sexuality under the microscope.

Veeresh contends that most of our problems stem from sexuality issues, so not surprisingly this aspect of human nature comes in for minute examination in his work. Indeed, it is a strong underlying theme in everything the Humaniversity does. I was aware of that before going to the *Aum Meditation* that fateful Sunday morning, and I am sure it was a major contributory factor in my feelings of nervousness as I drove to King's Cross.

The idea in the *Dance of the lovers* is compelling and simple. Sexy dance music begins and we are all free to move around choosing partners to dance with. In the dance we are encouraged, despite any inhibitions we might have, to express all our sexuality, to experiment and explore to find out what really turns us on, though we do, I hasten to add, keep our clothes on.

This Sunday in question the matter was complicated by the fact that there were more men than women, though we were told that we could dance in groups of more than two. The men were also asked to be sensitive to the women, and not to be too pressing in foisting unwanted attention on them, should this arise. It was unsaid, but clearly it would also be alright for people of the same sex to dance together, should this occur.

It may not sound like anything much to make a fuss about, but I do assure you, this was very, very confrontational and powerful stuff.

The music began and immediately the men who had done this before shot across to the more attractive of the women like bees to a honeypot. There was none of the usual English reserve or politeness and I was taken by surprise to see the law of the jungle instantly kick in like. It was immediately obvious this was going to be the survival of the fittest and the selection of the most beautiful. For the preceding few stages of the meditation things had been quite friendly, even civilised, but now it was basically and primally each one for his or her self.

It was amazing to see relatively uninhibited human sexual behaviour in action with the veneer of respectability and political correctness stripped off, and it certainly served to show me how relatively repressed and inhibited I was in my dealings with these matters. Although they did not go as far as performing sexual intercourse, though I am not sure why not, the more energetic of the men were behaving like predators.

The women had only three options, resistance, flight or surrender. They were completely engulfed by the male attention and, as far as I could determine, none made much of an attempt to go to a partner of their choice. That is not to say the women did not select. Interestingly, each woman found a way of giving energy to a man or men whom they genuinely favoured, while withholding it from those they did not. The message was clear, though spoken only in body language. In some cases the unfancied man would give up and join another couple or group, whereas others would hang in there in the forlorn hope of getting some serious attention. In a very subtle way, though the men where more proactive, the women certainly held the balance of power in most cases.

This immediately took me back to those cruel situations in school when I was always the last to be chosen – for the football team, the cricket team, the basketball team, whatever. Only when everyone else had been chosen would one grudging team captain have to choose and put up with me. Here in the *Aum* it was amazing to see, with a clarity that was actually quite alarming, that to press attention on a woman, a man has to be absolutely self-confident, or pretend to be, especially in a competitive situation.

The *Dance of the lovers* hit me squarely in the face because after leaving school I overcame my shyness enough to have many liaisons with women so I had conveniently forgotten those painful feelings from my schooldays when I had been nervous and unsuccessful around the opposite sex. Suffice to say that during the whole agonising ten minutes of this stage of the meditation I went through many mental evolutions, and it certainly heightened my awareness of my many issues on this subject. Veeresh was right, this area is loaded with issues which most of us hardly ever look at in our daily routines.

This is a vital area to explore in depth, we can't ignore it, and almost certainly it will be acutely uncomfortable at times, one way or another. Nevertheless, it's worth it if you want to feel completely comfortable with all aspects of yourself, including your sexuality. The only thing you can usefully do with uncomfortable feelings is to feel them. Then they can pass. As I have said many times, being in denial, pretending you don't have those feelings, is not a viable strategy. If you want to make root and branch changes to how you function, you can, but only when you have heightened your awareness and fully experienced all your feelings.

Here at the *Aum* I found myself wondering if I would be able to make the changes I required. I was a little worried I might falter. At the same time I noticed a little flicker of light and a sense of strength within. After all, I had my two greatest allies at my command, perseverance and dogged determination. Those two qualities, I instinctively knew, would always see me through, as they had done so many times before. To these I could now add laser-like focus and clarity of purpose, as well as a lot more of the necessary emotional experience.

It is worth remembering that the jungle is never far away. Somehow I had forgotten and now the basic *'me Tarzan, you Jane'* approach to sex was being recreated in the meditation room before my very eyes.

The *Dance of the lovers* stage in the *Aum* had been a powerful wake-up call and it gave me much food for thought over the subsequent weeks and months. One question that kept coming up in my mind for weeks afterwards was perhaps the most vital question of all: 'where does love figure in all this, indeed is there room for love in the primeval sexual jungle'? I shall leave you to ponder this and other monumental questions as we move on to Stage Ten, simply called *Om.*

Stage Ten: Om

Here, by the time we had hastily readjusted our attire, the atmosphere was transformed seamlessly as we stood in a circle hand in hand or arm in arm while a lighted candle was placed on the floor in the middle of the circle. Softly and with eyes half closed we began to chant the mantra, *'Om,'* and I began to feel a peaceful serenity drift over me at last.

Much has been written and said about *Om,* probably the best known and most widely used mantra in the Western world. A mantra is a wonderful device to help us keep our minds focused so they do not drift all over the place when we meditate. Also the vibration of the sound of *Om* being made in the body produces a sort of resonance that seems somehow to promote tranquillity, harmony and healing. It feels as if it's emanating from a very deep and profound place inside. You could even say when you intone the mantra *Om,* you are putting the voice of your deepest being out into the world with nothing in the way. *Om* seems to cut right through your conditioning, your issues, your strivings, in other words all the things that make you anxious, so that the real you is expressed unhindered.

Focusing on a sound and a vibration is a lot different from thinking, and can help very much in allowing a feeling of unity and wholeness or connectedness to creep over us. Mind, body, spirit, heart, our fellow humans and creation itself are inseparable, and chanting a simple mantra can help promote a sense of that.

Ever since the dawn of time, humans have craved harmony and found it within themselves and the Universe. The harmony that a chant creates seems to spread through the ether when massed united voices express that chant out loud. Even the most aggressive, dysfunctional contemporary rock music contains harmonies, for without it the music would be bereft of the power to communicate emotions.

Standing in the circle chanting *Om* that morning, having experienced the turmoil of the first nine stages of the *Aum Meditation* without respite, the feeling of harmony that now began to arise in me was most welcome and I was more than ready to receive its healing effects.

The sound of *Om,* gradually rising in volume and growing in intensity from moment to moment, was exciting for it seemed to have the power to uplift the whole group as it filled every tiny nook and cranny of the room. Some twenty-five people, for Dhyano and his assistants joined in at this point, all feeling a resonance within, were united in filling the space with harmonious vibrations. These, I felt, contained the potential to heal the wounds of anyone who had ears to hear.

It was a group expression of pure love, made up of all our individual expressions of pure love. There was a feeling of community and it certainly added up to a lot more than the sum of its parts. Not only the sounds and vibrations, but also the very rhythms of life seemed to be flowing through us. I was thoroughly enjoying this. In fact I was beginning to admit to myself the possibility that maybe, just maybe, the torture and difficulties of the previous stages of the *Aum* had all been worth it just for this experience alone.

For now I felt as if the meditation had been lifted onto a plane of pure spirituality. It had shifted up several gears and what had begun as a physical and emotional exploration had finally moved into the abstract realms of the spirit, yet the structure kept us grounded. The usual anxieties that so often make us restless and keep us apart from our true selves and each other had had a good run for their money. I, at least, was at last prepared to let go just a little into nothingness.

Which was just as well, for suddenly the penultimate stage was upon us, *Silence.*

Stage Eleven: Silence

I need hardly remark that silence is a feature of just about every meditation technique known, so I was no stranger to this. Of course, the obvious difficulty popped up as usual, what to do with the silence.

Following a period of intense, relentless activity, a time of silence coming straight afterwards is often when significant transformations happen for the alert meditator. Many things which up until then had been shrouded in mystery, conflicting emotions, confusion or doubt, gradually or suddenly come clear during or after the meditation. Very often at times like this we spontaneously let go into a moment of true stillness. Complete peace of mind, for me the ultimate goal, prevails as everything falls into balance naturally, even if only for a second or two, but sometimes for longer.

When a moment of absolute stillness occurs it's a transformative experience, for something changes or heals for ever.

As I have already stated, if you want to get to know yourself inside out, if you want true peace, balance and fulfilment, sooner or later you have to be still and silent and listen to your heart. But there's more to it than hearing your inner voice, for because sitting (or standing) in total silence and stillness is a situation in which a true transformation can take place.

But stillness cannot be contrived. The first ten stages of the *Aum,* as with the early stages of *Dynamic Meditation,* are designed to provide the optimum conditions in which stillness can spontaneously arise.

That morning as the spacey, new-age music for the *Silence* stage of the *Aum* softly filled the little hall in King's Cross, I had a practical demonstration of this. I was still feeling wounded from the break-up of a recent love affair. Suddenly it came to me, I understood. The reason why she had rejected me. She told me she had been afraid of losing herself, of having her identity swallowed up as the two of us became one, of losing control and having to let go into the intimacy that was becoming very strong between us. She had invited me to come towards her and I had opened myself to her in spite of fearing the possibility of rejection, and I felt betrayed and abandoned when she chose to push me away instead of facing her fear and coming closer.

Finally I understood the situation from her point of view and her behaviour made sense. That in turn helped me to accept her actions, painful though they were and driven by her own fears. This was a breakthrough for me, for in that moment I also realised that by understanding and accepting, I would soon let go of those painful feelings and move on.

What was particularly astonishing was that in that precise moment of understanding, there in the meditation, the anger towards this woman that had been gnawing at me began to melt, to be replaced with compassion. I was not doing anything about it, that was the curious thing. It was happening by itself like the process of water evaporating in the sun. It just happened by itself. And all this was revealed to me in an instant.

This is typical of the kind of thing that can occur during or after meditation.

I have long since given up trying to control my mind to be still during a silent stage in a meditation. Instead I just let it come up with what it will while I carry on witnessing. In this way, mountains of undesired mental baggage get processed, simply by allowing, watching and listening with no judgements.

Mindsets or erroneous beliefs that continually worry us when we try to work out answers rationally simply dissolve into insignificance and lose their potency when allowed to process themselves through the unconscious in the way I describe.

The mind cannot be quieted, the body cannot be stilled, but they can both be made exhausted and then you have no choice but to let go – this is what every master who ever lived has taught us in one form or another. The story of the Buddha illustrates this beautifully, for it was only after many years of searching in the world at large that he finally sat down and surrendered. In that moment all he had been searching for came to him. It arose from within.

Stage Twelve: Namaste

How would this *Aum Meditation* end, I wondered? I did not have long to wait before finding out because the final stage was about to happen. It was called *Namaste.*

In India, *Namaste* is a traditional greeting which means that the essential being within you greets and acknowledges with deep respect the essential being within the person you are greeting. It is a meeting of earthly mortals on the most heartfelt spiritual plane to honour each other's existence and is signified by a person putting his hands together in front of his face as if in a prayer posture and bowing to the other while giving the verbal greeting, *'Namaste.'*

How fitting that the *Aum* should finish like this. We were to move around the room so we would encounter each person in the group, one at a time, and make pairs, the two people in each pair making the greeting of *Namaste* to each other before moving into a deep, close hug of thanks, and then moving on to someone else to make another pair, and repeating the same procedure until each participant had greeted and hugged every other participant. It felt like wiping the slate clean – after all we had just spent over two hours yelling at each other, loving each other, crying, hugging, laughing, running on the spot, dancing, catharting and jointly and individually experiencing all kinds of emotional and spiritual ups and downs. We had bounced off each other, using each other as mirrors. Everyone had contributed what they could and we had helped each other grow and move towards a healing.

This was a way to acknowledge the respect we felt for each other for having the courage to go through this process, and to affirm that everything that had been done and said was simply to help ourselves, and each other, to grow and heal. The power of a tuned-in group of wholehearted participants is not to be underestimated. Now we were rightfully thanking each other for the support we had received.

This was truly a remarkable bunch of people. Many were disciples of Osho but some were not. Some were undergoing ongoing training in Veeresh's work to become Humaniversity therapists, though others were not. All are welcome.

There were two other first timers who no doubt had been every bit as petrified as I had been at the beginning. To my mind anyone, especially a newcomer to this kind of work, who has the courage and commitment to step into the unknown like this in search of growth and spiritual emergence deserves the utmost respect. I was especially glad to honour these two people with the *Namaste* greeting.

For myself, just the experience of turning up and having a go acted as a great tonic for my self-esteem, and this effect grew with each subsequent visit to the *Aum Meditation.* The legendary Veeresh magic was beginning to work on me – my therapist was right, I was beginning to believe in myself again, just as I am sure I must have done when I was a small child.

When I had originally walked into the room before the meditation began, I had of course made unconscious judgements about everyone else, as we all do – she was drop-dead gorgeous, he was annoying, he was repulsive, she was stupid, and so on. The mind fabricates, categorises, puts down, elevates, believes all kinds of fantasies to be the truth, and creates its own hell out of mere assumptions. Now, during the *Namaste* stage, I was clearly seeing the arrogance of this habit and I was looking at people with fresh eyes, as it were. It was honestly amazing to be able to greet every person present equally, with respect and without judgement, and to be similarly greeted.

Where had all those judgements gone? They seemed to have melted away while we were expressing our pain and joy. 'It was worth it just for those brief moments …' I wrote later in my diary.

What freedom is really about is not so much physical or political liberty, free choice, free speech or democracy, though of course these are essential; it is about a more personal inner liberation from judgements, mindsets, neurotic behaviour, anxiety, conflict, stress and imbalance. After all, once you have reached it, as long as you maintain your awareness this latter kind of liberty can never be taken away whatever happens, neither by military coup, ethnic cleansing, invasion, captivity, domination, suppression, censorship, nor even holocaust.

A few days after doing the *Aum,* whose name I later discovered is an acronym standing for *Awareness, Understanding, Meditation,* I returned for another session with my therapist, the woman who had first suggested I do it.

'When you first recommended I should go, I didn't want to because the idea scared the hell out of me,' I said. 'But I did it and now I want to thank you for suggesting it and pushing me to go. It was quite something.' I have always had a penchant for understatement.

'I know,' she said, smiling softly. 'I've done it myself.'

How can we experience compassion and love for ourselves and others, and how can we feel wholly integrated, if we neglect the parts within us that hurt the most? Only a person with love in their heart would come to such an event as the *Aum*. Without the love quotient the *Aum Meditation* would be too harrowing, and nobody in their right mind would do it.

Love enables us to take the risk, to launch ourselves into the void, to explore deeply into the unknown. Veeresh's therapists and group leaders are very careful to provide an infrastructure of solid support and safety. Dhyano, who was in charge that day, certainly did. The matter in hand is too delicate, too important and too explosive for irresponsible or insensitive handling.

Since doing the *Aum* at least six or eight times during that period of my life I have developed a much deeper understanding of what is going on inside. Best of all, *I discovered personal resources and choices I did not even know I had.*

Now it's time for me to share that empowering discovery, which is why I present to you the *Aum Meditation* as one of the most powerful personal development tools I have ever had the good fortune to encounter. Perhaps you will turbocharge your healing journey by experiencing it too.

Summary

- The *Aum* is particularly valuable for those who find it hard to access or express their emotional side. It's a powerful tool for reconnecting with your feelings
- The facilitators of the *Aum* encourage but never force you to go beyond your limits
- According to Veeresh, 'love is always the answer'. This fundamental truth lies beneath all worthwhile therapy, and Life Coaching too, for only love can heal
- When doing the *Aum,* be 'as total as possible' to achieve the best results
- Whatever happens in the *Aum,* whatever is said or shouted, don't take it personally

- During the first stage of the *Aum, I hate you,* you can express all the anger, rage and pain you feel, unhindered by self-judgement, repression, or the judgement of others. The person you shout at acts as a mirror
- Anger held inside not only masks our pain and other feelings too, it also poisons our inner being and dictates our unconscious behaviour in negative ways. Choices that should be ours are not at our disposal
- *'Waiting is meditation. Waiting with full awareness. And then it comes, it descends on you, it surrounds you, it plays around you, it dances around you, it cleanses you, it purifies you, it transforms you.'* Osho
- The beauty of the *Aum* is that no-one judges your outrageous behaviour or tells you to behave 'properly,' and most important, you are not judging yourself
- What a gift a cathartic opportunity is, to be sure
- Keeping emotions bottled-up is dangerous. It seems more likely that a person, if they really are sufficiently wounded and frustrated, will go crazy and become homicidal or suicidal if they *do not* let go and express their anger and aggression in a safe environment than if they do. Alternatively they might become ill and depressed
- Going through a *catharsis,* at least in the beginning, is something that should only be done in the presence of one or more trained facilitators
- If you choose to do this cathartic meditation, you won't go crazy because the conscious decision to do it puts you in control. On the contrary, you can voice your inherent craziness instead of trying to contain it, so you no longer create unnecessary fear, pain and conflict within yourself
- All we are doing in this process is making a conscious decision to open up so whatever is inside comes out spontaneously. We do not stop it or judge it, or even make it happen. We stand aside, we get out of our own way, we allow our inner beings to express themselves exactly as they are
- Unless physically in pain, discomfort or hungry, babies always stop crying when they receive what they need, even if it is only attention that is required. They don't need to be hushed up, they require their needs to be met

- It is important that you are able to express *the entire range* of your emotions because unless you do, you cannot feel fully alive. Feeling alive entails not only experiencing joy and bliss, but everything else too, like anger, pain, grief and sadness
- Some feelings, like jealousy or anger, are uncomfortable and hard to accept, but when you find it difficult even to cry or shout, feeling anything is a major breakthrough. The *Aum* is a lifeline for anyone who wants to relearn how to express their emotions
- There are no short cuts if you want to heal your emotional wounds and reach emotional maturity; we have to establish a new habit of allowing our emotions rather than denying them
- No matter how deeply buried and difficult to access our memories are, the hard disk of the human biocomputer can never be erased. Those hidden feelings are in there somewhere!
- Nothing works so well as a meditation for letting a person see themselves objectively
- It is not helpful to regard anything within yourself, even your conditioning or sabotaging behaviour, as 'the enemy.' Noticing and accepting them is essential
- Your sexuality is a vital area to explore, even if what you discover is uncomfortable. It's worth it if you want to feel completely comfortable with all aspects of yourself
- The only thing you can usefully do with uncomfortable feelings is to feel them. Then they can pass. Denial, the only alternative, is not a viable strategy
- When you intone the mantra *Om,* you are putting the voice of your deepest being out into the world. *Om* cuts through your conditioning, your issues, your strivings, all the things that make you anxious so that the real you is expressed unhindered
- Focusing on a sound and a vibration is a lot different from thinking, and helps in allowing a feeling of unity and wholeness or connectedness to creep over you
- Following a period of intense, relentless activity, a time of silence and stillness is often when significant transformations happen for the alert meditator

- When a moment of transformation occurs, something changes or heals forever
- Sitting (or standing) in silence and stillness is when true transformation can take place. If you want to know yourself inside out, if you want true peace, balance and fulfilment, sooner or later you have to be still and silent and listen to your heart
- Mindsets or erroneous beliefs that continually worry you when you try to work out answers rationally, simply dissolve when allowed to process themselves through the unconscious while you witness in silence
- Just turning up at the *Aum* and having a go acted as a great tonic for my self-esteem – I began to believe in myself again
- What freedom is really about is a personal inner liberation from judgements, mindsets, neurotic behaviour, anxiety, conflict, stress and imbalance. Once you have that awareness, this kind of liberty can never be taken away from you whatever happens
- How can we experience compassion and love for others and ourselves, and how can we feel wholly integrated, if we neglect the parts within us that hurt the most?
- Love enables us to take the risk, to leap into the void, to explore deeply into the unknown, for only love can heal emotional wounding
- The *Aum* helped me develop a deep understanding of what is going on inside, and I discovered personal resources and choices I did not even know I had

15

Boundaries, Barriers & Limits

Whether you believe you can or whether you believe you can't, you're right
Henry Ford

Dr Phil McGraw, in his book *Life Strategies,* describes vividly how we train others in how they can treat us.

At first this may sound ridiculous because few of us go round telling people, especially perfect strangers, how they can treat us in so many words. However, Dr Phil is absolutely right and he makes a point of vital importance if we are to understand what happens with regard to all our relationships. Most of us simply don't realise we give out clues and signals all the time as to where our boundaries are, what we are feeling about ourselves and others, our values and beliefs and what we find acceptable.

We broadcast these signals largely unconsciously, and others pick them up, in most cases also unconsciously, which is why they may never be mentioned. Nevertheless they are important because they deliver powerful messages.

Not everybody respects your boundaries, especially if they feel you are not serious about maintaining those boundaries, and we each know at least one person who, in our perception, always takes liberties. In a situation like this, it may be necessary for us to be more assertive than usual, but that means we have to make ourselves aware of what signals we are putting out.

Generally speaking, it's a good idea to make a habit of being assertive in daily life, but that does not mean it's OK to become self-obsessed to the point of narcissism. Always remember there's a world of difference between being assertive and being aggressive. It is perfectly possible to be assertive without being aggressive. Being assertive simply means making sure other people understand clearly what you are about, where you are coming from and where your boundaries are.

You'll soon know if you've got the balance right. If all your friends disappear and no-one wants to know you, you've overdone it. If anyone is overstepping the mark, you're not doing it correctly, or strongly enough. If people start treating you with respect, you've got it right. In real life you will probably have to adjust slightly to each individual.

Back to basics

Let's start at the beginning. The first step in defining your boundaries is to decide what you want and do not want in your life and to use those decisions as the basis for your guidelines or boundaries. This is yet another of those times when you need to know yourself inside out, because valid boundaries are based on your core beliefs and values and what comes from your heart. Proper boundaries are not based on misplaced feelings of guilt, conditioning or persuasion by other people. In other words, boundaries are effective for you and taken seriously by others when you believe in them.

It's not only about how we relate to others. It's also to do with how we relate to the world around us, for there are so many distractions and possible blind alleys on the path to happiness and fulfilment. In these modern times when we are presented with a vast array of choices, it is easy to waver, to allow ourselves to be led astray, get distracted or simply lost in confusion. Clear guidelines or boundaries are essential aids in every aspect of organising yourself so you keep your focus and know clearly where you are going.

Once you have a feel for your boundaries you can then practise simply stating your truth clearly, but non-aggressively. There's a bit of a knack to this, so don't be surprised if everything comes out wrong the first few times and you end up going to the other extreme. Soon you will find a balance.

Sometimes we are faced with a sudden challenge, or even a simple decision that needs an answer on the spur of the moment, and you are unprepared. It's a new situation so you haven't yet decided on a boundary. For example you've just come home from work exhausted, it's cold, dark and snowing outside, and you collapse into a comfy armchair in front of a roaring log fire. You really don't want to go anywhere.

Then your partner comes breezing into the room and says, 'Martha gave me a couple of tickets for the cinema tonight. I really want to go. It starts at 7.30 – will you be ready in half an hour?' Your heart sinks. You are exhausted, you don't want to move, you don't even like the movies, and yet, before you can stop yourself you hear yourself answering, 'OK, I'll be ready.'

Aaaaarrrrrrgggggggghhhhhh!!!!!! Instant self-sabotage! The Impeccable Warrior just died! You are not being honest, you are not being true to yourself and you are not taking responsibility. You are allowing yourself to be swayed because you'd feel guilty if you said no. But now you feel guilty because you are being untruthful. It doesn't make sense. You are not looking after yourself, any possibility of a boundary is out of the window, your awareness is below zero and your self-esteem will suffer.

I know it's easier said than done to say no to you partner when he or she is really excited about something they want to do, but there are hidden dangers for your relationship if this sort of thing happens regularly.

This kind of behaviour is the perfect recipe for building resentment and repressed anger which you will either turn in on yourself or fire at your unsuspecting partner or friend in an unguarded moment. If you keep doing this sort of thing it may even lead to depression and maybe even separation or divorce, and all the while you'll be puzzled, wondering why you don't feel so good about yourself.

'I did everything I could to please her (or him),' you say to yourself, hurt and bewildered. But it's at the expense of your integrity and that will become a major problem if you continue like this.

When we allow our boundaries to be transgressed without protest we are insincere and disrespectful towards ourselves, we are not taking ourselves seriously and perhaps we don't even believe we count as valid. Moreover, in such a state, we are also incapable of being true to anyone else.

Check yourself out

Yet there is a very simple remedy. I call it *checking yourself out.* Let's replay the above imaginary scenario but this time incorporating my *checking yourself out* technique and you'll see how it works.

Your partner says, 'Martha gave me a couple of tickets for the cinema tonight. I really want to go. It starts at 7.30 – will you be ready in half an hour?'

Before you say a word you immediately ask yourself, 'how do I feel about this?' and in this case the answer that pops up in your mind is 'I really don't want to go.' Now you know consciously what your boundary is and the next step is to decide how strong your feeling is. This is the vitally important point, *you are now making choices with awareness and that makes all the difference.* You may decide that just this once you'll go along with your partner's wishes because it means so much to him or her, or you may not.

If you decide you want to say no, the next stage is to find a way of tactfully communicating how you feel, while totally owning your feelings and taking due consideration of the other's feelings too. It's a delicate balancing act, but given plenty of awareness and sensitivity, you can do it!

Your answer might go something like this: 'To tell you the truth my love, I'm completely exhausted and not really in the mood. Would you mind awfully if we gave it a miss tonight?' Now you have asserted your boundary by making it known.

Now you have stated your truth so no matter what happens from now, even if you do end up going out, your self-esteem will be intact. Especially so if your partner is sensitive and intelligent enough to make sure you feel he or she has received and acknowledged your position. Even if your partner doesn't like it, they will respect you for it. You have put down your boundary, behaved with absolute integrity and made it known to all concerned, so whatever happens in the discussion that ensues no longer matters.

For example, you might eventually take the view that if you make an effort to go you might enjoy it after all; or you might decide after checking yourself out that you don't feel strongly enough to make an issue out of it; or you may dig your heels in and refuse to go, or suggest she goes with another friend while you stay home and put your feet up.

Of course, you partner will have a boundary issue as well, and we can only hope that he or she will have the integrity and courage to make it known truthfully. In such a situation, a proper discussion is possible in which each partner gets their emotional needs met. You have looked after yourself *and* acknowledged your partner's feelings. This is very important not only for you but also in all your relationships, for one of the most common complaints about wounded feelings I hear from people in relationships is that they don't feel *heard* or *seen* by their partner.

Another very common complaint is when a person can't understand why they feel angry or resentful towards their partner, or why their partner is behaving with anger and resentment towards them. A lack of honesty to oneself and the other is almost always the reason.

If you have a good and honest relationship with your partner in which you accept each other unconditionally, you will respect each other's boundaries. Then give and take becomes possible without generating bad feeling. The same principle applies in all relationships and all boundary issues. If you are not sure where you want to draw your boundary in any given situation, *ask yourself how you feel.*

Dangers

Now a word of caution, for there are many misunderstandings around the idea of boundaries which many mistakenly take as a vehicle for rigid self-control, of refusing to accommodate another person's point of view, or trying to control others. A person who feels insecure, for example, may refuse to make a necessary but scary move involving changing his mind, claiming he wishes his boundary on the issue respected.

Another danger is transgressing our own boundaries, often unconsciously, a move for which we no doubt have an awesome array of brilliant excuses and rationalisations. Sometimes we do this when we fear losing someone, or we fear we will be judged. This is especially true of people who feel compelled to be 'pleasers'.

Many partners, whether they realise it or not, use emotional blackmail against each other as a weapon of manipulation to cause a boundary to be compromised. This is a dishonest way to relate.

Unconscious behaviour hinging around boundaries causes us a great deal of discomfort. We know deep inside when we compromise our boundaries, or when someone else does, or something goes against our boundaries. We feel bad about it, even if we don't consciously notice that feeling. Hence the need to monitor yourself and ask 'how do I feel about …'

Many of us are unaware that when we bend over backwards to accommodate someone else at the expense of our own boundaries, we are actually creating problems by trying to be 'nice,' 'reasonable,' or 'civilised'.

There is nothing 'not nice' about stating your boundaries and sticking to them. People who stand by their boundaries engender our respect, for we recognise they know what they want, what they are doing and where they are going. They don't mess themselves or anybody else about. Monitoring how we feel about the issues that life presents us with by listening carefully to our inner voices helps us identify and define our boundaries.

Many of us have got into the habit of putting other people first, mainly unconsciously out of fear, but this automatically renders truthful relating impossible. Clear understanding between people only begins when we put ourselves first, not in a mean and selfish way, but when we state our truth with an open heart and stand by it.

Boundaries can, of course, be changed; they do not have to be cast in concrete. However, it is only sensible to change them if we feel sure the change is for the better, not just for the sake of avoiding a row, because we cannot be bothered to stick up for ourselves, because we want an easy life, or for fear of upsetting the other person.

Another trap waiting for the unaware is the danger of inadvertently using boundaries to be obstructive. Maybe for the sake of being curmudgeonly, to be deliberately non-committal, because we are afraid to appear weak, or because changing our minds to agree with someone feels like a defeat. The Impeccable Warrior sticks to his guns or changes his boundaries according to what *feels* right.

When we reach the stage where we feel good enough about ourselves to trust ourselves implicitly, we will not allow our boundaries to be rubbished by ourselves or by anyone else. We will feel perfectly happy about dropping one boundary in favour of another if the new one serves our needs better. Each of us needs to find a balance we *feel* comfortable with, for undue rigidity serves only to engender resistance between people.

It might be hard to accept this truth, but a partner or friend who cannot or will not respect your sincerely defined boundaries is not a suitable candidate for a satisfactory relationship with you, and never will be. Sometimes a partner wishes their opposite number to change, but a person can only be who he or she is, and no-one else. If we lose our boundaries we no longer know who we are and we lose control of our lives immediately. The same applies within friendships and business or work relationships.

That is not to say that we are defined by our boundaries. There's a lot more to the human race than a set of fences. My point is simply that we each need to be able to approach the world and our partners as individuals and to be accepted exactly as we are, boundaries and all, so we can relax and be ourselves. Only in that way can we shine our lights, grow and freely express our creative impulses.

Requiring a person to change to fit your expectations, requirements or specifications is a recipe for disaster, even if that person *tries* to fit the image you want. It simply is not sustainable and it's arrogant to expect a person to be anyone other than themselves. It's an infringement of their human rights.

That kind of behaviour is not what I understand by true friendship and certainly not real love either and no matter how insecure you might feel, there is no getting away from the fact that nourishment and nurturing are only of value when given unconditionally or not at all. It's important to realise that because if your boundaries are at all shaky you could easily fall foul of this problem.

Not only that, but if your boundaries are not clear, it's not only very difficult for you to feel a strong sense of who you are, but you also make it very difficult for others to relate to you, for they can't sense who you are either.

Am I being over extreme? I think not. No matter how beautiful or allegedly irreplaceable your partner might be, or no matter how strongly you believe you'll never find another person to love you, if either or both of you allow your boundaries to be continually violated by the other, there will be consequences. Either you will argue like cat and dog with no resolution possible; you will repress your anger and pain, breeding for yourself depression and resentment of the other; or more than likely, both. That's a vitally important point in a book about happiness!

Every time you allow a boundary to be overstepped, you collude with the transgressor and that does neither of you any favours. As in any dishonest scenario within a relationship, both parties have an issue to examine. It always takes two to tango. It is pointless and disingenuous to blame the other if you allow your boundary to be violated when you had a choice. And you *always* have a choice.

I learned this the hard way some years ago when I was the proud owner of a beautiful dark green Honda hatchback car which I loved to bits. It was a gloomy October Sunday afternoon in the Isle of Wight, and pouring with rain. My then partner, Saffron (not her real name), and I owned a static holiday caravan there. We had enjoyed a traditional Sunday roast lunch at the nearby yacht club in Bembridge, and were driving along a small country lane on the way back to the caravan site where we planned to pack and load the car before returning to London.

When we were about half a mile from the site, Saffron asked me if I would please miss our turning and instead continue on for a further couple of miles to a nearby garden centre. She wanted to buy a few plants for our garden back home. Then we would return to the caravan. Automatically, I responded in the affirmative though, if the truth be known, it was the last thing I wanted to do.

I was exhausted and hoping to find a few minutes to rest, or even sleep, before leaving the caravan to face the motorway home. I was cold, the road was treacherous, the visibility was restricted and the sky was dark. All in all, a very depressing wintry scene from which I wanted to escape as soon as possible. I certainly did not fancy any extra driving, no matter how short, nor did I want to hang around getting bored and even colder in a garden centre. That is the truth yet, without thinking, I agreed to drive on. *It never even occurred to me I could have said no.*

Perhaps I felt sorry for Saffron, who could not drive and was dependent on me for transport, who was crazy about plants, and who had done many nice things for me. More likely I was reluctant to say no for fear of starting a row. At the time it happened I was so depressed and cut off from my feelings, my responses to most situations were automatic. I had become a slave to my conditioning and I had got used to pleasing people, neither of which was Saffron's fault, but mine. I didn't realise at the time that I was functioning virtually on autopilot.

I should have said no, in the nicest possible way, for that would have been straightforward. If I had explained my reasons I am sure she would have understood and respected me for being real but I didn't want her to be disappointed. Ahh, the wisdom of hindsight! It doesn't take a genius to guess what happened next.

We drove on along the country lane and after three or four miles we realised we were on the wrong road. I stopped the car on a gravel patch in front of a gate at the side of a field, waiting for a break in the traffic so I could reverse back towards the gate and turn round. There was thick hedgerow either side of the gate making it hard to see what was coming. The spot was a little past the brow of a hill and not far beyond a bend in the road, which was narrow at that point.

The road was clear so I started pulling out and suddenly there was a car coming over the brow of the hill. I stopped at once but the front of my car was protruding into the road a little. There was no time to think about reversing back to safety. All I could do was wait for what felt like an eternity for the bang and the mixed sounds of tearing metal and shattering glass, muttering, under my breath, *'oh shit, oh shiiitttttt!'*

After the impact I was a little shocked and dazed, but very relieved there had been no injuries. Later, when I had to some extent recovered, I began to feel angry. If we had just gone back to the caravan, if she had not moved the goalposts and asked to go to the garden centre this never would have happened, I rationalised. If, if, if …

I was taken aback when, a few days later, in my therapist's consulting room in London, she told me it had been my fault (this was the same therapist who had recommended the *Aum Meditation*).

'I know I made a driving error,' I said, 'but apart from that, how is it my fault?'

'You didn't want to drive to the garden centre, right?' She enquired.

I nodded.

'You should have said no.'

Believe it or not, it hadn't occurred to me that saying no was an option, and at the time of the session I thought my therapist's point of view was a little extreme. But I was looking for someone to blame and after a few days of thinking about it, I grudgingly had to admit she was right. I had failed even to notice my boundary. When I did, I had allowed Saffron's request to take precedence over my boundary, which was a real put-down to myself, from myself.

So you see when I talk about conscious awareness, I know exactly what I'm talking about. I was so unaware and so unconscious at that time in my life I hardly knew which was up or what day it was, and believe me, the results were disastrous.

As a result of denying my truth that day I did myself a great disservice. I could have got us both killed and maybe other people too. I was the one who wrote off my beloved car and suffered the financial consequences, and all for the sake of a plant that we did not buy anyway because we never made it to the garden centre. What a painful lesson and wake-up call that was!

That wasn't all, for when I realised I had set myself up for this classic self-sabotage, purely through lack of awareness, I started feeling angry and berating myself for being so stupid. Eventually, I ran out of steam for doing that, realising that I was now pursuing another fruitless avenue by blaming myself. 'Learn the lesson,' I told myself, 'and be grateful for it.'

Referring back to what I have written in earlier chapters about expressing your feelings to the full, this was when I discovered that by expressing my sorrow and anger at full volume in the privacy of the therapy room and in *Dynamic Meditation* sessions, I was eventually able to let the anger pass through and put the incident behind me. Finally I told myself, 'just make sure to live your life for yourself, in the way you want to live it. Don't make compromises and don't be a slave to your conditioning. Be real and only say yes when you really mean it, whatever the consequences.'

When a boundary becomes a barrier

People who allow their boundaries to be walked over do not engender respect, they are trodden on like door mats and they feel like victims. Conversely, people who stick rigidly, insensitively or unreasonable to a boundary usually provoke antagonism, for others feel personally hurt or affronted. That's usually because the one on the receiving end feels he or she is not being heard. *It is easier to accept a person's 'no' when you feel you have at least been heard and valued by the person saying it.* Otherwise you feel the person with the boundary actually has a chip on his shoulder rather than a true boundary and is simply using it as an excuse to ride roughshod over your boundaries.

In a situation like that a boundary can become a barrier, and that's a different matter altogether.

Barriers in people can be hugely counter-productive. A barrier is essentially a powerful defence mechanism and like all defence mechanisms is, in effect, designed to protect your delicate psyche from getting wounded and your heart from being broken too many times. That's the intention anyway. A person who puts up a barrier makes it far more difficult for others to see and reach the real person that they are, the diamond within. They stop themselves from reaching out to others. Nobody can get through and a path of lonely isolation is assured.

We have already discussed how a defence mechanism almost always has it's origins in a person's very early childhood when as a child you got hurt or feared getting hurt, and it develops from there. The problem is that in adult life such a barrier or defence mechanism seriously limits you. If people keep asking why you are so defensive, or complaining they can't reach you, those are pretty major clues, and your cue to put your defence mechanism under the microscope.

Once you see it consciously and get to know it intimately, you can find the courage to let it pass. Like all unconscious behaviour it's only a habit. It's learned behaviour and it can be unlearned.

Boundaries, on the other hand, provide a reference point against which we can measure how we feel in any given situation. Boundaries help us maintain clarity about how we want to live our lives and help us stay on track.

If you feel you've got this issue out of balance, for example if people regularly confront you saying they can't get through to you, the only remedy is to heighten your awareness so you can see for yourself what you are doing. Then you empower yourself to choose to change your behaviour. Undoubtedly the best way to do that is with silent meditation, which I recommend you do regularly anyway.

Boundaries are also useful in helping us to communicate with ourselves and others about our feelings. They can actually make it feel safer to come closer, whereas a barrier inevitably shuts the other person out.

Boundaries can be usefully deployed with sensitivity and compassion and they support you, whereas barriers or defences are control mechanisms that keep people apart. Singer songwriter Paul Simon perfectly described the feeling of isolation that barriers create in his song, 'I am a rock, I am an island.'

If a person will not let you go beyond their defences, an intimate, trusting relationship becomes impossible. If you realise this is the case with your would-be partner and you want a fully nurturing, intimate relationship, it might be better to withdraw and find someone suitable. There is another very important element in this, which is when you quit trying to relate to someone unsuitable, you are more likely to start to move away from any tendency you may have towards co-dependency.

Over the years we discover that by defining our boundaries we feel much safer to drop our defences and approach people openly, for we start to believe in ourselves more, and to experience that feeling of integration I have mentioned. The reason for that is because we become far less dependent on the approval of others to make us feel OK.

From the experiences I have described in this chapter, and others as well, I began to realise some years ago the importance of spontaneously showing emotions as they arise, for they are a powerful indicator of where your boundaries are. They also show us and others that our boundaries are to be respected, for we have strong feelings about them.

Being assertive about boundaries means we insist on being taken seriously. It is very important for everyone concerned, ourselves included, to put this message out loud and clear, no matter how frightening the consequences might be. An issue might seem insignificant, a boundary not worth defending, but it isn't really. If we neglect a boundary even for an instant, even if we do it unconsciously, we deny of how we feel, meaning we put ourselves down.

As a Life Coach I see over and over again people putting themselves down little by little. It becomes a habit and it wears them down and destroys their self-esteem. Putting yourself down, like playing small, is a really, really counter-productive habit. It's insidiously undermining and if you allow yourself to do it, you will severely disempower yourself. It really matters, and that's why I'm covering this subject in such detail.

Finally, there sometimes seems to be confusion between boundaries and limitations. The difference is very simple, limitations are nothing but an imaginary point beyond which we cannot go. I firmly believe the only limitations we humans have to put up with are the ones we create for ourselves. If you believe you are limited, you are. But if you believe you are free beyond all limitations, you are.

I'll tell you how I know. I have a slight, invisible physical disability that makes it very difficult and tiring for me to walk long distances without pausing at regular intervals to rest. I will almost certainly never climb Everest, nor probably even walk in the foothills of the Himalayas. This is a limitation which I choose to acknowledge because I have no desire to climb Everest and to go through the difficulties that would entail. All that means is that I don't feel a calling to be a mountaineer.

Hill walking, rock climbing, white water rafting, even horse riding, are not fields in which I am likely to excel. However, because doing these things is not where my talent or calling lies, I am not attracted to doing them anyway. Therefore, for me that limitation is irrelevant, except in so far as it helps define what I have no interest in becoming good at.

Let's analyse this a little more precisely. It is probably true that anyone can do anything really well, given enough time, effort and determination. But if you don't have the aptitude or talent you will be pushing the river and there's little satisfaction in that, *so what's the point?* If instead you do something you *do* have the talent for (and everyone has something), then even though you may have to work to develop skills and knowledge, you flow with the river and feel immensely satisfied.

Where am I going with this? Simple. If you feel a limitation trying to stop you, pause for a moment and ask yourself, 'is this really right for me? Do I really care passionately about doing this? Is this my calling? Or is it just an ego trip?'

I'm sure you know what I'm going to say next. It's obvious. *If it doesn't feel right, drop it there and then.* Doing that will save you a lot of time and heartache. If it does feel right, persevere. If you're not sure, try for a little longer and *see how it feels.*

The folly of youth being what it is, there were times in my younger days when I felt a desperate need to transcend my disability, albeit on a more modest scale than ascending Everest and one day I decided to see the view from the top of the Malvern Hills. Most people, even elderly folk, take two or three hours to get to the summit of the Worcestershire Beacon, the highest of this range of hills, whereas it took me all day and a great deal of trouble and anguish. Coming down was fun though.

Like all youngsters, I needed to discover and find out about my limitations by testing them. Now I know I *can* go a lot further than I do in my normal daily life if I really want or have to, so I no longer have to prove anything to myself or anyone else and that feels good and makes acceptance easier. However, there are also times when this situation causes me considerable frustration, as, for example, when my partner, a very energetic woman, wants to go for a stroll by the river with our even more energetic Golden Labrador.

This usually costs me a great deal of effort, so first I ask myself if I really want to do it and, if so, she has to be prepared to put up with regular stops for resting. If she did not understand that or felt unable to accept it, she would not be suitable partner for me, or I wouldn't go for walks with her. Fortunately for me she is a caring person and she feels OK about resting when necessary.

This is important because there was a time some years ago when I used to get very wound up about the situation, feeling I was not a 'proper man' because masculine occupations like playing football were beyond me. However, I eventually realised I did not have to be the same as everyone else, in fact it would be far better to be different and do something I could excel in. I'm not remotely interested in football anyway, and one David Beckham in the world is quite enough, so why was I making such a big deal of it?

Eventually I realised I was giving myself a hard time for nothing and when finally I started being my own person I soon saw that perceiving my difficulty as a limitation was nonsense, for I am as valid as the next person and, most important, my condition has never stopped me expressing myself. I can and do excel in the things I am interested in and suited for, so why should I give myself imaginary limitations?

Of course it's not always that easy, because occasional lapses of awareness inevitably occur. When I wake up and get things in perspect-ive I feel I live a charmed existence. In fact, like so many disabled people I have met, my difficulty has given me grit, determination and perseverance, which are very useful qualities.

So that, in a nutshell, is why I don't believe in being stopped by so-called limitations. People who hide behind limitations are scared to live life to the full, and without wishing to sound smug, I live a far more fulsome life than many able bodied people.

Here's the key understanding that will enable you to achieve anything your heart truly desires: *if you can imagine something, you can create or achieve it.* As Albert Einstein pointed out, our imaginations are far more powerful than our thoughts.

By avoiding wasting time fretting and trying to do things for which you are not suited, you can give yourself more time and build up stronger motivation to develop talents and interests in the things you are good at and suited for. Projects that bring you satisfaction and fulfilment. In the field of creative endeavour, the sky is *not* the limit. There are no limits unless we choose to put them there.

Everything depends on our attitude, for we can choose to create limits or abolish them. We can let obstacles stop us in our tracks, or turn them to our advantage. Once we learn to do the latter, obstacles become irrelevant. When water meets an obstacle it flows around it or, if that is not possible, gathers itself till it has enough depth to flow over it. Water always follows the easiest course. I prefer to leave obstacles be and not waste energy needlessly struggling with them.

Somewhere deep inside I have always known that limits are for transcending, just as when I was a schoolboy I knew that rules were for breaking. Were we to live within our so-called limitations we would never achieve anything, and if we all abide by rules like sheep in a flock, nothing exceptional or remarkable would ever happen. Dr Wayne Dyer made an insightful comment on this subject when he wrote, 'if you follow the herd, guess what you end up standing in!'

There are endless examples of people who have achieved the impossible. In World War Two, the Royal Air Force medics told Douglas Bader he would never fly again after losing both his legs. He did, and very ably too, leading a squadron in the Battle of Britain. He had false legs produced and he made it his business to master their use so he could fly again, because flying was his passion.

Another example is Richard Noble, the man who, despite huge debts and terrific difficulties, built the first car to go supersonic. His achievement stands in *The Guinness Book of Records*.

Captain Joshua Slocum was not the sort of man to take any notice when he was warned, at the end of the nineteenth century, that it would be impossible to sail alone around the world, just because nobody had ever done it before. He not only did it, he then wrote the fascinating story of his exploits of travelling in his sloop, *Spray*.

Let us not forget the most famous navigator in history, Christopher Columbus, who was told he would fall off the edge of the world if he sailed too far west. I think he half believed it himself, but somehow he found the courage to follow his vision. What he discovered was, as we know, of massive significance to world history.

These people all had two things in common:

- a vision
- unshakable self-belief

We can all develop those qualities. The secret is to *do what you love and love what you do*. Then your achievements will be truly meaningful. Limitations are imaginary, which makes it easy to transcend them.

I like to think my son might be gracious enough to listen to his father for a moment, for this is my message to him, and all of you too: *never, never, never live within your apparent limitations. Decide what you want with all your heart and go for it for all you are worth, hell for leather. Don't hold anything back, and woe betide any obstacles that have the audacity to think they can get in your way.*

And never listen to anyone who says you can't. If you want it enough you can.

Here's my strategy in brief: *embrace your boundaries, eschew your barriers and don't entertain any concept of limitation.*

Summary

- We train others in how they can treat us
- The signals we unconsciously transmit deliver powerful messages
- You can be assertive without being aggressive. Being assertive means making sure people understand what you are about and where you are coming from
- Valid boundaries are based on your core beliefs and values and what comes from your heart, not from misplaced feelings of guilt
- Boundaries are effective for you and taken seriously by others when you believe in them
- Clear guidelines or boundaries are essential aids in every aspect of organising yourself so you keep your focus and know clearly where you are going
- Saying yes when you really mean no is the perfect recipe for building resentment and repressed anger which you will either turn in on yourself or fire at someone else in an unguarded moment
- If you're not sure what your boundary is, check yourself out by asking yourself, 'how do I feel about this?'
- If you have an honest relationship with your partner in which you accept each other unconditionally, you will respect each other's boundaries. Then give and take becomes possible without generating bad feeling
- Many people misuse boundaries as a vehicle for rigid self-control, or trying to control others
- Another danger is transgressing our own boundaries, often unconsciously, when we fear losing someone, or fear we will be judged. This is especially true of people who feel compelled to be pleasers

- Many people use emotional blackmail against their partners and friends to manipulate or compromise a boundary. This is a dishonest way to relate
- We know deep inside when we do, or someone else does, something that goes against our own boundaries, for we feel bad about it
- There is nothing 'not nice' about stating your boundaries and sticking to them
- People who stand by their boundaries engender our respect
- The Impeccable Warrior sticks to his guns or changes his boundaries according to what *feels* right
- A partner who cannot or will not respect your boundaries is not a suitable candidate for a satisfactory relationship with you, and never will be
- Despite their importance, we are not defined by our boundaries
- Requiring a person to change to fit your expectations is a recipe for disaster, and an infringement of their human rights
- Every time we allow a boundary to be overstepped, we collude with the transgressor and that does neither any favours. Both parties have issues to deal with
- It is pointless and disingenuous to blame the other person if you allowed your boundary to be violated when you had a choice. You *always* have a choice
- Make sure to live your life for yourself, in the way you want to. Don't make compromises or be a slave to your conditioning. Be real and only say yes when you really mean it, whatever the consequences
- It is easier to accept a person's 'no' when you feel you have been heard and valued by the person saying it
- A barrier is a defence mechanism designed to protect your psyche from getting wounded and your heart from being broken too many times
- Someone who puts up a barrier makes it difficult for others to reach the real person, and stops him or herself from reaching out to others. A path of lonely isolation is assured
- Like all unconscious behaviour, creating a barrier is only a habit. It's learned behaviour and it can be unlearned

- When we define our boundaries we feel safer to drop our defences and approach people openly, for we start to believe in ourselves more, and experience a feeling of integration. We know who we are, so we become less dependent on the approval of others to make us feel OK
- Being assertive about boundaries means we insist on being taken seriously
- Putting yourself down is counter-productive habit. It's undermining and if you do it, you will disempower yourself and destroy your self-esteem
- Limitations are an imaginary hindrance. The only limitations we humans have to put up with are the ones we create for ourselves
- If you believe you are limited, you are. If you believe you are free beyond all limitations, then that's what you are
- If you insist on trying to achieve something for which you do not have the talent you will be pushing the river, and there's little satisfaction in that
- If instead you do something you *do* have the talent for, then even though you may have to work to develop new skills and knowledge, you flow with the river and feel immensely satisfied
- People who hide behind limitations are scared to live life to the full
- *If you can imagine something, you can create or achieve it.* As Albert Einstein pointed out, our imaginations are far more powerful than our thoughts
- In the field of creative endeavour, the sky is *not* the limit. There are no limits unless we choose to put them there
- Everything depends on our attitude, for we can choose to create limits or abolish them. We can let obstacles stop us in our tracks, or turn them to our advantage
- Limits are for transcending, just as rules are for breaking. Were we to live within our limitations we would achieve nothing, and if we all abide by rules, nothing exceptional or remarkable would ever happen
- In the words of Dr Wayne Dyer, 'if you follow the herd, guess what you end up standing in!'
- People who have made significant achievements against the perceived limitations of their times all had a *vision* and *unshakable self-belief.* We can all develop those qualities

- The secret of meaningful success is to *do what you love and love what you do*
- Never live within your apparent limitations. Decide what you really want, and go for it, don't hold anything back
- Never listen to anyone who says you can't. If you want it enough you can
- Embrace your boundaries, eschew your barriers and don't entertain any concept of limitation

Questions to ask yourself

- How do I feel about that?
- Is this really right for me? Do I really care passionately about doing this? Is this my calling? Or is it just an ego trip?

16

Zenning is a Beautiful Feeling

By simply allowing, you become the bringer of space, and in that space wonderful transformation and healing takes place

Eckhart Tolle

In this, the last chapter before we move on to start building our second pillar, we look first at ideas for physically giving you more room to manoeuvre and operate creatively, though this will, of course, beneficially affect your psyche too. Then in the second part of the chapter we will discuss the merits of enacting a mental decluttering by finishing all unfinished emotional business.

Decluttering your environment

First, there is no doubt in my mind that creating a comfortable and user-friendly environment in which to live and work liberates your creative juices so they can flow more freely, and decluttering (or *zenning* as I call it) is a great place to start.

'To zen' simply means to make your home, office, car, boat, garage, loft, mind or whatever as empty of superfluous 'stuff' as possible. It's a concept inspired by the Zen Bhuddist tradition of living as simply and minimalistically as possible (without attachments), and needless to say, it's a lifestyle wholeheartedly embraced by the Impeccable Warrior.

I've done several major zennings myself over the years, and it's interesting to note – and it can't be a coincidence – that all my clients who make significant progress have done it too. Either they zen first and their lives suddenly take off; or they start to fly and then find they have to pause to zen so their progress is not hindered. While it doesn't matter which way round you do it, it makes sense to view zenning as great preparation for getting your life going, especially if you have something blocking you. One of its many benefits is that it helps you get into a productive mindset.

Quite simply, if you're in a mess it's much harder to think straight or even to know what you're feeling, and so you have a tendency to do crisis management (or non-management), chaotic thinking or hoping for the best, any or all of which can lead to panic or procrastination. At the very least it makes it far more difficult to gain clarity and focus, and that's a real problem. It's also highly inefficient, and that's a waste of your personal energy.

So what does zenning involve? It boils down to shedding anything that's superfluous and creating simple, user-friendly systems that empower you to quickly and easily find things or information you want. It's a process of radical simplification, and with simplification comes reduced stress. It could be as simple as tidying your desk or emptying your e-mail inbox, or as complicated as creating new filing systems or getting rid of unwanted furniture. It might include a fundamental life change, such as selling your house and moving to a smaller one after your children have grown up.

The symbolic value of zenning goes far deeper than it appears on the surface. There can only be one motive for accumulating superfluous possessions, things that are of no use to you any more, stuff that doesn't support you, items that clutter you and crowd you out; and that's a fear of letting go, which might be conscious or unconscious. Perhaps you feel you have suffered from lack or privation in your life. However clinging to material goods will not make you feel more secure or fulfilled, those qualities come only from within.

Maybe, in your unconscious perception, you felt a lack of love and emotional nourishment. Grasping physical objects will never compensate for that. On the contrary, finding the courage to let go will give you a sense of freedom that enables your priceless inner qualities and resources to begin to emerge. Then the real you, with all its beauty, power and potential, can flower. When that happens you will automatically attract all the support you could ever need.

One of my clients, a woman who had been divorced for several years, wanted to embark on a new relationship and at the same time move to a house which would be less rambling, easier to maintain, and more to the point, not full of unhappy memories. She put her old house on the market but had no sensible offers until she realised something was blocking her. She felt cluttered by mountains of belongings left behind by her ex-husband and three kids, all of who had grown up and left home. So she decided to have a zenning.

Fortunately, we had already spent a lot of time in one-to-one Life Coaching sessions working on strengthening her boundaries. Also she was sufficiently intelligent and aware to realise that by leaving their unwanted possessions in her house, her children and ex-husband had failed to take responsibility for their own lives by, in effect, dumping them in what was now her space. They had transgressed her boundaries, albeit inadvertently. Let's not forget it always takes two to tango – she had allowed it to happen, meaning she had also neglected to take responsibility for her boundaries. She had let things slide over a period of several years and now she was feeling resentful. This is indisputably a lose/lose situation.

After some reflection, she understood what she had done and decided to remedy the matter. From the moment she took that decision, she started taking responsibility. She contacted her three sons and ex-husband and told them they had two weeks in which to come to the house to remove whatever they wanted of their goods, and if there was anything left she would then order a skip and throw the rest out herself. Interestingly, two of the boys came and took a few objects, but not very much. Then, as good as her word, and with the blessings of all three sons, she spent several days clearing everything out from the loft and the rest of the house until the skip was overflowing.

Smaller objects she put in her car and took to the local dump herself and anything of value she sold on eBay or took to a local charity shop. While she was at it, she also had a no holds barred zenning of her own stuff. She told me that although being hard physical work she had a whale of a time because it felt so satisfying.

In less than a month her task was completed and she reported feeling liberated and empowered in the extreme. She was much more relaxed too, for what she had also done, in effect, was restored her ailing boundaries or built new ones. Oh, and guess what happened? Within two weeks of finishing the job she had a good offer on her house, and the deal went through to a remarkably stress-free completion.

The other side of the story is that she had been looking for a new house for many months and suddenly she found one that she said was perfect. Within two months of doing her zenning, she was happily living her new life in her new house with her new partner. Even better, her move was also remarkably un-stressful because she had only a modest amount of stuff to move and she didn't have to think of where to store things she didn't want in her new house. So goal achieved with minimum fuss and a happy and fulfilled woman!

Now of course I'm not saying her goal of moving house was realised just because of her zenning. It was achieved by her actions, plain and simple. The zenning helped her to focus, to think clearly, to clear all blocks physical, psychological, emotional and even spiritual, to feel empowered and make things happen at a lightning pace. She was like a racehorse jumping out of the starting stalls – liberated and running with all her energy flowing, bursting with her unstoppable creative approach to the task.

It's actually awesome to see a person supercharged and on fire like that, and it's incredibly exiting for the person doing it. *The same can happen for you and me. Have a zenning and set yourself free,* especially if you're feeling bogged down, confused and overwhelmed.

Incidentally, being the kind of person she was, there was no way she was going to stop even though her immediate goal was achieved. She then set about persuading her new partner to zen his flat where he had been living up to his eyeballs in clutter. She helped him through his initial difficulties in letting go of his so-called 'nostalgic' collection of 'stuff that might be useful one day.'

Soon he also started feeling better about the whole idea and in a remarkably short time he too began to develop a strong appetite for feeling free and unencumbered. He actually built a bonfire to throw his stuff onto, a highly symbolic way to kiss goodbye to your past.

Net result – his flat was so tidy and clear of mess he was able to rent it out, while he moved in with his new partner into her new house, but bringing none of his former clutter with him. She was delighted, because her new boundary stated that he was welcome but his superfluous possessions were not.

Tips for decluttering

1) Lots of people have difficulty deciding what to throw out, sell or give away, so they give up. Here's a suggestion: consider throwing out anything you haven't used or worn for a year. Ask yourself if

you are likely to use it within the forthcoming year. If not it's outlived its usefulness and out it goes, whatever 'it' might be. Be ruthlessly focused and it's unlikely you'll get it wrong.

2) Don't confuse yourself by wasting time looking through old papers or photos. Apply the same rule as above. If you haven't used or referred to it in a year and you're not likely to do so in the forthcoming year, sling it out. If you stop and read everything it could take many lifetimes to complete the job!
3) Be careful – for example don't throw out your wedding photos (unless you're divorced, in which case you might be delighted to dispose of them) or your spouse might be very upset, maybe even thinking you don't love him or her any more. Also don't throw away important documents like mortgage deeds, insurance documents, bank statements, income tax returns, passports or driving licences, unless they are out of date.
4) Don't throw out other people's stuff with first asking their permission.

Finishing unfinished business

Exactly the same principle applies to emotional issues and that's why it's very important to finish all unfinished business, or gain closure. Feeling free to move on at sticky points in your life can be greatly facilitated if you take responsibility for finishing or making an end to what you started, no matter how painful or embarrassing. That's what Impeccable Warriors do.

Finishing unfinished business is *emotional* decluttering or zenning. When a relationship ends, for example, only when you fully split up can you really feel free to embark on a new relationship or other adventures. Some married couples split up but delay getting divorced. This can lead to the still married partner in any new relationship feeling unable to fully commit to the other.

Similarly, if you change your job, you might want to work out your notice period for your old job as conscientiously and diligently as possible so you can move honourably to your next employment, leaving nothing behind for others to clear up. By behaving in this fashion you are able to move freely through your world unencumbered and with a sense of having done what's right.

This also has great benefits for your reputation, which might be important in a work context. Many years ago when I worked as a carpenter, I made a point of always finishing one job before moving on to the next and my customers loved me for it. If that meant delaying the start of the next job by a day or two I would telephone the next customer to explain, and usually they were happy too. They knew that it would be their turn next and their job would also be finished before the following one commenced. Many people in the building trades seem to be incapable of doing that and it's annoying for everyone concerned. If you are the errant tradesman, you will have disgruntled customers constantly on your case, instead of satisfied ones. This is a situation the Impeccable Warrior would abhor and it is obviously detrimental to your creative flow, let alone your peace of mind.

When I was involved in this line of work, it was in the days before the internet and mobile 'phones had been invented, at least for the average tradesman, and members of the building trade were notorious for being unreliable, unable or unwilling to communicate with their clients. So just by doing those two things – finishing one job at a time, and keeping people informed – I stood out from all the other carpenters in my area and lots of referrals came in my direction.

This was definitely win/win for me and my customers. Not only did I make a handsome living from a collection of very satisfied clients, but I had a great feeling of satisfaction and fulfilment every time one of my wooden creations was finished, be it a bookcase, a wardrobe or a fitted kitchen.

One of my present Life Coaching clients is a single mother with a five-year-old daughter. She is separated from her husband and not yet divorced. Her husband, who is a very manipulative character, seems to be having difficulty in comprehending and accepting that their marital relationship is effectively over. This makes tremendous boundary difficulties for my client. She feels, quite rightly, she can't simply cut off and have nothing more to do with this man because he and their daughter have a good relationship and they love and want to see each other, as one would expect. However, the symbolic gesture if my client were to get her divorce would undoubtedly help her convey a stronger sense of finality and would assist her estranged husband to accept reality. The boundary would be clearer, she would feel stronger and he would have less scope for manipulation, all of which would ultimately benefit the child too.

Of course, a divorce in this case would only be partial completion because the two parents still have to relate, at least until the child is a few years older. But there would be a much clearer basis for their new tripartite relationship, which is bound to be much improved.

If you find yourself in a position in which complete closure is impossible, at least for some years into the future, then it comes down to a strategy of damage limitation and self-preservation. In a case like this, supporting the child emotionally as much as possible has to be paramount. That's why much of the work my client and I have done together is around helping her to build clear and strong boundaries, which she has accomplished commendably. It is also very important for her to develop as much awareness as possible so she can see instantly when her husband tries to transgress those boundaries.

Some of those boundaries have been about making clear and strong access and living arrangements so she looks after herself properly, he cannot invade her space, and she can behave with integrity. By this I mean she can be scrupulously true to herself at all times, which she is now learning to do. This enables her to avoid getting sucked into feeling guilty or inadequate or any one of the 101 unpleasant feelings that single parents often suffer. When she feels able to initiate a divorce, she will make her life a whole lot easier.

My client's issue of setting herself up so she could be true to herself is of vital importance not only for her, but also to ensure her daughter experiences her as a worthy role model. Hopefully, though the child is bound to undergo a painful journey, she will at least learn about strong boundaries, finishing unfinished business and the behaviour of the Impeccable Warrior.

If you are in a similar situation you are bound to have times when you feel really angry, perhaps even furious and enraged, in which case it's a good idea to use one of tools described earlier such as *Osho Dynamic Meditation* or the *Aum Meditation*. Make sure your child is looked after elsewhere by someone who is trustworthy, so you can express your anger in private in a place where your child won't get hurt.

At the very least talk in confidence to someone you trust. Otherwise it's virtually guaranteed that your relationship with your estranged husband, wife or partner will degenerate into rowing, and your anger might inadvertently get dumped on the child.

Zenning and achieving psychological closure are essential life skills we can pass on to our children, who should also be taught to deal responsibly with their anger. By doing this we become great role models who will help them understand from an early age how to deal with at least some of life's many challenges.

Summary

- Creating a comfortable and user-friendly environment to live and work in liberates your creativity. *Zenning* is a great place to start
- *'To zen'* means to make your home, office, car, boat, garage, loft, mind or whatever as empty of superfluous 'stuff' as possible
- It makes sense to view zenning as preparation for getting your life going, especially if you have something blocking you
- If you're in a mess it's harder to gain clarity and focus, and that's a problem
- Zenning is shedding anything that's superfluous and creating simple, user-friendly systems that empower you to quickly and easily find things you want. It's a process of radical simplification
- There can only be one motive for accumulating superfluous possessions, and that's a conscious or unconscious fear of letting go
- Finding the courage to let go will give you a sense of freedom that enables your priceless inner qualities and resources to begin to emerge. Then the real you, with all its beauty, power and potential, can flower
- Have a zenning and set yourself free, especially if you're feeling bogged down, confused and overwhelmed
- It's a very good idea to finish all unfinished business to gain closure
- Finishing unfinished business is *emotional* decluttering or zenning
- Some married couples split up but delay getting divorced. This can lead to the still married partner in any new relationship feeling unable to fully commit
- If you change your job, work out your notice period for your old job as conscientiously and diligently as possible so you can move honourably to your next employment, leaving nothing behind for others to clear up
- When you finish your unfinished business properly you move freely through your world unencumbered and with a sense of having done what's right

- If you find yourself in a position in which closure is impossible, at least for some years into the future, you need a strategy of damage limitation and self-preservation
- Being true to yourself is vital when a child is involved so you are seen as a worthy role model. Then the child will learn about strong boundaries and the behaviour of the Impeccable Warrior
- If you are in a situation in which closure is impossible for now and you feel angry, do *Dynamic* or the *Aum Meditation* to express your anger in private so your child won't get hurt
- If you're angry, at the very least talk in confidence to someone you trust
- We owe it to our children to deal responsibly with our anger while creating strong boundaries and enjoying a sense of completion, so we can be good role models. Then they will understand from an early age how to deal effectively with at least some of life's many challenges.

Tips for decluttering

1) Consider throwing out anything you haven't used or worn for a year. Ask yourself if you are likely to use it within the forthcoming year. If not, out it goes, whatever 'it' might be. Be ruthlessly focused.
2) Don't waste time looking through old papers or photos. Apply the same rule as above. If you stop and read everything it could take many lifetimes to complete the job!
3) Whatever you do, don't throw out your wedding photos! Don't throw away essential documents such as passports, mortgage documents or insurance papers.
4) Don't throw out other people's stuff without asking for their permission first.

THE SECOND PILLAR

Your Passion

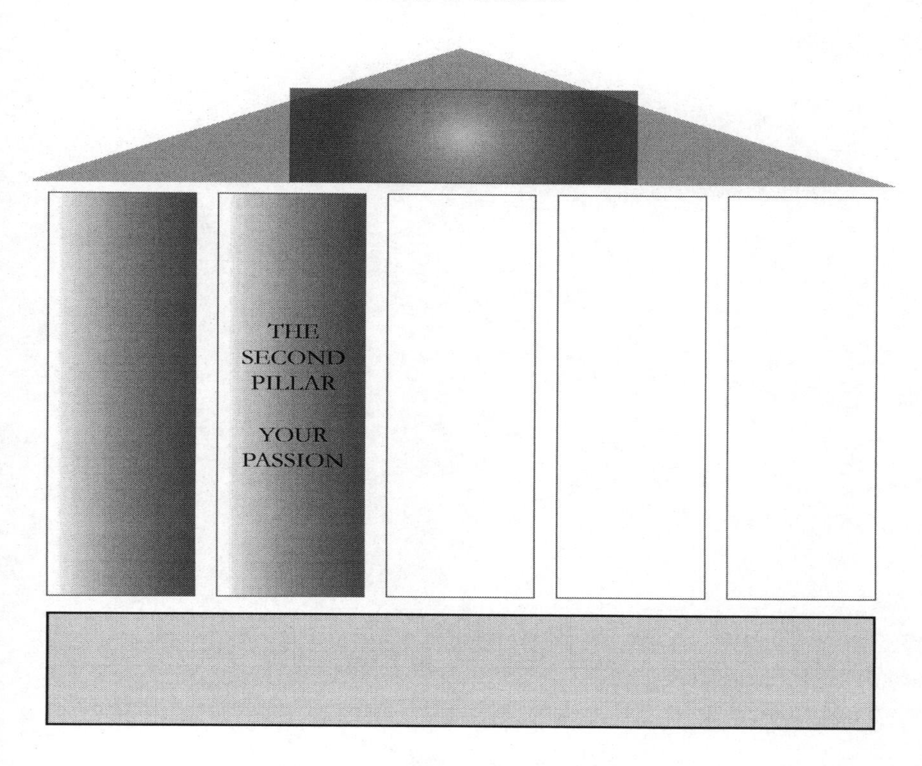

Now we've started to equip ourselves with tools and our awareness is sharpening up, we can start to build our second pillar, which is all about doing what you love and loving what you do. You may or may not yet be aware of what that is but don't worry. By the end of this section you will know how to find your passion and build strategies for action while developing the courage to pursue your new action plan.

We begin with an examination of that most misunderstood of subjects, goals, for it is vital we have a clear understanding of why they are so important and how they can best be used.

17

Understanding Goals

There are different paths that you can take in this life and choosing the correct path is supremely important. And as if that weren't pressure enough, it's no good choosing not to choose because that approach to life absolutely guarantees failure

Richard Branson

Many people believe that coaches are obsessed with goals, and there's much truth in that belief, and for very good reason. The reason why we love goals is that they, like your resistance, are your friends. They are extremely helpful in many ways, as we shall see as this chapter unfolds.

But beware, goals are not the be all and end all. *What is just as important as defining your goals, if not more so, is getting to know yourself inside out.* Then you can tell which goals are right for you and which are little more than red herrings.

A goal is nothing more nor less than a statement of what you desire to achieve – it defines what you aspire to. The important word here is 'desire', but don't forget desire on its own is not enough. It must be accompanied by appropriate action. The world is full of well intentioned, desiring non-achievers and it is said that the road to hell is paved with good intentions. I take it that refers to this life on this Earth at this time – it can be heaven or it can be hell, depending on what you make of it by your actions or non-actions.

Action is the only thing that can bring about change in your life. If you take no action there will be no change; if you do take action, something is bound to happen, though things may not necessarily change. It's simple cause and effect, but thinking and feeling creatively in deciding on what action to take is important too. Remember what Einstein clearly told us, 'we cannot solve our problems with the same thinking we used when we created them.'

Think about that for a moment. We *create* our problems by our thoughts, which implies we can *solve* our problems by changing our thoughts. It makes perfect sense because different thoughts will produce different actions and different actions will produce different results. Therefore if you don't like the results you are getting, change your thinking and change your actions. It's a balancing act because there will also be times when persevering with the same action will eventually bear fruit, as when mastering a new skill, so tune in to your inner voice to feel intuitively when it's right for you to persevere or when it's better to quit and do something different. You can do this on a case by case basis.

Even if you keep trying at something, you can still change your ways. Perhaps a subtle adjustment, a little tweaking, a tiny bit of fine tuning will get you on track towards the results you want. You can say to yourself, 'I'm going to try this again, but what can I do differently to make it better this time?'

A correctly stated goal is a great place to start. The following chapter describes two excellent ways to create powerful goals while framing them in the most effective way.

Any idiot can run round achieving goals, it's not difficult when you know how. *The real art of personal development is in achieving goals that make you happy, goals that really get you to where you want to be.* If you achieve the 'wrong' goals you might well find yourself saying 'I've achieved all this and I'm still not happy,' or even worse, you might feel you have actually hurt yourself. You have to be so careful in every detail of what you ask for, because that is exactly what you will be given.

I've already touched on the matter of 'right' and 'wrong' goals, but now it's time to analyse the subject in more depth. The best way I can do that is by giving a couple of examples. It's all about finding and following your path.

Let's take the example of one of my clients who was training to be a solicitor before we met. His top goal was to pass his final exams. He did everything necessary and worked hard but on the day of the exam he walked into the exam room and collapsed unconscious. This was alarming for a fit young man on the brink of successfully achieving his number one goal, and totally unexpected.

An ambulance came and took him to hospital, and during the journey he regained consciousness. While he lay in his hospital bed having lots of tests done, he had plenty of time for reflection and introspection. Finally, he realised the awful truth. 'I don't want to be a solicitor,' he cried. Hallelujah, finally the penny had dropped!

His parents came to visit him and he told them the news. But why, then, had he spent years studying law? The answer was simple. His parents had wanted him to be a solicitor. They very strongly 'suggested' this path to him and because he was afraid of upsetting them (he was a pleaser) he had taken the idea on board and tried to make it his own. Sometimes the conditioning a person receives is absorbed unconsciously, sometimes semi-consciously and occasionally consciously. In this case he was vaguely aware that the guiding light of the judicial system was not really right for him, but he chose denial as the least scary solution. That is, until his body protested and gave him a huge warning that was more frightening than the truth.

His fear was compounded by the fact that admitting to his parents and even to himself what he *did* want to do, was to him completely terrifying because of the reaction he anticipated from his parents. He could hardly utter the words. I imagine the conversation in the hospital might have gone like this:

> 'So what do you want to do then, son?'
> 'I want to be a writer.'
> 'A writer! A writer! What sort of a career is that for an intelligent boy like you?'
> 'Err, well, a journalist *actually*.'

As you can imagine, by the time the truth finally came out, his father was almost on the verge of an apoplectic fit. However, it was clear that now that his son had finally said it straight out he seemed fully recovered from his fainting fit, and was now cheerful and full of beans. Finally, his father realised that any further resistance on his part to his son's choice of career would be futile and he calmed down. Eventually he actually managed to be quite supportive.

By this time the young man started seeing me for individual one-to-one Life Coaching sessions. He was planning his writing career and he had a new goal, to become a best-selling author. After some discussion it became clear to me that this man probably did have the required talent and he certainly seemed energised by the whole idea, so more than likely it was a 'right' goal for him to pursue. His original goal of wanting to qualify as a solicitor was clearly unsuitable for him.

Now let's say you have a goal and you want to know if it's right for you. How do you find out without going to the lengths of having a physical or mental meltdown? Yes folks, you guessed it. We're back to my fundamental solid gold very simple key question to ask yourself, slightly adapted for this specific purpose, which is *'how do I feel about this goal?'* Really engage your imaginative powers by imagining you have achieved it and ask yourself, *'how do I feel now that I have achieved this?'* or *'How do I feel now that I am doing this?'*

A goal that is right for you comes from your heart, not from your mind. If a goal comes from your mind then either it's the result of conditioning or it's just an ego trip or a fantasy. Your only safe recourse is to trust your instincts and intuition on this. If something about the goal doesn't feel quite right, you don't need to know the reason why, just drop it. If you get a warm feeling or excitement, it's a sure bet it's right for you. It may not be perfect, it may not be your number one goal, but there's no need to restrict yourself to only one goal. Sometimes when you pursue something that feels right it may eventually become your second priority goal, while your genuine top or most important goal reveals itself gradually.

As a coach I always know when a client is homing in on his or her true goals or aspirations because I notice a complete change in body language. I have seen clients change from lugubrious, depressed, monotonous, introverted and lifeless in their behaviour, to lighting up like a Christmas tree and talking with animation, passion and enthusiasm. That change can come about in the twinkling of an eye.

When you hit upon something you are passionate about, the real you comes out and sparkles.

Here's another example, this time a story from my own life. When I earned my living as a carpenter there came a time when I decided I wanted to make more money so I could save a little. So naturally enough I formulated a goal saying I wanted more work.

Within a very short time I found myself working seven days a week. I was also charging higher prices and coining it in. 'Excellent! Brilliant result,' I thought to myself. But there was a problem. I began to resent having no leisure time and I started to feel exhausted. Of course, being inexperienced and youthful I thought I knew best and carried on, refusing to heed the warning signs.

Finally my body rebelled and I became ill with gout. I could no longer stand all day or carry heavy timber and tools up flights of stairs because of the pains in my feet, and sometimes in an ankle or knee.

Eventually I had no option but to cease my business and take to my bed for about three months, during which time I spent all the extra money I had saved on subsistence living while I earned nothing.

It was a salutary and painful lesson in every respect. While I was laid up in bed I also had plenty of time for reflection and introspection. I finally realised that although I had achieved what I asked for, it was not *really* what I wanted. When I recovered I had to start my business all over again from scratch, but this time I took it slowly and built it step-by-step until I reached a level of working five days a week. That's when I decided enough was enough and I kept my work load at that level.

I realised I had actually hurt myself by achieving the 'wrong' goal and that I had better be more careful next time. Incidentally, I realised I had made another classic mistake, which was in assuming the only way to receive more money is to do more work. Of course, if you make that assumption you are shutting the door to creating other income streams. But that's another story for another day.

Don't be deceived by your ego or your conditioning. When you work towards genuine, heartfelt goals your health will improve, all things being equal, and you will feel more abundant. Most important, your life begins to take on real meaning and purpose. You are doing what you were put here to do and you will be taking major steps towards a sustainable state of happiness. That's because you are going with your own inner flow, you are doing whatever makes your heart sing and your work becomes a love affair.

Why goals are so helpful

A correctly expressed goal gives you something to aim at, and it provides a benchmark against which you can measure your progress. But there's much more to it than that. A goal cements your intention so you know you are committed to taking the necessary action. It lets your unconscious know you are serious and it helps you develop a *'can do attitude.'*

Once you have your goal, it also helps you to keep focused, to stay on track and to maintain your motivation. For example, if several potential opportunities that you could pursue pop up simultaneously and you feel in danger of indecision or going off down a dead end street, you can simply ask yourself about each option, one at a time. 'If I do XYZ, will it get me nearer to my goal?' If the answer is 'yes' or 'probably,' then pursue that option. If the answer is 'no' or 'unlikely,' then ignore it. Using this technique you invoke your heightened state of self-awareness and it can save you a great deal of time and frustration on your road towards successful achievement.

Perhaps the most important function of a goal is to help you develop the optimum mindset for creating what you want. I hope you remember in an earlier chapter I explained how your mind manifests whatever is your dominant thought. A well formulated goal automatically gets your mind focused on whatever you want to achieve, because your desired achievement automatically becomes your dominant thought. This is so important it can't be overstated. If you can create and maintain the appropriate dominant thought, the achievement of your goal becomes virtually inevitable. Creating your correctly formulated goal is the most reliable way to do that.

Two great techniques for creating goals

You may have noticed I have emphasised that a goal has to be *correctly formulated* for maximum effectiveness. So exactly how is a goal correctly formulated? I have come across two great methods. One involves writing them down in a particular way, the other is by drawing or mapping them.

How to create a goal

Some years ago, researchers surveyed of a group of students at Harvard University and discovered, when they researched the same group some years later, that *almost 100 per cent of the students who had written their goals down had achieved them all.* Just to make their findings even more convincing, they also discovered that the vast majority of the students who had achieved their goals had written them down.

That means that though there were a few students who achieved their goals without writing them down, the students who did write them down enormously increased their chances of success.

Now of course you might say to me, 'I've been writing goals down for years and years and I'm still not a millionaire,' to which the obvious question is, 'what action did you take towards becoming a millionaire?'

Now I know this sounds obvious and I don't mean to patronise, but I feel I have to say this because so many of the people I meet just don't get it. A goal, written or not, is not a magic recipe, any more than a positive intention is. It's a tool or guide, no more no less, designed to define and clarify where you want to be. *You have to do the work of transforming your life.* There is no substitute for action, just as there is no substitute for experience, and there are no shortcuts.

Someone said to me once, 'hey, I put my vibes out to the Universe, man, I asked the Universe for what I wanted, a new job and a new girlfriend, but hey, it hasn't happened. These goals and affirmations don't work. What did I do wrong?'

Look at it this way. If you want to knock in a nail you need a nail and a hammer. The nail is the material with which you work, the hammer is the tool, and the whole enterprise is guided by your knowledge and experience. If you try to put the nail in without the hammer, it will be very difficult, perhaps impossible. If you use the hammer *you* have to physically wield it. If you get the hammer and just put it down, it will not knock the nail in on its own.

Expecting to achieve a goal without taking action is like laying the hammer down and expecting it to knock in the nail all by itself. It ain't gonna happen!

The first principle of goal setting

The first principle of goal setting is *write it down*. In fact, writing it down many times is even better. Then you can stick it in places where you will be reminded of it at odd times during the day. For example you can write it on several Post-it notes and stick them on your fridge, your bathroom mirror, your wardrobe, above your bed, on the side of your computer screen, even on the kettle! The more you are reminded of it to get it etched deeply into your consciousness, the stronger the effect will be.

Don't forget that writing something down automatically focuses your mind on what you are writing, so immediately you adopt the dominant thought you require.

The second principle of goal setting

The second principle is to *make your goals 'SMART' goals*. SMART is an acronym for Specific, Measurable, Achievable, Realistic and Timely. Let's look at what that means in detail by developing a hypothetical goal according to SMART principles.

Specific means making your goal as specific as possible, and expressed in positive terms. For example, instead of writing 'I'd like to have more money,' it's far more powerful to write, *'I want £5 million.'* You are defining the amount and the denomination, and positively stating 'I want' is far more powerful that 'I'd like to have.' The statement is unambiguous, positive and it leaves no doubt about your meaning and desire.

Measurable means you need a way of measuring your progress and of knowing when the goal is achieved. In this example it's easy, all that's necessary is a routine for checking your bank statements at regular intervals, or statements of investments, or if you are making money by investing in property then by having your property portfolio valued at regular intervals. Of course you also need to keep track of costs and expenses, so maybe having your accountant work out your annual returns is the solution. It doesn't matter how you do it as long as you measure your progress at regular intervals. If you find you're making significant progress you will feel motivated, if you are not you know you have to take remedial action. How do you know you have achieved it? When you are holding your bank statement, or looking at it online, and it shows £5 million credit in your name.

Of course the value might not be in the form of liquid cash in the bank, so at this stage you might decide to rewrite the goal accordingly. For example, you might write 'I want £5 million in a combination of cash and assets,' or if you really do want it all in cash, you might say simply, 'I want £5 million in cash.'

Now your goal is even more specific and it's certainly measurable.

Achievable is probably self-explanatory. I know I said we can create whatever we want, but if we are chasing a 'wrong' goal, it's a pointless exercise. It's not 'right' for you. That's what we mean by unachievable in this context. Bear in mind that there is nothing more demoralizing than working towards a goal that is unachievable. If you are over-ambitious or chasing ego-driven goals you make life much harder for yourself and run the risk of falling flat on your face. This is where it starts to be very important that you know yourself well, for what might be achievable, realistic and meaningful for one person may not be for another.

For example, the fictitious goal we are examining might be easy to achieve if you are Warren Buffet, Sir Alan Sugar or Bill Gates, but if you are a modest person from a poverty stricken background with little financial education it might seem more challenging and take a little longer. For somebody who would rather, let's say, be a physician, it might not be realistic. It really depends on how hungry, how devoted to gaining the necessary knowledge and experience, and how committed to action you are. That's why you need to know yourself inside out and to be scrupulously honest with yourself. You are far more likely to succeed and be happy if you pitch any goal at a level that accords with what you are actually like.

I'm certainly not suggesting you should hide from a challenge, but ask yourself first, 'is it worth it? Do I really want this?'

Realistic means your goal is not only achievable but reasonably grounded within the realms of reality, or even sanity. *Can you really imagine yourself doing this thing?* For somebody who has lost the use of his legs, a goal of climbing to the top of Everest is not realistic. Of course, technically it is possible and I believe it has been done by someone in a wheelchair, but why would you want to put yourself to such pain and struggle? Imagine the stress and anxiety you would cause yourself. *Is it really worth it?* Check yourself out with some serious soul searching, and be honest with yourself. Maybe you need an extreme challenge to prove something to yourself, or maybe you just love mountains. Maybe you are a mountaineer who fell and was permanently injured and now you want to get back on the horse, as it were, to conquer your fear. Whatever your motivation, clearly it's only realistic if you really want it so much you will do literally anything to make it happen.

Timely means you set a date and/or time to achieve your goal. Later, when you create your *action plan,* this timing will need to be extended to your actions, so you will then create an *action schedule.* This is important to guard against procrastination, dithering and indecision, otherwise the achievement of your goal could drag on for ever. You must hold yourself accountable.

Let's say that starting from zero you want to make the first £1.5 million towards your £5 million total in one year. So you put a date on it of one year hence. Your goal, which is now the first of a series of smaller goals, might now look more like this: 'I want £1.5 million in cash by June 28th. 2011.'

OK, that tells it like it is and nails it down.

By doing it this way you break your major goal down into a series of smaller sub-goals which you can tackle one step at a time. This makes your overall goal more realistic and more likely to be achievable. This tactical approach is especially helpful if you feel a danger of being overwhelmed by the seeming enormity of the task.

The third principle of goal setting

As I have said many times already, it's also very important to make sure your goals are aligned with your core values and beliefs. If not it will be very hard to achieve them, and even if you do, you are likely to remain unhappy. Maybe at this stage you could ask yourself, 'what do I want the £5 million for?' For the sake of argument let's say you want it for a new house where you live, a holiday home abroad, a new yacht and a visit to the carnival in Rio de Janeiro.

At the same time you check that these desires are really coming from your heart and you are not merely trying to keep up with the Jones's, or satisfy some ego fantasy of your own.

At this point you may work out that you can manage all those with only £3 million, created via two sub-goals over two years. You can then rewrite your overall goal to say 'I want £3 million in cash by June 28th. 2012.' Bear in mind, when you have achieved that goal there's nothing to stop you creating a new goal to make the other £2 million you wanted before. In fact it's a good strategy, because the second time you do it, you should find it easier and less stressful. Having achieved your first overall goal once by means of two sub-goals over two years, you will have the confidence to know you can do it again.

Before you start, ask yourself, 'am I the sort of person who can make big money in a short time.' Then you will be able to judge whether this goal and its timing are realistic for you or not.

Can you see the benefit of developing your goal this way? By reducing the amount you want you almost certainly achieve your goal more quickly, so even if you go on to the second goal you can, in the meantime, buy the house and holiday home, the yacht and the holiday and start enjoying them sooner. You have also arrived at a less daunting figure, so the fear of failure and the anxiety that produces is less. Perhaps most important of all, you have guarded against getting stressed out from being over-ambitious.

The fourth principle of goal setting

Having said that, beware of the mistake of asking for less than you want. It maybe because you feel guilty about asking for so much; perhaps you feel greedy, avaricious or in some way uncomfortable; maybe you feel unworthy; or maybe you simply fear failure so you go for something apparently 'easier,' or less demanding.

Assuming you feel passionate about your true goal, all of the above are merely manifestations of your saboteur. They are negative self-judgments and come from your conditioning. Hence you can safely ignore them.

How can I be so sure? Because you have carefully checked with yourself that these goals come from your heart and they align with your core values and beliefs. You have, haven't you? Don't forget, it's imperative to maintain your awareness and tune in to what you are feeling so you can immediately identify a true goal and recognise your saboteur as soon as he shows himself, and send him packing!

As with all things, a correct balance produces the desired result. If you ask for less than you want you will never be satisfied or happy. If you ask for more than you want you create unnecessary stress and extra work. *The art of goal setting is to ask for precisely what you want.* It really is as simple as that.

The fifth principle of goal setting

This principle acknowledges that you can go on refining your goal ad infinitum and one very worthwhile exercise is to edit it so it becomes as succinct as possible, yet without losing its full meaning. This way your goal is much easier to remember and you are more likely to think of it accurately and in its entirety more often.

The sixth principle of goal setting

Another great technique (the sixth principle) I learned from Christopher Howard, facilitator of the three-day programme called *Breakthrough to Success*, but many other coaches use this too. The idea is to harness the power of visualisation by bringing the achievement of your goal into the present. This then gives your goal the power, immediacy and reality of this moment. It means you visualise your goal as *already achieved*.

Let's say today's date is 28th. June 2010 and you are creating a goal to be achieved in two years from now. Using this technique this means your goal now looks something like this: 'It is now June 28th. 2012 and I am looking at my bank statement, which shows I am £3 million in credit.' As you can see, this simple sentence says it all. It states the amount and denomination specifically, it shows how the achievement has been measured, it has been checked for achievability, it's realistic and it has a timeline. As it's expressed in terms of the present, when you read or say it to yourself you imagine you have achieved it already. This technique is designed to fill you with confidence. Now all you have to do is take appropriate action.

The seventh principle of goal setting

The seventh principle is *you do not necessarily have to know how the goal will be achieved at the time you are creating it.* When you move on to develop your action plan, all you need to know to begin is what your first step will be. For the moment you don't even need to know that. This is the goal setting stage and the object of this exercise is to be sure of what you want to achieve or create and set about expressing it in words as succinctly as possible. So if you have a daring goal that makes your heart leap and it suits you to the core, don't abandon it because it *seems* impossible.

Osho put it very bluntly when he said, 'be realistic, plan for a miracle.' Never forget that this world and everything in it is built on miracles.

Goal mapping

This is another very powerful technique for creating goals. It's especially effective for people who learn and express themselves in predominantly visual ways for it uses your visual imagination to create your goals in the form of pictures that you draw yourself.

It is inappropriate and unnecessary for me to repeat or plagiarise Brian Maynes' material here, especially as it's a whole subject in itself. My only comment is you don't have to be any sort of an artist to use this technique. I tried it myself and I'm hopeless at drawing, but it worked very effectively for me nevertheless.

If you want to try it, all the details are in the book entitled *Goal Mapping* by Brian Mayne, and you can get lots of information by visiting www.liftinternational.com

Summary

- Goals are your friends, but they are not the be all and end all
- A goal is a statement of what you desire to achieve – it defines what you aspire to
- *Just as important as stating your goals is getting to know yourself inside out* so you can tell which goals are 'right' for you and which are red herrings
- Desire alone is not enough. It must be accompanied by appropriate action
- Action is the only thing that can bring about change in your life. If you take no action there will be no change; if you do take action, something is bound to happen, though not necessarily change. It's simple cause and effect
- Einstein implies we can solve our problems by changing our thoughts, because different thoughts will produce different actions, and different actions will produce different results
- If you don't like the results you are getting, change your thinking and change your actions
- Tune in to your inner voice to feel intuitively when it's right for you to persevere or when it's better to quit and do something different
- The real art of personal development is in achieving goals that make you happy, goals that really get you to where you want to be
- You must be careful in every detail of what you ask for, because that is exactly what you will be given
- *A goal that is 'right' for you comes from your heart, not from your mind.* Learn to trust your instincts and intuition on this
- If something about your goal doesn't feel right, you don't need to know why, just drop it. If you get a warm feeling or excitement, it's probably right for you
- When you hit upon something you are passionate about, the real you comes out and sparkles
- When you do whatever makes your heart sing, you are going with your own inner flow and your work becomes a love affair
- A correctly expressed goal gives you something to aim at, and it provides a benchmark against which you can measure your progress

- A goal cements your intention and your desire so you know you are committed to taking the necessary action, it lets your unconscious know you are serious and it helps you develop a *'can do attitude'*
- A goal helps you to keep focused, stay on track and maintain your motivation
- The most important function of a goal is to help you develop the optimum mindset for creating what you want by ensuring what you want to achieve becomes your dominant thought
- A well formulated goal automatically gets your mind focused on whatever you want to achieve. This is so important it can't be overstated
- If you can create and maintain the appropriate dominant thought, the achievement of your goal becomes virtually inevitable
- The art of goal setting is to ask for precisely what you want
- Be honest with yourself. You are far more likely to succeed if you pitch any goal at a level that accords with what you are really like
- Goal Mapping is another powerful technique for creating goals. It's especially effective for people who learn and express themselves in visual ways

Questions to ask yourself

- How do I feel about this goal?
- Imagine you have achieved it and ask yourself, 'how do I feel now that I have achieved this?'
- How do I feel now that I am doing this?

The seven essential principles of goal setting

- The first principle – *write it down*
- The second principle – *make your goals SMART goals*
- The third principle – *ensure your goals are aligned with your core values and beliefs*
- The fourth principle – *ask for precisely what you want, no more, no less*
- The fifth principle – *edit your goal until it becomes as succinct as possible, yet without losing its full meaning*

- The sixth principle – *visualise the achievement of your goal in the present, as if it is already achieved*
- The seventh principle – *you do not necessarily have to know how the goal will be achieved at the time you are creating it*

The five characteristics of a SMART goal

- ***Specific*** – make your goal as specific as possible, and expressed in positive terms
- ***Measurable*** – you need a way of measuring your progress and of knowing when your goal is achieved
- ***Achievable*** – there is nothing more demoralizing than working towards a goal that is unachievable. Remember, what might be achievable for one person may not be so for you
- ***Realistic*** – your goal not only needs to be achievable but reasonably grounded within the realms of reality, or even sanity, and it must be worth the effort
- ***Timely*** – always specify a date and/or time by which your goal is to be achieved so you can hold yourself accountable

18

Your Maximum Creative Flow

If you follow the herd, guess what you end up standing in.
Dr Wayne Dyer

Life becomes far more enjoyable and you achieve what you want more easily and with a lot less stress when you are in your *maximum creative flow*. But what is your *maximum creative flow*, how do you find it and how do you know when you are in it?

Some people just know what it is and instinctively slot into it, whereas others, those who have lost touch with who they really are, have to put in some work to find out (this is discussed in more detail in the following chapter). It's a question of being acutely aware of how you feel, and how closely what's happening in your life aligns with your core values and beliefs. The best way I can explain is to give an example.

Let's imagine you are born Wolfgang Amadeus Mozart. OK, I know it sounds ridiculous, but bear with me because this will illustrate my point perfectly. As a youngster, everywhere you go you hear beautiful music in your head, wonderful music pours out of you, so one day you say the obvious thing to your dad, 'when I grow up to be a man, I want to be a great composer.'

Now let's pretend your father is a bit unimaginative and risk averse and he just doesn't get it. His reply goes along the lines of, 'no, no Wolfgang, absolutely not. I've just lined you up for an apprenticeship with Joseph Hegel and Sons, builders to the gentry, so you can learn bricklaying. It's a much safer career, it's respectable and you will never go hungry.'

Let's press the pause button for a moment while we consider the scenario so far. As a Life Coach and someone who has been around the block a few times I can tell you that this exact situation comes up time and time again in real life. Someone else, usually your parents or teacher, thinks they know better than you what you should do with your life, and they are not backward in coming forward and laying their opinions vehemently on the line.

This is a recipe for disaster, especially when you are a defenceless child or adolescent. At such a tender age you are bound to suffer self-doubt. After all how do you know what to believe, how do you know you are right, how do you know you can trust your intuitive, instinctive gut feeling, how do you know your passionate interest is not just a passing fad? How do you know that no person other than yourself can possibly know what is best for you? You have no life experience. It is usual for children to believe and trust their parents, teachers, mentors and role models, so it's very easy for you to be manipulated without even realising it. The net result in many cases is that you are totally undermined and your self-belief and confidence fly straight out of the window, in some cases never to return.

Unless your passion is so strong and your talent or genius so obvious, as of course it was for Mozart, you may well agree that someone else's idea is better for you than your own. You might be persuaded to believe it's too risky to pursue your real passion, you might feel you are inadequate or incapable, or perhaps saddest of all, you might believe your passion is not worthy or does not carry sufficient gravitas to command respect. All in all, to persist with any ideas of your own might seem too scary. The worst scenario is if your parents insist despite your vociferous protestations and you are bullied into following a path that for you can be no more than second best whether you like it or not.

I have many clients who fall into that category and that, in my experience, is why the vast majority of those who beat a path to my door are people of somewhat mature years who realise they have spent too long *not* doing what they love. They feel damaged and sick at heart as a result. Their top goal, now that they have realised this, is to re-invent themselves so they can at last live out their passions and lead a life of meaning, purpose and fulfilment. Some are so far removed from who they really are that they can't remember what their passions are, what they truly want or what their calling might be. And so the detective work must begin, because as sure as the sun will rise tomorrow, it's in there somewhere. Deep inside, you *do* know what makes your heart sing, but you may have blotted it out and courage might be required to re-connect, to remember and to acknowledge what it is.

At last we come to the essence of what my work, and this book, is all about. As I said at the beginning, *we each already have the necessary ingredients within ourselves to be happy and fulfilled, so there is no need to achieve anything in the outside world on that score.* The search for happiness has to be focused within, and really it's a process of re-discovery and re-balancing. If you are to achieve the happiness you yearn for, there is no room for compromise. Second best simply will not do.

Once you find your passion and start to enact it, the supporting goals most of us focus on – a house, a career, a partner, wealth, abundance, recreational pursuits, and so on – can be achieved virtually as a matter of routine procedure. It becomes easy to decide which of these aspirations are worthwhile spending your valuable time on because you are only interested in the ones that come from your heart and support your passion. The rest can be allowed to fall away naturally.

Notice I refer to such goals as supporting goals, as opposed to primary goals, and this is an important distinction because, before the time of your heightened awareness and the discovery of your passion, or what your heart wants you to do, these might have been mistaken as primary goals. If that were to occur, then in your effort to build a life of enduring happiness, satisfaction and fulfilment, you would then be missing the fundamental ingredient – your passion.

Often someone will say to me, 'I don't know what I want to do or what my passion is,' and when that happens my instinct is disbelief. The person may sincerely believe that what they said is true, but they are short-changing themselves because we all know what we feel passionate about or what our gift is, but sometimes it's hidden or deeply buried so we don't know that we know. What to do if that's your situation? More about that in a minute. First let's finish discussing our Mozart example.

Imagine your father, Mozart Senior, kicks up such a fuss, lays down the law so strongly and generally makes your life hell so much that you give up all thoughts of music and do the bricklaying apprenticeship instead. Clearly this is not a great move because it's not your calling. Even if you study and learn all there is to know about bricklaying, even if you practise for hours until you master the skills, it's a pointless exercise because you will never be happy. You are not doing what is meaningful to you, you are doing something that is meaningful to your father, so let him learn bricklaying!

Moreover, if you do something that doesn't make you happy, your customers don't benefit either because they sense unconsciously that your heart is not in your work. Doing work that doesn't suit you is the epitome of what I call *pushing the river* and it's the exact opposite of getting into your flow.

If on the other hand, as young Mozart you are able to convince your father to your point of view, the possibility exists for you to excel and develop your talent or genius. Genius is nothing other than you tuning into your creative gift so precisely that it is able to express itself though you to the full. It's like water flowing through a pipe, you are a conduit and what is created flows through you. You have nothing to do with it.

When it's at its optimum, your *maximum creative flow* has two dimensions – you are flowing through your life, and what you create flows through you. When you achieve that subtle balance, I can only describe the feeling as awesome in the true sense of the word. Nothing can stop your flow, and what is created is magnificent.

OK, so back to you as the young Mozart. You have now won the permission to do your own thing so you start by composing simple pieces and you learn rapidly. Maybe you find a great teacher and study music in great depth. Eventually you master your art and develop your experience and start to create something so beautiful, original and unique it far exceeds anything anyone has ever heard before. At this time you are in your *maximum creative flow*, which is the exact opposite of pushing the river.

Of course, there are many factors that can obstruct your flow of creativity, for example worrying about money, a crisis of self-doubt, the trauma of divorce or bereavement, negative feedback or input, or a negative attitude, so don't be deluded. *Just because you may have found your maximum creative flow does not necessarily mean your life will automatically become a bed of roses overnight.* It means that *the possibility now exists* for your life to be a bed of roses. Think of yourself, in the beginning, as a seed that needs careful nurturing if you want to grow strong, healthy and happy. You must keep your focus.

In real life, as I am sure most of you know, Mozart's father was very quick to spot his young son's talent. When he was little more than five years old, Wolfgang was playing the clavier and composing simple pieces. His father promoted him vigorously, taking him around the crowned heads and patrons of European culture and showing off his prodigy to the full. Mozart was so switched on, his massive body of incredible work was created in a very short and troubled lifetime. Unfortunately, he was a man of excesses and was obsessional about his work to the extent that it seems he was completely unable to find any kind of inner balance. His personal life was a shambles, he alienated people and he died young, lonely and impoverished at the age of thirty-four. You could argue he had done what he was sent here to do and there was no need for him to stay longer, but of course we shall never know whether that is true or not.

Many great creative geniuses lived short and tortured lives, and in every case it was because they failed to find an inner balance. Obvious examples include Jimi Hendrix, Vincent van Gogh, Billie Holiday, Henri de Toulouse-Lautrec – the list is endless. By contrast Leonard Cohen, Michelangelo, Leonardo da Vinci, Eric Clapton, Mick Jagger, Rembrandt and Neil Diamond enjoyed (or are enjoying) long and august careers. From this we deduce that being in your *maximum creative flow* is only one side of the coin. A good balance is the other side. Both are absolutely essential if long-term happiness is your goal.

One of the best ways to achieve that balance is through meditation, so once again I refer you to Chapter 5 where my simple meditation technique is described. I urge you to ignore any resistance you might have and do it regularly. I assure you, the time spent will pay off handsomely.

Before we return to your *maximum creative flow*, let's quickly summarise the two golden rules for finding lasting happiness, because they are crucial and very relevant in the context of this chapter.

The two golden rules for finding lasting happiness

1) *To thine own self be true. Don't compromise and don't allow yourself to be derailed or manipulated. Go for exactly what you want, no more, no less.*
2) *Take a balanced approach. There's no need to become obsessional.*

I don't know what I want to do with my life

Sooner or later, when I get a client who is not happy with what they are doing, I will start asking questions such as, 'what are you passionate about?' or 'what makes your heart sing?' or 'what are you good at?' If the person is stumped, as is often the case, I might try, 'what do other people say you are good at?' or a brilliant question which I believe comes from peak performance expert Tony Robbins, 'if you knew you couldn't fail, what would you start tomorrow?' Finally, if the person is still stuck for an answer I might try, 'if money were no object, if you had no responsibilities, and you were absolutely free to do whatever you like, what would that be?'

Funnily enough, sometimes a simple question like, 'what did you do yesterday,' or 'what do you do at weekends,' or even better, 'what did you love doing when you were a child,' sometimes does the trick in providing that vital clue that can lead us through a tiny gap in the person's defences.

If you have lost touch with that special something that absolutely turns you on, you may well have to do a great deal of introspection. These questions are designed to help remind you, so ask them to yourself in private quiet moments and try to be open to whatever might pop into your consciousness. You may get a full answer or maybe just a tiny clue, but even the latter is enough for you to embark on a full scale enquiry. Maybe some research and experimentation will be necessary.

It is also possible you may get many answers and be unsure about which are the true ones, so trial and error may be part of your process. Don't hesitate to try things out, constantly monitoring yourself as you go by asking yourself, 'how do I feel about this?' Also, ask lots of questions to people who are already doing something similar.

Visualisation and role-playing is another great way to spark off your creative imagination. Let's say you have an idea that maybe hill walking is your passion. Visualise yourself walking in the Lake District or imagine you are ascending Kilimanjaro. Try acting it out as if in a role-play exercise, either on your own or with a trusted friend, perhaps even with your dog, just to try to get a feel. While you visualise, make it as real as possible and use self-monitoring questions to give you clues. For example, ask yourself, 'now I am walking in the foothills of the Himalayas, I can feel the dust, I can smell the sweet, sharp fresh air, I see the spectacular snow-clad, sunlit peak of Everest towering above me, how do I feel about this?' Don't be afraid to test things out either in your imagination, or experiment for real. Do you feel passionate about being there? Don't be put off if you get answers like, 'I feel terrified,' or 'I'm exhausted.' In spite of those feelings, in your mind's eye you still might love being there, in which case it was worth facing your fear and exhaustion.

Don't let money, or a lack of it, be an excuse to give up

Many people make the mistake of trying to think of something they love that they could do to earn a living or make money, but I'm not talking about money just yet. It may well be that you start doing something you love as a leisure pursuit and do something else for a living at first. Maybe you start doing what you love and some unforeseen way of remuneration grows out of it, or maybe you just do what you love for no other reason than you love doing it. In such a situation, your rewards will be abundance, but not necessarily money.

At this stage I implore you please to keep an open mind about matters of money. It's very important not to pre-judge, because the most unexpected things can and do happen when you follow your heart, but only if you allow them to by keeping your mind open. You might block unforeseen possibilities if you dismiss something because you can't see the end game when you are at the beginning, or because you are rigidly attached to a particular outcome that may or may not materialise. So don't pre-judge and don't let money be an excuse for not exploring something you are interested in. Most important, don't let money (or the lack of it) limit the scope of your thinking, feeling and imagining. Forget about it for the moment.

You may believe your aspiration is an impossible dream but I have seen people make an art form of achieving the impossible. So I repeat, don't pre-judge, and expect the unexpected.

Sometimes a person will say 'I'd love to do so and so, but I can't afford the training.' I repeat, don't worry about the money or how your goal can be achieved just yet – we're going to go through that step-by-step in the fullness of time. At the moment this is not anything to do with money, this is to do with finding your passion, talent, calling, gift or vocation. It maybe necessary to do some research or to work out a strategy or action plan before you start taking action. If you want that training badly enough, you will find a way, maybe in the most unexpected form. *At this stage all we need to find out is what we passionately want to do or be. The only thing that's important is to start believing it is possible.*

This subject is well illustrated by my own experience, which may be of interest. I separated from my ex-wife in early 1983 and landed up for a while living in a shared communal house in London with nine other people.

I knew I had spent too many years pushing rivers and travelling on paths that were totally unsuitable for me, and I had become quite depressed. My self-belief had taken many severe knocks and I was about as far away from my flow as a man could be. I was aware that I must now embark on a campaign of healing and recovery, whatever that might mean. Then one morning over breakfast I thought to myself, 'I'm on my own now, I can start my life all over again and I can do whatever I like.'

Hmm, exciting, except at that point I drew a blank. Then the following internal dialogue with myself began:

> 'So what do I want to do?'
> 'Dunno, can't remember.'
> 'Oh yeah, I remember. I want to have fun.'
> 'Errrr, how do I do that? Can't remember.'
> 'Right.'

Then I recommenced my breakfast. After a few minutes, as I sat pensively munching my cornflakes, a word came into my mind, seemingly all by itself, and that word was 'boats'.

With that tiny clue my memory was suddenly liberated and I remembered I had always been interested in boats ever since I was a child, and I had always wanted to learn to sail. I had buried this fascination because I thought it was impossible. As a child, I didn't know anyone who owned a boat, my parents were not interested in the slightest and somehow I had taken on board the belief that only the mega-rich could sail. I had also taken on the assumption that you have to own a boat to be able to sail. I realise now I had also assumed the belief that becoming one of those mega-rich people would be impossible for me. So by a series of erroneous beliefs and assumptions I had thwarted myself by believing it was an impossible aspiration and until that very morning over breakfast, to shield myself from my disappointment, I had kept my desire to go to sea firmly buried. So convincingly, in fact, that I had forgotten all about it – or so it seemed.

The simple truth is, we don't know what's possible until we give it a try.

When I left college I had started trying to establish a career, and when I got married and realised I was about to become a father, all thoughts of boating has been well and truly banished for ever, because we had no spare money and my time was fully occupied with my domestic focus.

To cut a long story short, the inner conversation I had with myself that morning led me very soon to start dinghy sailing on a lake, then dinghy ownership, then training in yachting and eventually through a series of boat purchases and sales, to yacht ownership. I spent a lot of money on training over the years and there was a thought of becoming a professional instructor or skipper, but in the end even though I got the qualification I decided to remain an amateur.

Why am I telling you this? Because I want to illustrate what pursuing one of my great passions has done for me. I am convinced that learning to be a skipper and going sailing has been greatly instrumental in the gradual dispersal of the depression I used to suffer. It has enabled me to discover many inner resources I never knew I had. Even my boundaries grew stronger and self-belief ceased to be a problem. Of course there were also other factors that contributed to those changes, but sailing gave me the satisfaction of significant achievement, and it still does.

As for the question of balance, as I delight in telling people, sailing is the perfect antidote to writing and coaching. Both the latter activities are totally sedentary and, much as I love writing and coaching, I would soon become a couch potato if I never went out and got some exercise, fresh air and physical challenge.

Even worse, if you pursue only your main passion and nothing else you will soon become stale and fed up, and let's be blunt, who wants to be coached by someone who is stale, and who wants to read a book written by someone who is fed up? Neither is an inspiring prospect! With that in mind, you could argue that my going sailing is actually good for my business and my clients, indirectly.

The converse is also true, for me at any rate. If I spent my whole life at sea and never did any writing or coaching, I'd soon be hankering for the shore, a nice warm bed that doesn't move, and a PC or laptop on a solid desk.

Returning briefly to the point of someone saying they think they know what they want to do, but they can't because they'd have to do a training or obtain a qualification before they could do it. At this point I usually have to restrain myself from shaking the person into waking up, and instead try calmly to point out, 'when you say 'I can't,' what you really mean is 'I choose not to,' or 'I won't.'

Simple, one would have thought. If you can solve your problem by being trained or educated, or getting qualified, just do it and then the door will open for you to pursue the passion you've dreamed about all your life. This is actually so in many cases and in most major Western cities nowadays it's possible to train in virtually anything you can think of. If it's a countryside pursuit you want to train in, then opportunities abound all over the place. We are virtually snowed under with opportunities, so please don't let me hear you say lack of training is stopping you. If necessary get a job washing dishes in a restaurant, or sweep the road and empty dustbins, to pay for your training. These are perfectly honourable occupations and they are absolutely valid strategies. Lots of people do exactly that, or its equivalent.

We've already mentioned the objection or self-sabotage pattern that sometimes kicks in next. At this point the person in question will decide categorically that they don't want to invest the money, and also perhaps the time, in training unless they can know for sure that they will be able to make a living out of their chosen path. They are not sure if they'll be good at it, or even that they'll love it as much as they think they will, or if there will be too much competition for them to be successful, or if they have what it takes.

This is when I usually fall silent and wring my hands in despair because if a person doesn't believe in themselves, their vision or their passion enough to take the plunge, if the risk seems so scary they simply can't bring themselves to come out of their comfort zone, then how will they ever get what they want. Sometimes, as Christopher Howard reminds us, you have to 'play all out' and see what opportunities arise. Of course there can be no guarantees of a desired outcome, except the guarantee that if you take no action, you will change nothing.

Even more alarming, this sort of person will then blame life or his desired path for being too hard and impossible to achieve, but the cold, hard truth is that the person has stopped himself. He has created a limitation for himself to avoid sticking his neck out and going for what he wants, and he refuses to remove it or work around it.

Training in something you love is the fast track to success, plain and simple, and it makes your life easy! But of course you have enough self-belief to follow through.

There is only the clarion call from your heart to rely on. If you are really worried about investing in yourself, here's what to do to become unstuck:

Visualise yourself doing your training and then going on to practise the actual discipline for real. Put as much detail as possible into your visualisation, then ask yourself the all important question we have asked so many times already, 'now that I'm doing this, how do I feel about it?' By asking your heart for guidance in this way and being scrupulously honest about the answer that arises, it will tell you what to do (or not do). Then it's up to you to find the courage to proceed.

Final warning: Beware the voices of fear coming from your conditioning and don't let them overpower the true voice of your heart. You might have to feel the fear and do it anyway. Tuning in with moments of silence and stillness while listening carefully for what sounds authentic and what lacks the ring of truth is the way to distinguish between them. Don't try to figure it out. Ask yourself, 'how do I feel about this?'

The Law of Attraction

This is a very misunderstood subject, so let's try to shine a little light on it. The Law of Attraction actually has everything to do with finding and acting upon your passion and getting into your *maximum creative flow*. When you do that, you attract what you need to manifest the things you want. That's how the Law of Attraction works.

The misunderstanding that commonly occurs is if you believe that the Universe provides you with what you want – just because you asked for it. Of course this is nonsense. It may seem as if that's what happened, but in reality *you* have created what you want by adopting a suitable mindset and then taking appropriate action.

So let's be absolutely clear about this – if you don't take action, nothing changes. You may practise positive thinking, you may do affirmations until you're blue in the face, you can write your goals down, you can change your mindset, you can pray, you can meditate, you can talk to God, whatever; but none of that will make a blind bit of difference if you don't take action.

The Law of Attraction will not do anything of itself. It's just a means, a psychological trick to help you attain the right mindset so you feel empowered and so you believe, to slightly paraphrase the words of President Barack Obama, 'yes, I can.'

Here's the most important bit and I want to emphasise it: *when you find and start enacting your passion and enter your maximum creative flow, you automatically start to create the desired mindset that empowers you to create what you want in your life.* The Law of Attraction is nothing other than a sweet sounding metaphor because when you get what you desire it feels as if your goal has come to you, and in a way it has. But it would be more accurate to say *you* have created what you want.

This is vital for your self-belief. You and you alone create the life you want. Once you take that empowering mindset on board and learn to use it, you no longer have to suffer from life happening to you, as it were.

Let's go to another of my boating examples: occasionally someone will say to me, 'Oooh, you're so lucky having a yacht.' This immediately makes me feel impatient, because of the bit they didn't say, which goes something like … 'and I wish I had one too,' which of course they could, if they wanted it seriously enough. Instead of feeling envious, if that person got off his backside he could make it happen! This is how the conversation typically continues:

Me: 'What do you mean, lucky? What's luck got to do with it? I worked my backside off to get that boat!'
Him: 'Alright, but you are lucky being a skipper and knowing how to navigate and all that.'
Me: 'What are you talking about? It's got nothing to do with luck! Do you have any idea how much training I've done and how many years of practise I put in before I felt even vaguely competent?'

OK, hold it right there for a minute. Let's emphasise this one more time: *Life's too short for wishing, hoping, having good intentions or being envious of someone else's 'good fortune.' Let's get over our victimhood, decide what we truly want and take action to make it happen.*

The man in the above conversation is talking as if I attracted a boat into my life, complete with the necessary knowledge to sail it on the high seas, as if by magic. In fact a great deal of soul searching and a lot of hard work, application, time and focus were required. The only reason I was able to keep going was because I knew I was in my *maximum creative flow,* even through the hard times, even when I felt overwhelmed by the enormity of what I was trying to master, and even through times of severe self-doubt and downright fear.

I was able to get into my *flow* easily because I was pursuing something I passionately loved doing, and my *flow* carried me through. If it had been merely 'a good idea', I never would have stayed the course.

I'm telling you this not to brag or to try to show how clever I am. I'm just trying to demonstrate how anyone with a passion and a devotion to their achievement can create whatever they want. Your passion is what keeps you motivated, because you have to really, really want your goal. Of course, it would have been much easier just to give up and gaze wistfully while other people go sailing by. I want my example to inspire you just enough to find your passion and use it to shape the world you want.

Let's finish the conversation.

> *Me:* 'Let me ask you a question. Is sailing your passion? Would you go to any lengths to learn how to do it? Is your heart saying you must get a boat?'
> *Him:* 'Well, not exactly. It just looked like a nice idea.'
> *Me:* 'Well in that case forget about boats and sailing. It'll never happen. Go and find out what your true passion is.'
> *Him:* 'I'd love to learn horse riding, but how could I ever own a horse?'
> *Me:* 'Now we might be getting somewhere. I don't know, but you do. Maybe you don't have to own a horse, why not learn to ride first? You used the word 'love'. If the idea of learning horse riding is truly coming from your heart, you will find a way of taking that essential first step. But first you have to believe it's possible for you.'
> *Him:* 'It is coming from my heart, but I just can't believe it's possible for me to do it.'
> *Me:* 'Then act as if you do believe in your ability to learn to ride. Just decide what to do first, get focused and get on with it.'

Whatever your passion, start with a realistically achievable goal. In this example, owning your own horse is an unnecessary major responsibility, not to mention the cost, and if you know nothing of horses and riding the idea is far more fraught with difficulties than it need be. To start with you can simply pitch up at a riding school and start learning. Later, when and if it arises, you can think about ownership. Remember, whatever your goal, think tortoise and hare and only take on bite-sized chunks. Then you won't give up because of feeling overwhelmed.

Exercise 15: How to create what you want in your life

(We have included a form at the end of the explanation of the exercise, but if you don't want to write in this book, you can download and print the form from www.thefivepillarsofhappiness.com).

HOW TO CREATE WHAT YOU WANT IN YOUR LIFE

Here in a nutshell is my simple seven step process to create (rather than attract) what you want in your life. With a little practise you should soon master the technique:

1) Define your passion, calling, talent, gift, vocation or whatever you want to call it. Start to believe in yourself, or *act as if.*
2) Create your goal and write it down succinctly, unambiguously and in the present, *using only positive terms*. Start to visualise yourself doing or being or having whatever your goal is.
3) Make a list of options, perhaps with the aid of some self-brainstorming, and choose the few that you feel the most attracted to as potential action points.
4) Create your action plan. *Write it down*, even if you only know the first two or three steps, and put dates by when you will have actioned each step. Make sure your steps and dates are realistic and achievable.
5) *Take your first step.* Then your second step. Then the third, and so on. Keep going.
6) Keep monitoring yourself as you go along to make sure that what is happening is still exactly what you want *(how do I feel about this?)*
7) Know when you have achieved your goal and celebrate!

CREATE WHAT I WANT (FORM)

Date:
My passion:
My goal:
Options:

Shortlist of options:
Action plan:
My first step(s):
How do I feel?
Goal achieved?

I hope I have demonstrated that the Law of Attraction is not some nebulous, abstract, magic force out there somewhere in the Universe. It's within you and it's your power to create whatever you want in your life. That's why it should really be called *The Law of Creation.* The trick is knowing how to use it.

Summary

- Life becomes far more enjoyable and you achieve what you want more easily and with less stress when you are in your *maximum creative flow*
- Believing someone else knows better than you about what you should do with your life is a recipe for disaster, especially when you are a defenceless adolescent
- Deep inside you know what your passion is but it may be hidden or deeply buried. Courage will be needed to reconnect, remember and acknowledge it
- The search for happiness has to be focused within, and it's a process of rediscovery and rebalancing
- If you are to achieve the happiness you yearn for, there is no room for compromise
- Once you find your passion and start to enact it, achieving supporting goals become a matter of routine procedure. It's easy to decide which of those aspirations are worth pursuing because you are only interested in those that come from your heart
- When you work at something that doesn't make you happy, your customers don't benefit because they can tell unconsciously that your heart is not in it
- Doing work that doesn't suit you is the epitome of *pushing the river* and it's the exact opposite of getting into your flow
- If on the other hand you follow your unique path by doing what you love, the possibility exists for you to excel and develop your talent or genius
- Genius occurs when you tune into your creative gift so accurately that it is able to express itself though you to the full
- Your *maximum creative flow* has two dimensions – you are flowing through your life, and what you create flows through you. In that state, nothing can stop you, and what is created is magnificent

- When you are in your *maximum creative flow,* it's the exact opposite of pushing the river and it means that *the possibility now exists* for your life to be a bed of roses
- Many great creative geniuses lived short and tortured lives, and in every case it was because they failed to find an inner balance
- A good balance is absolutely essential if long-term happiness is your goal, and one of the best ways to achieve it is through meditation
- Some research and experimentation may be necessary to assess how passionate you really are about something
- Don't hesitate to try things out, constantly monitoring yourself as you go by asking yourself, 'how do I feel about this?'
- Visualisation and role-playing are great ways to spark off your creative imagination
- Never let money, or lack of it, be an excuse to give up or avoid making a start in finding your passion, talent or calling
- It's very important not to pre-judge, because the most unexpected things can and do happen when you follow your heart
- At this stage the only thing that's important is to start believing it is possible
- We don't know what's possible for us until we give it a try
- There can be no guarantees of a desired outcome, except the guarantee that if you take no action, you will change nothing
- When you say 'I can't because I don't have the training,' what you really mean is 'I choose not to,' or 'I won't'
- Training in something you love is the fast track to success, plain and simple, and it makes your life easy!
- If you are worried about investing in yourself, visualise yourself doing your training and then going on to practise the actual discipline for real. Then ask yourself, 'how do I feel about this?'
- The Law of Attraction is about finding and acting upon your passion because when you do that you attract what you need to manifest what you want
- *You,* not the Universe, create what you want by adopting a suitable mindset and then taking appropriate action. If you don't take action, nothing happens

- When you find and start enacting your passion and enter your *maximum creative flow,* you automatically start to create a mindset that empowers you to create what you want in your life
- Anyone with a passion and a devotion to their achievement can create whatever they want. Your passion is what keeps you motivated
- If necessary *act as if* you believe in your ability to make what you want happen. Just decide what to do first, get focused and get on with it

The two golden rules for finding lasting happiness

1) *To thine own self be true. Don't compromise and don't allow yourself to be derailed or manipulated. Go for exactly what you want, no more, no less.*
2) *Take a balanced approach. There's no need to become obsessional.*

Questions to remind yourself if you've lost touch with your passion

1) *What are you passionate about?*
2) *What makes your heart sing?*
3) *What are you good at?*
4) *What do other people say you are good at?*
5) *If you knew you couldn't fail, what would you start tomorrow?*
6) *If money were no object, if you had no responsibilities, and you were absolutely free to do whatever you like, what would that be?*
7) *What did you do yesterday?*
8) *What do you do at weekends?*
9) *What was your favourite thing to do when you were a child?*

Try to be open to whatever might pop into your consciousness. You may get a full answer or maybe just a tiny clue, but even the latter is enough for you to embark on a full scale enquiry.

Monitor yourself as you try things out by asking:

10) *How do I feel about this?*

Exercise to create what you want

Exercise 15: How to create what you want in your life.

19

To What do you Feel Attracted?

> *Question: 'When is the best time to plant an apple tree?'*
> *Answer: '20 years ago, but failing that, right now!'*
>
> Ancient Chinese Proverb

If at this point you still don't know what your passion, calling or talent is, you can approach this from another angle by asking yourself another powerful question, 'to what do I feel attracted?'

Exercise 16: To what do I feel attracted?

TO WHAT DO I FEEL ATTRACTED?

This may well open new avenues of enquiry because it's not quite such a loaded question as asking what your passions are, so you are more likely to respond spontaneously, without being defensive. It's a bit like the *'tell me who you are?'* exercise we did a lot earlier in that you can start at a more superficial level and gradually penetrate deeper until something resonates. You are not enquiring about your life's purpose at this stage. You simply want to know what attracts you and there could be many things, so relax, don't pre-judge anything and don't be inhibited.

What is very important is to jot down your answers, so when you ask yourself this question make sure to have a pen and notepad handy. It's similar to a brainstorming session which you can do by yourself or with a friend, in which case one of you asks the other, *'what do you feel attracted to?'* It's much more effective if you spend five minutes writing down your own answers rather than letting your partner write them down for you or trying to memorise them. Meanwhile your partner who posed the question patiently listens in silence until it's his or her turn, then you can reverse roles for five minutes the other way, and so on.

It's also important to say and write down whatever comes out – uncensored, unjudged and without analysis, justification or inhibition, no matter how preposterous your answers may sound. As a hypothetical example, you may get a list that says, *'fast cars, tennis, fine art, women, impressionist art, architecture, maths, work with hands, Mahler, real ale, pubs, clubs, Thai food, films, East Enders, travelling, football, woodwork'.*

This may look like a random list, but when you cast your eye over it you may discern a pattern, something may jump out at you, or more than likely you'll spot something that is not part of your life right now but you would like it to be.

Exercise 17: What new things do I want to try?

WHAT NEW THINGS DO I WANT TO TRY?

You can then go through another exercise in which you ask yourself, *'which items on my previous list am I not doing that I would really like to have a crack at?'* and let's say *'football'* comes up. That doesn't necessarily mean you will start playing for Manchester United tomorrow, but there's no reason why you shouldn't go down to your local amateur club and join. Or maybe get some friends together and go to your local park for a five-a-side kick about.

Find an easy way to make a start.

Likewise, if *'woodwork'* comes up you could go to a woodworking exhibition, buy a few tools and magazines containing woodworking projects and start making something in your living room.

Six big mistakes many people make when deciding what to do with their lives

1) They say, 'I'd love to do xyz, but I could never make a living out of that'
2) They believe it's impossible, inappropriate or irresponsible
3) They believe they can't afford the equipment or the training
4) They take the whole thing too seriously
5) They let fear of failure or low self-belief stop them
6) They listen to negative people who say it's impossible, unsuitable, impractical, uneconomical, too precarious, etc.

At all times be very aware of what you are doing, thinking, saying and believing because there will always be consequences. If you allow any of the above six mistakes to stop you, you end up changing nothing.

Let's say you're an accountant and you fancy doing some woodwork. No one is saying you should try to make a living as a master carpenter, especially at this stage. What I am suggesting is you experiment and see what becomes of it by making a start at square one, at an elementary beginner's stage. For example, you could join a beginner's evening class or find a teacher. My point is that by regarding it as an experiment whose outcome doesn't matter, there's no need to take it too seriously, make yourself stressed out and stage all your hopes and dreams on it.

Your real aim in this exercise is to get a feel for whether you have the requisite talent or aptitude to pursue the activity as a hobby and maybe later as a profession, whether you enjoy it, and to see if your creativity starts to flow.

At this stage all we want to know, when you are pursuing the thing you are attracted to, is 'how do I feel about doing this?' Either you will love it, in which case you can pursue it further and see where it takes you, or you won't, in which case you probably won't go any deeper into it. If you keep doing this with each item on your list that bears investigation, sooner or later your passion will emerge or at least something will resonate. Most likely it will be something that was staring you in the face all the time.

It's also possible that something that's not on your list suddenly pops into your mind and just the thought of it resonates.

What I mean when I say *'something resonates'* is you register something that passes across your consciousness and your heart takes a leap or skips a beat (metaphorically, I hope). That means you may have to be super aware to notice it, but not so much that you make yourself tense, anxious and inhibited. *Alertness* is the key word. The aim is to open yourself up in a non-confrontational way so you don't go onto autopilot and shut down or build a defence mechanism. So be careful to find a good balance between alertness and tenseness.

At this point let's return to Exercise 16 and follow the progress of a fictitious pair of friends as they work through it, just to illustrate the kind of outcome that could occur:

Exercise 16 revisited: To what do I feel attracted?

TO WHAT DO I FEEL ATTRACTED?

This is the next logical next step. The following is an example of two fictitious friends going through Exercise 16 with the aim of producing further clarity, perhaps even an answer, in which one questions the other. If you decide to try this, remember the one being questioned should answer aloud as honestly and spontaneously as possible, and without self-censorship or judgement, while writing the answers down in brief, or in note form.

First session

Friend: 'To what do you feel attracted?'
You: 'Aeroplanes, brunettes, steak and chips, betting on the horses.'

That's a perfectly OK start, just write those things down and take a break or swap roles. After a few minutes try it again, only this time allow yourself to go a little deeper.

Second session

Friend: 'To what do you feel attracted?'
You: 'The novels of the Bronte sisters, eating out in a cosy restaurant with my girlfriend, seeing a performance by the Royal Shakespeare Company, maybe trying some acting myself.'

OK, you're getting somewhere. Clearly these answers are a little more profound and from a deeper place inside. *Has anything resonated yet?* Even if it has, it's a good idea to have at least one more session just to see what other golden nuggets might emerge from your unconscious. A few minutes later you have another go.

Third session

Friend: 'To what do you feel attracted?'
You: 'I love going to rock concerts, Beethoven's violin concerto ... oh yeah, I've always wanted to play the violin ...'

BINGO! That resonated!

It happens time after time in my coaching practice that when a person says they don't know what their passion is, or even what they are interested in or attracted to, in the end what rings their chimes is the very last thing they thought of. It usually comes as a lightbulb moment because for whatever reasons, they have buried it so deeply. I can always tell when they've hit on a true target, because the person's body language changes suddenly and fundamentally as they become animated and excited. Bear this in mind when you do the above exercise with your friend, asking them to tell you if and when there's a marked change in your body language. If there is, you will start to believe in your revelation yourself.

Even if you do this alone, literally asking yourself the question aloud and saying your answers aloud while writing them down, you will be able to feel when something resonates, as long as you remain alert, aware and sensitive. When it happens, the important thing then is to believe the signals coming from deep within your heart.

Now we come to the next stage of self-enquiry, in which you test out your discovery. Ask yourself, 'can it really be true, do I really want to play the violin?' Be honest with yourself and remember, nobody expects you to play like a famous virtuoso just yet (except possibly yourself), and if you are a perfectionist you are going to have to contain yourself. If you are your own sternest critic you will have to refrain, if you are afraid of failure be sure to regard this as an experiment. Also remember not to be concerned about the feasibility of your wish or how impossible it might seem, or how long and hard the rocky road ahead might be. At this stage you are merely testing the sincerity of your aspiration. *Is it coming from the voice of your heart?* Trust your intuition, your gut feeling, for your heart will know the answer.

At this stage you may be wondering why you didn't think of it before, or if you did, why you never acted upon it, and that's a very pertinent question. In truth you probably have thought of it, maybe many times, especially when you were a child, but dismissed it as impossible for whatever reason. Quite likely you've been repressing your desire for years. Maybe it was squashed out of you when you were a child. Whatever, the only thing that matters now is to get your hands on a fiddle and *give it a try.* Get a teacher, a teach yourself book, a DVD or a CD, or see if you can find a tutorial video on YouTube. Whatever you need to do, just do it. *No excuses!* If you say, 'I haven't got time,' or 'I can't afford it,' or 'maybe now is not the right time,' or anything like that, you are copping out. It doesn't have to be a Stradivarius, even a child's instrument will do. Just get hold of the best violin you can manage, give it a try and then ask yourself, 'how does this feel?'

I cannot stress strongly enough how important it is to *seize the moment.* As soon as you get a clue of something that resonates, you must take action straight away, in this case by buying, begging or borrowing a violin. Remember the story I told in the preceding chapter about how the word 'boats' came into my mind and gave me the clue I needed to achieve what I thought was impossible? Just that one little word led me to eventually crossing the Bay of Biscay under sail. But if you leave it too long before taking action, you allow the possibility of fear to consciously or unconsciously take hold of you again, with the danger of your revelation getting re-buried.

This whole process vividly illustrates the ancient Chinese proverb, *'a journey of 10,000 miles begins with a single step.'* If you've had to work hard to uncover your true passion, or possible passion, you must take your initial step without delay.

Sometimes I am challenged when I tell people they can achieve whatever they want. I suppose it's natural for some people to find this an impossible notion to believe. I repeat what I said in the previous chapter that the simple truth is, *we don't know what's possible until we give it a try.*

At this point we see again the importance of developing SMART goals. In my experience it is usual for people to only want to achieve something for which they have an aptitude, even if they don't realise their aptitude or why they feel attracted. I'm not saying you'll be the champion of the world in your chosen passion or *metier*, but there's no reason why if you want to play football or tennis, for example, you can't play to a sufficient level to thoroughly enjoy yourself. Even if you are disabled, it's possible – just look at the Paralympics.

If you are coming from your heart and not forcing yourself through ego conditioning, you will only choose a goal for which you have an aptitude. Imagine it's your heart's desire to be a solicitor, but you're training as an accountant because your father or teacher persuaded you. And let's say you just cannot pass those accountancy exams, no matter how hard you try. Instead of feeling like a failure because you can't achieve what you 'want,' simply acknowledge it's obvious you are barking up the wrong tree!

To recap, when asking yourself to what you are attracted, be 100 per cent honest with yourself, trust your intuition 100 per cent, and don't be put off by the idea that your aspiration seems impossible.

Who and what inspires you?

It's very helpful to have positive role models, for they are a terrific source of inspiration and they can help you believe in yourself and your power to manifest what you want.

When choosing a role model it's important to select somebody who you not only like and admire, but also a person who is visibly successful in his or her chosen field. Maybe somebody at the top of their game or profession who has chosen a path of excellence and impeccability, and most important, someone whose core values are in sympathy with yours. Then simply analyse their paths to success and learn, learn, learn.

For example, if you want to be a footballer perhaps a good choice of role model is David Beckham who, while perhaps not quite an angel, has clearly demonstrated excellence and success time and time again, and is very obviously devoted to his path.

On the other hand it may not be such a great idea to choose George Best as someone to emulate because of his alleged tendency towards alcohol addiction and other behaviour that probably does not fall under the accepted meaning of impeccability.

By the same token, if you want to become a wealthy financier or philanthropist perhaps you will choose George Soros, or if real estate and property development is what interests you maybe you will emulate Donald Trump. If you want to be an entrepreneur perhaps you will take the examples of Richard Branson or Sir Alan Sugar, if you want to be a tennis player perhaps you could choose Roger Federer, and if you want to be President of the United States, you could choose to emulate Barack Obama. Whoever you choose, don't be afraid to aim for the very top.

On the other hand somebody completely unknown could become your role model. For example, many years ago when I wanted to learn woodturning, I met an old retired master turner who became my role model and mentor. When I was a kid in school, my woodwork teacher was the one I looked up to for inspiration.

Notice I have used the word *'emulate,'* which is not to be confused with *'imitate'*. If you want to be truly happy and fulfilled all you need to do is to develop the *unique you* by finding and following *your unique path*. Imitating others is a gigantic waste of time and utterly futile, and even if it were possible, there's little satisfaction to be had in copying someone else.

When it comes to mentors or teachers, it really pays to find the very best one you can, even if you have to travel long distances. What you really want is someone who has been there and done it to a high standard, and as a result gives you inspiration.

When I wanted to learn sailing, seamanship, navigation and boat handling I went to some of the best sailing schools in the UK and some of my instructors were legendary, at least in my books they were. One had sailed round Cape Horn, so he made an excellent role model, another had survived the Force 11 severe storm in the Irish Sea during the notorious 1979 Fastnet Race, so naturally he also became a role model, and another had won prestigious awards for achievement in navigation.

There was another instructor who taught at the evening classes I attended to learn Celestial Navigation, one Commander Alan Sewell RN, a retired reserve Royal Navy officer. He inspired me, against all the odds, to learn this highly technical and seriously mathematical subject, simply by getting me angry enough to believe that if the other folks in the class could get it, so could I.

I was just as intelligent as they were, just not very good at maths, that's all. He got me feeling so challenged I was determined to transcend that self-limiting belief and get my head around it. I could hardly believe it when I passed the exam and received my certificate, and I am quite sure had it not been for him I would have given up halfway through the course.

All of the above goes to show, I hope, that it's a big mistake to avoid your passion, calling, gift or path, or drop it too soon after taking it up, for fear of failure, lack of money or for any other reason. Never be afraid to experiment, to test what you think is your passion and to assess your talent or aptitude if you are in any doubt. Expect to be challenged and relish the prospect. It's an opportunity to step up to the plate and raise your game. If you want to be truly happy and fulfilled, avoidance, making excuses, playing victim, procrastination, resistance or any form of denial are not options.

Never forget, every person who ever achieved anything significant and truly fulfilling had to face the daunting prospect of starting from square one, the first step on that journey of 10,000 miles, and keeping going.

Summary

- If you still don't know what your passion is, asking yourself, 'to what do I feel attracted?' may open new avenues of enquiry for you
- Answer the question spontaneously, and relax. Don't pre-judge anything and don't feel inhibited.

- It's very important to jot down your answers, so when you ask yourself this question have a pen and notepad handy. Don't try to memorise your answers
- Go through your list looking for patterns, something that jumps out, or something you'd love to try that you don't do now. Ask yourself, 'which items on this list am I not doing that I would I really like to have a crack at?'
- Find an easy way to make a start
- When you find something that attracts you, stage an experiment and start at square one. At this stage all you want is an answer to the question, 'how do I feel about doing this?'
- Keep doing this with each item on your list that bears investigation, and sooner or later your passion will emerge, or something will resonate
- *'Something resonates'* means you register something that passes across your consciousness and your heart takes a leap or skips a beat. You have to be *alert* to notice it
- When you hit on a deep, perhaps passionate, interest, your body language changes as you become animated and excited
- When you have a revelation, test it by asking yourself, 'can it be true? Do I really want to …?' Is it coming from the voice of your heart? Trust your intuition, your gut feeling, for your heart will know the answer
- *The only thing that matters at this stage is to get going and give it a try. No excuses!* If you say, 'I haven't got time,' or 'I can't afford it,' or 'maybe now is not the right time,' you are copping out
- Get the best equipment or teacher you can. Give it a try and then ask yourself, *'how does this feel?'*
- *It is essential to seize the moment.* As soon you get a clue of something that resonates, you must take action. Otherwise fear might jump in again and tell you it's impossible
- We don't know what's possible until we give it a try, so don't prejudge! Note again the importance of developing SMART goals
- When asking yourself to what you are attracted, be 100 per cent honest with yourself, trust your intuition 100 per cent and don't be put off by the idea that your aspiration seems impossible

- A role positive model is a terrific source of inspiration to help you to believe in yourself
- Ensure your chosen role model is somebody who is visibly successful in his or her chosen field, somebody at the top of their game or profession who has clearly chosen a path of excellence and impeccability, and someone whose core values are in sympathy with yours
- Analyse your role model's path to success and learn whatever you can
- If you want to be truly happy and fulfilled, develop the *unique you* by finding and following your *unique path.* Imitating others is utterly futile
- It's a mistake to avoid your passion, gift, path or aptitude, or drop it too soon after taking it up, for fear of failure, lack of money or for any other reason
- Never be afraid to experiment, to test what you think is your passion and to assess your talent or aptitude if you are in any doubt
- When seeking your passion, avoidance, making excuses, playing victim, procrastination, resistance or any forms of denial are not options

Six big mistakes people make when trying to decide what to do with their lives

1) They say, 'I'd love to do xyz, but I could never make a living out of that'
2) They believe their aspiration is impossible, inappropriate or irresponsible
3) They believe they can't afford the equipment, the training or the time
4) They take the whole thing too seriously
5) They let fear of failure or low self-belief stop them
6) They listen to negative people who say it's impossible, unsuitable, impractical, uneconomical, too precarious, etc

If you allow any of the above six big mistakes to stop you, you end up changing nothing

Exercises for finding your passion

Exercise 16: To what do I feel attracted?
Exercise 17: What new things do I want to try?
Exercise 16 (revisited): To what do I feel attracted?

20

Exploring and Experimenting

Disciple: 'Master, what should I do with my life?'
Master: 'Whatever you want'

We live in a world of opportunities and possibilities, many options are open to each of us and there are many choices to be made.

If the truth be known, for most of us there is only one main path to happiness and our most important mission is finding out what it is and making that choice, the *right* choice. By this I mean *the choice of path that is exactly right for you.*

As I have said many times, if you are one of those people who believes you don't know what your special gift is, don't worry. Your heart knows the answer. That's why I emphasise again and again the importance of tuning in to your heart and listening carefully to its still, small voice.

What if you are still stuck because you are so heavily conditioned and so inured in the wrong paths and turnings you have already taken in your life that you find it hard to distinguish between your true inner voice, the voice of your heart, and the many voices of your conditioning? What if you are feeling so wounded and damaged that you are afraid to make a stand for what you want in case you get hurt again? Or even worse, in case you 'fail'? What if you simply lack the confidence to trust and depend on your inner voice because you believe that at some point time in the past it led you astray? What if it still seems impossible to change anything?

All I can say is, if something led you the wrong way or let you down, it wasn't the voice of your heart, it could only have been the voices of your conditioning that led you up the garden path. It's so easy to deceive yourself, and even the most focused person falls into that trap sometimes.

Clearly some careful and diligent research or experimental detective work is required in which you try out various options that appeal while monitoring yourself carefully and patiently, until you become a master of the art of tuning in, witnessing and hearing your inner voice clearly. If you do that, sooner or later something will resonate, but when it does, you are going to need the courage and perhaps also the blind faith to act on the guidance you receive.

This chapter describes some of the ways in which you can zoom in and focus more closely to test out the choices you are considering. You may unearth some you never thought of before. This way you can be as sure, as it is possible to be, that the path you choose is the right one for you. If you already know in your heart what your path is you could skip this chapter, but I wouldn't recommend that because it does contain more tools and techniques you might find useful to get a deeper insight, and they will generally add to your growing repertoire of life skills. As a former carpenter, a DIY enthusiast, sailor, author and Life Coach, I can tell you for a fact you can never have too many tools!

Wheel of Life revisited

Way back in Chapter Six we discussed the *Wheel of Life*. Now that you have read this far it's probably a good idea to do that exercise again and see what, if anything, has shifted. It will also keep fresh in your mind the parts of your life in which you want or need to make changes. If you can't remember how to do the exercise, please refer to Chapter Six.

As explained in that chapter, any issue that comes up as a result of doing the exercise can be examined in more detail for even greater insight simply by making a new wheel out of the segment in question. Whatever exercise you do with the *Wheel of Life*, don't forget to put the date on it as this is valuable for later comparison. It's easy to mistakenly believe you've made no progress, but inevitably you'll find you have when you compare today's wheel with one you did say two or three months ago.

Don't forget when you discover progress, especially if it's measurable, write about it in your *Success Diary*.

Exercise 18: Brainstorming

BRAINSTORMING

This is usually done in an interactive group or workshop, but there's no reason why you shouldn't do it on your own.

If you are doing it alone, have a large piece of writing paper in front of you and a pen in your hand, while you sit in silence at your desk or writing table at a time when you know you won't be interrupted. Then you choose a subject you want to test or examine, something you might like to do with your life, a direction you might like to go in, a profession you'd like to consider, and so forth. Write down everything that has even the vaguest bearing on it as thoughts come into your head. It's important to be spontaneous and not to think too much because you want fresh ideas straight out of your inner creative storehouse, not only the same old stuff you've thought of a million times before. You want notions that come from your heart, but be careful, something from your heart may be something you've come up with many times before. What's important is to concentrate on ideas you feel strongly about. It doesn't have to be neat, tidy and logical, all over the page is fine. In fact, the more random, the better.

Basically you want to include anything that might give you a clue or a symbol that might eventually lead you to a new idea.

Let's take a hypothetical example. Let's say you have a burning sense of freedom of expression and you think you might want to be a journalist. You love writing and you are interested in current affairs but you're not sure if this is your real passion. On the other hand, you also love sport and wonder if perhaps you'd love to be a professional rugby player. Or perhaps a good path would be a journalist who writes about sport.

It is entirely possible that you might pursue more than one of these paths as your life goes on. Sue Barker was a top tennis player who turned TV presenter and has been very successful in both fields. Footballer Gary Lineker is another example of a star sportsman turned TV personality, and so is former snooker champion Steve Davis. In the beginning you don't necessarily know where your path will lead you, and meanwhile you have to choose where to begin.

Obviously the place to begin is where *it feels right to begin*, and that may well hinge on what opportunities come your way. Bear in mind that a place to begin that feels right to you may be viewed as unconventional, wrong or even potentially disastrous by others, but that does not necessarily mean you are wrong. There are many factors to consider, for example, do your naysayers have experience in this matter, do they know what they are talking about and do they have any evidence to back up their views? How strong is your vision and the voice of your heart? Do you have any experience of this, what hinges on it and how risk averse are you?

Let's say you want to start a new business and you stand to lose a lot of money if it goes 'pear-shaped'. In such a case I would hope you are going to be very careful, especially if you are inexperienced in this field. You might be well advised to find some experts and listen only to them before you decide. Also very important, find a mentor and one or more role models for extra guidance, feedback and support.

The brainstorming exercise is just that – an exercise, and it's designed to get you thinking creatively. In the final analysis, you and you alone must decide what action you will take, for we must all stand or fall by our own decisions.

Given that we need to be pro-active to be successful, and we like to think we have some control over where we are going, the brainstorming exercise is great for focusing down and getting clear about your feelings and ideas.

I would never give business advice to anyone, but what I do know is that it's essential to get to know yourself inside out and to learn to hear the voice of your heart if you want to home in on your 'right' path. Therefore use the brainstorming exercise and any or all of the other tools we've talked about, and don't forget to meditate. If you do those things and combine them with proper business and financial advice, you maximise your chances of success.

When you have finished your initial brainstorming, make a shortlist of things you'd like to try.

Let's go back to our example of journalism or sport. The secret of the exercise is to deeply explore your thoughts and feelings on each idea that interests you, one at a time. So first you brainstorm on the possibility of becoming a journalist, and then to do the same exercise again afterwards on the idea of becoming a pro rugby player. Once you have done both exercises and compared them, the results should speak for themselves.

This is how your rugby page might look:

Professional Rugby Player – Bill Sykes

7th. October 2011

Team player
Scrum Fun
Captain Try Bad loser
Love winning Tri-nations Touring Travel
Australia France Wales France
South Africa New Zealand
Injury
Marriage Children Family issues
Salary Wales
Love rugby Ball

Competitive	RoughDangerous	
Work-out	Running	Press-ups
Spaghetti	Rump steak	
Alcohol	Drugs tests	
Club		
Taking orders		

You now put the paper aside for a day or two and then come back to it. Then, from this higgledy-piggledy list you draw out, say, six to ten items that have meaning to you and might make feasible action points. You then make a shortlist, which might look something like this:

Professional Rugby Player – Bill Sykes

7th. October 2011

Team player
Captain
Love winning
Travel
Love rugby
Competitive
Running
Club

Now you can start to evaluate by asking yourself, 'how do I feel' about each of the items on your shortlist, and write down your thoughts, either as a narrative or as a bullet point list. You must be brutally honest with yourself if this exercise is to prove worthwhile. Your inner conversation might go like this:

> 'I'm quite a good team player and I do like being part of a team. I'd love to be a Captain one day – I'm sure I'd make a good one. I certainly have the will to win – I'm highly competitive and I'm sure those qualities are essential. It would be really exciting to travel, I've always wanted to go to Australia and there's no doubt I'm totally devoted to the game. Running is my weak point, I'd have to work at that. I could probably join a high-ranking amateur club and see if I can progress from there into the professional rankings.'

From this sheet of paper you can now make a list of action points, which you can later prioritise and furnish with date and time deadlines. This should give you plenty to work with. Here's an example:

1) Find nearest athletics track and practise running (date)
2) Start working out in a gym (date)
3) Find a good amateur club and join it (date)
4) Start playing rugby on a regular basis (date)

At every stage don't forget to ask yourself 'how do I feel about this?'

You will also want to do a similar exercise regarding the idea of becoming a journalist, so when both exercises are finished it's probably best to leave them for a day or so to let things settle. It is a good idea at this point to meditate because ideally you want to let your heart pull you in the direction you want to go. You can rest assured both your conscious and unconscious minds will be working overtime by now, and something revealing is almost certain to come up when you meditate, or perhaps when you are asleep that night.

Let's pursue our example further by assuming you choose to continue further along the rugby path. You now have your action plan, which you can refine and mould into something that feels right for you. Start to build your own unique vision as to how you can make this work. Remember, even the most brilliant plan is useless unless you take action. In this case, most important is to *start playing the game.*

Two important points to remember:

1) Even though you are giving this your best shot, don't forget it's an experiment, at least in the beginning. You are testing your love of the game, your passion, commitment, talent and your determination. You will soon find out if your heart is really in it. *Instead of sitting at home and wondering what to do with your life you are actually putting how you feel to the test for real, in a real life situation.*
2) Don't be put off if you are not instantly an expert, the star of the club or even any kind of celebrity. As with all things that are worth doing you have to work at it. You have to climb the learning curve, develop your fitness and expertise, and earn the respect of your fellow team members. You will make mistakes. You will suffer injuries. Even if you love playing the game, there will be moments when you hate it and you convince yourself you made a mistake. But don't be too hasty. Meditate often in moments of solitude to get some distance and perspective. Then, in time, you will come to know the truth about this being the right path for you or not.

If you are not sure which path you want to pursue, this process of detective work is very important and it's definitely worth going the extra mile to be sure. It may seem laborious but if you can't imagine what it would feel like to be doing the thing you are thinking of, then this gives you an opportunity to find out for real. Be open to any result being possible and remember, *the only worthwhile yardstick is how you feel.*

During my lifetime I have tried out many, many paths, although in the beginning I didn't realise they were experiments. However, nothing is wasted. In my life now as an author, coach, workshop facilitator and meditation teacher, every scrap of experience I have ever had stands me in good stead, including experience that has nothing to do with my present line of work. For example, when I started to take an interest in Osho I had no idea that one day I would earn money from teaching people to meditate! That was a massive surprise.

I have learned so much about myself from the many activities and paths I have sampled, I have discovered so many inner resources, I have learned so many skills and I have come to be self-reliant. It gives me great pleasure to be self-reliant. I really do believe if my motivation is strong enough I can turn my hand to anything and nothing feels impossible. This is a very different story from the quivering jelly I was when I started out as a teenager. That's why I suggest, if you have a list of things you are interested in and you are not sure what to go for, brainstorm all your ideas onto paper, then make a shortlist and try things out.

Don't forget to enjoy your journey, never be afraid to experiment and don't worry about the possibility of 'failure'. I honestly believe *there are no failures, only learning opportunities.*

This finally brings us back to our example of becoming a rugby pro. Even if you eventually decide to drop the idea of being a pro and remain an enthusiastic amateur, nothing will have been lost because of all the reasons mentioned above. What's more, you will never have to put up with that awful feeling of wondering whether you should have gone for it. If your heart so directs you, you'll be satisfied to play as an amateur and watch the professionals while you do something else for a living, something that really makes your heart sing.

More about brainstorming

If you get an idea that you'd like to try a particular something, such as a specific career path, leisure activity or project, but you are not sure how to go about getting started, you can use the brainstorming technique for that as well.

Let's say as an example you get a feeling that it would be a good idea to lose weight. There are many ways you could approach this, many paths are possible but you don't know in advance which, if any, would suit you. Brainstorming can help you find your direction with how best to go about this project.

One word of advice before you start. Try not to refer to losing weight or weight loss, which are negative terms and put you psychologically at a disadvantage because they imply deprivation, and by association, suffering. It is good to find a positive title, such as pursuing a 'Health and well-being project'.

Exercise 19: Brainstorming a project

BRAINSTORMING A PROJECT

This is what your page might look like:

Health and well-being project – Bill Sykes

7th. October 2011

Dieting Weight-Watchers GI Diet
Eat less Weigh myself More protein
Less carbohydrate Atkins diet
Sausages Low fat Diet Coke Yogurt
Coffee
Skimmed milk No more croissants
No sugar Sweeteners Grapefruit
Boiled, not fried
Give up marmalade Paul McKenna weight-loss system
Self-hypnosis Auto-suggestion Acupuncture
I am enjoying feeling slimmer
I am enjoying feeling more healthy I am enjoying feeling more mobile and agile
Yoga
Calories
I don't like chocolate Bananas rule the waves
Bananas are not just for monkeys
Chicken Tikka Marsala

Coleslaw Lesley Kenton Diet
Deepak Chopra Natural Weight book Herbal tea
Join a gym
Work out Swim Walk Run
Avocados Avoid restaurants
Vegan Vegetarian Macrobiotic
Sushi
Egg, bacon, mushrooms, tomatoes, hash browns, sausages and loads of grease
Low cholesterol Cornflakes

You now put the paper aside for a day or two and then come back to it. Then, from From this random list you draw out say six to ten items of things you *could* do that appeal to you and seem feasible as action points and make a shortlist. At the same time you might draw up a list of things to stop doing. Your lists might look like this:

Health and well-being project – Bill Sykes

7th. October 2011

To do	**To stop eating**
Weigh myself	Sausages
Eat less	Exchange Diet Coke for Regular Coke
More protein	Croissants
Paul McKenna	More herbal tea, less coffee
Auto-suggestion	Restaurants
Lesley Kenton juices	Less chocolate
Yoga	
Deepak Chopra	
Swim	
Walk	

From this you could draw up an action plan as follows:

1) Weigh myself and write my weight in my diary once a week (date)
2) Stop eating sausages and croissants (date)
3) Exchange Diet Coke for Regular Coke
4) Drink one coffee per day (date)

5) Drink as much herbal tea and/or raw juices from Lesley Kenton recipes as I want per day (date)
6) Eat in a restaurant once a week (date)
7) Smaller portions, more protein, less carbs (date)
8) Eat one square of chocolate a day (date)
9) Read Paul McKenna's and Deepak Chopra's books on weight control (date)
10) Join gym for yoga classes and swimming. Walk to gym (date)
11) Do affirmations* and other auto-suggestion techniques (date)
12) Meditate for half an hour three times a week (date)

* Chapter 25 describes in detail how to do affirmations.

As with all techniques related to goal setting, it is very important to write down your action plan. A simple list like the one above is fine and very quick to do. Put dates and times in the plan and put them in your diary too, and hold yourself accountable so you know for sure when you will be starting yoga or whatever. This way you are far less likely to sabotage yourself by double booking the date and time concerned.

Notice how I changed negative to positive in the to-do list. So instead of saying cut chocolate consumption to one square a day, which reminds you of what you are missing or sacrificing, I wrote, eat one square of chocolate per day. This gives you something to look forward to. You give yourself far more encouragement if you keep everything in positive terms and avoid focusing on what you will lack. Instead of saying reduce coffee etc. I wrote down drink one cup of coffee per day, and as much herbal tea as I want, and eat out in a restaurant once a week. That gives you a feeling of abundance and makes it much easier and more enjoyable.

This is a very important point when you are dealing with any addiction such as over-eating or comfort-eating (which this may or may not be): if you stray from the straight and narrow, don't beat yourself up. Simply note you have strayed and bring yourself back to your chosen path. If you get feelings of deprivation, such as chocolate withdrawal, remind yourself you have chosen a path of increased fitness and health, not a path of deprivation and lack. Always, always, always, accentuate the benefits you will get from the project, especially at crisis moments.

While we are on the subject, exactly the same principle can be applied to giving up smoking or any similar addiction. Rather than focusing on your deprivation, remember the health and financial benefits, and any other benefits you can think of.

Prioritising and time management

All too often we create a 'to do list' with so many items on it that we don't have a hope in hell of getting them all done in the allotted time (remember SMART goals are realistic and achievable). When that happens it's all too easy to berate yourself for the items that were left undone and then to wonder why you feel overwhelmed and demoralised. Also, putting too many items on your list can cause procrastination – you can't decide what to do first so you end up paralysed, doing nothing. This is a counter-productive situation, and nothing will change if you fall prey to it.

If you stop and think for a minute you will realise that any kind of procrastination or indecision is an avoidance or denial technique and you are choosing it unconsciously. They are further manifestations of your saboteur, and very subtle ones at that. So subtle, in fact, that you could go on for years doing the same thing without realising what's really happening and why you feel continually frustrated. It's a deceptive situation because it feels as if making a 'to do list' is a good idea and we look forward to ticking off all the items listed.

Typically, a lack of proper planning almost always means that only urgent items get done. Even they may be abandoned, done in haste, without due care and attention, and at the cost of much stress and anxiety. Stephen Covey makes a point of explaining the folly of this behaviour in his book, *The Seven Habits of Highly Effective People,* because it leads to crisis management. As Covey points out, it's much better to plan properly, well in advance, so *matters are dealt with when they are important, but before they become urgent.* If other items are not deemed important, either they can be dropped from the list or planned for so they get actioned when they become important. By using this method, no item should ever become urgent – in theory at any rate. Therefore you can be more efficient in the way you operate while giving every action it's due attention, and you'll be a lot less stressed.

If lack of planning is your habit, I hope you now have the awareness to see that once again you are sabotaging yourself if you carry on in the same way.

Dreams and aspirations

Dare to dream big and never compromise. If there's one golden rule about making your dreams come true, then surely this is it. Take Osho's advice, *'be realistic, plan for a miracle.'*

What possible reason could you have for settling for second best? You've been doing that all your life and you're not satisfied. That's obvious because you are reading this book. The main reasons people aim too low or too small are that they don't believe they are capable of achieving exactly what they want, they feel unworthy, the goal is impossible, they are afraid of failure (or something else), or because for whatever reason they are unwilling to step up to the plate and play all out. There are many other possible reasons too.

If you allow yourself to dream anything other than big, you are selling yourself short. You are not behaving with integrity like the Impeccable Warrior because you are not being true to yourself, you are withholding something of yourself from entering full-bloodedly into the game of life, you are not doing justice to the amazing and powerful mental equipment you were born with. Also, you are not doing the rest of us any favours either because we are deprived of your full contribution.

If you want to achieve your top goals, have *faith – faith in yourself* and *faith that your achievement will come to pass.* I don't mean religious faith. Figure out what the game is, learn the rules, practise the moves, and play it with all your energy. There can be no half-measures and there's no room for self-doubt. Look at yourself and ask, 'am I dreaming big, am I stating my top goal, and I telling it like it is?' Be honest with yourself and remember, if you find your confidence is wanting, the strategy to employ is *act as if* ….

In other words you tell yourself, no, you *convince* yourself, that you are supremely confident, and you will find the courage to dream big as you formulate your goals. Later, as you go though the action phase, gradually your true confidence will grow and you will no longer have to *act as if.* Nothing builds confidence better than experience, and experience comes with taking action.

Be creative

If you want something and you are daunted because you believe too much faith and effort will be required to achieve it, ask yourself, 'what has to happen or what has to change for me to find the courage to take my first step?' Perhaps it's your defeatist mindset that has to change first. Once you realise what needs to change, you have no more excuses. Don't be afraid of coming up with something that's unusual or unconventional. The last thing we want is more of the same, so *be your original, unique self* as you draw up your list of things to experiment with.

Moreover, in all likelihood many of the skills you already have are transferable to the new areas of endeavour you want to try, with little or no adaptation. In my coaching practice I find myself saying time and time again, 'are you sure you are trapped? I get the feeling you are much further along the path towards your dreams than you realise. It's just a question of seeing your strengths from a different viewpoint.'

Remember, if a time comes when you feel trapped, it is absolutely true to say that you are your own jailer, which means that you are also the one who has the key.

When you follow the wrong path you feel trapped. When you stop and turn to the right path you feel liberated. That's what it boils down to. Maybe you need a strategy, maybe you need to manoeuvre yourself across gradually or may be not. Either way, it really is as simple as that.

Set yourself free, liberate your imagination, change your mindset, let yourself out of jail and soar like a bird. I don't want hear, 'but my problems are worse than other people's,' or 'that worked for her because she's special,' or anything like that. 'She' indeed is special and so are you. I have never yet met anybody in my three score years on this planet who, once connected to their true self, is anything other than extraordinary, and that means you too. And before you protest, saying, 'but you don't know me personally, you don't know what I'm like, you don't know anything about my problems,' bear in mind that I don't need to know you personally to know that you are special and powerfully capable, because we all are.

Asking for feedback

As you progress through your experimental phase there can be times when it's hard to step back to get a distant perspective on what's really going on. If you are experiencing that difficulty it's a good idea to ask for feedback from someone you trust, someone who will be objective, someone who will be like a mirror, and simply reflect back to you what they see.

This can be an area fraught with hidden dangers so make sure your awareness is sharp. Here's a hypothetical example: you're a would-be musician, a singer-songwriter, and your goal is to get a recording contract from a record company. You write a song that you think is good as it ticks most of the boxes a record company would require. However, you are not quite sure if it might need some tweaking, or if it would be best to leave it well alone.

You ask a friend for feedback, by which I mean someone who knows what they are talking about, for example someone with some knowledge and experience of the music business, or at least an avid enthusiast of your genre of music. You get your guitar or you sit down at the piano and you perform the song to your friend.

Now your friend might love it or hate it but that's irrelevant because that's just his opinion based on personal taste, it's not objective. You want to know if it's fit for purpose and of a professional standard, not whether one person likes it or not. Even worse he might say he loves it because it comes from you, someone he loves, and wants to be supportive. So now it's not even a true opinion.

What is the value of this to you? His like or dislike of the song is of no value. You are trying to decide if it's good enough to submit to a record company so you want feedback as to whether it's suitable. If, on the other hand, he comes up with some suggestions as to how it could become more appealing to the record company *based on his knowledge and experience,* that's invaluable!

The point is, this is your creation and only you, in your heart of hearts, know whether the song truly reflects what you are trying to communicate. You must learn to trust your own judgement or to be more precise, your gut feeling, your intuition and your instincts. That's why I counsel never ever follow anyone else's advice (and that includes my advice incidentally), otherwise you are back into a situation in which you behave according to what other people think is right for you.

By all means ask people for feedback, perhaps even for their opinions, for they might suggest something you hadn't thought of, but put their input into the mix to be considered and balanced with your own gut feelings and opinions, don't just accept it as the gospel truth. Ask yourself how you *feel* about their input and then *make your own mind up.* If you follow your heart you will never go wrong.

Of course that does not necessarily mean the record company will welcome you with open arms, but if your approach is rejected it simply indicates there is something you could to learn to your benefit before you go back to the drawing board and change or improve something. It might also mean that somewhere, in some detail, you are not precisely aligned with your core values or what is coming from your heart, otherwise your enthusiasm could have won the day.

Don't take it personally. Get over your disappointment, learn, and try again.

It's exactly like the situation an author finds when his book proposal is rejected by many publishers. It doesn't necessarily mean he should give up, nor does it mean that what he proposes is rubbish. It simply means he has to renew his self-belief, try again and be even more creative. It takes considerable focus, vision, devotion and faith. Each time he re-submits his proposal, the would-be author must search his heart and mind to find ways of making his book proposal better than it was the time before. It may also mean he has yet to find the right publisher.

If publishing a book is a heartfelt path for this person, sooner or later he will have raised his game high enough and will find a publisher somewhere who resonates with the work he proposes.

There is an argument that says if the friend you asked for feedback realises your confidence is wavering, he should do something to encourage you, maybe by praising your talent, the song, the proposed book or whatever. However, for genuine results when you are trying to achieve something that demands the highest of standards, your encouragement has to come from yourself. Your conviction, your belief in the work you do, your determination to give your gift to the world, your drive to be of service, those are the qualities that will get you to your goal, not insincere 'encouragement'.

Potentially everybody has the necessary qualities but they may need to be uncovered and developed. You can get support, you can get feedback, but those qualities can only come from you. If you believe you have them but can't seem to access them, the tools and techniques in this book will, I hope, help you get on track. If you are still stuck, try working with a coach.

Many years ago I felt I was the only one whose problems were so severe that I alone would never be able to achieve anything of note. My therapist said to me, 'What makes you so unique? What makes you so arrogant as to believe you're a special case?' That woke me up and taught me to stop making excuses.

If your friend really wants to be of service he or she will give you honest, objective feedback, plain and simple.

Constant self-monitoring

As you progress through your experimental phase it's important to keep monitoring yourself. *How does it feel to be doing what you are doing, thinking what you are thinking, feeling what you are feeling?* At any given moment you could decide to do more of it, drop it forever, or stop doing it until you've dealt with another pressing task, *depending on how you feel.*

Sometimes when I am sailing along a coastline we leave harbour in thoroughly enjoyable blazing sunshine and after a while the sky darkens, the wind freshens picking up the waves, and big cold spots of rain start falling. At this point, as I pull on my waterproof clothing, I ask myself and my crew if I am still enjoying this. Sometimes the answer is yes, in which case we carry on, but sometimes it is no, and that's when I start heading for the nearest harbour. It doesn't mean I'll give up sailing forever, it simply indicates that once it ceases to be enjoyable it becomes a pointless exercise and it would be preferable to do something else that is enjoyable instead. I have no reason to sail other than for enjoyment, and I am perfectly content in the knowledge that sailing will resume when we deem the conditions are conducive to enjoyment.

Exercise 20: Your successful life now

YOUR SUCCESSFUL LIFE NOW

Another useful self-monitoring exercise is to get a blank sheet of paper and a pen and *describe what your vision of the successful life you want looks like now. Then on another sheet, compare it to your present life as it actually is.* This should give you clues as to whether you are on the right track and how far you have to go, or what needs modifying or changing. You may well find you are not as far away as you think you are. Don't forget to put the date at the top of each sheet.

Exercise 21: Your five-year vision

YOUR FIVE-YEAR VISION

Once you have done that, get another sheet of paper, put today's date at the top and *describe your vision of how you see your successful life in five years time.*

What does it look like, sound like, smell like, taste like and feel like exactly. Then *compare that vision with today's vision and today's life as it actually is.* This exercise again should help you evaluate how your experimentation is going. Do you seem to be homing in on the right track?

Four points to remember

1) Whenever you do self-monitoring exercises like these, always put your name and today's date on your sheet of paper so you can repeat the exercise at intervals and compare the results with earlier ones to evaluate progress.
2) Don't forget the purpose of this experimental stage is to help you be sure, by a process of detective work, elimination and self-monitoring, of what path your heart wants you to follow. Therefore, if you are trying out something and you decide it's not for you, don't hesitate to drop it immediately to make time for trying the next thing. Conversely, if you find yourself enjoying what you are trying out, go more deeply into it.
3) If you had been brought up free of conditioning and neurotic hang-ups, which none of us were, you would be so connected with your heart you would know your path intuitively, or you would have intuitively done this research when you were a teenager (please excuse me if you are a teenager). If, however, like me and lots of the people I know, you hit middle age or later and you realise you never did this, it's important to go back and do it now. *Your emotional maturity can never be complete and fully satisfactory if you leave gaps in your emotional and psychological development.* No one is to blame, that's just how it is for some of us. Luckily, it's never too late.
4) Finally, *keep meditating!* It will help you stay on track, find or maintain your balance, and allow more clarity to develop.

Summary

- For most of us there is only one main path to happiness and our most important mission is to find out what it is and make the *right* choice
- If you don't know what your special gift is, don't worry, your heart knows the answer

- If you believe your inner voice led you the wrong way or let you down, that wasn't your inner voice, the voice of your heart; it was the voices of your conditioning
- If you have lost touch with your inner voice and are not aware of your path, then careful and diligent experimental detective work is required. Monitor yourself until you master the art of tuning in, witnessing and hearing your inner voice clearly
- Do the *Wheel of Life* exercise again and see if anything has shifted since last time. It will also keep fresh in your mind the parts of your life in which you want or need to make changes
- Remember that any issue can be examined in more detail for greater insight simply by making a new wheel out of the segment in question
- Put the date on your wheel – this is valuable for comparison. When you discover measurable progress, write about it in your *Success Diary*
- The best place to begin exploring is *where it feels right to begin*
- If you have a list of things you are interested in and you are not sure what to go for, brainstorm your ideas onto paper, then make a shortlist and try things out
- *There are no failures, only learning opportunities*
- If you stray from the straight and narrow, don't beat yourself up Simply note you have strayed and come back to your chosen path
- If you get feelings of deprivation, remember you chose this path and focus on the anticipated benefits
- Nothing will change if you have too many things on you 'to do list' and you become overwhelmed
- Plan well in advance so matters are dealt with when they are *important,* but before they become *urgent*
- Dare to dream big and never compromise – 'be realistic, plan for a miracle'
- The main reasons people aim too low are that they don't believe in themselves, they are afraid, or they are unwilling to play all out
- If you allow yourself to dream anything other than big, you are selling yourself short

- If you want to achieve your top goals you must have *faith – faith in yourself and faith that you will make your achievement come to pass.* There can be no half-measures and there's no room for self doubt
- Don't be afraid of coming up with something that's unusual or unconventional
- Many of the skills you already have may well be transferable to the new areas of endeavour you want to try, with little or no adaptation
- Remember, if a time comes when you feel trapped, *you are your own jailor.* You are also the one who has the key
- We are all special, unique and extraordinary, including you!
- Ask for feedback from someone you trust, who will be objective, and like a mirror, simply reflect back to you what they see
- Be careful, only ask someone who knows what they are talking about, and ask for feedback based on his or her knowledge and experience
- If you create something, only you in your heart of hearts know whether it truly reflects what you are trying to communicate
- Learn to trust your own judgement, gut feeling, intuition and instincts
- Never follow anyone else's advice. Ask people for feedback and their opinions, and put their input into the mix to be considered with your own gut feelings and opinions. Then *make your own mind up*
- *If you follow your heart you will never go wrong*
- If your approach is rejected maybe you have something more to learn. Go back to the drawing board and do something differently. In some detail you might not be precisely aligned with your core values or what is in your heart. Check it out using self-monitoring questions
- Don't take it personally. Get over your disappointment and try again
- When you are trying to achieve something that demands the highest of standards, your encouragement has to come from you
- Your conviction, your belief in your work, your determination to give your gift to the world, your drive to be of service, those are the qualities that will get you to your goal
- If you hit middle age or later and you realise you never went though your teenage exploration phase, it's important to go back and do it now. That's because *your emotional maturity can never be complete and fully satisfactory if you leave gaps in your emotional and psychological development*

Important points about brainstorming

- When *brainstorming* be spontaneous, and think as little as possible.
- The point is to write down anything that might give you a clue or a symbol that might eventually lead you to a new idea
- The secret is to deeply explore your thoughts and feelings on each idea that interests you, one at a time
- Be brutally honest with yourself and build your own unique vision as to how this could work
- You will significantly increase your chances of success and make your desired achievement easier if you create a written plan
- Don't forget it's an experiment, especially at the beginning, and don't be put off if you are not instantly an expert
- *The only worthwhile yardstick is how you feel*
- If you'd like to try something such as a new career path, leisure activity or project, but you are not sure how to go about starting, the brainstorming technique can also be used to determine your first steps
- You give yourself more encouragement if you keep everything in positive terms, avoid focusing on what you lack and focus instead on how you will benefit

Important points about prioritising and time management

- It's all too easy, if you put too many items on your 'to do list,' to berate yourself for the items left undone and then wonder why you feel overwhelmed and demoralised
- If you wait for things to become urgent, you end up doing nothing but crisis management

Important points about self-monitoring

- Ask yourself, 'am I dreaming big enough, am I stating my top goal, am I telling it like it is?'
- Be honest with yourself and if you find your confidence is wanting, the strategy to employ is *act as if* ...
- If you feel daunted because you believe what you want will require a lot of faith and effort to achieve it, ask yourself, 'what has to happen

or what has to change for me to achieve this?' Most likely it's your defeatist mindset that has to change first

- When you ask someone for feedback, ask yourself how you *feel* about their input
- Get a pen and paper and describe *what your vision of the successful life you want looks like. Then compare it to your present life as it actually is*
- Once you have done that, get another sheet of paper and describe *your vision of how you see your successful life in five years time.* What does it look like, sound like, smell like, taste like and feel like exactly? C*ompare that vision with today's vision, and today's life as it is*

Exercises to detect your path

Exercise 18: Brainstorming
Exercise 19: Brainstorming a project
Exercise 20: Your successful life now
Exercise 21: Your five-year vision

21

The Three Golden Rules of Risk-taking and Decision-making

Life is like a game of cards. The hand that is dealt you represents determinism; the way you play it is free will

Jawaharlal Nehru

You may have heard the term, *'emotional intelligence'*.

When I broached this subject recently in a talk I was giving, someone suggested it was nonsense on the basis that the two words are opposites. When I asked the lady concerned what she meant, she explained, *'emotional'* is to do with right-brain activity, intuition, kinaesthetics, empathy and feelings; whereas *'intelligence'* concerns rationality, logic, objectivity, coldness, analysis, and it excludes emotion, and in this woman's opinion, never the twain shall meet.

There may be some truth in this if you take the term literally and you want to play semantics, but I'm more interested in the meaning conjured up by the sound of the phrase, or the image that is suggested.

The lady has a point, in the sense that many of us tend to think predominantly with one hemisphere or the other. What I'm concerned with here is a balance between the two sides, emphasising one hemisphere or the other on a continually shifting fulcrum, as appropriate to your situation at the time. Viewed in this light, *emotional intelligence* is a highly descriptive term and, more important, a very real and useful skill to learn. It's a holistic, rather than dualistic, approach.

What I mean when I use the term is that you are thinking rationally while at the same time balancing your logical thought processes with what your intuition or feelings are telling you. Sometimes an issue is best decided by your intuition of what feels right when deciding between two possible courses of action, both of which are rationally plausible or viable.

Sometimes when we are challenged with a problem, an issue or a goal, we come up with a possible solution based on reasoning. When that happens it's a perfect time to ask yourself the self-monitoring question, *'how do I feel about this?'* When you entertain that question and apply it to your rationale you are using *emotional intelligence*. You have a practical, logical solution, but the decision as to whether it's right *for you* is coming from your heart. You could call it intuitive, but intuition is only one side of the equation.

Emotional intelligence is especially useful when it comes to taking risks. How often have you been told, 'you'll never achieve anything if you're not prepared to take risks,' so you take a risk and promptly fall flat on your face. The reason for that, I finally realised the hard way, is because you are not combining your intelligence and intuition when evaluating the risk. Our careful judgement has to go into the mix too, and more often than not our decision has to be subjective as well as objective.

I return to my earlier points about the danger of taking someone else's advice, and the importance of doing what is right for you. One person can take a risk and the outcome will be a huge success, while another person takes exactly the same risk, and everything goes pear-shaped for them.

Let's get a bit more specific by quoting an example. In 1984, a couple of years after the collapse of Laker Airways, most sane and rational entrepreneurs in the UK would have considered the idea of setting up a low-cost, no-frills airline to fly across the Atlantic to be certain financial suicide. Unless, that is, your name is Richard Branson.

This, a very much simplified version of the story, illustrates the importance of having a vision, coupled with enough drive and energy to follow through with action based on sound rationale. Richard Branson, according to his autobiography, had a vision of how such an idea for an airline could work. Instinctively he knew there was a large market and he was convinced he knew how to communicate with that market and persuade it to support his idea. Allegedly, most of Branson's closest advisors did not share his vision at the time and believed their boss had taken leave of his senses, but Branson was not listening to negative advice. If you have a vision and it's so strong and you are so passionate about it and you believe in yourself 100 per cent, there is no point listening to people who do not share that vision, even if they turn out in the end to have been right. If you have a vision and you take the appropriate steps, you also have a better than average chance of being right. An entrepreneur achieves nothing unless he has the courage of his convictions and dares to put his money where his mouth is.

At this point a few words of warning seem appropriate: if you are thinking of striking out for yourself in business do not be deceived by new-age speak. In any new business or entrepreneurial undertaking there is risk, vision or no vision. That's because vision alone is not enough. It is essential that every action you take must be aligned with your vision or inspiration or you could fall off the tracks. As usual, supreme awareness has to be your mantra, and even then any new venture must be viewed as an experiment. It's impossible to contrive or manufacture a vision, for it has to come from your heart, and if you don't have a vision that has arisen naturally then don't even think about taking a risk. That's my honest opinion. Better to continue your inner journey until something real clicks. I'm not trying to put anyone off – exactly the contrary. I just want to make sure we stay grounded in reality.

You should also consider the possibility that you get your business up and running and it's highly successful, and then there's an earthquake or massive flood that wipes out everything you built. When you decide to go for it, go in with your eyes wide open. A risk is a risk however you dress it up and it can be a big mistake to underestimate risk.

Branson started his airline Virgin Atlantic, and as a result rewrote the rulebook about the aviation business by doing something that had never been done before. He started giving his customers staggering value for money and the best possible quality of service at unheard of competitive prices. It seems that Branson loves to compete and prove that he can do it better than his competitors – it's as if he loves to give them a wake up call, saying, 'come on guys, you can do better than that! Look, here's how you do it!'

Just look at the following quote from his autobiography, *Losing my Virginity*: 'My interest in life comes from setting myself huge, apparently unachievable challenges and trying to rise above them ... from the perspective of wanting to live life to the full, I felt that I had to attempt it.' Is that inspiring or what! He did it to feel fully alive!

My point is that *it's very important to know exactly what you are like* when it comes to evaluating risk-taking (that's another very good reason for getting to know yourself inside out). Let me give you another example, this time of the opposite extreme.

A client of mine, let's call her Barbara (not her real name), is an alternative health practitioner and her goal was to get more clients. We looked at the service she provided and decided it was very good, so no problem with the 'product'. Then we started looking at how she promoted herself, and straight away we ran across problems. We looked at her website and the first thing I noticed was that there was no photograph of her on it. When I questioned her on this she said, 'oh no, I don't want my picture on it. I don't want to be too pushy.' She was painfully shy.

So I explained if I were suffering a backache and looking on the web for someone to give me a healing massage treatment, I might be reassured by a sympathetic face on somebody's website and be drawn to contact that person. But she was adamant. Then I pointed out there was no picture on her leaflet either. Same response. She had deliberately avoided having her picture on her leaflet.

Then I suggested she might ask some clients for testimonials to put on her site and her leaflet, but again she refused to even entertain such a possibility. 'Oh no, I couldn't do that. It wouldn't be fair to pester my clients, and it's unethical. *It wouldn't feel right.'* That last sentence was the punch line.

The idea that it's 'unethical' to ask a client for an endorsement or testimonial if they have benefited from your service is beyond my comprehension. After all a client always has the prerogative to say no if they want to. However, when she said 'it wouldn't feel right,' I knew she'd succeeded in carrying off a masterstroke of self-sabotage. For she knew perfectly well I would never advocate she should do something that doesn't 'feel right.' She had, in effect, shut me up and that takes a bit of doing, if I may say so! Trying to point out what she was doing or to suggest another way of looking at it proved futile because she absolutely refused to go there. Something about raising her profile was way too scary.

I asked her, 'you want new clients but how do you expect them to find you if you deliberately make yourself invisible? You are making their life really difficult, as well as your own. You have this gift, this facility for healing people, why are you keeping it to yourself and refusing to share it?'

The poor woman was too terrified to go any further. She simply refused to stick one tiny toe out of her comfort zone. It was an extreme case of risk aversion, probably stemming from a deep-seated feeling of unworthiness, and the exact opposite of Richard Branson.

At this time it became obvious to both of us that irrespective of wanting more clients, Barbara's real issues that she urgently needed to address were how to feel better about herself, how to feel worthy and how to start believing in her self. That's what I mean when I talk about getting to know yourself inside out, so you can find out what really are the right goals for you right now, and what is stopping you from shining.

If you have that kind of an issue it will always stop you in your tracks every time you try to be successful, no matter how strong your vision or how great your talent, until you address it and deal with it fully.

From the above conversation we evolved a strategy whereby Barbara created two short-term goals concerning expressing her anger and shame and thereby gradually changing how she felt about herself. We also evolved medium to long-term goals for her about creating a new website, leaflet and business card. She could develop these over a period of time to reflect the fabulous person she would discover she really was, *while her self-discovery was taking place.* All this would be a preparation for the major long-term goal of ultimately starting to attract new clients.

Is that an exiting way of revolutionising your life while at the same time discovering and marketing yourself? I think so. It certainly beats hiding your light under a bushel!

Most of us ordinary mortals accept the fact there's only one Branson, and if you're not him it's important to acknowledge that being who you are is absolutely fine. Perfect in fact. It's unrealistic, unreasonable and unnecessary to go to the opposite extreme and remain a shrinking violet if you want to make changes in your life and achieve things that you feel passionate about. There has to be a balance, and where you draw the line is up to you. All I would say is, if you are contemplating taking a risk, get to know yourself inside out and evaluate it using *emotional intelligence.* Create a strategy to come out of the woodwork in a way that accords with your ability to cope with risk.

Here then are my three golden rules of risk-taking and decision-making:

The three golden rules of risk-taking and decision-making

1) Only do what feels right
2) Be guided by your heart as well as your head. Use *emotional intelligence*
3) If you are not sure if you are hearing the voice of your heart or the voices of your conditioning, drop everything and meditate

Spontaneity versus control

Nobody likes to be labelled a control freak. Nobody, that is, except me. I freely admit I like being in control. That's why I wanted to be a boat owner and skipper, rather than a crew on someone else's boat. That's why I prefer to be self-employed. It's part of who I am and I enjoy that. But it's important to know when to let go, or to quit while you're ahead.

When I was a teenager in the so-called 'Swinging Sixties', the hippie cry was, 'hang loose man, go with the flow, let the brakes off, don't be so much in control.' I am reliably informed that at the entrance to the meditation hall at Osho's ashram in Poona, India, (at that time he was known as Bhagwan Shree Rajneesh) there was a notice asking people to leave their minds, with their shoes, at the door.

This is all well and good when taken in the spirit in which it is intended, that is, allow space for some spontaneity in your life and live more from your heart, drop your attachments, ego, resistance, neurotic reactive behaviour, and all that sort of baggage.

Unfortunately many of the people who went to visit the ashram, and Osho's second ashram in America, missed the point and ended up virtually ceasing to think for themselves. They abdicated personal responsibility for their lives, their behaviour, their core values – even their feelings – in their haste to 'surrender to the master', even though the master expressly counselled against that.

The hippie ideology of the 1960's was also gravely misunderstood. For example, peace and love and free love were wonderful hippie ideals but they resulted in many unwanted babies and teenage single mothers. If *emotional intelligence* had been applied at the time of conception, it is likely the parties involved would have used contraception. I hate to sound preachy, but when children come into the picture the rules of the game change and things become much more serious because children are easily damaged. When you take a risk on getting pregnant, you are potentially taking a risk that concerns someone else's life. When a couple take responsibility, they can still have fun but without unhappy consequences. I mention this not to be moralistic or to lay a guilt trip on anyone but because this book is about how to find happiness, so I feel duty bound to point out how failing to take total responsibility for everything we create is likely to lead to heartache and unhappiness.

So how do we reconcile this conundrum? We want spontaneity in our lives yet we want to be in control. We want to go with the flow but we want to take responsibility.

As usual it comes down to awareness, because only awareness can give you the necessary perspective to create a suitable balance. In this way, thank goodness, good old-fashioned common sense will come to our rescue if we invite it to. When you combine *emotional intelligence* with awareness, following your heart becomes second nature. You behave intuitively, your life flows and once you get used to it, you don't even have to think about it.

Finally, please don't take what I say as a judgement. If you are a single parent of either gender, or involved in any way with an unplanned pregnancy, I hope you won't use what I have said to beat yourself up, put yourself down, do a guilt trip on yourself, perceive yourself judged or feel in any way badly about yourself. Acceptance has to be the name of the game. What's done is done. I tend to work on the assumption that we are all doing the best we can, and no one can ask for more than that. As I have said many times already, it's impossible to learn and grow without making mistakes.

Summary

- *Emotional intelligence* is balancing your logical thought processes with what your intuition or feelings are telling you
- Sometimes when we are challenged with a problem, an issue or a goal, we come up with a possible solution based on reasoning. When that happens, it's a good idea to ask yourself, *'how do I feel about this?'*
- *Emotional intelligence* is especially useful when it comes to taking risks
- One person can take a risk and the outcome will be successful, while another takes exactly the same risk, and everything goes pear-shaped. Therefore, never act on the advice of others. Always take responsibility for your own decisions and *only do what feels right for you*

- When considering saying yes to a big decision, it's important to have a vision
- If you have a strong vision that you are passionate about, there is no point listening to people who do not share that vision
- If you have a strong vision and you take the appropriate steps, you have a better than average chance of being successful
- An entrepreneur achieves nothing unless he has the courage of his convictions and dares to put his money where his mouth is
- In any new business or entrepreneurial undertaking there is risk, vision or no vision. It's a mistake to underestimate risk
- Vision alone is not enough. Every action you take must be aligned with your vision or inspiration
- Supreme awareness has to be our mantra, and even then any new venture must be viewed as an experiment
- It's impossible to contrive or manufacture a vision for it has to come from your heart. If you don't have a vision then don't even think about taking a risk Better to continue your inner journey until something clicks
- It's essential to know yourself well when it comes to evaluating risk-taking
- When children come into the picture, the rules of the game change and things become much more serious because children are easily damaged
- When you take a risk on getting pregnant, you are potentially taking a risk that concerns someone else's life
- Failing to take total responsibility for everything we create is likely to lead to heartache and unhappiness
- Only awareness can give you the necessary perspective to create a suitable balance between spontaneity and control
- When you combine *emotional intelligence* with awareness, following your heart becomes second nature. You behave intuitively, your life flows and once you get used to it, you don't even have to think about it
- Acceptance is the name of the game. It's impossible to learn and grow without making mistakes

The three golden rules of risk-taking and decision-making

1) Only do what feels right
2) Be guided by your heart as well as your head. Use *emotional intelligence*
3) If you are not sure if you are hearing the voice of your heart or the voices of your conditioning, drop everything and meditate

THE THIRD PILLAR

Your Passion

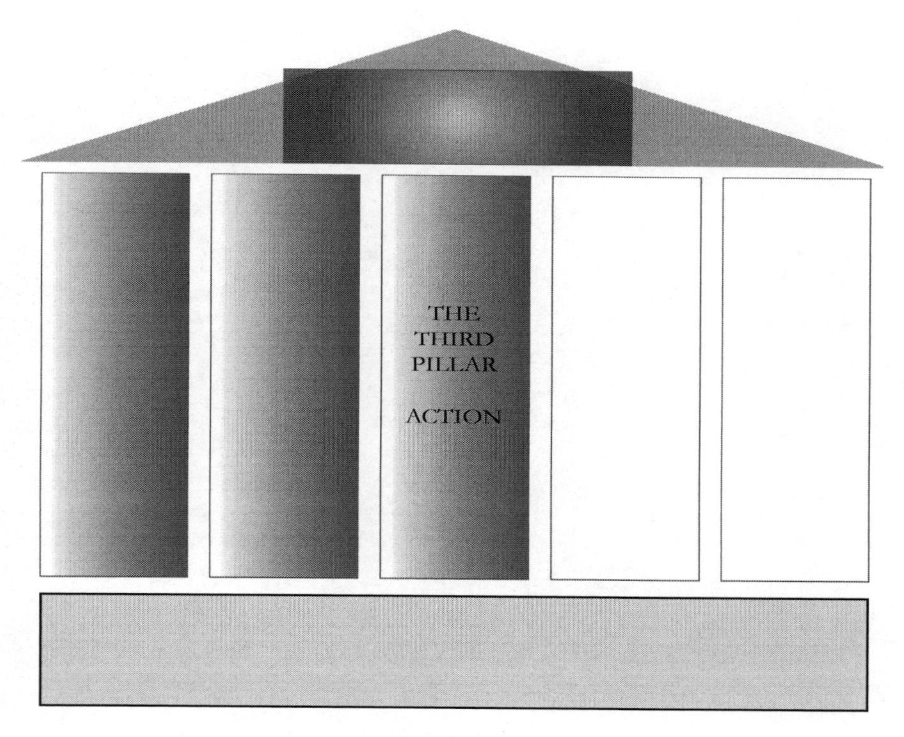

I hope that by now either you know what your passion or gift is, or you are well on track towards finding it. That means at last we have arrived at the action stage. It has been said many times that all great creative endeavour is five per cent inspiration and ninety-five per cent perspiration, which is another way of saying that unless you take action and keep going, all your efforts up to now will come to naught.

Remember the story of The Tortoise and the Hare (see Chapter 30).

Its message is to make a plan, make a start and keep going till you get there!

Let's begin by looking at ways of making an action plan.

22

Action Plan

If you fail to plan, you plan to fail
Old saying, anonymous

Why is planning so important? Very simple. It gives you a psychological edge by reinforcing your intention (especially if you hand-write it down), it strengthens and adds detail to your vision, it makes your life easier, and it helps you stay on track. Also it helps you determine your first and subsequent steps, it reminds you which way you are going, it eliminates or reduces the possibility of being overwhelmed, and it makes it far more likely you'll end up where you want to be. Mainly that's because an action plan helps you to create the appropriate mindset for yourself. By making a *written* plan you make a commitment to yourself, a powerful statement of intent, even if it's on an unconscious level, that you will do whatever it takes to be successful.

Writing your plan, however simple, is important because as we have already noted, the act of writing makes you think deeply and develop your thoughts about what you want to achieve. It makes you more aware of your feelings around the subject so you feel them more strongly and helps to imprint your intention into your mind. It also helps kick-start the process of thinking up options concerning which actions, exactly, you could take, or what experiments to try, to ensure you get there.

You may remember in an earlier chapter we saw how you create more of whatever your dominant thoughts are. Making, and especially writing, a plan helps to get relevant productive thoughts powerfully fixed into your psyche in a dominant position.

Yet many of us delay or even avoid planning, and we do so at out peril. Probably the most common excuse or mistake is to believe, 'I haven't got time for planning,' which is almost as common a misconception as believing 'I haven't got time for meditation.' Of course my answer to both of these is, 'yes you have,' because doing both these things will help you save time in the long run and make a successful outcome far more likely.

When you get overloaded with work or even leisure activities and you start to feel overwhelmed, it's hard to think straight and know what to do next; then it's easy to lose your motivation. Know the feeling? A plan can help you get yourself together so you know what you need to be doing at any given moment. It saves you time in the long run because you have thought out what to do in advance.

Lots of people also make the mistake of thinking that once something is planned it's set in stone and can't be altered. 'I can't operate in such a rigid environment,' one client told me. So if necessary or appropriate, change the plan. In fact change it at regular intervals, as often as you like, *if that's what you want to do.* No harm in applying some common sense here.

It's worth pointing out that if you realise you are about to do something you don't want to do just because it's in your plan, then in all probability there's no point doing it. Better to change the plan so you do something you do want to do. We must assume responsibility for all our actions, even ones that are written in our plan. Be careful though, it could just be your resistance or your saboteur leading you into avoidance.

There are lots of reasons for *not* planning and I don't intend to go into any of them here, save to say that every one of them is an excuse and you are kidding yourself if you believe otherwise. If you want to avoid procrastination; if you want to use your precious time efficiently and effectively; if you want to avoid crises, panics, unnecessary stress, re-inventing the wheel and making unnecessary mistakes; planning is the answer. I know I said it's OK to make mistakes, but there's no need to go looking for ones that can be avoided with a little applied awareness.

A plan can be as simple as writing a shopping list. Just think how irritating it is to come home after a hard slog round your local supermarket only to find you forgot to buy butter. It's cold, dark, windy and raining outside but you have to go out again.

A plan can mean simply writing appointments and deadlines into your diary as they arise, so you don't end up double-booking yourself or missing an important meeting. It's so simple and it safeguards your wellbeing. Over the years I have tried all sorts of Filofax's, Palm Pilots, Laptops, PC's, mobile 'phones and other devices for recording appointments and deadlines but I have concluded you can't beat a traditional pocket diary and a wall planner for seeing short and long-term plans at a glance. For addresses, a card index is as easy as falling off a log. Unlike an electronic organiser it doesn't need batteries and it doesn't die when someone spills coffee all over it. Find out what works for you and use it religiously.

Danger point: If you are the sort of person who will spend ages writing an elaborate plan and going to enormous lengths to perfect it, you would do well to ask yourself if you are using it as a hiding place. In other words you might unconsciously make it into another manifestation of your saboteur to help you *avoid* taking action. It's another form of *analysis paralysis,* or denial, or plain old-fashioned procrastination. Get the plan finished to a point at which it's workable, then take action.

In your unconscious mind the inner dialogue goes something like this: 'Ooooh, this project is too scary, I don't want to do it. I might fail. Anyway I can't do it yet because my plan's not perfect!' We all know very well that no plan will ever be 'perfect' in the eyes of someone who is obsessed with perfection. You could delay the moment of action forever, using this ploy to fool yourself that because you are making a plan you are doing what is necessary.

You can probably guess what I'm going to say next. *Balance. Find a balance in all things. That is the way to go.*

Let me give yet another example from my own life. As I write this chapter, I am creating a new website for my coaching practice and I want it to be perfect before I publish it on the internet. It's only natural. But because I know only too well what I'm like I have set a deadline for publishing it whether it's ready or not. When the time comes I daresay it will have a few glitches and I'll see where I could have made it better (just like this book), but what really matters is that it will be a vast improvement on my previous website. I will continue to develop and improve it but in the meantime I want it up there working on my behalf.

It's exactly the same principle with making a plan. Once it's good enough to let you see a way ahead, start taking action. You can always tweak the plan as you go along.

Making a plan

It may seem obvious, but when you start thinking about planning, the most important element to keep in the forefront of your mind is your desired result or achievement.

Let's start with a simple example. Every week either I or my partner does our household grocery shopping in a local supermarket. Obviously the desired result is to come home with the requisite food-stuffs to refill our fridge, freezer and kitchen cupboards with enough of our favourite foods to last a week, after which time we will undertake our next shopping trip.

This is accomplished by means of a simple list. We keep a small notepad and some pens on the kitchen worktop and as soon as we run out of something, or when we anticipate running out of it, whichever one of us notices that will add it to the list, which gradually grows as the week goes by. Whoever goes shopping simply takes the list with him or her and gets everything on it.

If you want to get really clever, before you leave home you can re-write the list in the order in which you will pass the items on the shelves so you never have to retrace your steps in the supermarket. This arguably is the most time and effort-efficient way of doing the shopping but it does require memorising the layout of the shop in advance. Where this degree of attempted perfection comes unstuck is when the store manager gets it into his head to move an item or even a whole section and swap it with another section, an event that can drive a perfectionist control-freak shopper into near hysteria. That's when you need your plan to be flexible and you in a mood of acceptance.

It can also happen that the shop is out of stock of one vital item. Is that going to defeat you or shake your resolve? No of course not. You find it in another shop, or go without it. A plan does not always work out exactly as intended.

In a case like this you depart from your plan because to try to stick to it would be futile. But that doesn't mean your plan was useless. It served you very well and supported you in getting the major part of the job done, while ensuring that the remainder of the job that had to be done by improvisation and initiative was not overly challenging.

OK, now let's look at a plan for embarking on a new career. The first thing to do is to state your goal, for example, 'I want to move out of the furniture business and build a new career in property investment.' Before you go any further it's important to develop that into a SMART goal, which you can easily start doing by writing the letters of the acronym down the side of the page and entering appropriate sentences or bullet point notes next to each letter, like this:

Goal

S (Specific)	Two-bedroom flats at least 50 years old (not new build)
M (Measurable)	A portfolio of six flats worth at least £1 million in total, each one cashflow-positive and tenanted
A (Achievable)	Budget of £100,000 for six deposits over two years
R (Realistic)	Six 80% buy-to-let mortgages required. £150,000 budget for refurbishments and costs
T (Timed)	To be achieved within two years, by 27th. November, 2013

From this you define your goal as: *'It's 27th. November, 2013 and I own six buy-to-let flats worth a minimum of £1 million in total, each one cashflow-positive and with reliable tenants.'*

(This is a fictitious, hypothetical example and not to be used for investment.)

Assessing you present situation

- Need to learn a bit more about this business
- Haven't got much cash
- Feeling very nervous
- Am excited and enthusiastic to get cracking

Assessing your options

First you need ideas of where to find six two-bedroom flats at least 50 years old in suitable locations with a total value of at least £1 million after refurbishment and costing not more than £500,000 (the deposits represent 20 per cent of the purchase price). Here are some possibilities: estate agents, property auctions, newspaper advertising, shop windows, internet, word of mouth.

Next you need to find a place to obtain six mortgages (they don't have to be found all at once and they don't all have to come from the same place. In fact it might be better if they don't). Here are some possibilities: financial advisors, banks, building societies, internet, loan sharks.

Finally, you need ideas to raise the capital for the deposits, as you don't have enough.

Again here are some possible ideas: your own savings, family, bank, friends/ colleagues, financial institutions, business partners.

Once you own your first property you will have to find builders and decorators, letting agents and so on, but that second and third tier of detailed planning can wait, though it's probably essential to include a budget for that in your initial planning. It's not a good idea to jump the gun by taking on too much before you start. Just bear in mind that you will need to plan again in detail for the later phases of your project.

An overall plan containing all the numbers to the best of your knowledge, but not necessarily all the details, will probably be essential for raising finance.

Looking at the above options, probably a *strategy* is by now beginning to emerge in your mind. This is where it becomes even more essential to know yourself inside out. Have you ever done this before? How risk-averse are you? Can you afford to risk losing money? How confident are you that you can pull it off? Should you find a less risky/better strategy? Is this strategy enough of a challenge to keep you motivated? How are your self-belief and self-esteem? Don't forget to keep asking yourself, 'how do I feel about this?'

So let's look at a strategy whereby you initially want to scrape together your first deposit and organise a mortgage in principle so you can go to an auction or find a property through an estate agent by a certain date, with the intention of buying your first two-bedroom flat. You can now start to develop a three point short-term action plan, as follows:

Short-term action plan

One

- Search through my papers tonight to see if I can raise enough from my savings, shares, dormant bank accounts etc., for a deposit
- As a fall back option contact bank to make an appointment for tomorrow to ask for a loan to be used as a deposit
- Organise a family meeting/tea party on Sunday to ask if any relatives would like to chip in to an investment opportunity

(Notice that each action point has a time, day or date as appropriate. This helps to make sure you get on with it in spite of fears, reluctance, obstacles and so on.)

Two

- Make a list of banks and building societies offering competitive rates for mortgages and put in an application by Wednesday 5th. March 2011 to apply for a mortgage in principle. *(When you buy property at an auction, you must have your finance in place beforehand because if you bid and win a property you are committed to completing your purchase within a very short time. The date chosen here is fictitious, but the date you choose for real should allow ample time to have the funds ready for your first auction.)*

Three

- Conduct an internet search to find local property auctions taking place between Monday 4th. June and Friday 8th. June and put the dates in my diary. Go to the auctions when directed by my diary. *Find out exactly what the rules are for buying property at auctions*
- Start other property searches – visit local estate agents, *find out the exact procedure for buying property through an agent and through private advertising,* look in shop windows. Scan the local papers and internet advertising. *(There's potentially a lot of money at stake here, which means if you want the best deal without problems it's important to be thoroughly prepared.)*
- Find a reliable solicitor who specialises in conveyancing, and an independent surveyor, and put them on standby in case one is needed at short notice

Schedule

Make a schedule of appointments and deadlines to make sure you get everything done by the required dates, and put all key dates and times in your diary. If you then do what your diary tells you to do, as and when the dates come up, you will automatically take the appropriate action at the right time. *Do not rely on your memory,* or you are in danger of forgetting something important, or making a double booking, either of which could jeopardise the whole undertaking.

Even with a diary, a plan and a schedule, you will still have to make unexpected decisions. With something as important as committing large sums of money to any investment, my suggestion is always to use your common sense and *do not commit yourself to any major decision until you are in possession of all the relevant information and you feel absolutely positive about going ahead.* Don't act because you are being bullied, persuaded, harried, embarrassed, sold to or made to feel guilty or for any reason other than your own motivation. At every stage of the game keep asking yourself, 'how do I feel about this,' bearing in mind that whatever you do, *it's your decision and your responsibility.* If you are so far out of your comfort zone that you are getting panic attacks, sleepless nights and unbearable anxiety, slow down. Take it easy, get things in balance, find a reliable mentor, meditate and be guided by your inner voice. Then maybe you will be in a fit state to make a responsible decision, that is, a decision that's right for you, when the time comes.

The amazing creativity of your mind

There is a simple technique I often employ which, when you understand the principle and develop the knack, will enable the amazing creativity of your unconscious mind to go into overdrive suggesting all manner of possible solutions to your problems or issues. This practice of harnessing the creative power of your unconscious sometimes takes the form of coming up with new ideas, thought forms or mindsets, and at other times with new ways of applying existing ideas. The technique can be used at any stage of any creative process, especially when you need a fresh perspective. Incidentally, I regard a creative process as any activity that comes from your heart, even property investment.

I can best illustrate this point by giving an example, and once again I choose the example of my new website. Creating this website is a new adventure which has taken me a long way out of my comfort zone because I am certainly not an IT expert, nor am I a designer, and I've never really done it before. However I can write copy, I can take good photographs and on a good day I can even follow instructions. So eventually I developed the confidence, or rather *I acted as if I had developed the confidence,* using another of my favourite mantras, 'how hard can it be?' and decided to try by using a ready-made template and design wizard from my website hosting company.

I'm not going to bore you, or myself, with the technicalities, but suffice to say one evening while I was working on the project I reached an impasse. I just could not get something to work, I couldn't see what I was doing wrong and I couldn't understand what I was supposed to do. So after trying for half an hour or so, I gave up and went into the other room to watch television to unwind before going to bed.

In the middle of the night I woke up with ideas buzzing around my head so I sat up in bed and meditated for a while, and then went back to sleep. Then at about five a.m. I awoke again and bingo! An idea had been born. In fact there were three ideas, for suddenly I thought of three possible ways I could make the thing work. I got up and briefly wrote down the three ideas and finally I was able to get back to sleep for what little was left of the night.

Writing ideas down when they come in the night is important for two reasons. First, it puts your mind at rest so you can get back to sleep without fear of forgetting the ideas; second, in the cold light of morning, you can look at what you have written, decide if your ideas are worth trying and instantly see ways of fine tuning those ideas to make them even better.

That morning when I got up I went straight to my PC in my pyjamas and lo and behold, I was able to see how one of the ideas could solve my problem. So later, after a hearty breakfast, shower and putting on some clothes, I spent an hour doing what needed doing. Success!

OK, you might say, nothing brilliant in that! But it was brilliant, because if this had happened ten years earlier, instead of going to bed I would have sat up until five a.m. trying to crack the problem. I would have used the same thinking over and over again, getting nowhere and feeling frustrated, gradually letting my confidence ebb away, ultimately giving up, feeling exhausted the next day, and all for no result.

This way I had given it a try for a short while, just long enough to implant the problem into my unconscious mind, then gone to bed and let my unconscious mind work on the problem while I slept at least for some of the night. Then I woke up with three possible solutions and despite feeling a little sleepy the next morning I was buoyed up with a positive mindset and went on to easily achieve what the previous night had seemed impossible. Result – not only problem solved but also confidence increased and a strong feeling of satisfaction and empowerment.

If I achieve my goal, solve my problem or resolve an issue, I don't mind paying the price of being a little sleepy the next day. But to feel whacked out and have no result, which was the alternative – that's hard to cope with. Worst of all, I would still be held up on my project and in a lesser mental and physical state to deal with the problem.

I believe that by giving up temporarily and going to bed I was taking responsibility for looking after myself properly and giving my imagination a chance to get going, whereas if I'd insisted on working through the night, I would have repeated my old pattern of trying to be a control freak, thereby sabotaging myself good and proper.

The essence of the technique is to *sow the puzzle, problem or issue into your unconscious mind by working on it for a short while.* Don't waste hours getting nowhere. Then you can let your unconscious mind get on with solving your problem for you while you sleep.

You may think I'm exaggerating, or maybe that it's no big deal, but I assure you this sort of thing happens to me quite often, and you can do it too. I'm trying to think of a good way to express my message in a new leaflet, for another example, and suddenly the words for the headline come to me in the middle of the night during my sleep after I have been puzzling over what to say for a short time the evening before. Sometimes great ideas come in the night when I didn't even realise I had a problem! In fact, the majority of my best creative ideas come to me in the middle of the night. That's why I'm always yawning. But who cares? It works for me and it might work for you too.

This technique needs a little practise. Instead of getting anxious and wound up, work on your problem for a little while and then forget about it and do something else. Chill out, relax, read a book, go to bed, whatever, and let your unconscious take over. It's a terrific technique to use when thinking up options for your action plan.

Staying on track

An action plan is a device to get you started in the right direction while directing plenty of energy into actions that will get you results. Therefore, in theory, once you are away on your trajectory the plan has served its purpose.

However, you can get even more value out of it if you make your plan ongoing. Then you can review your progress against your plan from time to time as you go along, while also using it to make sure you are staying on track. That's why the plan might need to change from time to time. The idea is that the plan comes alive as you start to enjoy your journey, not just your anticipated arrival.

You can go as far as you want with this process – I remember in the 1970s when I worked in two public relations companies we used to produce weekly progress reports for each client. Each report itemised the projects we were undertaking for the client in question and highlighted in columns who was due to take what action next, and when. This was to ensure each person concerned took responsibility for actioning something by the appropriate time, and that the project would be ready, or finished, on time.

If you are in business you might want to do this too, but if you are working on personal goals and achievements you might consider this as overdoing it. In part it depends how determined you are to succeed and how much structure you need to support you.

A similar and very helpful time management tool for day to day use is a simple *weekly action schedule.* This is similar to a school timetable or a spreadsheet, in which the days of the week are listed down the left-hand column, and the times of the day split into hours across the top. Actions can then be entered into the appropriate day/time square. It's like a diary in effect, but you can view a whole week on one sheet of paper and pin it to your notice board.

Something I find very useful, which is really like an expanded action schedule or diary, is a *wall year planner*. It shows me at a glance my major commitments and deadlines for the year so I can plan in advance easily and know where I am supposed to be at any give time. You could alternatively use a simple *calendar*.

How far you go with your ongoing action-monitoring tools is up to you. Wherever you decide to draw the line, make sure you draw it somewhere and start taking action.

One more thing I would strongly advise – once you've made your action plan, or even only started on it, write about it in your *Success Diary*. The same applies every time you make any positive progress, when you start actioning the plan and at every step on the way. This will greatly reinforce your positive mindset and strengthen your determination to keep going even in the face of setbacks until you reach your goal.

Summary

- *Writing* a plan helps you to create the mindset that helps you get to where you want to be
- A *written* plan is a commitment to yourself that you will do whatever it takes to be successful

- Writing makes you think deeply and develop your thoughts, it makes you aware of your feelings and helps to imprint your intention onto your mind
- Writing a plan helps to get the thoughts that will propel you firmly towards success powerfully fixed into your psyche in a dominant position
- Writing a plan, like meditating, will save you time in the long run
- A plan helps you to know what you need to be doing at any given moment
- When necessary or appropriate, change the plan. Do it as often as you like
- If you are about to do something you don't want to do, change the plan
- Reasons for *not* planning are excuses
- If you want to avoid procrastination, crises, panics and extra stress as well as use your precious time efficiently and effectively, planning is the answer
- A plan can be as simple as writing a shopping list
- A plan can mean simply writing appointments and deadlines into your diary as they arise, so you don't double-book yourself or miss an important meeting
- For addresses, a card index is simple and easy. Find a system that works for you and use it religiously
- If you take for ever writing an elaborate plan and going to enormous lengths to perfect it, you might be using it as a hiding place, a means of avoidance
- Find a balance in all things. That is the way to go
- Once your plan is good enough to let you see a way ahead, start taking action. You can always tweak the plan as you go along
- When you start planning, keep your desired result or achievement in the forefront of your mind
- The first step in creating a plan is to state your goal and develop it into a SMART goal. From that choose which actions you will take
- Now you can develop a *strategy* or *action plan* to determine how to approach your project, bearing in mind what you are like so every action is congruent

- Keep asking yourself, 'how do I feel about this?'
- Knock your plan into shape. Many drafts may be necessary
- Next, create your *schedule*. You can do this using a conventional diary, calendar, wall planner, timetable or spreadsheet. *Do not rely on your memory*
- Use your common sense and if there's a lot at stake *don't commit yourself to any major decision until you are in possession of all the relevant information and you feel absolutely positive about going ahead*
- Harnessing the creative power of your unconscious can be used at any stage of the achievement process, especially when you need a fresh perspective
- Writing ideas down when they come in the night puts your mind at rest so you can get back to sleep, and in the morning you will instantly see ways of fine tuning your ideas so they work even better
- The essence of the technique is to *sow the puzzle, problem or issue into your unconscious mind by working on it for a short while.* Don't waste hours trying in vain and getting nowhere
- You can get even more value out of your plan if you review your progress against it from time to time to make sure you are staying on track
- With a long-running project involving others, you may find it useful to produce regular progress reports
- How far you go with your ongoing action-monitoring tools is up to you. Just make sure you start taking action sooner rather than later
- Once you've made your action plan, or even made a start on making your plan, write about it in your *Success Diary*
- As you progress towards your goal, write about that too in you *Success Diary*

Techniques

- Harnessing the creative power of your unconscious while you sleep

23

Your First Step

As you begin changing your thinking, start immediately to change your behaviour. Begin to act the part of the person you would like to become. Take action on your behaviour. Too many people want to feel, then take action. This never works

John Maxwell

It's time to take that all-important first step, but first you have to decide what that step will be. Whatever you do, *don't think about it too much* or you risk encouraging the onset of *analysis paralysis*, which wants to keep you stuck. Indecision almost always comes from over-thinking or taking a negative view, an example of the latter being when you see your first exciting challenge as a problem rather than an opportunity. If you indulge either or both of those tendencies, you are making life much harder for yourself than it need be and even worse, you increase the likelihood of your remaining stuck for good.

If your first step involves doing something you've never done before, let's say making a 'phone call to someone you are attracted to and asking for a date, or starting cold calling on the telephone, you will probably find it scary enough without making things unnecessarily difficult. When you are about to enter uncharted waters, you need every psychological advantage you can get, so *don't think too much, act as if you are supremely confident and act on instinct combined with common sense.* Find that delicate balance where you behave intelligently while being guided by how you feel. And if it's a major undertaking, don't forget, you have your plan to guide and support you.

Of course, nothing is cut and dried in the awareness game, and herein lies another danger so be careful on this point. When I suggest being guided by how you feel I don't mean, 'I feel afraid, so I'm going to run away and hide and not take this step after all.' It is essential to keep focusing on the positive at all times. For example, try these thoughts instead: 'I accept that I'm afraid, but if I can overcome my fear and talk to this person I feel so attracted to, I'll feel like a million dollars, even if I'm rejected.' Or, 'If I make these cold calls I'll be supporting my business and overcoming my fear, so even if I am unsuccessful I will have learned that I can act in spite of being afraid.'

This applies as long as you believe you are doing what is right for you, and you regard every move you make as an experiment and a worthwhile step along your personal learning curve. As I have said many times before, the Impeccable Warrior does what is necessary no matter what the difficulties, and therefore never has grounds to reproach himself. Whatever happens, you emerge with your self-esteem intact.

If, on the other hand, you run away and give up on your most heartfelt desires, you might avoid rejection but you can never feel good about yourself, no matter how hard you try. The fear never really goes away if you try to brush it under the carpet.

This is where your action plan proves its value, because by referring to it before taking your first step it gives you confidence. It supports you, reminds you of your intention and keeps you pointing in the right direction. If you are lucky enough to have a good coach, he or she too will support you and encourage you to make a start.

If you think I'm joking or exaggerating about making a plan to ask for a date, think again. If you are so nervous that you feel you might fall apart as soon as you approach the other person, a plan will help boost your confidence considerably.

Have you ever experienced feeling frozen, paralysed or overwhelmed when faced with starting something new and scary; so much so that you feel defeated before you even start? When that happens, look at your action plan and focus on taking your first step. Chunk your task ahead down into small steps and get started on tackling them one at a time. *Never underestimate the power of small steps.* Think *'Tortoise and Hare'* and remember *small steps will get you there!* But don't forget the all-important caveat, *as long as you keep going.*

Watch out for your old conditioning, sometime mistaken for human nature, looking for a way to sabotage you. Imagine you have one hundred things to do in a day and you do ninety-nine of them really well and only one goes pear-shaped. Which one are you going to focus on? Which one will stand out in your mind? I'll take a bet it'll be the one that went wrong, of course. Then you will berate yourself for 'failing' while totally ignoring your ninety-nine successes, which should be making you feel good about yourself.

If, as a result of the above scenario, you fall into the trap of thinking, 'I'm a miserable failure, I'm totally incompetent and hopeless,' you know perfectly well that this is blatantly untrue and completely unjustified. However, that depends on you maintaining your heightened state of awareness so you actually notice what you are doing and how irrational it is.

You do yourself a massive disservice if you insist on putting yourself down, for in effect you are then unconsciously trying to mislead yourself. That's because ninety nine successes far outweigh one 'failure'. You are not taking a balanced view. You are falling into your old habit of beating yourself up because you still have a self-image of seeing yourself as a failure, and though it might seem bizarre, we always feel safer when we conform to our perceived self-image.

Someone once argued with me that the one pear-shaped result could have been by far the most important one. That may be true, but it doesn't alter the fact that ninety-nine things went right, so give yourself credit for that.

It is never a good idea to put yourself down for any reason.

The main purpose of your *Success Diary* is to help counter this tendency by enabling you to begin to see the truth that you are basically and intrinsically, on balance, a successful person right now. Not in five years time when you have achieved some fabulous goal, but right now. The fact that you are living and breathing proves you have already been successful at least in the essentials for survival, and are continuing to be so.

You may remember we discussed earlier how you manifest more of whatever is your dominant thought. That's why it's highly counterproductive to fill your head with thoughts of failure, for those thoughts will lead you further and further down a negative road and I'm sure you don't want that.

Here's the important bit, and it's the reason why I keep on stressing the importance of awareness. *Now that you realise and understand this* (that is, you now have the awareness) *you can now choose to focus only on the positive,* (that is, any or all of the ninety-nine things you did really well). Put them in your *Success Diary* and give yourself due credit for being an achiever and hey, guess what, you will start to feel much better about yourself.

It is entirely by doing the things you want and love to do while noting your success as you go along that your self-esteem, self-belief and self-worth start to grow, and you begin to relax and feel more confident. This is also the start of inner peace beginning to replace inner conflict, the beginning of excitement ousting fear and anxiety, and of balance triumphing over wild extremes.

Let's take a real-life concrete example. When I decided I wanted to learn to sail, as I said earlier I had no idea how to go about such a challenge, but after thinking about it for a while a series of options presented themselves in my mind as possibilities. I realised it would be a long process and I should start with the simplest, least scary and least expensive steps. This was long before I'd ever heard of Life Coaching or action plans. It was around 1983, yet intuitively I knew I should approach it in small steps or I would be overwhelmed by the enormity of it.

So I went to the library and borrowed a book with a sailing dinghy on the cover that promised to explain the basics of how to sail, which I read and mostly understood. I also remembered that when I was a child there had been a man on the television called Barry Bucknell, a carpenter and specialist presenter in the up-and-coming field of DIY. He had designed a small dinghy in association with the *Daily Mirror* newspaper especially for home building, called the Mirror Dinghy, which could be sailed, rowed or driven by an outboard motor. 'Maybe I should look for a second-hand one of those,' I thought to myself.

The equivalent of *Ebay* in those days was a weekly newspaper full of classified advertisements called *Exchange & Mart*, so I duly bought the latest copy and started looking through the sailing boat section to see what was on offer. I was specifically looking for a Mirror Dinghy for sale, and quite a sizeable number were listed, but I actually found something else far more interesting, an advertisement for an august institution entitled Iver IPC Yacht Club. It was a club whose members sailed Mirrors and Miracles (I hadn't a clue what a Miracle was, but it sounded exciting) on a small lake near Iver, Buckinghamshire. Crucially the advertisement said, 'Every Wednesday new members evening, beginners welcome.' It sounded very 'highfalutin' because it called itself a 'Yacht Club,' but it was, I soon realised, a very friendly small dinghy sailing club.

I ran to the 'phone and within seconds I'd secured my invitation to visit the club, about three-quarters of an hour's drive away from my home, on the very next Wednesday evening. Then I had to wait four days. I was almost beside myself with impatience. That was the beginning for me.

I tell this story to illustrate how, when you hit upon something that excites you and comes from your heart and you start taking steps, all sorts of unexpected doors open for you and you feel energised. This journey began with small steps and continued with many more small steps plus the occasional large step, and at each twist and turn new and exciting opportunities presented themselves.

From this it is clear there are two essential factors in revolutionising your life for the better:

1) Find your creative path
2) Take action

It's so important to get to know yourself inside out and check that your goals and aspirations are coming from your heart. If you embark on a path that is not really yours, for example you have been persuaded into following a 'safe career' when really you'd rather be a polar explorer, your road ahead will be difficult and painful with many pitfalls, and few doors will open easily for you. Progress will be slow and hard won. More important, there will be no joy and no fulfilment in it, and probably little meaningful creativity. Any success you experience will feel hollow and exhausting, a Pyrrhic victory at best.

If you are finding it hard to make progress with your goals, stop and check. Are you really listening to, and acting upon, the guidance of your heart?

Dealing with setbacks

Everyone, even the most highly successful people in our world, experiences difficulties and setbacks. It's how you deal with them that separates the achievers from the victims. Once again, a 'can-do' mindset is essential. An essential tip to remember is to use the tools I have given you in the earlier parts of this book. That's what they are for, so don't keep them unused in the closet.

The reason I know this without a shadow of a doubt is because I used to be a victim myself. Life used to happen to me, it seemed totally random, massively unfair, very hard, my life was a mess and believed I was powerless to do anything that would bring me joy. The concept of changing things seemed like something that other people did. Then one day I got fed up with feeling like that and I vowed to myself I would 'sort my life out' even if it took me until the end of my days. Somehow I had garnered just enough awareness to begin to see a little of what I was doing to myself, and I hated what I saw. Just a glimpse or two was enough to get me started.

Let's repeat this often neglected point yet again: when you are not sure if what you are doing is right for you, ask yourself, 'how do I feel about this?' If you are feeling nervous about doing something new, *act as if* and take action.

There are also many other questions you can ask yourself, as appropriate, such as 'what on Earth am I doing here?' or 'why do I feel so awful about doing this?' or 'if I do this, will it move me nearer to my goal?' or 'does this goal really feel right for me?' Also, let yourself know when things are going well, for example, 'wow, this feels great.' Invent your own questions and allow yourself to be as creative as you wish in your soul-searching.

One of the most important tools of all, whatever you feel, is to *acknowledge how you feel.* If you feel angry, admit it to yourself and own your anger fully (that does not mean you can dump it on the first person who triggers you off). If you feel sad, happy, frustrated, afraid, courageous, depressed, ill, sick at heart, *whatever,* acknowledge how you feel and own it fully. Find ways of expressing yourself without harming yourself or others. Get it out of your system.

Stay centred, don't be distracted

The temptation can be strong to go off following interesting ideas and so-called opportunities that are 'off piste,' as it were. Maintain your awareness so you can spot potential red herrings before you go for one, and instead stay centred. Ask yourself, 'is this really relevant, will this get me nearer to my goal, do I really want to do this?' and act strictly in accordance with your inner guidance. Otherwise you could waste a good deal of time.

A big mistake is to become consumed by all the blogs, teleseminars, webinars, websites and other e-mails that can come your way in a working day. These are massively time consuming so be very discriminating. Allow a maximum of, say, half an hour first thing in the morning to check your e-mails – then get on with your current project according to your real priorities. Take a lunch break, check them again briefly after lunch, and get back to the matter in hand. E-mails and the web can destroy your focus before you even realise it.

That's not to say you shouldn't have some leisure time in which you have fun for it's own sake and not for any higher purpose. There's a time for fun and a time for getting on with it, just as there's a time for rest, relaxation and recuperation, and a time for action. Use your awareness and intuition to keep a balance that feels healthy in your heart of hearts. Ask yourself, 'am I making progress, or am I frittering away my valuable time?'

It's also very important to keep meditating at regular intervals. Osho used to talk about 'meditation in the marketplace,' a practise in which you remain centred and with heightened awareness at all times, even in the midst of the hurly burly of daily work or family life.

I know I've said it a hundred times, but it's impossible to over-stress the power and importance of this – meditation will help you grow your inner strength and clarity of purpose. It will help you keep things in perspective and feel empowered, it will help you decide on your next step and your order of priorities, it will help you greet new challenges with a sense of adventure, and it will uplift your spirit so your journey remains fresh and joyful. In short *meditation will help you stay on track and hear the guidance of your inner voice, the wisdom of your heart, and enjoy travelling on your creative path.* So don't think just because things have started going really well you don't need to meditate any more. A soul thrives on meditation at regular intervals, like a car needs petrol.

Feel the fear …

A scary goal is a challenge that enables you to enlarge your comfort zone. The other side of fear is excitement, and you can't be bored or depressed when you are excited.

I used to have a theory that if a challenge wasn't scary it probably wasn't worth doing. Nowadays I wonder if maybe that's a bit extreme, but that's probably because I've learned to enjoy worthwhile challenges rather than fear them. I suppose that's because I actively want to rise to the next level. I have come to realise that I can do whatever I want if I have sufficient genuine heart-driven motivation.

When I was a kid in school my reports used to indicate I didn't excel in most academic subjects, which I took to mean that everyone thought I was unintelligent or stupid. At the time I didn't realise, probably because my teachers never remarked on it, that I was as bright as the next child and perfectly capable of learning. I just wasn't interested. In the few subjects I was interested in, for example English Literature, I got along famously. It was probably because I discovered and loved the quintessentially British characters of children's literature of the 1950's and 60's, like Just William, Billy Bunter and Biggles at about age eleven, that I later learned to love Chaucer and Shakespeare.

Children and adults alike need encouragement more than anything else. The verb *'to encourage'* means *'to fill with courage'* so if you are a parent, observe carefully to see what your children are naturally good at and naturally drawn to and encourage them to do as much of that as possible. When I was in school my hero was my woodwork teacher, but woodwork is not an academic subject and we were given minimal time to learn and practise it. How I wished and wished I could have had more time in the woodwork shop instead of having to play football and cricket. I hated both those games with a vengeance, not because there was anything intrinsically wrong with them, but *because I was not suited to them.* I have never been a team player, I never will be and I have no wish to be. I just wanted to make things with my hands.

So now you are an adult and so am I and there is nothing going to stop me now from doing whatever I want. I suggest there is also nothing to stop you doing likewise, *except perhaps yourself.* Don't let the ghost of your head teacher stop you, or your parents, or any other social conditioning that makes you feel afraid or inept. If you feel fear, face it head on, acknowledge it fully and then move on to take those all important first steps. If and when the fear creeps back in later, acknowledge it again and keep going on your path towards the fulfilment of your full human potential.

Constant self-monitoring

Don't forget the reason why you are reading this book. It's because you want to build yourself a happy and fulfilled life. All the achievements in the world don't amount to a hill of beans if you are still unhappy. Constant self-monitoring is essential, and if you find maybe this path is not bringing you the joy you yearn for, don't hesitate to change direction, radically if necessary, or even to start again from square one.

Here, as a convenient reminder, are some self-monitoring questions you can ask yourself. Of course, you can adapt them as you see fit:

- Am I in my *maximum creative flow*?
- Am I enjoying my journey?
- Does the end goal still have the magic appeal it had at first?
- Am I feeling discouraged because of fear?
- Am I feeling disappointed?
- Am I feeling encouraged?
- Do I honestly believe I can do this?
- Exactly how do I feel about this?

Don't hesitate to fine tune your plan and what you are doing if necessary, or start all over again in a new direction if that's what feels right. You are doing this for you, so if it doesn't give you what you want, it's a pointless exercise. On the other hand getting it 'right' for you, even if you have to try again many times, is obviously essential.

Strengthening your motivation

Finally let's reiterate, you will make your action plan even more powerful if you include a written schedule at least for your opening moves. Detail exactly when you will take each step. It's very important to *hold yourself to account* to make sure you do what you say you are going to do by the stated time or date. Otherwise how are you going to start believing in yourself, and how can you expect to get results? The Impeccable Warrior always honours his commitments, including his commitments to himself. This is essential for solid self-esteem and self-worth, as well as self-belief. The structure of such a forward-looking plan is immensely supportive in making sure you do what you intend within a reasonable timeframe.

If you decide you chose the wrong path and you want to stop what you are doing and start again on something different, you then have a responsibility to yourself to make that change of direction *without delay*. When you do that, you can always hold your head up high – not in an egotistical way but in a self-respecting manner.

Even if your first step in your new direction is to do more research, planning and decision-making prior to taking direct physical action, that's absolutely valid if it's a necessary preparation towards eventually moving you nearer to your goal. You don't want to go off at half cock. Put it in your plan.

Sometimes a person is highly motivated but fear overpowers their intention, resulting in procrastination, or *analysis paralysis,* or even giving up. If that happens to you, there is a question you can ask yourself which will probably help you overcome the problem, which is: 'what needs to happen, or what do I need to do, for my motivation to get stronger?'

Various answers are possible, such as:

- Take more, stronger action
- Feel the fear and do it anyway
- Meditate to become more centred, clearer and more empowered
- Do some more research so you feel better informed
- Take a holiday and try again as soon as you come home
- Develop a more positive mindset

If you really open yourself to the questions, many different ideas might come to you. The important thing is, whichever answer(s) appeal to you, **TAKE ACTION**.

Let's repeat this final point yet again just to make sure we never forget it: *only action produces a result.* The same action will almost certainly produce the same result, so if you don't like the results you are getting, change your action. This means if you make a mistake it's OK, just try doing it differently next time. It also implies you also need to change your thinking and change your mindset. Also, strongly question anything within yourself you recognise as a self-limiting belief.

Summary

- Don't over-think your first step, or you risk *analysis paralysis*
- When facing a new challenge *act as if* you are supremely confident and *act on instinct combined with common sense*
- If you run away and avoid your most heartfelt wishes, you might avoid rejection but you can never feel good about yourself. Don't try to brush your fear under the carpet

- Use your action plan to support you
- Chunk your task ahead down into small steps and tackle them one at a time. *Never underestimate the power of small steps*
- It is never a good idea to put yourself down for any reason. Your *Success Diary* will help you to see that you are, on balance, a successful person
- Filling your head with thoughts of failure can only lead you down a negative road, instead you can choose to focus only on the positive
- By doing things you want and love to do while noting your success as you go along, your self-esteem, self-belief and self-worth start to grow. You will begin to relax and feel more confident
- At the same time inner peace begins to replace inner conflict, excitement starts to oust fear and anxiety, and balance begins to triumph over extremes
- When you act upon something that excites you and comes from your heart, all sorts of unexpected doors open for you and you feel energised
- Two essential factors in changing your life for the better are: *find your creative path* and *take action*
- When you are on a path that is not really yours, your way will be difficult and painful with many pitfalls. Progress will be slow and hard won. More important, there will be no joy or fulfilment and probably little creativity
- It's how you deal with setbacks that separates the achievers from the victims. A 'can-do' mindset is essential
  It's vitally important to acknowledge how you feel and own it fully
- Maintain your awareness so you can spot potential red herrings and instead stay centred
- Don't be distracted by e-mail and the internet
- Meditation helps you stay on track and hear the guidance of your inner voice, the wisdom of your heart, and enjoy travelling on your creative path. A soul thrives on meditation at regular intervals
- If you are a parent, observe what your children are naturally good at and naturally drawn to and encourage them to do as much of that as possible

- There is nothing to stop you doing whatever you want, *except perhaps yourself*. If you feel fear, face it head on and then take your first steps. If fear creeps back in later, acknowledge it again and carry on regardless
- If you want to build a happy and fulfilled life, all the achievements in the world don't amount to a hill of beans if you are still unhappy
- Constant self-monitoring is essential; don't hesitate to change direction or even to start again from square one if it's the right thing to do
- It's important to hold yourself to account, so include a written schedule for your opening moves, detailing exactly when you will take each step
- If you decide you chose the wrong path and you want to start again on something different, make a commitment to yourself and change direction *without delay*
- *Only action produces a result*
- The same action will almost certainly produce the same result. If you don't like the results you are getting, change your action, as well as your thinking and your mindset

Tools for dealing with setbacks

- If you are feeling nervous about doing something new, *act as if* and take action
- If you're not sure what you're doing is right for you, ask yourself:

  What on Earth am I doing here?
  Why do I feel so awful about doing this?
  If I do this, will it move me nearer to my goal?
  Does this goal really feel right for me?
- When things are going well, tell yourself : 'Wow, this feels great,' and write about it in your *Success Diary*.

Questions to ensure you stay on track

- Is this really relevant?
- Will this get me nearer to my goal?

Self-monitoring questions

- How much am I enjoying this?
- Exactly how do I feel about this?
- Am I in my maximum creative flow?
- Am I enjoying the journey?
- Does the end goal still have the magic appeal it had at first?
- Am I feeling discouraged because of fear?
- Am I feeling disappointed?
- Am I feeling encouraged?
- Do I honestly believe I can do this?

Questions to boost your motivation

- What needs to happen, or what do I need to do, to make my motivation stronger?
- Strongly question anything within yourself you recognise as a *self-limiting belief*

24

The Knowledge and Experience You Need

Courage is being scared to death ... and saddling up anyway
John Wayne

If you live in the Western world and you are a grown adult with average intelligence, lack of relevant knowledge is really no excuse for not following your creative path, and neither is lack of experience. In England where I live, for example, you can train in or learn virtually anything you can think of, and many things you can't. If you are creating something new for which there is as yet no training, there's always something you can learn from earlier pioneers or mentors.

It is quite likely you are in a situation in which you can't just get out of bed one day and suddenly start living your passion if you've never approached it before. If you want to be a musician, for example, at the very least you need a musical instrument and lots of practise, and a great deal of application will be required before you can even think about performing in public. However, if lack of knowledge is your only inhibiting factor, your life is easy because there's a set procedure you can follow which will deliver you to your goal, assuming you have the necessary talent. It's called getting a training (or education).

We are not talking here about domestic or family scenarios that make it hard to adapt or change, such as having a mortgage, a spouse and five kids to support, for in such a case you almost certainly need a strategy and your manoeuvring might have to be highly tactical. I'm talking about another way of feeling stuck – *believing* you don't have the knowledge, training, qualifications or experience you need, and that it can't be remedied.

I use the word *'believing'* because you might be one of those people who, no matter how much you know already, never feel you have enough knowledge and experience even when you get to the point at which you could quite easily make a start. What you lack if that applies to you is confidence or self-belief, so watch out for that potential trap. It's just an old pattern, a manifestation of your saboteur, but it can stop you in your tracks if you let it. Never forget that making a start, no matter how hesitant or humble, is the key to getting onto your road towards success and happiness, and the sooner the better.

Maybe you're a perfectionist who refuses to ply his new trade or art until he can do it 'perfectly' and his knowledge is 'complete.' If that is so, get over yourself and get on with it. Neither knowledge nor experience can ever be complete so therefore your delay is futile. You are avoiding or postponing.

Yet another possibility is the 'I'm too old, it's too late, you can't teach an old dog new tricks' scenario. This really is nonsense and it deserves no sympathy whatsoever. I once met a seventy-five year-old woman who had just graduated with her first degree, and an eighty-year-old who had recently trained in anthropology and was about to embark on writing his first book on the subject. Obviously it only makes sense to train in something you are suited for – it would be crazy for our seventy-five year-old to start a ten-year training to be a doctor because she'd never be able to practise. The point is that these two people derived tremendous satisfaction merely from achieving their lifelong dreams. At their time of life they were sufficiently sage to enjoy the journey for its own sake, not only for the result. They felt empowered and fulfilled.

So if there's a simple procedure to open the door towards your goal, like getting a training, you owe it to yourself to grab it with both hands without delay. When you get trained, somebody with the knowledge you require is handing you what you need on a plate, and that's priceless. Don't make the mistake of believing it's only worthy to pursue a course that leads to a profession, career or a job. Doing it just for the joy of learning, or to pursue a leisure activity or sport can be reason enough.

All of the above objections are various manifestations of your fear. Fear is not to be sniffed at or belittled, some of us go through agonising difficulties because of it. But it will block you if you don't watch out. It's important that you recognise your fear for exactly what it is – a construct of your mind. In all probability it's not real – or justified.

If fear is holding you back, look it squarely in the face and ask yourself what you are afraid of. When you acknowledge that, your fear will have less of a hold over you.

Please don't think me rude, but I am obliged at this point to ask you the key question: 'are you going to sit around lamenting your lack of knowledge and make yourself believe your dream goal is too difficult or impossible so you have a golden excuse to give up? Or are you going to put your resistance under the microscope, get off your backside and find a way forward?'

If you have read thus far you will know by now that you can do whatever you like if you really want it and have the talent or aptitude. So if you still aren't galvanised, by a process of deduction it can only be because of some sort of fear or resistance. You are making excuses and procrastinating. So let's take a look at that in more depth.

I had a client who dreamed of opening a healing centre with a group of likeminded people, yet she'd spent her entire working career in high pressured office environments, latterly as a middle management executive, a position she hated. Finally, suffering untold stress and anxiety, she had been made redundant and decided now was the time to do something completely different.

She knew exactly the kind of healing massage she wanted to do and she'd already done a little of it on her friends in a non-professional capacity. But she was not trained for it and she lacked the diploma she wanted.

I asked her, 'What's to stop you from enrolling in the training course?'

'Oh I couldn't do that,' she replied. 'It's expensive and I might not get enough customers to make a living. Also, I don't know for sure that I'll be good at it or even if I'll enjoy it,' she told me.

Bear in mind we had already checked very carefully and at some length that the idea of opening a healing centre and doing healing massage was coming from her heart, and I felt pretty sure it was. Unfortunately, she was feeling very insecure and unsure about risking the money for the course, let alone for opening the centre. Of course, life doesn't come with a guarantee.

'How will you find out?' I asked her.

'Ahh! Catch 22,' she replied.

'Exactly!'

The inescapable truth is you can't know in advance, you can only trust and follow your heart and evaluate how you feel about taking the risk, and any business start-up, which is what this would be, carries a risk, like it or not. You should also consider that if you end your days not having at least tried what you yearned to do with all your energy, passion and enthusiasm, you may not feel so good about that.

Clearly, in her mind, moving forward along this path was a total impossibility, yet she was very obviously gifted and highly creative in this direction. She could well afford to pay for the training from her redundancy settlement but she was so terrified of dwindling her savings she could not see her need to invest in her own advancement.

As I understand it, unless a person has reached retirement age, redundancy money was originally intended for this very purpose, to empower a person to retrain and find a new career or line of employment.

At this point it is well worth remembering the wise words by John Maxwell quoted at the beginning of the last chapter:

> *'As you begin changing your thinking, start immediately to change your behaviour. Begin to act the part of the person you would like to become. Take action on your behaviour. Too many people want to feel, then take action. This never works.'*

Please note the key words, 'this never works.' If you want written guarantees in advance of taking action, you are putting the cart before the horse, and that doesn't work either.

It is worth emphasising that her opening phrase, 'I couldn't do that,' shut her down straight away. Watch out for that pitfall because if you fall prey to it, it will sabotage you every time.

I pointed out to my client that she had already made a start despite her misgivings by giving therapeutic massage sessions to her friends, who had given her very positive feedback.

'How did you feel when you were giving those massages,' I asked her?

'Great,' she replied.

What more can we say? The evidence is looking good.

If you are not prepared to invest time and money in yourself, and if you demand guarantees before you make a start, you are not putting forward a very believable message to the world or to yourself.

If you want to make radical changes, if you want the satisfaction and fulfilment that comes with achievement and excellence in your chosen field, sometimes you literally have to put your money where your mouth is. If you allow yourself to be guided by your heart and make moves to support yourself, there will be responses from the world at large to match your self-supporting action. But you have to make the first move and to do that you have to either believe in yourself, or *act as if* you believe in yourself. It's as if you are stepping up to a podium and yelling, 'This is me and this is what I really want!' In reality it's yourself you are addressing.

This is an essential part of being proactive – obviously it makes sense to prepare first, but sooner or later you must take your power and your courage in both hands and do whatever it takes. Even if you start of by making lots of mistakes, learn and press on.

This kind of pro-active behaviour is also a vital ingredient in creating the correct dominant thought. Even if you are afraid, you must find it within yourself to have the courage of your convictions. There is no other way.

You can do this. I heard of a man in a wheelchair ascending to the top of Everest; I came across a person disadvantaged by thalidomide who developed a successful career as an artist; I have seen incredible paintings done by disabled people who have learned to use their feet and mouths to paint with. I myself have changed careers and directions in major ways several times, and I assure you I am no more special than the next person. I just learned the value of developing a *'can do'* attitude and I got fed up with complaining and feeling powerless.

Whatever is necessary and appropriate, if you have the passion in your heart and the talent in your being, you can do this. That includes getting the knowledge and experience you need. Knowledge and experience are empowering, so don't hold back.

There is no substitute for personal, first-hand experience. It can't be taught. Yet specialist knowledge might be needed too. It's up to you to find the balance so you develop both. Learning and doing are great ways to sally forth on your joyful journey towards creative fulfilment. At first you may feel impossibly challenged, but soon things will begin to flow and your confidence will grow.

Don't forget to stop, be still and listen to your heart at regular intervals. Then you'll know if you're on the right track, even when doubts creep in.

Summary

- Lack of relevant knowledge is no excuse for not following your creative path, and neither is lack of experience
- If, no matter how much you know already, you never feel you have enough knowledge and experience to make a start, what you lack is confidence
- Making a start, no matter how hesitant or humble, is the key to getting underway on your road towards success, and the sooner the better
- The quest for perfection in this context is just avoiding or postponing, once again because of lack of confidence
- More avoidance also lies behind the 'I'm too old' scenario
- If there's a simple procedure to open the door towards your goal, like getting a training, you owe it to yourself to grab it with both hands without delay
- Don't make the mistake of believing it's only worthy to pursue a course that leads to a profession, a career or a job
- It's important that you recognise your fear for what it is – a construct of your mind. In all probability, it's not real
- If fear is holding you back, acknowledge that and ask yourself what you are afraid of. When you own it, your fear will have less of a hold over you
- Will you lament your lack of knowledge and give up? Or are you going to put your resistance under the microscope and find a way forward?
- If you are not prepared to invest time and money in yourself, and if you demand guarantees before you will make a start, you are not putting forward a very believable message to the world or to yourself
- If you want to make radical changes, if you want the satisfaction and fulfilment that comes with achievement and excellence, sometimes you literally have to put your money where your mouth is.
- If you allow yourself to be guided by your heart and make moves to support yourself, there will be responses from the world at large to match your self-supporting action

- Sooner or later you must take your power and your courage in both hands and do whatever it takes
- Pro-active behaviour is a vital ingredient in creating the correct dominant thought
- Knowledge and experience are empowering, so don't hold back
- There is no substitute for personal, first-hand experience. It can't be taught. Yet specialist knowledge might be needed too. Learning and doing are great ways to move forward
- Stop, be still and listen to your heart at regular intervals. Then you'll know if you're on the right track

25

Affirmations, Manifestation and the Law of Attraction

The way in is the way out
Anonymous

There is nothing magic, supernatural or ethereal about affirmations, but they are an extremely powerful tool in helping you develop a positive mindset. They help you focus like a laser and they place fruitful dominant thoughts into your unconscious for your mind to work on. I would even go so far as to say that affirmations, when used correctly, should be regarded as one of the most important tools in your quest to reprogramme yourself for success. I have no doubt you will do yourself a priceless service if you master the art of correctly using affirmations, for then you will hold in your hand one of the major keys to your future happiness.

In his book *Think and Grow Rich*, author Napoleon Hill puts much emphasis on the practice of *auto-suggestion* which, in essence, is how affirmations work. Indeed I know the power of auto-suggestion first-hand because my father was a hypnotherapist. His work depended for its success entirely on the power of suggestion and when I was about eight-years-old he taught me how I could hypnotise myself to harness and apply the power of auto-suggestion to myself for various benefits.

Doing affirmations is another great way to use auto-suggestion, and it's the way I would suggest for those who are not hypnosis professionals.

When you do affirmations (full instructions to follow), all you are doing is planting a suitable dominant thought into your mind. The new mindset that develops supports you and your behaviour by prompting you to take the necessary actions for the achievement of your goals and aspirations.

Of course, it's still your responsibility to take action to make things happen. The good news is that affirmations, correctly applied, will cause you to do that almost automatically *via the unstoppable power of your mind.* It's a bit like changing your default settings, if you will pardon the computer analogy, so that it becomes easy to adopt behaviour and actions that are constructive instead of sabotaging. It is very much in your interests, therefore, to learn how to apply that power.

It took me many years to understand how your mind can create virtually anything it wants. I have heard and read countless personal development gurus who claim it's true, but I was always sceptical. That's because I never fully understood. But one day the penny dropped.

I used to believe, for example, 'if I decide I want a new house, how can my mind create such a thing? How can I own a new house just by thinking about it? Surely this is nonsense. Houses are created by architects and builders and if you want one you have to buy it, inherit it, or build it yourself.'

The next stage, sadly, would always be that I would consign the project, in this case a new house, to the box marked *'impossible.'*

Finally, one day, I got it and it is now absolutely clear to me that your mind is unimaginably powerful, and indeed it can create virtually anything. Let's go back to our new house example to see how it can work:

- I get an idea – I want a new house
- It seems impossible – I can't afford it, I'm not a builder, I don't have any elderly relatives about to quit their mortal coil and therefore no inheritance in prospect
- Eventually I learn various methods of changing my mindset and suddenly lots of creative ideas flood in showing me how I might be able to do this after all
- I start to develop a *'can do attitude.'* My favourite can do attitude question to myself is, 'how hard can it be?' It sounds like a negative but it isn't. It's just a way of asking yourself if you are creating unnecessary difficulties and obstacles. *(As soon as you entertain this question, you're at a pivotal moment, for this is the instant of transformation when the impossible can begin to feel like a practical proposition)*
- I come up with an idea of how and from where I could get a mortgage. I could help cover the repayment costs by taking in a

lodger. Maybe I could find ways of earning a bit more money. Other options appear and suddenly my new house is very much on the cards

Please notice, *the only thing that changed was my mindset.* None of my other circumstances have changed in any way whatsoever. Therefore it is fair enough to say that the route towards achieving my goal of owning a new house was revealed to me by the power of my mind. All I have to do now is follow through by doing what it tells me to do.

Very often an important goal is a stretch and a challenge, but that doesn't make it impossible. The more you rise to challenges that come from your heart, the more you will grow to relish a good challenge. It's exciting to expand your comfort zone.

In that sense, my new house has been created by the power of my mind. *You can do that with regard to any goal you care to dream up,* as long as it accords with your core beliefs and values and you feel passionate enough about it to let it become a near obsession. Affirmations have helped me countless times over the years.

Before we leave the topic of how creative our minds are, let's have a quick look at some amazing achievements that have been made real through the power of the mind.

When I was a child the idea of lunar travel was the stuff of fantasy comic books, nobody had ever thought of the internet, and serious sea travellers wore heavy waxed canvas Sou'Wester hats with oilskin waterproofs, as breathable Gortex and fleece materials had not been invented.

Now technology has changed beyond recognition, for we have new methods, materials, machines and equipment. What has created all this? *The power of people's minds, nothing else.* Every invention or new service started with one great idea. The laws of physics, chemistry and mathematics have not changed. It's simply that we have learned more about them and imagined new ways of putting atoms and molecules together. We have discovered much about how things work – and all this is through the power of our minds.

You might say this is obvious and you've heard it a million times before, and maybe that's so. I mention it here because it's vitally important that you don't *underestimate in any respect the power of your mind.* If you do, you run the danger of dismissing affirmations as new age claptrap, psychobabble or fairy stories. You don't have to be another Einstein. *If you want to change your life, if you want to achieve the seemingly impossible, it's easy.* Anyone can do it if you understand how to take control and gainfully employ the power of your mind.

To understand how auto-suggestion works, imagine that the unconscious mind is like a piece of blotting paper or a sponge, in other words, super absorbent. Any input it receives is soaked up and when that input dominates the other material that's already there, the unconscious mind puts it together as a dominant thought. *By controlling the input, you decide what thoughts your mind creates.* Simple.

That's why, if you read newspapers you will start to take on a negative view of the world and perhaps become depressed. If you stop reading newspapers and do something else instead – let's say you take the dog for a walk in the woods in the warm sunshine – your depression leaves you almost without you noticing. You are now receiving pleasant and nourishing input so you start to feel better. Your endorphins start flowing. It really is as simple as that. You decide.

The corollary is that if you want to achieve something that's important to you, all you have to do is feed your mind the necessary input. Your mind will then create that achievement for you by prompting you to do whatever is required. It will give you ideas about what to do next by coming up with all sorts of options for action from which you can choose – this time with the power of your conscious, rational mind.

The much talked about law of attraction, or the law of manifestation, works on exactly the same principle, so by doing affirmations, you are in fact aligning with those laws.

How to create an affirmation

An affirmation is nothing more than a desire or intention expressed in the form of a written statement. Creating one is very similar in principle to goal setting in that it needs to be positive and in the present tense. It's also important to make sure your affirmations are personal, brief, strictly to the point and easy to memorise. All you need is a pen and some paper.

Let's take a look at some examples which will demonstrate first how *not* to do it, and then how we edit what we have written to correct our statement.

- **Personal:** *I wish I could lose some weight.* (It's personal but also negative, conditional and in future tense)
- **Positive:** *I am going to eat only healthy foods.* (Now it's positive but its still way off into the future)
- **Present:** *I eat only healthy foods.* (Almost perfect. It's personal, positive and in the present. But it could be a tiny bit shorter)
- **Brief/to the point:** *I eat healthy foods.* (Bingo! That sums it up succinctly and it's very easy to memorise)

Note: The more briefly the intention, thought or statement is expressed, the more effective it is, as long as it tells the whole story.

Before we go on to see what we do next, there is one very important caveat. The affirmation must come from your heart and be imbued with your emotion or passion, otherwise it won't work. In other words, if you create the above affirmation because your spouse or partner is nagging you to lose weight you might as well forget it because you're wasting your time. Similarly if there's a negative or fear-based motive behind it, for example *'I want to lose weight because I'm afraid of dying,'* you are unlikely to experience success. Try rephrasing it to *'I love my life,'* or *'I love feeling healthy.'* When you create your affirmation, the sentiment expressed might not be true at the moment, for example, you might hate your life right now but aspire to love it soon. Nevertheless it is important to phrase your affirmation in such a way that your aspiration is stated in the present tense, as if it is already so.

Affirmations are best used to bring about a change of mindset or to implant a suitable dominant thought. There is no reason you won't succeed as long as you follow the guidelines, which have been tried and tested in one form or another over many centuries by countless spiritual seekers, personal development practitioners and high achievers the world over.

Next step

Once you have your affirmation, we return to the power of writing. The simplest way to work with your affirmation is to get a book full of blank pages, exactly as you did for your *Success Diary*, open it at the first page and write the date at the top. Then you write out your affirmation by hand at least ten times. The act of handwriting, as opposed to word-processing or typing, is important because as with every writing exercise we have described in this book already, it has the effect of imprinting your message powerfully onto your unconscious mind, and that will considerably reinforce your intention.

You do this in private as soon as you get up in the morning and last thing before you go to bed at night, and if you can find the time at lunchtime do it then too. In this way, you actually plant your idea into your unconscious mind. This is what is meant by the term *auto-suggestion.* Your unconscious will get to work on granting your wish whether you realise it or not. Don't forget, you must have some emotional charge in your affirmation – in other words you have to really want it – for it to work properly.

All the writing, drawing and visualisation exercises we have covered in this book have the same purpose – *auto-suggestion.* For maybe the first time in your life you are now in control – you no longer leave things to chance. *You* decide what message goes into your psyche and *you* create your own dominant thought or thoughts. At the same time you shut out negative input by, for example, not reading newspapers and avoiding horror films or movies featuring gratuitous violence, and so on. You can support your efforts even further by doing other positive actions, for example voluntary work to help others, the environment, or whatever feels important to you. However, unless you are a politician, I would suggest you avoid political activity, at least until you get your positive dominant thoughts firmly embedded.

Other things you can do with your affirmation include writing it in large letters on lots of Post-it notes and sticking them around the house – on your fridge, bathroom mirror, doors, in the middle of your car steering wheel, on your briefcase, on your PC monitor, on your laptop – indeed anywhere you can think of where you will see it at odd times during the day and be reminded of it. That's another reason why very short is best.

You can memorise it and repeat it to yourself at odd moments, for example when sitting on the loo, waiting for a bus or even driving on a motorway. If you are alone, you can recite it out loud like a poem, over and over again.

If you do all of the above, you'll be amazed at how much more positive and enthusiastic you start to feel about your goal. The change can be radical, and often is.

There's no end to the creative ways you can use your affirmations.

For example, I felt I needed to shed a few pounds and I decided to try using the system described in Paul McKenna's book and CD, *I Can Make You Thin,* mentioned in Chapter 20.

Without going into detail, the CD is very effective in planting helpful suggestions into your mind that can help you change to the required mindset to make this weight-loss system work. However there was one rule that I found hard to observe because it cut across a lifelong, deeply conditioned habit – stop eating as soon as you are no longer hungry, even if there's food left on your plate. All my life my habit had been to eat until I was full up, which is subtly different from stopping when I was no longer hungry, and I got away without putting on much excess weight until I reached the age of about forty-three. Then my body chemistry must have changed and I started gradually putting on weight, which didn't feel good.

So I came up with two affirmations, *'I eat when I'm hungry,'* and *'I love feeling light and healthy.'* These I wrote out ten times in the morning and ten times at night, and stuck them to the door of my fridge, where I would be bound to see them if ever I went after more food. I also stuck them on the side of my shaving mirror, so I stared at them every morning while shaving. It took a while, but after about two to four weeks I got used to eating far smaller quantities *without feeling hungry.* The emotional void that drives comfort eating, that feeling of deprivation, sacrifice or loss had gone and guess what? I slowly shed over a stone and a half and felt infinitely better!

There was also considerable benefit to my self-esteem and self-belief, because that's what happens when *you* empower yourself, *you* take control and *you* start to get the results you want.

I am in no doubt that the affirmations helped me to stay on track until I altered my mindset in the right direction. Many of the weight-loss gurus say nowadays that losing weight using methods that rely on will power alone will never work long-term. That's true and it's because the person's mindset has not changed, and in the end we always revert to acting in accordance with our frame of mind. Changing deeply ingrained habits requires powerful tools coupled with supreme awareness and perseverance.

Finally, it might amuse you to know that when I started writing this book I used a slightly different version of this technique. First, needless to say, I created and wrote down a goal, or series of goals, about producing this manuscript. Then I wrote down three phrases that suddenly popped into my head in a fit of exuberance as I rolled up my sleeves to get cracking, and I stuck them under the goal. Then I stuck the whole piece of paper, complete with scrawled phrases, right next to my computer screen where I was bound to see them regularly. They are still there and they are faithfully keeping me at it!

The three phrases say *'I have let go of my safety net!' 'I am jet propelled!' 'Ain't nothin' gonna stop me now!'*

And finally, here I am at the end of Chapter 25. It can't be a coincidence that since I wrote those affirmations, my feet have barely touched the ground!

Summary

- When used correctly, affirmations are one of the most important tools in your quest to reprogramme yourself for success. It will repay you handsomely to master their use
- Doing affirmations is a powerful and risk-free way to harness the power of auto-suggestion
- Affirmations enable you to plant a suitable dominant thought into your mind. The new mindset you create supports you and your behaviour by prompting you to take the actions necessary for achievement
- It's still your responsibility to take action to make things happen. The good news is that affirmations correctly applied will cause you to do that *via the unstoppable power of your mind*
- Your mind can create virtually anything you desire
- Don't underestimate the power of your mind, or you run the danger of dismissing affirmations
- *If you want to change your life, if you want to achieve the seemingly impossible, it's easy.* Anyone can do it if you understand how to take control and gainfully employ the power of your mind
- If you want to achieve something that's important to you, all you have to do is feed your mind the necessary input and it will create that achievement for you by prompting you to take whatever action is required
- An affirmation is a desire or intention expressed in the form of a written statement. It needs to be positive, in the present tense, brief,

personal and easy to remember – and to be effective it must come from your heart

- The more briefly the intention, thought or statement is expressed, the more effective it is, as long as it tells the whole story
- If there's a negative or fear-based motive behind your affirmation you are unlikely to experience success. Try rephrasing it
- When you create your affirmation, the sentiment expressed might not be true at the time. Your affirmation aims to encompass your aspiration and bring it into the present
- Write out your affirmation by hand at least ten times, and at least twice a day
- The act of handwriting, as opposed to word-processing or typing, has the effect of imprinting your message powerfully into your unconscious mind
- When you master the practice of *auto-suggestion,* you will be in control – you no longer leave things to chance. *You* decide what message goes into your psyche and *you* create your own dominant thoughts
- Another way you can use your affirmation is to write it on Post-it notes and stick them around your home so you can see it frequently. You can memorise it and repeat it to yourself over and over again whenever you can
- There's no end to the creative ways you can use your affirmations

THE FOURTH PILLAR

Relationships

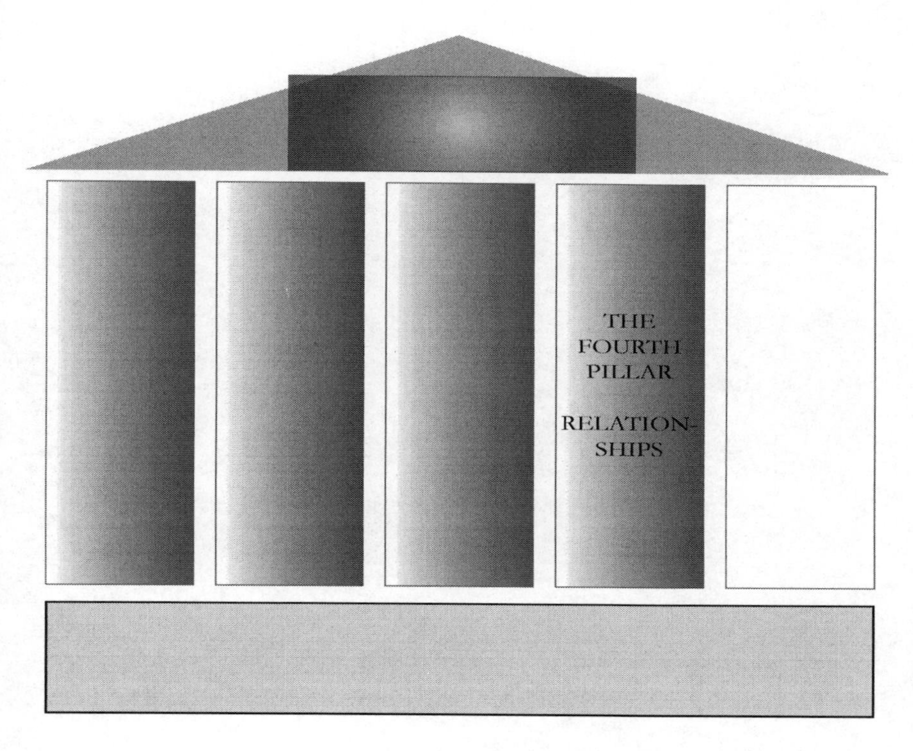

Most people would agree there is no way your life can be complete, successful or even viable if you neglect to master at least the most basic relationship skills, unless you yearn to be a recluse. It's a huge subject and it probably merits a book in its own right. Here we focus on the most important basic principles of building better relationships of all types – principles that can transform your experience of relationships from puzzling, frustrating or downright disastrous, to highly enjoyable, satisfying and fruitful.

26

A Suitable Partner

When we feel responsible, concerned and committed, we begin to feel deep emotion and great courage

Dalai Lama

Let's start by talking about romantic relationships. For the sake of brevity I talk here mainly in terms of relationships between men and women but I mean to include all types, for the same or similar principles apply in single sex partnerships too.

With the best will in the world, not every relationship can be made to work. Nor are there any guarantees that one that works today will work tomorrow.

Humans being what they are, the reverse can also be true. The lady may not want to know the guy today, but tomorrow she may fall in love with him, or vice versa. The most important point in this state of affairs is sensing when a relationship can never work and is therefore not worth pursuing, or when it could work given time, or when mutual attraction could grow, in which case it might be a good idea to persevere.

It's important to bear in mind that it is unrealistic and unfair to expect another person to change, for that has to be our guiding principle. Can we accept the other person as they are?

The implication of this when choosing someone with whom to have a meaningful relationship is that it makes sense to select a person who is 'suitable,' or maybe it would be more accurate to use the words 'already acceptable,' so you have no need for them to change. This chapter discusses exactly what we mean by suitable, how we know if someone is suitable, and how we can go about finding a suitable partner.

When in relationships, the only way to safely navigate around these problems in a way that works for all concerned is with supreme awareness regarding our feelings on a day-to-day basis. Constant self-monitoring is needed so we can keep in touch with what we want and how we feel. This enables us to adopt the behaviour of the Impeccable Warrior, absolutely essential in every type of relationship.

This also implies that your intended partner also needs to behave as an Impeccable Warrior, or at least to try to. To explain a little more clearly what I'm getting at here, most people who have not embarked on a path of living with heightened awareness will inevitably be driven, to a greater or lesser degree, by unconscious behaviour, which in many cases is manipulative, or sabotaging in other ways. Now that you have come some considerable way down this road, you are going to find it very hard, if not impossible, to live with that. I don't mean that as any sort of a judgement, it's just that I have learned from personal experiences and those of my clients what is likely to work and what isn't.

Only from a standpoint of knowing how we feel at any given moment can we engage in honest two-way verbal communication. We need this, along with sensitive and observant readings of the other person's body language and an understanding of their moods and feelings. Some people believe they are unable to do this, but all that is required is saying truthfully what is on your mind, and being a good observer and listener too, both of which might need practise.

Very often relationships break down because either or both parties fail to communicate regularly and honestly. This is sometimes because the people concerned are out of touch with their true feelings, or if they are in touch, they fear expressing them to the other person. Communication, especially around emotional issues, is essential within relationships, so if necessary learn and hone that skill and don't hesitate to use it regularly.

It is also sometimes the case that a relationship falls apart even when the two parties are being honest, because they realise they do not love each other after all or they no longer want to be together for some reason, or sadly, one partner feels that way.

In a situation like either of the above, there will almost certainly be sadness on both sides about letting go and saying goodbye. However, by facing the truth and going separate ways because of that truth, each person emerges with integrity, and that makes all the difference regarding how we feel about ourselves. This kind of Impeccable Warrior behaviour, in which we deal cleanly with everything that arises from our relationships, is important, for although either or both parties will feel pain, there is nothing more demoralising, disempowering and generally de-humanising than remaining in a dead relationship. It is impossible to flourish and grow in such non-nourishing circumstances.

By acting honestly in response to our feelings we eventually find it possible to view such a painful experience as splitting up as a positive one, and gratefully digest the lesson that is given before moving on. As we have seen in earlier chapters, when we allow ourselves to experience our feelings instead of trying to suppress them, they pass and we can progress.

Honesty in relationships begins with ourselves, and first we need to look inside and discover as clearly as possible what we actually want and need in a partner, and from a relationship. Unless we do that, there is the danger that we'll habitually grab the first potential partner that comes along out of an unconscious desperation. Then there is no way we can know if our needs are likely to be met unless we make ourselves consciously aware of what our needs are. If it turns out that they are not met, we will always experience a background feeling of dissatisfaction, frustration and resentment without really understanding why we are not feeling the bliss and contentment we expected to feel.

As we have already noted, it is unfair, fruitless and arrogant to expect another person to change. How can they and why should they? The fact is that our needs will never be met unless we choose a suitable partner, someone we can accept, warts and all, without the need for them to change. What is more, they have to be someone who can likewise accept us.

You cannot relax and be yourself if you perceive, consciously or unconsciously, that you are not being unconditionally accepted by your partner. There will always be a niggling friction and a feeling of unrealised expectations.

If you cannot accept a person and everything about them without that acceptance having to be contrived, you do not truly love them. You may love an image of what you want them to be, or what you think they are or might become, or possibly you are self-absorbed in a veil of blinkered narcissism, but you cannot be in love with the real person because you are not seeing and accepting the real person. The principle of unconditional acceptance, in my experience, is the key, the golden rule for any relationship to stand a chance of offering enduring happiness. Any other notion is pure fantasy.

Many was the time, when I was growing up, that I felt angry with my mother for accepting many of the things about my father that I found unacceptable about him at the time. Also on many occasions I was completely baffled as to how my father put up with behaviour from my mother that would drive me to distraction. I used to feel they were both colluding in mutual hypocritical compromises, and I discovered that many of my young friends felt similarly about their parents.

However, now I am a little more mature and better able to see with perspective, I see that these were my projections. Moreover, having gone through my share of anger and rebellion during my youth, I now feel completely at peace with my parents. I at last understand that they simply decided to accept each other, and that is why their marriage lasted some fifty years until my father's death, despite whatever problems may have arisen along the way.

What we often fail to understand when we are young and still rebellious, and quite naturally so, is that partners approaching each other from a heartfelt space of unconditional love for each other, which must have been the case with my parents, is far more important than irritating issues about people's idiosyncrasies. Of course only maturity teaches that.

It is right that when we are young and inexperienced we should split hairs over all the things young people argue about, for that is the only way we will ever find out how we feel, who we are, and what is important, and thence what we find acceptable or unacceptable. My partner does small things that drive me mad, but she loves me right down to my toes. I'm not complaining, I'm laughing for we have plenty in common and the bigger picture massively overpowers the small niggles. However, in my younger days, these differences could have become issues that provoked terminal confrontation. When I feel irritated I remind myself of what I have to be grateful for. I got exactly what I wanted, I'm the cat who got the cream. That's the bigger picture!

When we mature and more aware and we resolve some of our more troublesome issues we become happier with who we are, and then we find it natural to relax and accept, for other people's foibles need not challenge us any longer. Indeed we can celebrate our eccentricities. We all have foibles whether we choose to acknowledge them or not.

A very useful point to bear in mind is when we see something in someone else that we find irritating or unacceptable, it's almost always a direct reflection of something you see or used to see in yourself that you find irritating or unacceptable. Finding it in another reminds you, perhaps unconsciously, of something about yourself you'd rather repress or forget. So when someone irritates you, bear in mind that they might be triggering an issue in you that needs examining.

If you feel you might be co-dependent it is important to remember that the co-dependent person will always try to change the other and/or themselves in any relationship and, through lack of awareness and other psychological factors, will almost certainly choose unsuitable partners again and again. The pattern repeats itself relentlessly unless awareness is brought to bear. In such circumstances, unhappy, unfulfilling and non-nourishing relationships are inevitable. (If you want more understanding about co-dependency, read *Women Who Love Too Much* by Robin Norwood. Read it even if you are a man).

The phrase 'suitable partner', as I intend it, basically means a partner through whom we are likely to get our needs met, and whose needs we are likely to be able to meet. For example, I decided I wanted a partner who had enough courage and a big enough heart to let me come close, and who would want to come close to me. When I finally met a woman who seemed to fit those criteria, I made my approach. However, there were three or four women I had met on previous occasions who, though very attractive, I did not approach because I felt they would not have the courage to share true intimacy for very long. Intimacy requires a fair degree of self-acceptance.

This seems obvious with the benefit of hindsight. However in earlier days, before I understood something of how these things work, my unconscious behaviour prompted me to make moves towards almost any attractive woman who seemed attracted to me, suitable or not.

Indeed, the concept of suitability did not even enter the picture, for it never occurred to me. Perhaps I unconsciously assumed that if a person was attractive she was suitable, but I finally realised that's not necessarily enough. The different approach I mentioned above in insisting on a courageous, big-hearted woman, was a new way of behaving for me and I really had to think about it, for it seemed strange, even painful, to let attractive women go by.

Understanding, insight and awareness automatically bring about new or different behaviour patterns, because by definition we realise our old ones are counter-productive or sabotaging. In this context we can achieve what we want simply by deciding to identify our real needs first, and then choosing a suitable partner who at least appears to be compatible with those needs and who appears to have similar needs. Because of our developing awareness we now do this through conscious choice, rather than grabbing anyone attractive in desperation. In this way there is no need for anyone to try to change who they are.

Incidentally, this seemingly dry, rather academic approach does not mean I eschew the importance of what's going on in your heart. Far from it. The approach I advocate combines what your heart is telling you with what's on your mind – in other words, *emotional intelligence*. This way your heart can take wings with more likelihood of a positive outcome. I call it flying with your feet nailed firmly to the ground.

If you still think my approach is clinical, mechanical, robotic, heartless or cynical (I have been accused of all of those), consider the following: if you are with another person and you cannot accept them unconditionally, it is not their fault. It is not yours either, though the responsibility is yours, not theirs. If you were to stay with that person you'd have to try to control and manipulate them, to mould them to some image of what you think you want them to be, even if that were unintentional and unconscious. Conversely, if the other person cannot fully accept you, they would be bound to want you to morph into someone you are not, consciously or unconsciously.

As I have already pointed out, trying to control someone else is the greatest indignity and disrespect one person can ever visit upon another, for it is inhumane to deny someone the full flowering of their individuality, no matter how unacceptable we may judge that to be.

You don't have to like what they are like, of course. That is your prerogative. Better in that case to admit it and go elsewhere rather than blaming the other for not being how you want them to be, for you will never succeed in getting them to be the way you want. It is neither desirable nor possible.

Of course, you might not want your present or prospective relationship to represent an enduring commitment, especially if you are young. You may not yet have had sufficient worldly experience to know what you want, or maybe you just want to have fun for a while. That's fine and a necessary part of the learning process for some of us, as long as you acknowledge that to yourself and the other person in full honesty.

You could argue that getting your heart broken a few times is an essential part of growing up and learning about relationships and about yourself. That's one reason why being young is often such a painful time.

Most people find being deceived extremely painful. By honestly letting your needs, desires and intentions be known, the other person can then decide if they find them acceptable or not. Hopefully, they will have the courage to quit if the latter proves to be the case.

Until we have had some experience of lovers and partners, it is unlikely for most of us that we will really know what we want. A certain amount of sexual and partnering experimentation is almost certainly a must for most people, just as we may need to experiment to find our talents. Nevertheless, honourable behaviour is necessary for the sake of our, and the other person's, self-esteem. In Cupid's kingdom, just like everywhere else, the Impeccable Warrior gets what he wants and needs without damaging himself or others.

It is also important to recognise that sometimes our needs change as we grow, and someone who once seemed suitable may no longer be so. Truthful, courageous partners will acknowledge this too and move on, if it happens.

There used to be a myth and widely held belief when I was a lad, that there was just one special person out there for each one of us. This person's destiny was to live in perfect harmony with us, and only us, till death us do part.

I hope by now we all realise the absolute nonsense of that narrow mindset, for there are many potential suitable partners for each of us, most of whom can bring us untold happiness if we would relax and allow it to be so.

Time after time it has happened to me that I have given my heart to a woman and she has become my neurotic focus, maybe for years, until it became painfully obvious that one or both of us was failing to get our needs met. Then would come the heartbreaking splitting up, which was always very painful – until the next woman came along and the cycle repeated itself.

Then one day I woke up and realised that each and every one of those women had been utterly beautiful in her own way, and each had given me something and allowed me to give her something back of immense and immeasurable value. Though the pain might still be there, perhaps at times even more poignantly, somehow that realisation made it alright. Perhaps because there was now a purpose to all that pain?

This insight eventually helped me to break the co-dependency cycle, for I became less afraid to let go of a relationship in which it became apparent that our needs had changed, or were not being met. At the same time, this awareness helped me to become more self-sufficient. All these factors combined to make reconciliation possible with the other person in the relationship break-up, leading to a feeling of completion.

Usually it is fear that makes us want to hold on, but that is not a good enough reason to remain in a dead relationship, for time and time again I have been shown that holding on in such circumstances brings nothing but more suffering. When you realise that even in separation, acceptance becomes possible, you will understand that even the pain becomes acceptable. With that understanding we will appreciate that when it is time to move on it means that something even more beautiful is just around the corner. Each time we know a little more about what we want, and knowing ourselves better inevitably leads to a fuller and happier life, for the simple reason, we can ask for and receive, more of what we want and need. We will have a greater understanding of what makes a suitable partner.

I have experienced this many times over, and many of my clients report similar experiences. The principle is always the same; what leads to unhappiness in a relationship is when one or both protagonists are driven by unconscious behaviour.

As a perfect example, we may hang on to a relationship which is not happy for fear of letting go and being alone. Does that sound familiar? We may fear we will never find someone else or someone better suited; we may be jealous at the idea of our ex-partner in someone else's arms; we may be afraid of losing our house or children; we may enjoy the sex. There is an endless list of reasons for staying in a dead relationship and while all are perfectly understandable, none lead to fulfilment.

My concern here is to discuss some of the issues that affect the building of happy and fulfilling relationships on a deep level. As long as that is our primary interest, it is time to face the truth. If we feel we are not getting our needs met and are not likely to, it is time to move on. We would do well to remember that whatever happens, we have to live with ourselves, like it or not, and the most important relationship we can ever have is the one we have with ourselves. When we sustain unhappy relationships with others, we merely set ourselves up for a miserable relationship with ourselves, and that cannot be conducive to a happy, high self-esteem driven way of life.

From my perspective, my divorce was a particularly ugly and harrowing affair. When it was over, as I stood knee deep in a wasteland of the broken dreams that surrounded me, I promised myself I would never get married again, nor father any more children, until I had 'got myself sorted out.'

For years it made no sense, for I believe my ex-wife and I loved each other very deeply, yet we couldn't live together. It all seems perfectly simple now, it's obvious we were not suited to each other temperamentally, for though we had some common ground, we had very different needs, and what we wanted out of life was radically different. Of course, we didn't realise that at the time. Understanding this helped me accept the truth.

This is far from being a tale of woe, for that and other experiences have shown me that every relationship I had ever been blessed with has been a gift, and perfect in its own way. It's as if I've collected my own personal portfolio of case histories, each of which has contributed something essential to what I've learned about getting my life as I wanted it. Unlike what we learn in school, these lessons were alive and fascinating for being full of the drama of human emotion. That's why I firmly believe that no experience we have in our lives is ever wasted.

It took a long time, but finally I understood the message from the mystics when they say that everything in existence is exactly as it should be and everything that happens to each of us happens exactly as it should happen. An experiment can never fail. We might not get the result we want, but if we keep n open mind we always learn a truth. It is important to remember that without experiments, we learn nothing.

Every relationship is an experiment, and every relationship has at least one beautiful lesson to give us from which we can learn. Understanding is a wonderful thing, which is why I continue to labour the point about awareness. I only hope each of the women I have known feel as positively as I do.

Finding a suitable partner

Many people, and I was one of them, have a haphazard approach to relationships and they end up puzzled, confused and bereft when their love affairs drift onto the rocks. Let me tell you a story from my own life that illustrates how I woke up to this idea of a suitable partner and how to recognise when you find one. Then I'll describe a couple of powerful tools that can seriously empower you in the field of relationships, so you begin to behave with awareness and start to get the feeling you actually know what you are doing.

The day finally came, some fourteen years ago, when I felt ready for an intimate, loving relationship again. It felt like an act of acceptance and for the first time in my life I intuitively began to invoke the laws of manifestation to find a suitable partner. I became very clear about what I did and did not want in a partner. I also became very finely attuned with ways of doing affirmations and creating goals and wish lists to manifest whatever my heart truly desired, so it seemed the obvious thing to do.

Wish lists

After a few days thinking about it and asking myself how I felt about the ideas that were coming up, I produced the perfect specification of the woman I wanted for a relationship, which I sat down and wrote out as a list. The list contained every detail I could think of and as days went by I fine tuned and added to it, and re-ordered the priorities.

I knew then it would only be a matter of time before an attractive woman of around my age, with dark brown hair and eyes, a warm heart, a great sense of humour, compassionate and clearly bent on her true path would come into my life. She would also want me exactly as I am; would want to share my passion for sailing; be doing personal development of some kind; love music; be scrupulously honest; want to go deeply along the path of awareness, love, intimacy and communication; have a good appetite for sex, music, dancing, good food and movies. Not only this, she would also be capable of understanding me and letting me love her unconditionally. Someone with the courage to be real. All the above qualities I specified on a bullet point list, which I called my wish list.

I even specified her approximate height and the many interests I wanted us to have in common, that she should enjoy the cuisines of the world, that she should be non-religious, and anything else I could think of. Most of all I wanted someone with whom I could flow and harmonise, and someone who would give and receive nurturing in a generous way.

I was very clear in every respect I could think of, for I was looking in earnest for someone suitable and available for the kind of relationship I wanted. I had spent a good deal of time in introspection to discover what exactly I wanted. I was preparing for my next adventure, my next experiment – going deeper.

Of paramount importance is availability. A person who is not sure whether they are available cannot be a suitable partner if you are looking for commitment, for it never works, no matter how much we might wish it would. So I added to my list that the lady must be available.

This paragon, I reasoned, would have to be someone I had never met, because few of the above criteria applied to any of the women I knew already. Nevertheless, the ways of the world being unpredictable as they are and not wanting to leave any stone unturned, I decided to explore further by inviting each of the single women with whom I was acquainted, to whom I felt attracted and who might be available, out to dinner. One at a time, of course.

There were five in all. In each case I simply relaxed over the dinner table and talked in an effort to reveal something of myself, and listened as each woman did likewise. I made it perfectly clear beforehand I merely wanted to go out on a friendly basis, and to see what energy, if any, was there. I had a simple litmus test, which was to ask myself at intervals as the evening progressed, 'do I sense any chemistry between us?'

With each of the five women it turned out that I did not, but I was happy for I got to know five beautiful people a little better than before and made good friends with each of them. The women were happy too, for those evenings of good food and convivial company, characterised by free and open exchanges, were blissfully stress free on both sides because no-one was pretending or trying to impress.

Dates and one night stands are excellent when you are not sure what you want. However, we do have a tendency to present our egos to each other under such circumstances, instead of our hearts. Perhaps even on a date we could try it a different way by remaining open and revealing ourselves and our hearts. Not only would this make us magnetically attractive but there would also be a lot less emotional tension compared to a date in which we try to impress. It's bound to lead to a far more interesting evening, even if a heart connection doesn't materialise.

These five evenings also added to my insights and helped me refine my wish list even more keenly. This is very important, for the more accurate your specification is, the more likely you will get exactly what you want.

One afternoon shortly afterwards the telephone rang. It was an old friend, in fact one of the five women with whom I had gone out to dinner, inviting me to a small tea party at her house. I said I was sorry but I would be away sailing that weekend. However, a few days later my sailing plans fell through, so I telephoned her and asked if the invitation was still open. It was, so I went to her tea party.

There was a motley collection of people there, mostly couples and one or two babies. After a while, however, I became aware of a woman with very strong features and dark brown hair and eyes, sitting alone on the sofa. She was looking at me. Hey! I suddenly twigged, this might be her! The one I had been asking for! I went over and we started talking.

A month later we met in Southampton where she joined me and another friend on my boat for a few days sailing. Two mornings later, the boat tied up in Portsmouth harbour with the early morning spring sun peeping over the harbour wall, and we found ourselves in a deep embrace. Yes, she certainly seemed to be suitable in every respect, and for sure she was available. I was deliriously happy, and so was she. I was amazed at how closely she fitted my wish list, yet she was completely unlike anyone I had known before or could have imagined. Has I not made the wish list and refined it, I might have made a fateful mistake and passed her by.

Now let's get this in perspective, for when someone comes to me for coaching whose goal is a new partner and I suggest they make a wish list, very often they think I'm barking mad, or they think it's impossible, or they have strong resistance for some other reason. The wish list is not hocus pocus, nor does it represent some sort of delusional practice of putting wishes out into the ether so that existence can magically give you what you wish for. The wish list is a powerful tool, plain and simple.

The wish list is designed to help you become crystal clear in your mind exactly what you want in a prospective life partner and to make that your dominant thought so that when you run in to such a person you will recognise his or her potential immediately. When you spend a little time creating one of these lists for yourself, you will know immediately, when you meet an available man or woman to whom you feel attracted, whether or not he or she has the potential to be a suitable partner.

This is not merely an exercise in ticking boxes. Liberal dollops of emotional intelligence, sensitivity and common sense need to be applied if you want meaningful results. Most importantly, be prepared to modify your list in the light of new insights and experiences as time goes by. There is no way of knowing how soon you will meet someone suitable, but in my experience it's usually pretty quick, that is, within a few days or a fortnight, as long as you go out and mix with people in the traditional way, like people used to do before the onset of internet dating.

Let's take a hypothetical example. Imagine you begin your list and it starts looking something like this:

I want a partner who is:

- Kind and compassionate
- Intelligent
- Six foot two inches tall
- Loves children and wants to have some with me
- Loves dogs and wants us to get one
- Will share my passion for tennis, who will play against me and with me in mixed doubles matches
- Wants to learn golf with me

Now let's say you meet a woman of around six foot two and she appears to be wonderful in every way, but then it transpires she hates dogs but desperately wants a cat. At this point you can ask yourself, *'how do I feel about that?'* If you decide it's really important to you to have a dog and you are allergic to cats, then clearly the woman is not a suitable partner. However, if you don't mind that much and you quite like cats anyway, perhaps you would feel OK about giving way on that point as long as other more important points were covered. It's up to you to decide what's important to you, but don't be swept off track. What really matters is being honest with yourself. The purpose of the wish list is to help you stay on track.

You may think as you read this that the dog issue is insignificant, and it might well be to some people but not to others. However, danger lurks here because if you feel strongly that you want a dog and your partner refuses, this can lead to much resentment and can become a big bone of contention (no pun intended). It really matters that you are honest with yourself about how you feel on every issue.

Now let's look at this in more detail. Let's say you meet another six foot two lady and your heart starts to melt, but when it comes to discussing canine friends it turns out she wants a Poodle and you want a Labrador. Again you ask yourself, *'how do I feel about this?'* If you decide the breed of dog matters very much to you, then it's back to the drawing board once more. This time you realise it would be wise to change your list so that the line that says:

- Loves dogs and wants us to get one

Changes to:

- Loves Labradors and wants us to get one

The more detail you specify, the more likely you are to get exactly what you want. You might even decide to define the sex and colour of the Labrador if it means that much to you.

The internet

The time is now at hand for me to transcend my resistance and drag myself kicking and screaming into the 21st. Century by discussing some of the myriad potential opportunities for finding your suitable partner via the internet, using social media and/ or online dating.

Please understand, I speak as one who never takes himself *too* seriously, so I find it hard at my age (61 at the time of writing) to entertain the idea of inviting you to follow me on Twitter while keeping a straight face, yet that's what I'm doing now. I would also be honoured and delighted for you who are taking the trouble to read this book to join me, my friends and contacts on Facebook, LinkedIn and Ecademy. I have actually created a profile for myself on each of these social media or virtual networking sites and you can find me there (contact details at the end of this chapter), though to avoid any possible misunderstanding I must hasten to add, I am not looking for a partner, suitable or otherwise!

Finding a partner through the internet is the only ingredient in this book of which I have no personal experience, but many of my clients, friends and associates have, and with varying degrees of success, so I picked their brains and their hearts by way of research before writing this section.

There are many factors to consider. One is that some people use the internet as a hiding place to avoid exposing themselves for real in public. That's OK in the beginning if you are very shy, and even if you're not, but it seems important you acknowledge that and understand that conducting a relationship in cyberspace is not a substitute for personal contact. It's a tool you can use for finding suitable people and arranging your initial meeting. That means after making the first few initial contacts on the internet you need to get together in person.

I am also reliably informed that the internet is wide open to abuse and we hear stories all the time, some of which are true, of teenage or even pre-teenage girls being 'groomed' by men who have no intention of behaving like Impeccable Warriors. It is also not unknown for people of either sex to lie about their age, marital or financial status, sexual orientation and in some cases, even their gender. Plus of course there are always gold-diggers and other types of men and women who may not necessarily have your best interests at heart. Therefore everything said here about how best to use the internet must be taken with a huge caveat – BE CAREFUL.

So what are the advantages?

If you have followed my suggestion of creating a written specification that describes your perfect partner in detail you're going to love this, because in an online dating service or any of the social networks you will need to describe the kind of person you are looking for. So you will already be well equipped for the challenge because you have your wish list to refer to. Also, when people start responding to you, you will be able to tell straight away who might appeal and who will not.

The trouble you have taken to get to know yourself inside out will also stand you in good stead, because you will need to create a profile of yourself. This is to enable others to decide if you might be a suitable partner for them.

In both cases you will probably only be allowed a fairly small number of words, so a good way to create your online profile, or profile of someone you're looking for, is to use some keywords and bullet points, or what I call 'text-message speak,' not necessarily normal prose with complete sentences. Those of us who are past our first flush of youth may find this challenging, but don't be deterred. Go on line, log on to the network or dating service you wish to research, find out what's necessary and just start to play the game. In some cases, the King's English may be more appropriate.

It is important to consider why some people are unsuccessful and others get the results they want. In my observation, a person who writes something of who they are on a fairly profound level and who responds to another who also describes who they really are quite deeply, is far more likely to find a potentially suitable partner with whom he or she resonates. In other words don't present your persona, present your real self. Be aware that a list that says 'I like going to the movies and I love dancing to rock and roll bands and I go to Indian restaurants' is not going to showcase your individuality and charm, because lots of people fit that description.

It's a bit like 'niche marketing.' If you present something of your real self you put yourself in a small minority or niche because not many people do that, and this will help you 'target' a suitable partner, because they will be in a corresponding small minority. You will appeal only to the kind of people who are genuinely interested in what you have to offer, and vice versa. This means you automatically filter out those who are not suitable to you so you won't feel so overwhelmed. It will probably also lead to a satisfactory result more quickly.

Another important point is to be careful not to put yourself down. Present an accurate and positive picture of who you are, plain and simple, and behave impeccably at all times, whether online or offline.

I think I've said quite enough on this subject now, save to remind you, this is an experiment, just like all the experiments in your life, so don't be too fixated on a 'successful' outcome. The internet is just another tool or avenue for you to explore if you wish, and it may or may not bear the fruit you want. And don't feel you have to do this just because others in your peer group might be doing it. There are many ways to achieve what you want.

The marriage barometer

Here's another really important tool for people already in a relationship. If you or your partner are thinking of getting married or co-habiting, but you're not quite sure if you want to take on the necessary level of commitment, here's my barometer to help you decide. In effect it's a list of deeply insightful questions you can ask yourself so you can clarify your feelings. It's also very helpful if you feel your relationship is struggling and you are wondering whether to persevere or to give it up:

Self-monitoring questions to evaluate your relationship

- Do I feel loved for who I am?
- Do I love my partner unconditionally?
- Do I feel accepted exactly as I am, without being required to change?
- If not, do I honestly feel OK about that?
- Do I accept my partner exactly as they are, without requiring them to change?
- Do I feel listened to?
- Do I make sure my partner feels listened to?
- Do we have significant shared interests?
- Do I feel uplifted, supported and nourished in my partner's company?
- Does my partner feel uplifted, supported and nourished in my company?
- Do I feel free to express my individual personality and creativity in my partner's company?
- Do I love and accept myself?
- Do my partner and I work as a team?
- How exactly do I feel about my partner?
- How do I feel about my relationship in general?
- Do we agree on whether to have children or not?
- If so, do we agree on how to balance children and careers?
- If it turns out we can't have children, will we still love and want each other?
- How do I feel about giving up my freedom as a single person?
- Will I take the risk of opening my heart to this person?
- Will they open their heart to me?
- Can I cope with intimacy, and can my partner?
- Are we both ready to learn to communicate our feelings?
- Will I hold up a mirror to the other person and encourage them to grow?
- Will they do the same for me?

- Am I prepared to live impeccably, according to the guidance of my heart?
- Will I be true to myself – and my partner?

In the final analysis, always remember matters of love cannot be worked out by your rational mind. Trying to think these things out rationally almost always leads to confusion and loss of focus. Only your heart knows what is right for you and in matters of the romantic kind it is more important than ever to listen to it carefully and follow its guidance. The above questions are designed to help you do that, but don't forget that other powerful tool, meditation.

Once again allow me to repeat that meditation enables you to be still and silent so you can hear your inner voice, the voice of your heart, above the clamouring of your conditioned mind. Meditation helps you to see the bigger picture and get a true and balanced perspective on what's really important to you. Don't hesitate to use all your tools, especially if you feel confused.

Summary

- It is unrealistic and unfair to expect another person to change. Can you accept the other person just as they are?
- A sustainable, fulfilling relationship begins with choosing a suitable partner
- Constant self-monitoring enables us to adopt the behaviour of the Impeccable Warrior, essential in all of relationships
- Relationships often break down because either or both parties fail to communicate regularly and honestly, especially about emotional issues
- It is impossible to flourish and grow in a dead relationship
- When we allow ourselves to experience our feelings instead of trying to suppress them, they pass and we can progress
- Honesty in relationships begins with discovering what we actually want and need in a partner, and from a relationship
- It is unfair, fruitless and arrogant to expect another person to change. How can they and why should they?
- Our needs will never be met unless we choose a suitable partner, someone we can accept without the need for them to change

- If you cannot accept a person and everything about them without that acceptance having to be contrived, you do not love them
- The principle of unconditional acceptance is the key, the golden rule for any relationship to stand a chance. Any other notion is pure fantasy
- When we mature most of us become happier with who we are, and then we find it natural to relax and accept, for other people's foibles need no longer challenge us
- The co-dependent person will always try to change the other and/or themselves in any relationship. They will choose unsuitable partners again and again. Increased awareness is the only solution
- A 'suitable partner' means a partner through whom we are likely to get our needs met, and whose needs we are likely to be able to meet
- Understanding, insight and awareness make it possible for us to break our patterns, if and when we realise they are counter-productive or sabotaging
- We can achieve what we want simply by deciding to identify our real needs first, and then choosing a partner who is compatible with those needs
- Combine what your heart is telling you with what's on your mind – in other words, use *emotional intelligence*
- Until we have had some experience of lovers and partners, most of us will not really know what we want. Therefore a certain amount of experimentation is a must for most people. Nevertheless, honourable behaviour is necessary
- Usually it is fear that makes us want to hold on, but that is not a good enough reason to remain in a dead relationship
- Even in separation, acceptance becomes possible. Even the pain becomes acceptable, for when it is time to move on we know that something even more beautiful is just around the corner
- What never fails to lead to unhappiness in a relationship is when one or both protagonists are driven by unconscious behaviour patterns
- Our most important relationship is the one we have with ourselves
- When we sustain unhappy relationships with others, we merely set ourselves up for a miserable relationship with ourselves

- Every relationship is an experiment, and every relationship has at least one beautiful lesson to give us from which we can learn
- Opening our hearts, rather than presenting our egos, makes us magnetically attractive and reduces emotional tension when on a date
- The wish list is a powerful tool for getting clear in your mind exactly what you want in a prospective life partner
- When you create your own wish list, you will know immediately when you meet someone who has the potential to be a suitable partner
- Matters of love cannot be worked out by your rational mind, for only your heart knows what is right for you
- Don't forget that meditation is a powerful tool for listening to your inner voice, the voice of your heart

Tools

- Wish list
- The marriage barometer (self-monitoring questions to help you evaluate your relationship)

27

Helping Each Other Grow

By one's self the evil is done, by one's self one suffers; by one's self evil is left undone, by one's self one is purified. The pure and the impure stand and fall by themselves, no one can purify another

Dhammapada

Self-perception

I daresay we have all noticed that it is extremely easy to see other people and their foibles as they really are, but notoriously difficult to see ourselves and our own through objective eyes.

When we get up in the morning most of us go into the bathroom and look at ourselves in the mirror but few of us are really looking at our true qualities when we do this. We examine the bags under our eyes, we lament our wrinkles and the obvious signs of ageing, we fret over our hair loss and we mourn our fading youth as our bodies seemingly degenerate before our very eyes. Sometimes these self evaluations are so fleeting and habitual we barely notice we are making them, at other times we labour over them at length. However, judging ourselves purely on our physical appearance gives us a totally unbalanced view of who we are.

There is a certain functionality about this process too. Men are usually looking to see where to shave while women usually look to see where make-up is needed, to disguise their so-called blemishes. Many women refuse to leave the house, or even to be seen by others within their home, until their war paint has been applied. Men are just as vain – perhaps more so – endlessly combing in the forlorn hope of disguising those bald patches that most women can spot a mile away. In this way, most of us are fixated on trying to enhance our personas and we ignore our less visible qualities.

Supermarkets and pharmacies sell huge and growing quantities and varieties of cosmetic products, for men and for women. We are obsessed with our physical features, about which we make endless judgements – usually negative. Many of us spend a fortune on cosmetics yet we struggle to afford the time or money to attend a personal development seminar or training – something that could permanently enrich our lives.

Others take an unbalanced view in the other direction, thinking they are super-cool, the best thing since sliced bread, god's gift to the opposite sex and generally drowning in narcissism. Either way, our outward appearance tends to dominate the way we perceive ourselves.

Many people become fixated on at least one feature in particular that they do not like. Their nose is too big, they have a double chin, bags under their eyes, bushy eyebrows, buck teeth, acne or whatever. Self-judgement is endemic and it's almost always negative. Is it surprising then that so many people suffer from depression and low self-esteem?

Unfortunately, all too often we forget to acknowledge the other bits we do like and we fail to remember we are wonderful human beings with functioning brains and limbs, and brimming over with creativity. Warts and all, each of us is a miracle on legs.

Even if we are disabled and our brains and bodies are damaged, we are alive, and that is miracle enough. For a human to be alive, even on a life support machine, a fantastically complicated set of physical and chemical processes has to function. Every human who has the gift of life has feelings, and that makes us nothing short of wondrous.

If we can develop sufficient awareness to realise and remember we are amazing whatever our circumstances, we begin to see ourselves as we really are, for that *is* how we really are, and we start to love ourselves in a way we all deserve. When we see ourselves like that we can no longer avoid the glaringly obvious conclusion that we are all, without exception, beautiful people.

When we see a new born baby, we gather round to marvel at this masterpiece of miniaturisation. We were all little wonders like this baby once upon a time, so what's changed? I'll tell you what's changed: now we are even more marvellous, for we have grown and developed and become far more sophisticated.

The most truly amazing processes happen as living creatures grow and develop, and they carry on until we die. We do it without being told how. Like every living organism in this universe, our beings are expressing their multi-dimensional, miraculous qualities day by day, moment by moment.

Negative conditioning being what it is, however, it is incredibly difficult to persuade the majority of people to see themselves as beautiful. Sometimes we agree in theory that we are valid and worthy of love, but in our hearts we simply cannot believe it. A very young American woman once told me, *'existence wants you just the way you are.'* At the time I thought she was daft, but eventually I realised that, of course, she was absolutely right.

Self-judgement is supreme arrogance – as if we mere mortals could improve upon perfection, or know how to make ourselves better than creation has done. Who are we to judge, we who have developed the fantastic skills of how to make weapons, kill each other and reduce the Earth to a polluted planet? We seem to be driven towards living in conflict and destroying the environment we need in which to exist, instead of co-habiting in a state of acceptance and harmonising with our environment.

We are in denial when we refuse to accept our own perfection, something we do all the time. Dogs run around in circles chasing their tails, ostriches believe they are invisible when they bury their heads in the sand, and we humans are obsessed with striving for perfection when we are perfect already.

This habit of putting ourselves down is unintelligent in the extreme and a powerful energy drain. Here's the essential secret I discovered some years ago: *when we learn to accept ourselves, conflict simply fizzles out and our energies are released for expressing our creativity.* This is far more satisfying.

Sadly, the ingrained programming of unworthiness runs so strongly in most of us that it is very difficult for us to see beyond it and acknowledge there is another possibility, that we are lovely.

Some of you are by now, I am sure, vehemently disagreeing with me, saying again this does not apply to you. 'Dave, you don't know me,' you say. 'You don't understand what it's like to be me. I'm a special case, I'm especially unworthy and unacceptable, absolutely beyond redemption. Happiness and feeling OK is a great idea but that only happens to other people.'

Yes, I do understand. Of course I do because I've been there myself! That is exactly how I used to feel until I realised I was being self-indulgent and fruitlessly hanging on to my neurosis. I was attached to my pain because I felt safe with it. To let it go would be to take a jump into a frightening unknown. We are told as children not to boast and not to be conceited, and that's fair enough. But that does not mean we shouldn't credit ourselves for being perfectly OK exactly as we are.

At this point somebody usually challenges me by saying, 'surely you don't believe Hitler was perfect!' Of course, I don't condone what Hitler did. To me it was personal, for some of my distant relatives suffered terminally in the concentration camps.

But that was not the real Hitler. It can't have been, for the original essence of any of us is by definition innocent. Unfortunately for himself and millions of others, the *real* Hitler was completely obliterated by his neurosis, and it drove him to act out all that crazy stuff. Don't get me wrong, I would never in a million years stick up for Hitler – or Stalin, Mao Tse Tung, Saddam Hussein, Pol Pot, Idi Amin or any of the other brutal ego maniacs you might care to mention that litter the history.

No doubt all these people suffered severe emotional wounding in very early childhood. I'm not a psychiatrist so I don't know the details and to be honest, I don't have any sympathy for them anyway. But one thing is obvious in each and every one of the above cases, the *real* person was not the one performing the actions.

Mirroring

Now you may ask why I am going into such detail about the nature of our self-perception in a chapter about relationships. The reason is that a relationship can provide you with a powerful tool that you can use to develop a truer perspective of who you really are. That's because the true function of a partner, lover or spouse is to hold up a mirror to the other.

A considerable amount of awareness is necessary if we are to understand and accept the notion that each of us is acceptable already without having to do anything to prove it or earn it. This is why the concept of the mirror in a relationship is such a blessing, for when we refuse to look further than the end of our noses, the mirror can help us get a view of what is really going on. Of course Hitler's behaviour was unusually extreme, but perhaps if the real Hitler had been able to really see and accept what his persona and neurotic, wounded self were doing, things might have turned out very differently.

If you believe in your persona, if you believe your conditioned self, your personality, is the real you, you will never find peace and fulfilment. Moreover you make it very difficult to have totally satisfying relationships too. If fact more than likely you are heading for more trouble.

In any relationship, when each party is honest and courageous enough to reflect back to the other what they are really doing, as opposed to what they think they are doing, the person receiving the feedback is then able to see their unconscious behaviour as it really is. However, to benefit from this you need to be *sufficiently trusting, open and receptive.* It's like speaking into a tape recorder and then playing back the tape. The machine plays back what your voice really sounds like, not what you think it sounds like. There will almost certainly be a startling difference between the two.

In this context 'the mirror' is a metaphor for someone or something that reflects the nature of your true self back to you. Relationships can be of incalculable value to those who wish to learn and grow towards self-acceptance when both parties have the integrity to truly reflect each other's patterns. If in turn we have the courage to be receptive, we are then enabled to see clearly what we are actually doing and how we work. The mirror is a valuable aid in helping us to cultivate our awareness, and for that reason, when we reflect back objectively to our partners, we give them a tremendous and loving gift, even when our mirroring comes in the form of an angry reaction.

Unless we become supremely aware or we feel threatened, most of us spend much of our time functioning on automatic pilot. We live large chunks of our lives without even noticing what we do. For example, many a time I have climbed into my car and arrived at a friend's house, only to realise on my arrival I had not noticed how I got there. I might even have to think for a second or two to work out where I was. When this happens, although absolutely sober, I realise I was not consciously aware of the journey. Though something in me registered when to slow down, speed up, change gears or stop at the traffic lights, most of the time I was driving I was preoccupied, thinking about something else. And nine times out of ten, I do not even notice I'm doing that.

Interesting, if there's an emergency during the journey, such as a child unexpectedly stepping out in front of my car, suddenly my attention is be sharply focused and I'd be concentrating intently on avoiding an accident. As soon as we feel threatened, we have no trouble in being instantly focused like a laser while putting our full attention totally into the here and now.

Very often in the routine of daily life, I cannot tell someone what I said to them five minutes ago, unless it happened to be something of profound importance to me.

How many times has it happened to you that you are deep in conversation with someone and there's an interruption. After dealing with it you return to your conversation, and the first thing you say is, 'now what was I talking about?'

Mirroring can work in very simple ways. For example, your best friend says, 'women drive me mad. They just nag, nag, nag.' If this surprises you, maybe you say, 'do you ever listen to yourself? Did you hear what you just said?' Or, 'do you really mean that?' Perhaps your friend trotted out his statement having hardly thought about what he was saying. Maybe he had a row with his girlfriend and is now angrily reacting by unconsciously blaming all women, refusing to take responsibility for how he feels and sorting out his problem like a mature adult.

Your answer to his comment thrusts his sweeping generalisation back into his face for re-examination with more awareness. *Without making any judgement* you are requiring him to pay attention and take responsibility for the words coming out of his mouth, and examine their veracity. Unconscious talk can hurt others.

Once or twice I've heard women talking to each other and one says, 'I don't trust men. They're all rapists at heart!' This makes me furious and hurt. 'Excuse me ladies,' I might say, 'I'm a man and I never raped anyone!' to which I once actually got the outrageous reply, 'no, but I bet you'd like to!'

How incredibly arrogant it is to assume you know how someone else feels! All prejudice is born out of unconsciousness and it does nothing but lead to more hatred and mistrust in the world. When you invite someone to re-examine what they just said or did, you offer them the opportunity to step up to a higher level of conscious awareness, if they will, which is perhaps the most loving act one person can do for another. That's what mirroring does and if you are in a relationship and you love each other, you will make sure the mirroring you do is honest and courageous, always positive, non-judgmental and non-blaming.

Dumping and blaming

Though mirroring can help us in our quest to find out who we are, where we sometimes come unstuck is when we unwittingly project our own fantasies or hang-ups onto others, or when others do that to us. This is not true mirroring, it is what therapists refer to as 'dumping.' Dumping occurs when we judge or blame someone for something that is not their responsibility, but is usually ours.

In my observation, there is much confusion about this issue. Basically, dumping means you have overstepped the other person's boundaries by trying to shift your responsibility for an issue onto them instead of accepting it yourself. This is usually in an unconscious bid to make the other person feel guilty, while avoiding feeling bad yourself. Take the example of two friends in the finance business. One says to the other, 'it's your fault I lost my money. You advised me to invest in those shares.'

To which the other friend, who is blessed with a modicum of awareness and knows how he feels, replies angrily, 'it was your decision. Don't blame me.'

In this way the latter of the two characters is protecting his own boundaries, integrity and self-esteem, while simultaneously acting as a mirror to show his friend that he was dumping. Though these interchanges between people usually happen spontaneously and automatically, what is actually happening is that the responsibility is put squarely back where it belongs. The note of anger alerts the first friend to the fact that there is something the second friend wants him to look at.

It's essential to be clear about this. Trying to help someone see something in themselves by blaming them is as fruitless as trying to resolve an argument by blaming. Either asking an objective question, for example 'did you realise what you just said?' or saying how you feel, usually solves the problem.

Here's another example of how reflect or mirror without dumping: 'I feel angry when you say that' is a true statement and I'm not actually blaming you for how I feel. In saying that I take responsibility for my feelings and simply express them, while at the same time inviting you, in a non-confrontative way, to re-examine what you are saying. Of course you might react defensively, that's up to you, but the invitation is there like an olive branch for you to look again at what you said.

Conversely, if I say 'you make me so angry when you do that, I wish you would stop doing it,' I'm in effect saying it's your fault that I feel angry and I want you to change your behaviour. I'm blaming you for how I feel and pushing the responsibility for my feelings onto you, and trying to control you by requiring you to behave in ways that I want you to behave. You may find it hard to agree with me on this, but can I ask you please think about it. 'It's your fault that I'm angry' is almost never true.

It is not an accurate reflection but a manipulative way of trying to stop another person doing something you don't like and it's almost always counterproductive, because the person you are addressing merely becomes defensive, aggressive or passive aggressive. Either way, they are unlikely to take anything meaningful on board and might well retort with the comment, 'that's your problem!' which of course, it is.

A relationship is a potential dumping minefield and unless we are aware and careful of what we do we can easily fall into the trap of projecting, manipulating and colluding, all of which inevitably lead to unhappiness and stunted inner growth. Happy, loving and successful relationships need true reflections and their protagonists need the courage and awareness to be honest.

Most of us are so wounded and firmly attached to our own self-image we would not recognise our true reflection if it got up and bit us on the backside. We believe in the distorted self-image we create because we believe that who we really are 'is not acceptable,' to ourselves nor to the world at large. Only a beautiful persona is deemed by ourselves to be good enough to be worthy of love, and most of us invest huge funds of energy into maintaining one.

Self-acceptance

This is unfortunate because as we have discussed many times in this book, the ultimate relationship and the most meaningful one is the one we have with ourselves. To be happy with ourselves and not in a state of perpetual inner conflict, self-acceptance is essential.

Let me give you a classic example of this. I have been in my present relationship for some fourteen years now, but during the first five or so years I sometimes used to think, *'she couldn't possibly love me if she knew what I was really like.'* I did not realise for a long time she knew perfectly well what I was really like and that actually I was the one who did not acknowledge what I was really like! Truth is, she has always loved the real me. Ironically, my persona, when it appears, merely serves to put her off. Luckily for me, perhaps because she's a psychotherapist, she is fully aware that it's only a persona. All that, needless to say, is an essential part of what makes her a suitable partner for me.

Switching off a façade, made strong by decades of conditioning, is no simple matter, for you can only do it if you accept and trust yourself as you are totally. The very discovery of the existence of your façade is momentous, for it undoubtedly represents the essential first step in becoming 'real.' Fortunately, because my partner faithfully reflected back every time I presented my false self, I began to recognise it more clearly. Before long, it began to feel faintly ridiculous, and even though I still could not drop all of it for a long time, I gradually began to understand that I had a choice. For me, that was the second vital step in cracking what was a deeply ingrained habit of trying to hide my vulnerability.

Sure enough, little by little over a very long period, my internal tape that told me maybe I was unlovable began to fade into the background.

The final stage is acceptance, not just of the real self, but of the persona too. Instead of judging myself harshly, I gradually began to love and accept the edifice my unconscious had so cleverly manufactured to help me survive emotionally during my very young, defenceless years. I began to find the courage and trust to let the warmth of my heart shine through and melt my defence barriers away. Now, as long as I remember to maintain my full awareness, I have the choice to be defensive or open in any given situation, depending on whether or not it feels safe and appropriate to be vulnerable, for now I have both ways at my disposal. Naturally I still need the occasional nudge, and of course I do the same for my partner.

Only truly courageous individuals have the guts to look squarely into the mirror and realise they love and feel compassion for what they see.

I had dinner recently with an old friend whom I had not seen for three years. In that time he had separated from his second wife and, hurt and angry, he was fearfully anticipating a second painful and expensive divorce.

'Relationships are so complicated,' he complained. 'I don't know why they go wrong. At first we got on like a house on fire, but a few years later we were sleeping on opposite edges of the bed, not even touching each other. And sometimes I slept downstairs.'

Clearly my friend was hurting. 'I don't understand women,' he continued. 'I just can't figure out what they want. I bend over backwards to support all the kids, I buy us a nice house in a good area, I get her a decent car to run around in, we had great holidays, what more does she want? Why is she not satisfied?'

'Did you make sure she felt loved and listened to?' I asked my friend. All I got was a blank look followed by the retort, 'oh great! I should have known you'd be on her side!'

Now that's what I call projection. I never said I was on anyone's side. I merely asked a question that might shed light on his enquiry. I finally realised he did not want to understand, he did not want mirroring or feedback, he merely wanted to let off steam and to try to absolve himself of his part in this.

Many is the time I have also heard women saying they do not understand men. Moreover, I can heartily empathise with both points of view, for it took me many years to even begin to understand women, and even longer to understand myself. I used to think both men and women should come with an instruction book! Fortunately, there is now an excellent instruction book for men and for women, entitled *Men Are From Mars, Women Are From Venus* by John Gray.

Gray highlights many of the ways in which men and women differ from each other, both in their needs and in the ways in which these needs are manifested. Reading it certainly helped me understand where men and women are coming from and how they so easily misunderstand each other. I made a mental note to send a copy to my friend.

Actually, relationships are in essence very simple, but there are important provisos. Things work best when we choose suitable partners and then decide to go with the flow. We need to be crystal clear about what we want and communicate that to our partners. It is very, very easy to make relationships complicated, difficult and frustrating through unawareness, obstinacy or co-dependency. In these latter circumstances, the mirror is either distorted and everything we see in it is ugly, or it does not exist, or we refuse to look in it, or a combination of all three.

What exactly do I mean when I talk about going with the flow? We're back to our opening principle of choosing either a path of acceptance or a path of resistance for our passage through life. When we choose a partner who we genuinely accept wholeheartedly we obviously choose a path of acceptance and then we flow with the river. If then you have a lapse in your awareness and forget what's important to you, it's easy to slide into a negative and judgmental cycle of dissatisfaction in your relationship. You focus on the less significant bones of contention instead of the important things you love about your partner. That's what I call choosing a path of resistance, it's born out of unconsciousness, and it's what I mean by the metaphor of 'pushing the river.' Almost always it arises because you have not fully accepted yourself, and you are unconsciously projecting onto your partner characteristics about yourself that you cannot accept.

No one holds a gun to our heads to force us to go with the flow. Someone once argued with me that if we always choose to go with the flow, we exercise only 50 per cent of our options. If you want to waste your time pursuing that argument, may I wish you the best of luck. To me, going with the flow is just a matter of common sense. There came a time I got tired of doing things the hard way. *I love having an easy life.*

Whichever way we look at it, when we ignore the mirror we do ourselves and our partners a great disservice, for we are denying ourselves and each other the possibility of growth and understanding.

Relationships with others are learning experiences which can help teach us how to make the relationship we have with ourselves a satisfying one. If, like my friend, we have a negative self-image, meaning we do not love and accept ourselves, we cannot help reflecting that negative image back to the other person.

In such circumstances, inevitably we demand something from the other that can only come from within ourselves. It may be some sort of validation, something to convince us we are really OK people, even though we do not feel OK because we are wounded. We think we need a crutch from the other person to ensure our survival. We blame the other, or punish them, or make them feel guilty, when things do not work out how we want them to. When this happens there can be no mirroring, for narcissism takes over.

The same thing often happens in reverse, incidentally, when we find ourselves judging others harshly or expressing negative views about them. When we do that we express a reflection of how we feel about ourselves. Or to put it another way, we see in the other person something we don't like or accept in ourselves and this makes us feel uncomfortable, so we retaliate by attacking. An attack is, in essence, what a judgement or negative comment about someone else is. We are angry with the other person for what we perceive as them irritating us, when in fact they are merely a trigger (or mirror) for the irritation we've been carrying inside for years.

Whichever way round you look at this, there is no escaping the essential truth that *if we cannot accept ourselves we will inevitably fail to fulfil our human potential, and nothing can make us happy.* If our partner leaves us, we are devastated for now another person can accept us either, and there is nothing and no one to fill that aching void of missing self-belief, self-esteem and self-worth. Moreover, it confirms our belief that we are unlovable and we might as well cease to exist.

When I was a young boy in school, as I mentioned in an earlier chapter, I was always the last one to be picked for someone's football team because I could not run fast. I couldn't walk fast either and when our Geography or Biology teacher took the class out to the local woods to observe nature and the world around us, I used to struggle up the hill as best I could. I would arrive, puffing and panting, ten minutes after the rest of the class had made themselves at home in a clearing which we made our ad hoc woodland classroom.

How I wished I could be an integrated member of my peer group, but because I always lagged behind physically, I always felt like an outsider. I felt there was no way I could join in. I felt unaccepted and unacceptable. Even I could not accept what I was like. I just wanted to be 'normal' like all the others.

This state of affairs caused me great embarrassment for there was no visible sign of my disablement, which at the time I did not understand myself. Kid's games, especially boy's games, tend to be very physical and my failure to join in was not for want of trying. I just felt inadequate, and the problem was compounded by the fact that I did not understand what was happening to me, nor why.

From these and other similarly painful experiences, I developed the habit of trying to hide my inability to walk long distances, or do sport involving running, by trying to avoid the issue. I would not even admit to myself that there was something different about me and I persevered with physical challenges to prove my manhood (or boyhood) to myself, as well as to my schoolmates. However, it only brought me more pain and misery, though I was unwilling to admit that too.

I tried to present a cheery aspect long into my adult life, though if the truth were known, most of the time I felt far from cheerful. It was only when I began to admit the truth of how I felt about my condition, to myself and others, that I began to feel better about myself. To my amazement, people seemed to love me the more for my honesty, for the simple reason I was being real and letting them see me, pain, vulnerability and all. Admitting to being disabled seemed very scary to me at the time, and to some extent it still does. It was only the valuable support of true friends and partners over the years coaxing, encouraging and mirroring me that persuaded me out of my shell.

My perception as a school child was 'in a world in which everyone else has a correctly functioning body, I don't.' Of course, I had the whole thing way out of proportion. Only in recent years, by trusting my friends and taking the courage to glimpse into the mirror just a little at a time, I began to perceive myself more accurately, as someone perfectly capable of expressing my creativity, participating fully in life and being happy. I quote this story as a great example of the power of mirroring and the importance of partners in any relationship to help each other to grow.

For me, feeling happy began when I realised there was no virtue whatsoever in being like other people, or like anything or anyone other than who I am. Slowly it began to dawn on me that being myself was something I could excel in. I have my unique self to offer, complete with all my funny little ways, and I like it. It's such good fun being a little eccentric and watching people's bemused reactions as they try to assess whether I'm for real or not.

Of course if you don't love yourself you can't enjoy anything much, indeed being different will make you cringe, so something in the relationship I have with myself has been transformed. This has had a powerful and beneficial knock-on effect in all my relationships.

The huge effort of presenting a façade has dropped now, most of the time at any rate, for I invest virtually all my energy into doing my own thing, which is just another way of being who I am. This allows me to relate honestly, sincerely and openly.

Interestingly, around the time I started re-examining all this in the early 1980's, I unexpectedly found a sport I could not only cope with, but excel at – sailing. That was when I discovered the power of training and experience as aids to restoring shattered self-confidence and self-esteem, and thence to promoting self-acceptance.

It doesn't actually matter what you train in as long as you are passionate about it, which is why, at the grand age of forty-eight, it seemed so important when I passed my RYA Yachtmaster exam. After four attempts I had achieved this standard, which I would say is quite high. I had found a sport I loved and could cope with. It is a sport that does not have to be competitive but which enables me to express my physicality; a multi-dimensional thinking man's sport with a spirit of adventure and lots of fresh air; a tactical and strategic activity in which the individual can cruise rather than race and therefore excel without having to outdo other individuals; an activity requiring good communication, team building and leadership skills; and with a fascinating emphasis on harmonising with nature.

This also indicates that personal development and the path to heightened awareness is not only about meditation and psychology. Expressing yourself through physical activity is important too.

So now we are talking about different kinds of relationships. Yes, there's the relationship I have with myself, but there's also my relationship with the sea, my crew and sailing companions, my boat (I'm convinced she's a living being), and my relationship with my peer group, which is the yachting community. I applied myself to years of demanding training, I had done exams in a classroom and now passed a challenging test at sea. I was deemed competent to skipper a yacht on offshore passages, officially, and I have the piece of paper to prove it!

Why is this important? This really helped me to believe in myself and meant far more to me than any university degree could have done.

This is what I am trying to illustrate: *the path towards accepting and believing in yourself without reservation is to do, think and feel whatever your heart tells you to do, think and feel,* and that means being proactive and putting in whatever effort is necessary. It does not mean sitting around thinking, wondering, hoping, analysing and fearing. Interestingly, when you do whatever it takes to follow your heart, you will at some point automatically enter your *maximum creative flow* and you will enjoy the challenge of achieving what you aim for, even though you may experience moments of fear and self-doubt.

When you find the courage to do what your heart wants you to do, whatever that might be, there will always be a beneficial outcome. I'm not saying you shouldn't go to university, incidentally. Of course, a good education is a joy and a blessing, but only go if your heart wants you to be there. If not, don't waste time pretending or doing it for someone else's benefit or expectations.

What has all this to do with relationships? Well, there are many factors that come into play regarding our relationships, and many viewpoints to consider, especially if you want a multi-dimensional understanding of the subject.

Sometimes we are scared to look closely into the mirror, for we are sure we will only see pain, negativity and ugliness. So we avoid looking too closely into ourselves and instead put our energy into focusing on outer things – other people, entertainment, work, alcohol, drugs, whatever. We behave as if we are hail-fellow-well-met, busying ourselves and, in so doing, conveniently sidestepping the essential issues of loving and accepting ourselves.

I am not suggesting we should wear our hearts on our sleeves or go round mawkishly licking our wounds in public, but living in a state of constant denial is fruitless and painful. It kills creativity and spontaneity and encourages the twenty first-century curse, depression. If you are in pain, admit it and then move on. Better still, go out and do something you love – but don't deny how you feel.

We hear it all the time – one friend tells another of her broken heart because her lover left her. Her friend immediately advises, 'better keep busy, then.' One could paraphrase, 'at all costs avoid your feelings, especially around me. Otherwise you might remind me how much in pain I am feeling.' Clearly, neither woman wants to look into any mirrors. Sometimes even the reflected pain of others is too much for us to bear.

Take a look in the mirror, what do you see? A pained, pathetic, disempowered victim who loathes him or her self, or an alive human being capable of loving and worthy of being loved, simply because of being there. Maybe a bit of both are present, so why should so many of us typically only see 'the negative' and not 'the positive?' Finding the courage to look in the mirror our partner holds up helps us accept every aspect of ourselves, until eventually we only see ourselves as positive. That is the power of acceptance. When everything you see in the mirror is perceived as positive, everything else beyond the mirror, especially your partner, also becomes unconditionally acceptable.

From this we learn the curious truth that self-acceptance and acceptance of our partner is actually part and parcel of the same thing.

Imagine …

Imagine a relationship in which each partner takes time regularly to look in the mirror presented to them by the other, and continues to work through the more destructive of their self-sabotaging behaviour patterns and self-limiting beliefs. These patterns and beliefs were once unconscious but are now being bathed in the healing light of awareness, thanks to the mirroring process facilitated by each partner for the other.

As we have said before, with awareness, self-love and self-acceptance become possible. This is one of the biggest challenges a person can face: dare you admit to being lovable? Take up the gauntlet and then imagine the effect this will have on your relationships.

The exciting thing about the attitudes in the relationship described above is the healing potential of the love that is released when we begin to accept ourselves and each other. Once the process begins we can drop the mask and begin to relax. Then true happiness and fulfilment come at last within our grasp, and that applies to every one of us and all of our relationships.

When this couple comes together, they are a unit yet they are two individuals, each standing on his or her own two feet and taking personal responsibility for everything that happens in their lives and everything they manifest separately and together. They are not depending on each other for survival, or even happiness and fulfilment, yet they share their inner resources unstintingly. Both parties are fulfilled and fully functioning humans in their own right. When they come together, they each bring something immensely valuable of themselves to their relationship.

These two people intuitively understand that the only reason, apart from procreation, for being together is to hold up a mirror for each other, to help each other grow towards a deeper spiritual fulfilment. They both know perfectly well that if the other left or died, though there would be sadness, life would continue to be wonderful. And for no other reason than that life is wonderful.

On this basis, a relationship is blissfully simple. When we are true to ourselves, we are automatically true to the other. Although we might be deeply in love, we see things in a more detached way. We are in touch with reality for we have our feet on the ground and are therefore less subject to the vicissitudes of insecurity that come from being co-dependent, which is the alternative way of being in a relationship.

I am aware this sounds like a wonderful fairytale fantasy and for some it's much easier said than done, and I am sure some of you will find it impossible to believe. It does differ radically from the fantasy that seemed to prevail when I was growing up with in which men and women were supposed to fall in love with 'that special someone' and carry on in that blissful state 'happily ever after' as if by magic.

The scenario I describe contrasts sharply with that fiction, for it is by no means automatic, nor magic. It depends on awareness and honesty and therefore you may have to change the deeply ingrained habits of a lifetime to make this possible. It has to be worked for, desired with all your heart and given top priority. There are no free lunches on this one, but it need not seem so hard when you remember, the only real change anyone can go though is a change of mindset from resistance to acceptance.

In this book I put forward the evidence of my own experiences and that of many people I have known for the benefit of those who wish to share them. I have tried many ways to make relationships work, and spent many years seeking answers. If you are one of those who cannot believe that relationships can be simple, no matter, why not just try it the way I describe and see what happens?

Often relationships get into trouble when one or both parties fail to understand the need to find self-fulfilment, and they blame the other for not meeting their needs. Self-fulfilment is a basic human need which we must, by definition, satisfy for ourselves, yet it is often overlooked through sheer unawareness or fear of failure.

No other person, not even the most doting of lovers, can supply our need for self-fulfilment. We have to do it for ourselves. Nevertheless, if you are in a loving relationship, you can derive enormous assistance from the power of mirroring.

The mirror helps to cultivate the awareness we need to find that fulfilment. Therefore, if we want our relationships to be meaningful and profoundly satisfying we must find the courage to lovingly and clearly reflect back what we see, however uncomfortable, but don't forget the positive as well as the negative stuff. At the same time, we must prepare to accept our own reflections as they are transmitted back to us.

Breaking or changing patterns of behaviour seems difficult, but it is possible through awareness and acceptance. We repeat our patterns again and again unless and until we become aware of them, for the human unconscious always behaves in repeating patterns and cycles until you consciously change something.

Hence, people who suffer a pattern of relationship breakdowns usually go into successive relationship breakdowns as the years go by. It takes courage, time, patience and dogged determination, but looking in the mirror can help to break patterns like these.

It helps if we find as much support as possible. Our parents, friends, lovers, teachers, therapists, mentors, coaches and gurus all play their part in reminding us to keep looking in the mirror. I have never met anyone who has not benefited tremendously in the long run from looking into the mirror long and hard. The mirror is a vital tool for provoking us into awareness.

Summary

- Judging ourselves purely on our physical appearance gives us a totally unbalanced view of who we are
- When we remember we are amazing whatever our circumstances, we begin to see ourselves as we really are, for that *is* how we really are. Then we start to love ourselves for who we are
- We are obsessed with striving for perfection when we are perfect already
- When we learn to accept ourselves, conflict simply fizzles out and our energies are released for expressing our creativity
- The true function of a partner is to hold up a mirror to the other
- If you believe in your persona, or that your conditioned self or your personality is the real you, you will never find peace and fulfillment
- When each is honest and courageous enough to reflect back to the other what that person is really doing, the person receiving the feedback is then able to see their unconscious behaviour as it really is, *if that person is sufficiently trusting, open and receptive*
- 'The mirror' is a metaphor for someone or something that reflects back to you your true self

- Relationships can be of incalculable value to those who wish to learn and grow towards self-acceptance, as long as both parties have the integrity to truly reflect each other's patterns
- The mirror is a valuable aid in helping us to cultivate our awareness, and when we reflect back objectively to our partners, we give them a tremendous and loving gift
- It's incredibly arrogant to assume you know how someone else feels!
- All prejudice is born out of unconsciousness and it only leads to more hatred and mistrust in the world
- When you invite someone to re-examine what they just said or did, you offer them the opportunity to step up to a higher level of conscious awareness
- If you are in a relationship and you love each other, make sure the mirroring you do is honest and courageous, positive, non-judgmental and non-blaming
- Beware of unwittingly projecting your own fantasies or hang-ups onto others, or when others do that to you. This is dumping
- Dumping occurs when we judge or blame someone for something that is not their fault or responsibility. Most likely it's our responsibility
- Asking an objective question ('did you realise what you just said?'), or saying how you feel, are usually effective ways of mirroring
- 'It's your fault that I'm angry' is almost never true
- Most of us are so wounded and firmly attached to our own-self image we cannot recognise our true reflection
- Our ultimate relationship and our most meaningful one is the one we have with ourselves. To be happy, self-acceptance is essential
- Because my partner faithfully reflected back to me every time I presented my false self, I began to recognise it more clearly. Gradually I began to understand that I could choose to drop it
- It's very easy to make relationships complicated, difficult and frustrating through unawareness, obstinacy or co-dependency. In these circumstances, the mirror is either distorted and everything we see in it is ugly, or it does not exist, or we refuse to look in it, or a combination of all three

- If you have a lapse in awareness, it's easy to slide into a negative and judgmental cycle of dissatisfaction in your relationship. You focus on the bones of contention instead of the things you love about your partner. This is choosing a path of resistance and it's born out of unconsciousness
- When we find ourselves judging others harshly or expressing negative views about them we project a reflection of how we feel about ourselves
- There is no virtue in being like other people, or anyone other than who you are
- Getting a training and some experience is a powerful aid to restoring shattered self-confidence, self-belief and self-esteem, and helps to promote self-acceptance
- Personal development and the path to heightened awareness is not only about meditation and psychology. Expressing yourself through physical activity is important too
- The path towards accepting and believing in yourself without reservation is to do, think and feel whatever your heart tells you to do, think and feel. That means being proactive and putting in whatever effort is necessary
- Interestingly, when you do whatever it takes to follow your heart, you will eventually enter your *maximum creative flow* and enjoy the challenge of achieving what you aim for
- If you do what your heart tells you there will always be a beneficial outcome. Don't waste time pretending you want to do something when you don't, or doing it for someone else's benefit or expectations
- Living in a state of constant denial is fruitless and painful. It kills creativity and spontaneity and encourages depression. If you are in pain, admit it and then go out and do something you love
- Finding the courage to look in the mirror our partner holds up helps us accept every aspect of ourselves, until eventually we only see ourselves as positive. That is the power of acceptance
- When everything you see in the mirror is perceived as positive, everything else beyond the mirror, especially your partner, also becomes unconditionally acceptable. From this we learn that self-

acceptance and acceptance of our partner is actually part and parcel of the same thing

- Dare you admit to being lovable? Take up the gauntlet and imagine the effect this will have on your relationships
- What's exciting is the healing potential of the love that is released when we begin to accept ourselves and each other. Once the process begins we can drop the mask and begin to relax
- In a relationship comprising two individuals who are fulfilled and fully functioning humans in their own right, each brings something immensely valuable of themselves to their relationship
- When we are true to ourselves, we are automatically true to the other. *On this basis, a relationship is blissfully simple*
- The changes required for happy, healthy relating need not seem so hard when you remember, the only real change anyone can go though is a change of mindset from resistance to acceptance
- No other person, not even the most doting of lovers, can supply our need for self-fulfillment. We have to do it for ourselves. The mirror is a vital tool for provoking us into the awareness we need to find that fulfillment

28

Boundaries and the Middle Way

> *Genuine love not only respects the individuality of the other but actually seeks to cultivate it, even at the risk of separation or loss*
>
> M. Scott Peck

In an earlier chapter we discussed the essential need for boundaries in our individual lives, and relationships are no different. It is perhaps even more important to maintain strong boundaries in our relationships if they are to endure fruitfully.

Balance

I have no intention of repeating material we have already covered, but there are a few points on this subject that do need special emphasis in the context of relationships. The first essential is to realise that finding the middle way is not the same as compromising. The middle way, or the path of balance, is a very helpful attitude in any relationship. Compromise is not.

Contrary to what many of us were told when we were growing up, life, if it is to be lived happily and successfully, most certainly does not work very well as a compromise. Compromising means putting up with second best or less. In such a situation, fulfilment is clearly not possible.

Usually, if we allow ourselves to live in compromise it is because we do not fully believe in ourselves, we have woolly boundaries and we suffer low self-esteem. We believe the prophets of doom who tell us 'you can't have everything.' We allow people to treat us like doormats, we behave like victims and we let ourselves be manipulated and controlled by others or by events. The net result is we rarely get what we want and need, and life seems a perpetual struggle.

This is programming for self-sabotage, and if we believe we can't have exactly what we need and want, we needlessly accept limitations imposed upon us by others. These limitations have nothing to do with who we really are, they do not belong to us, and they will hold us back if we let them.

When someone says to me, 'but don't you see, you want it all and you can't have everything?' my response is 'why not?' To this date, no one has yet been able to furnish me with an even half-convincing argument and I am still waiting for a satisfactory answer to my question. The world I live in is infinitely bountiful and abundant. Who are these self-appointed judges who dare to tell me I should limit myself and play small?

Of course there is no answer, at least not one that holds water. 'You can't have everything' is an outmoded and outdated mythical belief that should have died in the Middle Ages. It probably arose because some of us have focused on acquiring more material possessions and power than we need or want, which makes us avaricious. That's an unconscious and non-impeccable way to behave and it won't bring you lasting happiness.

So maybe it's true to say you can't have everything your ego wants, but that's not what I'm talking about here. Maybe I should qualify my belief by defining it like this: *you* ***can*** *have everything you sincerely need and want if your desire truly comes from your heart.*

The reason I know this is, as countless sages have pointed out, we already have everything we need. It's just a matter of noticing that we have it and dropping our resistance or erroneous guilt that gets in our way of enjoying it.

If you think you cannot have your heart's desire you are not thinking and feeling for yourself – you are merely accepting dictum that has been foisted on you all your life. Lots of people have exactly what they want – but only because they sincerely believe in what they are doing. They come from their hearts and go out on a limb, taking all necessary risks and facing every fear, to live their truth in every detail.

The late Frank Sinatra springs to mind as somebody who appeared to believe totally in himself and what he had to offer. Though I didn't know him personally it was obvious, he polished his gift and used it to give unstintingly of himself to his audiences through his work. As a result, whenever he walked out on stage, he held the entire audience in the palms of his hands. He established worldwide fame and a reputation for himself as arguably the greatest male popular singer the world has ever known. Quite simply he gave pleasure to countless ordinary people.

I loved him because he never compromised. He did what he loved and was good at, and he demanded the highest standards of himself and those he worked with. It's obvious just from hearing his records and seeing his movies and TV appearances that Sinatra worked with tremendous focus and tireless dedication in a tough environment *and he let the world know he believed in himself.* He delivered a consistently high quality product, he gave everything he had to give and because of that his audiences loved him and believed in him too.

The converse also applies. Anything we try to present that comes from someone or somewhere other than from our own self does not have the ring of veracity, and never will. Therefore, if you are not being true to yourself, you are compromising.

OK, so where am I going with this rather convoluted argument? I am trying to emphasise the importance of refusing to compromise.

It's essential to understand this principle in relationships. I don't mean we must become stiff, unbending and obstinate when we relate to our partners. If you remain true to yourself and always behave with integrity so that everything you give to your partner comes from your heart, he or she will automatically respect you for it. Isn't that an excellent basis for building strong relationships?

What is really happening when someone asks us to compromise? They are asking nothing less than that we deny our feelings and ignore our truths, for whatever reason. The problem is unless you live with absolute integrity, like the Impeccable Warrior, it's impossible to feel 100 per cent good about yourself. The tendency then is to blame your partner or build resentment towards them because they asked you to compromise, even though it was your decision to do so, and that's not an honest way of relating.

Your behaviour is always your responsibility so when your partner asks, 'couldn't you be a bit more like this,' or 'why aren't you more like that?' look to your boundaries before deciding. Ask yourself, 'how do I feel about this' and always remain true to yourself. This may come at a price, for example your partner might feel frustrated because they haven't been successful in manipulating you into trying to change, and you may even split up, but in the end he or she will respect you for it. Much more important, you will respect yourself for behaving with absolute integrity.

Here's another important point to consider: if we agree to what is for us a compromise, and we've all done it so we all know this is true, we are colluding in the other person's insincerity and then two people will feel not good about themselves instead of just one.

One of my clients told me that I was nitpicking on this point, but I have seen so many relationships founder even among couples who were deeply in love because these very issues were not taken care of, so I make no apology for going into detail.

Boundaries

Defining and defending your boundaries in a relationship calls for skill and sensitivity. There is no need to go to the extreme of closing your heart in a defensive, protective strategy. Living with your heart closed is not much fun for anyone. Neither is there any need to be nasty, for as we saw earlier, it is perfectly possible to be assertive without being aggressive. When you are focused, open and centred you can relax, for nothing threatens your boundaries. You take care of them intuitively. *In most cases something of this rubs off on your partner* so it's less likely your boundaries will be challenged. Assuming they can and will accept you for who you are they will sense your boundary and, if they respect and love you, they will rarely overstep the mark.

That is unless they are unconscious, out of touch with their feelings or suffering emotional wounding, in which case we're into a different ball game. It's very difficult to relate successfully to someone who has little awareness of their own behaviour, and if they are reacting from being hurt it's unlikely they can accept anyone, because they probably can't accept themselves. In such a situation I can only suggest they begin a healing and awareness process of some kind, if they feel sufficiently motivated.

The suitable partner issue arises here. The sad truth is that if we are in a neurotic state we are going to have to resolve many of our issues before we can consider ourselves suitable material for successful relationships. When I was going through my divorce in the early 1980s, I promised myself I would never get married again until I had sorted out my emotional problems and decided what to do with my life. I certainly didn't want a second disaster, and I believed there was a high probability of that happening if I didn't make essential changes first.

The problem for many of us is that we have histories of not being clearly in touch with who we are and what we want and therefore we often don't realise when we have weak boundaries. This is hardly surprising, for it is not possible to put a firm boundary around something you do not perceive or something you're not sure how you feel about. I used to experience this simply as confusion until I saw that you have to know how you feel before you can know your boundary and trust your intuitive boundary preservation instinct, as it were. Otherwise the danger is ever present that you might transgress your own boundaries unconsciously, or unwittingly allow them to be transgressed.

There can be few among us who have not been hurt by someone riding roughshod over our boundaries. The enormous popularity of assertiveness training in recent years is easy to understand, for there are many of us who urgently need to learn to be assertive before we can hope to experience any kind of happiness.

It follows that, though it might be tempting, making a habit of compromise is a serious mistake, for the only way you can be true to yourself is by marching exclusively to the tune of your heart. Many of us see learning to be assertive as a good way of ensuring we do just that, and indeed assertiveness can be a very valuable tool when correctly understood and applied.

Assertiveness

So what exactly do I mean by assertiveness? Assertiveness is nothing more than the technique or habit of carefully tuning in to your innermost needs and wants and learning to communicate them clearly and honestly, to manifest them and to stand by them with steadfast integrity. It does not mean bolstering your ego so you always get your own way at the expense of others, nor does it mean closing your heart to others in your efforts to defend your boundaries, and it doesn't mean going on a power trip.

Assertiveness is not a defensive position. It certainly does not rest on an attitude that everyone is out to compromise your boundaries so you must defend them at all costs. On the contrary, it's a pro-active stance that proclaims, 'this is who I am.'

A person who really gets to know, understand and trust himself, and who behaves in such a way as his self-esteem is elevated, will become assertive automatically, for self-sabotage or letting others damage him ceases to be his habit. He simply tells it like it is.

Assertiveness is not merely a superficial or artificial remedy for a problem that has its roots deep inside. If you want to be naturally assertive it is necessary to apply healing to those damaged roots, or you remain profoundly wounded, making joyful, creative human functioning to your full potential impossible. If you contrive assertiveness without really feeling it, you merely replace one persona with another. In such circumstances, no matter how hard you try, your so-called assertiveness will always be a tremendous effort and can never flow naturally. It will never feel authentic.

Contrived assertiveness does have a value though, which is to wake us up to the fact that our boundaries are shaky, that we and others are compromising them and that there is a deeper problem to be addressed, which is why we seem to be unable to produce natural assertiveness. Contrived assertiveness may afford us some insight into the nature of that deeper problem and give us a starting place for getting to grips with it.

The flow I speak of with naturally arising assertiveness expresses itself via a sort of humble confidence, and is what I refer to as balance, or the middle way. It is not extremist, it is neither positive nor negative, neither aggressive nor passive, it is simply a flow. When a river goes around a bend, the fastest flowing water is always the deepest, or looked at the other way around, the deepest water is always the fastest flowing. This is because the deep part of the channel is where the flow is least impeded by the friction of the river bed. In the same way, when we drop our resistance we flow deeper and our passage through life is more empowered and less obstructed.

Too many times we hear the cry, 'that's your problem!' bandied about. When we believe in ourselves and respect our own boundaries, when we trust unreservedly in our inner voices and act on them, which is basically what assertiveness should be about, it is no problem for us to treat our fellow humans with care and compassion. We do not dismiss them as if we don't care about them by cutting them off with a dismissive 'that's your problem,' we respond with care, compassion and above all, firmness, but without being rude and making them feel worthless and rejected. There is no danger of becoming entangled in other people's problems or being brought down by them. True assertiveness keeps us centred and helps us remain aware and clearly focused, no more, no less, no matter what goes on around us.

More often than not, 'that's your problem!' is actually saying, 'I don't want to hear about your problems because I don't trust myself not to be brought down by them. I'm erecting a rigid boundary because I don't want to be reminded of my own pain. I don't want to get involved in case I'm sucked in and unable to break free.'

Recently in a café I overheard the opposite. A woman was telling her boyfriend about something that had upset her, though clearly it was nothing that he had said or done. She wanted to share. After listening attentively he replied, 'I'm sorry.'

He was not apologising, he was empathising. He was letting the woman know he had heard her on a deep level and resonated with her pain. Plain and simple. He did not get drawn into a protracted discussion or analysis, he had simply expressed the compassion he felt for his partner. He had thus taken care of her emotional needs, whilst looking after himself and his needs at the same time, a much more balanced and intelligent approach to assertiveness than the former example and one much more conducive to maintaining the obvious basic harmony of that couple's relationship.

Sometimes, of course, we are 'the other person,' the one with the problem. Again, if we trust in ourselves we know we have the ability to share our pain without dumping on others or sucking their energy. We know we have the facility to deal with it without depending on others for we know how to share so we need not feel isolated.

Unfortunately, lapses of awareness that happen to all but an enlightened handful can lead us, at one time or another, into an extreme refusal to listen with compassion when our friends are hurting. This totalitarian attitude in which we close our hearts leaves us all isolated, hurt and angry.

At times like this, we are quick to shut down with a retort like 'that's your problem,' but we do not like it when our friends refuse to really listen to *us*. It is the kind of attitude that breeds conflict rather than understanding and it is no way to successfully conduct meaningful relationships. When that happens you know it's time to resurrect your awareness.

In my view, there is no excuse for behaving with a lack of compassion. If that is what we find ourselves doing, we had better urgently check ourselves out deeply inside and start doing something to heal whatever wound is making us do that.

Even with the best will in the world, sometimes a friend or partner approaches, wanting us to lend an empathic ear, at a moment when we sincerely have no time to spare. We're late for a lecture or we have a job interview and we must get on. In such circumstances, like any other, honesty is the only sensible recourse. We will not jeopardise our boundaries or our relationships if we acknowledge the other person's feelings and explain our situation clearly and succinctly, for example, 'I'm really sorry you have this problem but I haven't got time to listen properly now. Can we talk later? I'll be able to give you my full attention then.'

In the space of approximately five seconds we have let our loved one or friend know we hear, acknowledge and respect them, and then we went about our business. The other person feels taken care of and we have looked after ourselves. With simple honest and open behaviour like this, everyone wins.

Alternatively, if it's a matter that can't wait, you could say, 'I'm sorry to hear you and Mary are not getting on well. I have to get to work now or I'll be in dead trouble, but meanwhile why not talk to Lucy, she'll understand. I'm not trying to palm you off, honestly, I'll catch up with you this evening after work and then I'll be able to listen properly.' You've done everything you can to respect your friend while avoiding a potential self-sabotage. If the other party can accept that, all well and good. If they cannot, so be it. You have nothing to reproach yourself for.

It's important we're careful not to patronise our colleagues, clients, friends and lovers, or anybody else for that matter, but instead develop the art of lovingly supporting them without compromising our own interests. Try to remember how you felt last time you were alone with a problem. Imagine how you will feel next time you are given a cold brush-off, now that many of your friends have been to assertiveness trainings of some sort. Trainings are fine, as long as we remember we are all fellow members of the same human race. It costs us nothing to acknowledge others and their feelings so that they feel validated. In fact, it benefits our self-esteem as well as theirs.

The middle way

More than anyone, the meditator knows that balance is automatically achieved through true self-empowerment. The person who sincerely believes in him or her self, who is centred in his or her being in a way that meditation can promote, intuitively follows the middle way with no fear of being deflected from their path. Being focused, their boundaries fall into place by themselves. This is the Impeccable Warrior in full flow.

The person who knows him or her self inside out understands that life is too short to take a fundamentalist attitude, to be so rigid as to choose the path of resistance and thus to cut off the ebb and flow of the life force within. By finding balance, the middle way, they show they care about themselves and also about others and every living organism.

When we tune in to the middle way, the abundance in nature vigorously supports our passage through life and leaves us free to resonate with others. When we live this way it is natural for us to respond positively to the needs of others. More often than not the attitude we transmit is picked up by the people we relate to, inspiring similar behaviour in return, and our relationships take on a new dynamism.

Balance is the road to peace and fulfilment. An intelligent and sensitive approach works really well, for it allows the river to flow fast and fulsomely without danger to our boundaries. Perhaps a potentially fruitful path and a great place to start for someone wanting firmer boundaries while also seeking the middle way is to make meditation a regular daily event. That way we build our awareness at the same time as getting clearer about what we want and don't want so that when we interact with others we automatically start to come from a place of integrity.

The same principles apply on a global scale to relationships between the world's nations, and between ethnic and religious groups within single nations. Throughout history, wars have been caused by people posturing and seeking ego aggrandisement. Unfortunately, it is always the innocent bystanders who suffer the most from the brinkmanship and one-upmanship that prevails.

In the late 1990's extremists on all sides of the argument in Northern Ireland started showing signs of modifying their formerly entrenched positions and began to move shakily towards a fragile agreement. To do this they were all obliged to meet on middle ground, but it was only able to happen after years of attrition. It seems it was necessary for the men of violence to first see the futility of their extremist activities, but the politicians who advocated non-violence eventually saw that they also had to change their equally entrenched attitudes. It always takes two to tango.

Even now, more than a decade later, we wait to see if the various factions feel able to continue embracing this middle way by maintaining their precarious rapprochement, or whether they will return to their old ways, wedded to feelings of insecurity and unable to trust in the new process. Sometimes it takes several generations for ancient hatreds to die down. In Northern Ireland, just as in every other conflict zone, somebody had to make the first move, but now it's down to everyone involved to maintain the peace by forsaking entrenched, dogmatic positions and continually choosing balance, which they will only do if they want peace sincerely.

Barack Obama, President of the United States, seems to have got this message, for he appears to be trying a different approach to solving conflict. The way of the heart, the middle way, is nothing other than the way of common sense. The middle way cuts straight through ego, straight through politics, straight through outdated hatreds and straight through ethnic, racial and religious dogma.

We can only hope that in Northern Ireland, where so many emotionally wounded people live in the hope of a decent life, peace is beginning to be seen as more important than political and ethnic differences and that people are finding weddings and birth celebrations, and even their daily toil, a lot more fun than going to funerals. Dare we hope that in this enlightened age the possibility now exists for us to allow the middle way to lead us to satisfactory solutions in all our relationships?

Trust

Slowly, slowly we learn, both on a personal and on a global level. Trust is required, and sometimes trusting seems like the hardest thing in the world to do. Trust is certainly something very hard for old enemies to embrace. The truth is, we have no choice but to take the risk of trusting unless we want to live out our days from beginning to end in perpetual conflict.

Here's a key observation from my life and the lives of many others I have known: *once we have tried everything else some of us discover the middle way, and then we finally realize that simply by treading this path we always get what we want. As long as you trust and remain focused on the path, there's no need to worry about anything.*

When I discovered this I felt enormous relief. At the same time I also realised that *to be able to trust, all I had to do was to drop my resistance to trusting.*

Our fear of making ourselves vulnerable and exposed, so everyone can see who we are, is usually what stops us from doing this. The person who believes in himself, trusts his own boundaries and travels a middle path, has no problem dropping his resistance to trusting, once he has enough awareness to understand the benefits of doing so.

When I realised this myself, I found it the funniest of ironies that to make your life happier and less stressful you don't have to work harder or do more of anything – quite the contrary, the trick is to do less, to stop making an effort! It sounds counter-intuitive – crazy maybe, but it's true nonetheless.

What exactly do I mean by that? *Trusting simply entails dropping your stress. Dropping your resistance simply means letting go.* How neat is that? To summarise in one short word, *RELAX!*

Trusting, I realised one day, is a normal, natural state for we humans, whereas not trusting is a deeply unnatural, neurotic one caused by early emotional wounding. It's a natural reaction. I came to this realisation the hard way, after first exhausting myself by clinging on to my fear of trusting for many, many years. Once we begin to trust, there is no longer any need for fear to arise. Indeed, when we let go of fear, trust is revealed as something that has always been there. All this becomes possible when you get to know exactly who you are and create firm boundaries as a result.

Once we truly understand and experience how it feels to live in trust, and really take it on board, we realise with a blinding flash of liberation that trusting is absolutely safe. Sadly, most people never reach that liberating moment, refusing even to entertain such a notion, for our Western society brings us up to believe we can trust no one, and that belief is so deeply ingrained most of us never question it. Unconsciously, most people take it for granted that it's not safe to trust.

This is of paramount importance because living in distrust is no way to live a happy, joyful and fulfilling life, and it's certainly not a fruitful way in which to conduct relationships. In earlier chapters we discussed how we tend to manifest more of what our dominant thought is. If your mind contains the thought that people are untrustworthy, if you expect people to be untrustworthy, if you fear that you yourself might turn out to be untrustworthy, then you are very likely to attract a high proportion of untrustworthy people into your orbit.

Even more important, don't forget our perceptions of the world around us and the people in it are a reflection of our own inner world and how we feel about ourselves. If we refuse to trust others this reflects our distrust of ourselves. If you suffer low self-esteem, self-belief, self-worth and self-confidence, and if you experience depression, it is almost inevitable you will live in fear and distrust – of others and of yourself.

If you see yourself mirrored in the above description, do not despair. Acknowledge to yourself how you feel and work though the exercises in this book again. Especially important is meditation, which can have a very healing effect. It gives you tremendous insight if you persevere and do it regularly. You will eventually come to see yourself in a true and positive perspective.

How can we trust?

We have no hope of living according to the middle way as long as we abdicate responsibility for our lives to our politicians, parents, teachers, clerics or anyone else, or try to imitate anyone else. Only when we each awaken and start to take responsibility for our own lives will the remotest chance arise of us and the world moving towards a state of balance, and thence into a process of healing.

So now the eternal conundrum rears its ugly head again. How do we trust, and exactly how are we supposed to follow the middle way to find this Utopian vision I describe, when all too often we feel lousy, resistant, angry, hurt and utterly mistrustful, and we feel as if we are under attack? Do we simply turn the other cheek? I don't think so.

Too many times in years gone by I have woken up in the morning to find myself burdened with my resistance, loaded with fear and bowed down with antipathy for the world, my fellow humans and my life. I am sure this sort of thing happens to us all at certain periods in our lives. Sometimes we simply find ourselves angry with our partners, hurt by our friends, jealous of our neighbours, afraid of our bosses, worried about the economy. There are hundreds of ways in which we feel our pain and lose touch with our flow each and every day.

Many people hate the work they have to get up and do, just to pay the rent or the mortgage, just to put bread on the table, just to keep body and soul together. When you feel like that, life is drudgery and you feel full of hatred and bereft of love. Then just when it looks like things couldn't get much worse, someone like me pops up and starts talking about living in trust! Doesn't it make you want to throw up?

At such times compassionate interaction with others and airy-fairy notions about some nebulous middle way are out of the question, for we feel the whole world is against us. We have built a world in which we have returned to the jungle where dog eats dog and life's a bitch, and our first instinct is to draw up the battle lines.

Many is the time I was told by friends in my younger days, 'stop whingeing and get real!' But people telling me that was of no help whatsoever. In the end, it was precisely because of my intimate acquaintance with the state of despair I describe that I decided one day that I would get real. The reality I discovered is that *each and every day we choose how we live our lives.*

If we continue to do a job we hate, it is because *we have chosen to do it.* If we feel trapped it is because *we* have shut down our creative imaginations and built ourselves a prison; if we hate the world, it is because *we* choose to blame her; if we feel that life is hard, it is because *we* have chosen to avoid taking responsibility; and if we feel neglected and abandoned, it is because *we* have slammed the door on love. These are, by definition, extreme positions, and ones *we* have created entirely by clinging to our distorted perceptions and our refusal to trust, because of our fear. If these are the choices we are unconsciously making, is it then surprising that we feel depressed and disempowered? The important point is to wake up and realise with awareness what unconscious choices we make so we get a chance to change them.

What then of the middle path? Are we to ignore these painful feelings and pretend we can lightly tread this middle path with our hearts full of love, when in fact we feel so angry and upset we'd like to murder someone? Of course not. When we feel like that, our hearts, and our boots, are laden with lead as we drag them despairingly around.

When we continue with work we hate, we blame the work, the boss, our colleagues, and our work environment, for being horrible. But do our bosses seek us out and press-gang us into doing their work? Is someone holding a gun to our heads? Absolutely not. We hold ourselves to ransom when we allow ourselves to be seduced by the golden handcuffs and, by so doing, we back ourselves into an extreme position. Then we blame outside circumstances or others because we feel trapped. And why? Because we are too unaware, too untrusting, too lacking in self-belief to believe we can choose whatever we really want.

Sometimes we convince ourselves we are forced to be in the position we are in because we have responsibilities to dependants, and so on. Even though this might seem like a good reason, we are wherever we are as a result of earlier choices. Though we may not realise it, we begin making choices from the moment of our conception. Shouldering our financial responsibilities to our dependants is wonderful and commendable, but let us not forget our responsibilities to ourselves.

Before I'm pilloried, let me clarify I am not advocating we shirk our responsibilities to our children and families – exactly the opposite. I'm saying by taking care of ourselves we put ourselves in a far stronger position to cater for the needs of our dependants. They not only want and need our financial support but also our joy and our emotional support, for only when we are fulfilled can we become the positive role models our kids and dependants need.

If humans are clever enough to build a huge Hadron Collider to accelerate and collide the tiniest of particle beams, surely a person can change from a profession he hates to one he loves?

Of course it takes guts to change course in mid-stream, for it is scary to admit we hate a career we have been pursuing for many years, and to turn our backs on it. But in recent years many more people are doing just that. In fact the vast majority of the clients in my Life Coaching practice are going through mid-life career changes, and many are looking to embark on new long-term relationships. They range from age thirty to seventy-five, so they obviously agree with me that it's never too late to demand happiness.

I have changed direction many times during my working life. In the early days I would only do it when I finally felt forced to change, for I could no longer carry on as I was. Jokingly I tell my friends that I have had more 'brilliant' careers than they have had hot dinners.

One day, early in my working life, it occurred to me that I was working myself to the bone for an ungrateful boss in a job I hated, and getting absolutely nowhere. In my youthful inexperience I did not know how to improve things, but an intuitive realisation told me I had nothing to lose if I quit, for no job could be worse for me than the one I had. I was getting more and more depressed and that worried me even more than the prospect of forfeiting my meagre income.

At the same time, I started going to therapeutic human potential groups in London and so the whole process of liberating myself slowly began. It was the late 1960s and the heyday of the Esalen Institute in California, where cutting edge developments in psychotherapy, Eastern philosophies and the human potential movement were evolving under legendary characters such as Fritz Perls (the founder of Gestalt Therapy), Alan Watts, Abraham Maslow, Carl Rogers and many other visionary pioneers.

All our beliefs about everything to do with the nature of our existence, how we got here, how we evolved into conscious beings and what might be the meaning of life was up for questioning and re-examination, and the effect began to be felt in London, where I lived. This was the next step on from Darwin, Freud and Jung and it was a crucially important period in the history of modern psychology, personal development and all matters of mind, body and spirit. In short, visionary people were reaching out for new understandings of what it meant to be human.

At first I found these groups in London decidedly unpleasant, for I was encouraged to say and show how I felt, and I felt awful. Not only did I *not* want to look at those painful feelings, I did not want others to see the state I was in either. I felt embarrassed and ashamed of myself because I was doing nothing I considered to be worthy, and the work I had been doing I felt was valueless. That's why I quit.

Nor did I want to look anyone in the eye, for my belief in myself was woefully lacking. I kept going to the groups because I desperately wanted to start feeling better and, sure enough, as time passed and I learned to trust myself and the others just a little, I began to see that it was just about possible after all to take a few brief glimpses at some of those deeply repressed painful feelings without going into a terminal or suicidal depression.

The results were fascinating for, to my surprise, within a remarkably short space of time I began to have odd moments of feeling high and elated. These happy feelings did not last very long because I was still acutely worried about being unemployed, and I was still unaware of what I wanted to do. I was looking avidly for solutions and felt scared that my whole life might consist of one long nightmare struggle to stay one step ahead of the bailiffs.

I had not yet realised that by simply touching base with those feelings of fear and insecurity, they would eventually move to the background so that possible solutions and options would begin to unfold in all sorts of unexpected ways. I was to learn a significant and helpful lesson, which was that nothing gets processed by avoidance, but painful feelings can be healed by experiencing them fully and letting them pass.

We avoid because we are afraid our feelings will be too overwhelmingly painful, and indeed they often seem so at the time. Those early groups helped me see that our only possible chance to free ourselves is to go totally into how we feel.

For some considerable time maybe, these feelings can send us seesawing to crazy and sometimes frightening extremes, as if in an emotional cold turkey – deep depressions, wild elations, profound pain and anger, mind-blowing ecstasy, and more. Like a body being ravaged by a fever, you are at their mercy during the time it takes for them to pass, which is why it pays to have the support of a group, a therapist or a coach to help you to trust your own process, to surrender to it and to encourage you to keep going, even through your deepest despair.

If this sounds scary, take heart, for extreme experiences like these can never be sustained as long as you let them flow through. Sooner or later your fever passes and a state of surrender arrives, leaving behind a situation of inner purification.

Ultimately, after facing your fears and living your pain to the full, a kind of blessed internal silence descends, a blissful relief where once there was conflict and turmoil. The process may have to be repeated many times and it may take some considerable time for the fires to burn themselves out fully, but in the state of peace in which we finally end up, we ultimately arrive at the middle way.

The fire analogy is a good one, for each time another firestorm passes, a little more purification and a little more healing take place.

When the moment comes that we have allowed our feelings to pass through enough times, the fires are finally starved of fuel. When that happens, they can burn no longer.

Of course the above describes an ideal scenario and it assumes you keep going till you find the peace you crave. But many people start on this path and don't keep going, but even so a partial cleansing can be achieved, and that is also well worth having.

By the time the first period of my life had elapsed I had become so used to living in a state of inner conflict that I found this strangely peaceful and harmonious state of being, when it finally arrived, a little unreal at first. But I grew to love it and to realise it was absolutely real. Meditation is an excellent vehicle for enabling this process to happen which is why I came to see the practice of meditation as a sublime gift that had saved my sanity and shown me a path to peace and balance.

Have ever asked yourself, 'why do I always end up torpedoing my relationships despite my best intentions?' or 'why do my relationships always end in tears?' or 'what do I have to do to be able to sustain a joyful and fulfilling relationship?' If so, you would do well to take note of everything we have discussed in the last three chapters, for it may furnish you with the understanding you need to find your solution.

Finding a suitable partner, holding up a mirror to help each other to grow, defining your boundaries, looking after your own personal growth and development and travelling the middle way – these are all essential hallmarks of a happy and sustainable relationship.

Living in a state of trust has never hurt me and it is rare nowadays for me not to trust. Indeed I can honestly say, hand on heart, I am far happier now than I have ever been. Of course I still experience pain, anger, sadness and all that, and I know when somebody is lying and in that sense is untrustworthy. It just isn't a problem now.

Finding our balance enables us at last to make friends with ourselves and 'step out of the war', as Jack Kornfield, in his book entitled *A Path with Heart,* put it. As I said before, there was a time when I felt ashamed of myself, but no longer. Now, as I travel the middle way, conversing with my heart as I go, I am never lonely for I have the finest companion a man could wish for, my wonderful, sparkling self!

Summary

- It is just as important to maintain strong boundaries in our relationships as in our individual lives if they are to endure fruitfully
- Finding the middle way is not the same as compromising. The middle way, or the path of balance, is very helpful in any relationship. Compromise is not
- Life does not work well as a compromise; for compromising means putting up with second best or less
- Usually, if we allow ourselves to live in compromise it is because we do not fully believe in ourselves, we have woolly boundaries and we suffer low self-esteem. This is a programme for self-sabotage
- If we believe we can't have exactly what we need and want, we needlessly accept limitations imposed on us by others
- You *can* have everything you sincerely need and want if you are coming from your heart
- Truth is, we already everything we need. We just need to notice that we have it and drop our resistance or guilt that gets in our way of enjoying it
- If you think you cannot have your heart's desire, you are not thinking and feeling for yourself – you are merely accepting dictum that has been foisted on you all your life
- Lots of people have what they want – but only because they sincerely believe in what they are doing. They come from their hearts and go out on a limb, taking all necessary risks and facing every fear, to live their truth
- If you are not being true to yourself, you are compromising. It's essential to understand this principle in relationships
- If we agree to a compromise, we collude in the other person's insincerity and then two people won't feel good about themselves instead of just one
- Defining and defending your boundaries calls for skill and sensitivity
- When you are focused, open and centred you can relax, for nothing threatens your boundaries. You take care of them intuitively

- If you are in a neurotic state you are going to have to resolve many of your issues before you can consider yourself as suitable material for successful relationships
- It's not possible to put a boundary around something you do not perceive or something you're not sure how you feel about
- Assertiveness is the technique or habit of tuning in to your needs and wants and learning to communicate them clearly and honestly, to manifest them and stand by them with integrity. It's a stance that proclaims, 'this is who I am'
- A person who gets to know, understand and trust himself, and who behaves in such a way as to elevate his self-esteem, will become assertive automatically
- If you contrive assertiveness without feeling it, you merely replace one persona with another. Then your so-called assertiveness will always be a tremendous effort and can never flow naturally or feel authentic
- Contrived assertiveness wakes us up to the fact that our boundaries are shaky, and that there is a deeper problem which needs addressing
- The flowing assertiveness of which I speak expresses itself via a sort of humble confidence, and is what I refer to as balance, or the middle way
- The deepest water is the fastest flowing. When we drop our resistance we flow deeper and our passage through life is more empowered and less obstructed
- True assertiveness helps us remain aware and clearly focused
- There is no excuse for behaving with a lack of compassion. If that is what we find ourselves doing, we had better urgently check ourselves out and heal whatever wound is making us do that, if necessary with professional help
- When a friend wants us to listen and we sincerely have no time to spare, honesty is the only sensible recourse. We will not jeopardise our boundaries or our relationships if we acknowledge the other person's feelings and explain our situation clearly
- The meditator knows that balance is automatically achieved through the self-empowerment that meditation can bring

- The person who sincerely believes in himself, and who is centred in a way that meditation can promote, intuitively follows the middle way and because of his focus, trusts his boundaries will fall into place by themselves
- The person who knows himself understands that life is too short to take a fundamentalist attitude, to be so rigid as to choose the path of resistance and to cut off the ebb and flow of the life force within
- When we tune in to the middle way, the abundance in nature vigorously supports our passage through life and leaves us free to resonate with others
- Balance is the road to peace and fulfilment
- Though it might seem difficult, we have no choice but to risk trusting unless we want to live out our days in perpetual conflict
- Once we have tried everything else, some of us discover the middle way, and then we finally realise that simply by taking this path we get what we want
- As long as you trust, there's no need to worry about anything
- To be able to trust, all you have to do is drop your resistance to trusting
- The person who believes in himself, trusts his own boundaries and travels a middle path has no problem dropping his resistance to trusting, once he has the awareness to understand the benefits of doing so
- *To make your life happier and less stressful you don't have to work harder or do more – quite the contrary, the trick is to do less, to stop making an effort!*
- Trusting simply entails dropping your stress. Dropping your resistance simply means letting go. How neat is that?
- Trusting is a normal, natural state for we humans; not trusting is a deeply unnatural, neurotic state caused by early emotional wounding
- Once we truly understand and experience how it feels to live in trust, we realise with a blinding flash of liberation that trusting is absolutely safe. On the rare occasions when it isn't, your intuition will raise your defences
- Our perceptions of the world and the people in it are a reflection of our own inner world and how we feel about ourselves

- We have no hope of living according to the middle way as long as we abdicate responsibility for our lives
- Only when we each awaken and start to take responsibility for our own lives will there be the remotest chance of us and the world moving towards a state of balance, and thence a process of healing
- Each and every day we choose how we live our lives
- We feel trapped when we are too unaware, too untrusting, too lacking in self-belief to understand we can choose whatever we really want
- We begin making choices from the moment of our conception
- When we are fulfilled we become positive role models
- It takes guts to change course mid-stream but in recent years more and more people do, for they've realised it's never too late to demand happiness
- Nothing gets processed by avoidance, but painful feelings can be healed by experiencing them fully and letting them pass
- Each time another firestorm passes, a little more purification and a little more healing take place
- Finding a suitable partner, holding up a mirror to help each other to grow, defining your boundaries, looking after your own personal growth and travelling the middle way are all hallmarks of a happy and sustainable relationship
- Finding our balance enables us at last to make friends with ourselves and 'step out of the war'

29

The Minefield of Sexuality

Go deeply into your sexuality
Osho

We are all well aware that one of the primary functions of mankind is to procreate in order to maintain the integrity of the species. Humans are especially lucky, for of all the living creatures on this earth, we are one of the few species that have the conscious awareness to realise we can enjoy the process. Humans are one of the very small number of beings that sometimes use sex consciously as a creative expression of love, or simply for recreation.

Unfortunately, much heartache can be created when two people arrive at a stage when they feel ready for a long-term, committed relationship, yet one or both don't have the sexual experience and maturity to know exactly what they want and like in sex. Matters are only made more painful when and if they fail to communicate between themselves about the subject.

Sadly, because of these and other reasons, far too many of us do not enjoy sex to the full. Many are only partially fulfilled, others are totally frustrated and some positively hate the reproductive act. This is a vital issue we cannot ignore in a book like this. All too often partners fail to resolve their problems and their relationship ends up in the divorce courts, with potentially disastrous results to themselves and any children that may have entered the picture.

There are many possible reasons why people don't always enjoy sex or get what they need from it, and low self-esteem or self-worth are among them. Important though they are, since we have already discussed these at length elsewhere, I propose leaving those issues aside for the moment while we focus on other important aspects.

Probably the other most common problems are lack of communication between the protagonists in a relationship, coupled with a reluctance to experiment and a fear of intimacy. Time and time again I have encountered these characteristics in people I have worked with. My theory is that both these phenomena spring from the long and insidious history of Western civilisation in which manifestations of human sexuality have been systematically repressed and corrupted by society, and surrounded by stigma, embarrassment, guilt and shame.

Attitudes to sex

It's the fear of making ourselves vulnerable and therefore open to being hurt that usually drives the fear many people have of intimacy and intimate communication.

As a result, the time is urgently upon us to re-examine our attitudes surrounding all matters of sex and sexuality in an effort to free ourselves to explore and communicate. How else can we liberate ourselves and future generations so we can enjoy our sexual relations to the full? I can't help feeling, if we are in favour of having monogamous nuclear families as the basis for our society, that we should undertake this exploration and experimentation *before* we get married.

In case you are wondering, I am indeed talking partly from personal experience. It was only after my own painful divorce in 1983 that I realised I had not sown anywhere near enough wild oats before marriage and that was one major contributing factor to our resulting disaster, which was hardly surprising – in retrospect! It was a strong lesson and wake-up call, to put it mildly.

It seems amazing, and a sad realisation, that even in this day and age, there is still a huge taboo around matters sexual. This I have deduced not only from my professional experience but also from reading between the lines when I witness what happens with friends, acquaintances and ex-lovers, as well as from listening to clients who want to discuss relationship issues. I see the same again when gauging people's reactions when I broach the subject of sex. Often people react as if I have said something outrageous when I have merely stated a fact or asked a mildly provocative question on some sexual issue.

It would be all too easy to dismiss this as merely my perception because of my being 'typically English,' but other nationalities are equally reticent in their own ways. Around the time when the videotapes were released of President Bill Clinton's testimony about the alleged Monica Lewinsky affair, I happened to be talking to a French woman and I asked her opinion. She told me that the French find this kind of lurid detail when someone's private life is made public distasteful in the extreme. 'The private life,' she told me, 'is private!' Having delivered her final word on the subject, she screwed up her nose in disgust – not at what Clinton might have done, but because it had been made public.

In Holland, by contrast, it seems that anything goes. It's gone to the other extreme, for the Dutch are so up-front about sex and sexuality that lovemaking seems to have almost lost its magic. Sex is certainly not confined to the private bedroom in this land where every conceivable type of sexual taste or fantasy can be catered for very commercially and virtually in public, and not only in Amsterdam.

With regard to our own private lives, how are we to know what we want or like unless we experiment? Surely we must find ways to overcome our coyness if we are to relate honestly in lovemaking, and experience mutual satisfaction.

The judgements and perceived judgements of others, and our own self-judgements about our sexuality and our sexual predilections, hit us where it hurts, whether they are real or imagined. We are enormously sensitive around sexual issues and this is evident because as soon as we are judged inadequate, perverted or in some way 'incorrect' in our desires, our very validity as humans is called into question.

Experimentation

This is why I advocate my firm belief that the primary business of any self-respecting pre-marital youth, and this applies just as much to girls as to boys, has to be to explore and experiment in all spheres of life, to rebel and to seek new experiences. Thank goodness this is precisely what many are now doing! But of course care is needed. Are they going about it in ways that will ultimately prove helpful and not damaging?

Very few teenagers have a clue about what they want, much less what they need, and for most of us the noisy cavorting and getting drunk that many teenagers do is a necessary stage of growing up. It is very helpful in the process of enabling us to eventually develop a sense of who we are and who we are not. It's also a vital stage in learning to welcome intimacy, something that many couples fear like the devil.

Unfortunately, because of our distorted views, the mixed messages society puts out, neurotic conditioned behaviour and a general lack of conscious awareness, the rebellion sometimes goes badly wrong. There are unwanted pregnancies, sexually transmitted diseases, rapes, child abuse, domestic and other violence, drug or alcohol addiction and other heartbreaking scenarios, some of which even end in suicide. At the very least the result can often be rock-bottom self-esteem.

This vitally important issue is not going to go away so it behoves us to address it – not only for ourselves but for the sake of our children and future generations.

The former Poet Laureate, Sir John Betjeman, was asked in an interview shortly before his death if he had any regrets. He replied from his wheelchair, without the slightest hesitation, that he only regretted not having had enough sex in his life. When he was growing up, recreational sex among the young and unmarried in middle and upper class Victorian England was frowned upon and deeply repressed, at least in public. Any kind of 'deviation' from the perceived norm was simply unspeakable, something that fed Betjeman's sexual fantasies and his poetry at great length. Oscar Wilde also discovered the cost of departing from the social mores of the day, but with different and far more serious consequences, some years earlier.

I hope from the above we can begin to take on board the idea that young men and women are absolutely right to celebrate their lustiness to the full – lord knows it doesn't take long before we get too old. There is one vital caveat, however, which is that protecting yourself from unwanted pregnancies and unpleasant sexually transmitted diseases is not a matter for debate, it's a must.

There's another problem too. However much experimentation we may perform, until an element of awareness around what we are doing is introduced, there won't be much benefit other than hedonism, and the taboos will remain. By contrast, sexual union with awareness enables young people to learn to share real intimacy. What could be better for our world than that?

Unfortunately, sometimes young women are seen by men as conquests rather than fellow soul travellers who need to express their passions, discover themselves and make sense of the world they inhabit just as much as men do. I also meet some young women who, in a sort of defensive, retaliatory reaction, adopt a similarly aggressive and predatory attitude towards sexual adventures as young men sometimes do. I am not discussing moral issues here, I merely pose the question, are they really having fun? It doesn't always look like it to me.

If that sounds terribly Victorian, that is not at all how I mean it. It is a wonderful idea for uncommitted friends to have sex with each other as much as they like, and with as many different partners as they like, as long as they protect themselves. I merely make a plea for awareness because, try as we might, sex without feelings is impossible.

Sensitivity to ourselves and towards each other is essential, or we are bound to get hurt again. When we close our hearts and function solely on ego, we merely create and store up more pain. Have we not got enough already?

Here's yet another problem. Only too often, sex is used as a hiding place where we can avoid addressing the real issues that are making us depressed or unhappy. Sex can be a wonderful palliative, a placebo, to help us live with our pain. Nothing wrong with that as far as it goes, but let us not be under any illusions that using sex as an ego boost or an anaesthetic is a path towards long term happiness and fulfilment. It is not.

That's because ego-driven sex is by definition narcissistic, due to a lack of awareness towards sensitive issues, such as each other's feelings. If both sexes could begin to trust and understand that no ego damage is caused when we treat ourselves and other humans with due respect, we would all feel a lot freer to celebrate our aliveness, while experimenting to our heart's content. Then, rather than generating more pain, by behaving with awareness we begin to heal.

Perhaps I am idealising, but I believe that if we change our attitudes by simply telling each other honestly what we want and how we feel, this will lead to greater insight and understanding on both sides. As a result here would be fewer broken hearts, greater freedom and enjoyment, even a decrease in unwanted pregnancy and rapes.

This must be balanced by the realisation that it's unrealistic to expect a teenage man, overwhelmed as he is by a deluge of hormones, to be able to take a mature and balanced view about having a sexual relationship with a girl, whether at home or on holiday. Care must be exercised for very few young teenage men are sufficiently emotionally developed, experienced and equipped to sustain enduring loving relationships. In most cases, their early sexual experiences are part of their learning process. The boy may tell the girl he loves her, and very often he believes he does, but in all honesty in the vast majority of cases, he simply has not lived enough to be able to comprehend the flood of powerful emotions he is experiencing. Moreover, in all probability, neither has she.

In one sense, sex and love are two entirely separate issues, and yet the two are irrevocably entwined. To try to separate out sexual practice as if it were an activity entire in itself leads to an artificial and incomplete sort of nourishment in which the heart and soul are the losers. Yet for young people, hormonal activity overwhelms everything. We need to understand this if we are to avoid judging the behaviour of our young people unfairly.

What is the answer to this? I believe it's a compassionate, understanding and non-judgemental view from parents, teachers and other concerned role models towards our children as we teach them the importance of awareness and treating others with respect at all times. Additionally, it would be very helpful if someone would explain to our young teenagers what exactly is happening to them in emotional, spiritual, psychological and physical terms during the stages of their development from puberty onwards. I'm sure they are sufficiently intelligent to understand, and most would be fascinated and delighted to be able to comprehend what they are going through.

Another reason conflict arises in young people is because the converse is also true. Our conditioning is very powerful and sets itself up in competition with our hormonal development, which is one reason why so many of us experience conflict and confusion as we develop. For example, many girls still seem to be ready and eager to step into stereotypical fantasies of love, romance and marriage without really understanding the implications, or even questioning them seriously, because the example of what their more mature role models do is so powerful. Then they are surprised, confused and hurt when in many cases, their dreams end in tatters around their feet.

They have not questioned themselves deeply enough to know who they really are and what they really want, a potentially disastrous basis for marriage. That is why I told my children to take their time to explore and experiment with care to their hearts content first.

This need for self-discovery is just one of the reasons why puberty and adolescence is so often a time of enormous confusion for members of both sexes. Most mature adults find sexual experimentation with one long-term partner rewarding, but only if they have lived fully through their formative years and taken the trouble to learn all they can about themselves.

Not everyone who experiences these problems is young, but the same principles apply no matter what your age. People want and need sexual experience. Youth is the perfect and appropriate time for experimenting with different sexual partners. However, many people arrive in their mid-thirties, forties, fifties or beyond without enough sexual experience and, as a result, they find it hard to sustain loving relationships, or to understand why they will not work. For those of us who find ourselves in this position, there is only one solution. To go back, as it were, and relive our youth in the way we should have lived it at the time but did not because we did not realise it was OK to have a lot of sex.

There are no short cuts to emotional and sexual maturity. If you want the expertise you have to do the apprenticeship and put in the practise. If you don't experiment sexually in your youth, you may find after a lot of heartache and failed relationships that you have to do it in adulthood. *There is no substitute for experience.*

The vast majority of people I know personally in my peer group have suffered at least one divorce, which is why they all seem to agree that life really does begin at forty, or thereabouts (that is, post-divorce). A lot of the people I meet realise they lost precious opportunities for experimentation, learning, growth and development when they were young. Having now separated or divorced, a brave few find themselves having to go back to the drawing board, as it were. This development is both beautiful and exciting, for because of it, gradually they learn how to make our present relationships work. The major benefit of undertaking self-discovery during our more mature years is that it's much easier to incorporate the ingredient of awareness.

The big lesson I got from getting divorced was that, apart from love and awareness, *experience in all aspects of life, not just sex, is vital in making our lives and long term relationships work.* We have to know ourselves and we have to know what we want before we can emotionally prosper and flow.

All the love and goodwill in the world is no substitute for experience, for although those two ingredients are vital, only through experience can we begin to know our own personal truths. That is the purpose of experimentation. In the arena of relationships, as in every other area of our lives, there are no rights or wrongs in the positive/negative sense. Never forget that all outcomes to all experiments are opportunities for learning, growth and development.

Experiments help to broaden our understanding, which is why the bedroom should be our crucible for discovering the nature of love. We may kid ourselves we have sexual freedom, but as long as beautiful women look away in fear when they see men looking appreciatively at them in the street, we are still repressed and sex is still taboo.

It is an unfortunate side-effect that both men and women, when they suffer emotional wounding, tend to take a defensive view of each other. This is understandable because someone who has been hurt will naturally want to guard against being hurt again. Unfortunately, a defensive or aggressive stance eliminates any possibility of intimacy. This can lead to a perception, held by some, that there is irresolvable conflict between the sexes and there always will be. This is patent nonsense, of course. Problems between people can always be resolved, but only if both parties are prepared to risk being vulnerable and open to hearing the other person. Otherwise, all you are left with is something that feels like a kind of fear dual, or a power struggle, in which the one with the strongest ego 'wins.'

To me it seems obvious that nearly all the barriers that prevent men and women from simply pleasuring in each other's company, the factors that inhibit us from getting close, are artificial. They come from learned behaviour evolved because through our fears we have perceived a need to defend our vulnerability. That is why the way of the heart requires courage and resolve. We must cast aside our armour if we are to succeed in our quest for happiness in our relationships. Of course, no one can eliminate the risk we might get hurt again.

Risk or not, the way of the heart, when allowed free reign, is the only path that can lead you towards greater intimacy and that, though it may seem paradoxical, is what sets us free. Nothing worthwhile was ever attained without risk.

All I am advocating really is that we allow ourselves just a little more freedom to behave spontaneously. Surely, with all we have discussed up till now, we can trust ourselves enough to look after our boundaries and behave like Impeccable Warriors in all matters of the heart. Then whatever happens, we'll enjoy the moments we are given and we'll be alright – we'll learn something, we will grow.

Another complaint I hear sometimes is boredom in the bedroom. This is sometimes a result of refusing to connect with our creative imaginations, perhaps because of taboo (it doesn't feel permissible to be creative, or we feel guilty about experimenting), or because political correctness may have sanitised our sexual behaviour. It could also be a simple case of the raw animal attraction wearing off, but it seems unlikely it would just fade away if it were genuinely present once. If this is your situation, then your urgent issue is about putting some raunchy excitement back into your sex life.

One thing I can suggest is looking at how the men behave in Argentina, Brazil, Holland, Italy, or even France? I daresay British women reading this might find what I'm saying a bit Neanderthal, but I am not recommending we menfolk indulge too much in stereotypical machismo. Let's not forget the middle way in all this. I'm describing a scenario in which we get a bit more romantic and overtly amorous, that's all. Let's remember the union between men and woman is a joy to be celebrated and not a situation in which to get hung up in guilt and inhibition.

My appeal is to courageous individuals, those receptive beings who are prepared to take the quantum leap of laying aside their ego defences to start living according to the dictates of their hearts. What I mean is simply doing what comes naturally, sensitively, but without too much thinking. If we do more of that, our relationships will take off into exciting new realms, and that will inevitably be reflected in our sexual unions.

Contrary to popular belief we need less repression, not more laws telling us how to behave. When we tune in carefully, our hearts will tell us exactly how we should behave, therefore we need to develop our tuning skills and our awareness. Human emotions cannot be controlled, and unless they are given full expression with awareness, dangerously explosive situations can develop. But with awareness there's no need to worry, for in my experience, and that of many people I know, when we allow ourselves to express ourselves freely in all areas of our lives, and free ourselves from repressive taboos, the urge for destruction and violent behaviour simply evaporates.

In our hearts, each and every one of us knows how we want to have sex, especially after we have done some experimentation and asked ourselves the question that runs like a thread through this book, 'how do I feel about that?' What we need then to be happy is to find the courage to communicate about our heartfelt wishes with our partners, even if we are inhibited by guilt, shame and fear.

As in all aspects of our lives, giving ourselves the freedom to experiment helps us distinguish between what is real and what is conditioned in the ways we react and behave sexually. That in turn gives us the opportunity to choose what we want in the light of our first hand experience, rather than behaving in accordance with the conditioning we may have unconsciously accepted as if it were our own.

Trust

To really let go of our inhibitions during sex so we behave spontaneously from our hearts, we need to be able to trust. We need to trust that the other person will treat us honestly and with sensitivity, and we need to trust ourselves, so that whatever we feel we want to do in bed we will do with awareness and sensitivity. We also need to trust that our desires are valid, no matter what it is we want, as long as no one gets hurt. Once again, a suitable partner is a prerequisite.

When we behave with awareness, communicating honestly with our partners and with ourselves, nobody gets damaged. However, when we feel unworthy, guilty or shameful, it becomes impossible to be true to ourselves and behave with integrity. This also applies when we mistakenly believe we are obliged above all else to please the other, for fear they might withdraw their love.

Of course, our conditioning cannot be dismissed that easily. For most of us it takes tremendous courage to even begin to trust and behave with awareness. What evidence do we have that by putting ourselves into such a vulnerable position, things will work our alright? How do we know, for example, that if we men let our sexual fantasies run riot, we might not end up raping or venting our anger on the woman next door?

It's a very good question and here, at least, is my answer, based on years of experience and observation. If you give vent to your emotions on a regular basis, perhaps with the assistance of some of the tools mentioned in earlier chapters, and go deeply into your sexuality in consensual situations, no one will come to any harm. When damage arises it's because you have tried to repress or suppress your feelings and, like a volcano, you can end up with an uncontrollable explosion. Sooner or later the energy has to come out somewhere.

If you feel you might explode, and I mean at any time, not just when relating, go and do *Dynamic* or the *Aum Meditation,* find a quite space somewhere on your own to beat up some cushions, go to the gym and hit a punch bag, go for a run or do something preferably physical by yourself to express your anger safely. Then return to your relationship and *talk about how you feel.*

Never under estimate the power of talking to express yourself, and the importance of being heard. That means if your partner wants you to listen, be sure to listen attentively and let them know they have been fully heard and empathised with.

Anger and violence

It's important we acknowledge that every one of us has a potentially violent, angry streak, and that includes women. That acknowledgement enables us to take responsibility for finding ways of expressing that energy harmlessly, even creatively. Amazingly, just that acceptance helps our fear dissolve and our aliveness bubble up.

Rape fantasies spring, in most cases, from feelings of inadequacy. Broadly speaking, rape is one of the psyche's strategies men use in an attempt to convince themselves they feel they have power and control over women, when in fact they really feel emasculated. Most men have the physical power to make women subservient to their desires, or so they think, and that power fantasy can send some men into an aroused and potentially orgasmic state. Only when, and if, they wake up will they realise that this is an illusion, for truly empowered people find their power from within themselves and do not have to prove themselves at the expense of others.

This is one major reason why it's very important that we become intimately acquainted with our sexuality, including our sexual fantasies. Knowing our fantasies and recognising them for what they are helps us get reality into perspective, a vital milestone on the road to true empowerment. Only letting go into who we really are, trusting our hearts, communicating in depth and behaving with awareness will allow feelings of true empowerment and self-esteem to grow. Once a person feels empowered within him or her self, ideas of domination as a means of establishing personal power and authority simply evaporate.

I pondered long and hard on this subject until one day I heard a discourse by Osho in which he advised his audience to 'go totally into your sexuality.' It was then that I realised the obvious truth that was staring me in the face – repressed anger can lead not only to violence, but also to suppressed fantasies which arise from our conditioning. These in turn can lead to losing our perspective on what's real.

How are we to distinguish between reality and fantasy until we experience the concepts and practices about which we are curious, and witness the difference? How can we accept reality when we have distorted it? It is impossible, for a distorted reality does not make sense to the heart. Such acceptance, if there is any, is only in our minds and not in our hearts, but that is where it needs to be if it is of any validity.

Most of us have become so used to believing in our fantasies, it has become impossible to distinguish what is fantasy and what is reality. Hence Osho's brilliant idea. Put your sexuality under the microscope. Experiment with it in the laboratory of your bedroom. Examine it. Shine a spotlight on it. Share with your partner so you can help each other explore what feels right. Only by living and experiencing our sexuality and our sexual fantasies to the full, something that most of us fear and only dream of doing, will we find out experientially what is real and what is not. Remember, one person's reality is another person's fantasy.

Awareness is paramount, for the experiment will only prove meaningful if you allow your heart be your monitor of how you feel as you proceed.

For the sake of clarity and safety, a caveat is required at this point. As consenting adults, exploring fairly innocuous fantasies with our partners is OK. However, urges that have more serious social consequences, such as paedophilia, sado-masochism or flagellation, must be dealt with in the therapy room, not the bedroom. They need to be explored with a trained therapist, psychologist or professional who is specifically trained to help you with this, and not with your partner and certainly not with a child. These kinds of extremes are way beyond the remit of this book, which deals only with practices that are physically, mentally and emotionally harmless and legal, when approached in an appropriate manner.

While touching on this subject, the dangers of ignoring or repressing unexpressed pain are legion. If we are worried we might do something we will regret by letting go during sex, there are many simple ways of harmlessly dealing with that problem.

By looking inside we might discover we are angry, for example, but by employing some of the techniques described in earlier chapters, such as the *Aum Mediation*, one-to-one psychotherapy, or simply shouting and beating up cushions in private, we can find ways of expressing our anger and other emotions to the full within a supportive and safe structure. *If in doubt, always seek support from a qualified practitioner.*

I, and many of my acquaintances, use Osho's *Dynamic Meditation* from time to time as a sort of safety valve. When anger builds up we can go to a designated room where we will be given the great luxury of being undisturbed for a whole hour while having a thoroughly good catharsis, followed by a period of wonderful stillness. *With anger, better out than in is the golden rule,* but it needs to be put out safely and responsibly without dumping. Apart from anything else, dumping is counter-productive, an avoidance of responsibility and it's the height of unawareness.

Whatever your fantasies, there are places to go where expert loving and supportive healing can be found. Support is essential, for any kind of healing only happens through love.

Fantasies

Fantasies are a big issue in the bedroom, yet exploring our fantasies even in safe ways is neglected by the vast majority of people. We can hardly experience sex as blissful and joyful when we are out of touch with what we really want, or are too shy to ask for our fantasies to be acted out just to see how they feel and to help us find out what really turns us on.

Judging by what I hear from clients and others, bedroom fantasies are probably the most taboo-ridden and guilt-laden areas of our lives. When unexpressed and unexplored they become a constant source of feeling shameful and disempowered. As in all other aspects of leading happy and fulfilled lives, everything we do in exploring our fantasy life also leads back to doing as much as we possibly can to nurture our awareness. It is very easy to be driven by our fantasies when we do not explore or express them.

I don't propose to suggest the vivid details of exactly how you can act out your fantasies, save to say it's imperative to let your imagination have free rein. And don't forget to maintain your awareness, even when you're having fun.

In the Osho Humaniversity, the therapeutic community in Holland led by Veeresh, (we talked about him in Chapter 14), issues around sexuality have a very high profile, and anyone who goes there is certain to be confronted in this area, though always in a powerfully supportive, safe and loving context.

Those I have spoken to who have been sufficiently courageous to rise to the challenges they met in the Dutch therapeutic centre have learned, understood and experienced a tremendous amount about their personal lives as sexual beings, and have grown considerably in their spiritual lives too. The therapists in the Humaniversity are engaged in the valuable and essential work of undoing centuries of negative conditioning. This is about dropping learned behaviour that keeps us prisoners and separates us from our birthright, which in this context means expressing and experiencing our sexuality to the full.

If you really feel confused or uncertain in this area, it may well be worth considering a visit to this establishment get a firmer handle on it. You can find more information by visiting their website at www.humaniversity.nl but be warned, as in the *Aum Meditation,* you may encounter some strong confrontation.

The object of the experiment we call going deeply into your sexuality is to free yourself from the domination of your fantasies so you can choose to express them when appropriate and because you want to, because fantasies can be fun, not because you are driven by unconscious behaviour or beliefs.

Now if after all this discussion you are still blushing at the ideas I propound, here's a great idea, given to me by a friend who lived in Amsterdam, for couples who would secretly like to experiment but who feel too inhibited to do so. You just rent or buy a soft pornographic video or DVD and watch it in your bedroom, while in bed together. Either while the video is playing, or after it is finished, you and your partner conduct a sort of game with each other of imitating what you have seen on the screen. It might feel scary at first, or stupid, contrived, or embarrassing, or just light-hearted, but this exercise has a deadly serious purpose – to stimulate your imaginations, to help you lose your inhibitions, and to inject some light-hearted fun that will spice up the sexual side of your relationship which might otherwise fall apart through sexual boredom or frustration.

Some couples discover that they enjoy 'unconventional' or 'unacceptable' or 'politically incorrect' sexual practices so much that acting them out makes their lives complete. Going totally into your fantasies is a powerful way of discovering this part of who you are, and of giving yourself permission to get everything you need and want in your sexual union.

Explore, act on instinct and discover how to make sex exciting – like it must have been in Tahiti before Captain Cook arrived, before civilization and religion drowned it in judgements and tried to make us all feel guilty. Try out any ideas from books and films that appeal to you.

The basis of the Adam and Eve story is, supposedly, that these two lovers tasted 'original sin.' In other words, sin did not exist until these two characters experienced carnal knowledge together, for if you go along with the story, they were presumably the first people in the world ever to have sexual intercourse. If that were true, of course, there would be no human race had the fateful couple not fallen into temptation and committed the dastardly deed. Then where would we be? Yet Adam and Eve are supposed to feel guilty for getting our human race started. Clearly, the whole idea is nonsense, yet as a result of this and other fairy tales many people are brought up to believe in literally, they are made to feel guilty when they have sex.

Let's go a little further down this road of parables. The parents of Jesus Christ apparently had no need of sex. In fact as I understand it, Joseph seems to be depicted as virtually asexual, a simple carpenter cuckolded by god, while Mary was an innocent virgin. What a surprise they must both have had when they discovered she was pregnant! We are asked to believe that Joseph and Mary are squeaky clean, for unlike Adam and Eve they did not stoop to the allegedly vulgar level of sexuality.

It seems to me, unbeliever that I am, that the writers of the New Testament were so concerned to present Jesus with impeccable credentials that they sanitised the facts regarding his conception. In short, they must have rewritten history to suit their own ends. It would not surprise me to find out that Joseph was actually a lusty, energetic, normal male, while Mary was as overflowing with desire as any woman who loved her husband and wanted a baby.

All of this entirely misses the fact that Jesus *was* born with impeccable credentials and would have been under any circumstances – because we all were! He was a human being, wasn't he, and therefore by definition a perfect creation – just like you and me. There is no need for embellishment.

Upon the basis of fictions like the Immaculate Conception story, we have been fed over the centuries a stream of distorted, erroneous beliefs that have led many people into feeling sinful, dirty, perverted, fearful, guilty, ashamed and disgusting in such a way as to kill their innocent and spontaneous enjoyment of sex. The reality that we, and the ways in which we choose to express our sexuality, are perfect is overlooked.

Expressing our sexuality fully is a key ingredient in the recipe for being happy and fulfilled. If we surrender to our inhibitions, we run the risk of remaining frustrated for life. Our individual, personal sexuality is no-one else's business, it is a matter we must take into our own hands, for only you know what is right for you. By seizing the initiative and experimenting without recrimination, you re-empower yourself to enjoy sex to the full.

Every time you have sex, you embark on a voyage of discovery. You discover yourself and your partner just a little bit more each time, especially if you act with awareness. Even if you still feel guilty, by becoming aware of that feeling and where it comes from, the guilt gradually loses its grip.

Spending a long time in a loveless relationship, which once happened to me, can have disastrous effects on a person's self-esteem and sense of identity. Only when the relationship ended and I met a woman to whom I was attracted like a magnet did I remember the thrilling, alive feeling of letting your hot passions run riot and of firing energetically on all four cylinders, as it were. Our relationship lasted for only four months, but during that valuable time we had together, the raw excitement I felt during this episode literally put me back on the map of humanity. Once again I felt I was a viable member of the human race.

Important though that was, the best thing of all was we were both learning the art of relating honestly, and that meant when the final split occurred, we both felt a sense of completion. It was as if all unfinished business between us had been taken care of, and despite the inevitable pain, I came away with what I can only describe as a *clean* feeling. I was left with a strong sense of who I was, and the knowledge that I would be alright on my own. This clean feeling was a new experience for me and it was entirely because on both sides we had employed the behaviour of the Impeccable Warrior. We had done a lot of mutual mirroring, finally learning the lesson of *right relations,* and found ourselves able to put it into practise.

The bedroom, the cradle of love, is the ideal place for experimentation, finding sexual fulfilment and learning honest relating. It is also the birth place of creativity. It is a place where you can truly ask yourself and the other person, what do I need and what do you need? During my relationship with this woman, we addressed these questions in great depth.

Many more mature people cite the 'Swinging Sixties' as a time when sexual relating was finally liberated from its taboos and was allowed free reign. In fact, nothing could be further from the truth, for that era merely signalled the beginning of a slow awakening that was a long time coming and has yet to reach full fruition. To quote an ex-hippie friend of mine who was eighteen in 1967, 'that was when we began to discover how messed-up we were.' Most of us gradually became aware that something needed to change, but we had no idea how to enjoy sexual liberation. Sure there was a lot of sex going on, but a long learning process had to be undertaken before most of us could hope to feel free of guilt and conflict.

As many of the 60's generation found out, the struggle for sexual liberation was and is a tough battle indeed, but ultimately it is one well worth fighting. Whatever it takes, and with whatever support we need, sexual freedom is a gift available for the taking by each and every one of us. And this applies not only in the field of sex, for I can't help feeling that any stand we take against any of the conditioning that is foisted on us can only be a good thing, for we are making a bid for freedom. That is to say, freedom from neurosis, guilt, shame, self-limiting beliefs and all the many issues that stem from our sabotaging learned behaviour.

Yet again I am reminded of the teaching of the Buddha when he so wisely tells us to 'step out of the war.' That's the real secret to absolute liberation. I guess a person can only do that after he or she has done some fighting, received some scarring, developed enough wisdom and perspective to simply wash his or her hands of the whole business, walk away and start doing his or her own thing.

Meanwhile, if you don't feel you can do that because you are still in conflict, don't be afraid to ask for help. There are many groups centred on exploring sexuality, or if you prefer the privacy of the consulting room, many therapists and counsellors can give help and support on sexual issues.

Anyone who has watched ducks and drakes on their local pond will understand. With nature there are no holds barred. Animals just get on with it whichever way they need to for successful reproduction. There may be a courtship ritual, there may be competition between males or females, but they don't stand on ceremony and they don't seem to suffer embarrassment or shame.

Before finishing this chapter, one final interesting and amusing story that illustrates how absurd judgements about other people's sexuality can be:

It is well known that in highly religious Hassidic Jewish circles, men and women are not allowed to dance with each other at public celebrations such as weddings, for dancing, as we all know, is a sexy thing to do. It could put impure ideas into the minds of men and women. So one day a young man, a Hassid or learned scholar, seeks out his rabbi to ask for some advice. He is clearly very interested in sex, but wants to be careful not to do anything that might offend god.

'Rabbi, as you know, I was recently married,' the young man began. 'My wife and I both enjoy making love, but we do not want to accidentally offend god. Can I please check with you, is it OK to have sex lying down?' 'Yes Chaim, of course it is,' the rabbi replies. 'You're a married man now. Please god you should do it many times, and in good health.'

Feeling encouraged, and finally beginning to overcome his embarrassment, Chaim blurts out a second question, 'thank you rabbi, but is it also OK to do it from behind?' he enquired. 'Yes Chaim, of course, no problem with that,' the rabbi replies. 'Carry on and please god you should have many healthy babies.'

'Thank you, rabbi,' exclaimed Chaim gratefully, rubbing his hands with glee. 'I have one last question if you don't mind. Is it OK to do it standing up?' 'Ah,' exclaimed the rabbi, pausing to stroke his beard thoughtfully. 'That I am not so sure about. That worries me a little. There could be a problem. You see, doing it standing up could lead to dancing!'

This might seem amusing, but in fact it's ridiculous and even alarming for it has an uneasy ring of familiarity. In many countries around the world people, especially women, can be punished, ostracised, made destitute – even murdered, for disobeying that society's code of sexual ethics. In some cases even for marrying someone from a different caste or ethnic group. By any humanitarian standards, this is clearly outrageous.

In all aspects of our lives, we and we alone are the only ones fit to decide what is or what is not alright for us. Each of us defines the behaviour of the Impeccable Warrior in his or her own terms. The only valid guiding principle can be your own core values, which are unique to you, and how you feel about each and every issue that arises. You certainly don't need anybody, not even a cleric, telling you how you should behave.

When we begin to express our sexuality to the full in our relationships, we come to life. For many people, this can be the beginning of conquering their depression and starting to experience their lives as joyful, fun and creative. The message is clear: *live every moment of your life to the full*; go totally into your sexuality; study the sexual practices described by Vatsyayana, author of the *Kama Sutra* and examine the Tantric masters of India, Tibet and China; do everything possible to find out whatever you can about your sexuality. Then start looking inside to discover what you want, talk about it with your partner and start getting what you need.

Soon you will be celebrating the feeling of aliveness that comes with an active, creative and exciting sex life which will be a reflection of a fulsome, fulfilling and sustainable relationship.

Summary

- Much heartache can be created when one or both partners don't have the sexual experience and maturity to know what they want and like in sex

- Matters are only made more painful if partners fail to communicate between themselves
- Many people are not satisfied in sex. This is a vital issue we cannot ignore or we risk our relationships failing
- Many people are reluctant to experiment, and fear intimacy. It's the perceived danger of making ourselves vulnerable and therefore open to being hurt that usually drives that fear
- It's time to urgently re-examine our attitudes surrounding sex and sexuality in an effort to free ourselves to explore and communicate. Almost always it's far less painful if we undertake this exploration *before* marriage
- We are very sensitive around sexual issues and this is evident because as soon as we are judged inadequate, perverted or in some way 'incorrect' in our desires, our validity as humans is called into question
- The primary business of any self-respecting pre-marital youth, and this applies just as much to girls as to boys, has to be to explore and experiment in all spheres of life, to rebel and to seek new experiences
- Few teenagers have a clue about what they want, much less what they need. Their rebellious and 'outrageous' behaviour is a necessary stage of growing up, getting to know who they are, and discovering where they fit in
- Young men and women are right to celebrate their lustiness – but they must protect themselves from unwanted pregnancies and sexually transmitted diseases
- Sexual union with awareness enables young people to learn to share real intimacy. What could be better for our world than that?
- Young women are fellow soul travellers who need to express their passions and discover themselves as much as men do
- Sex without feelings is impossible. When we close our hearts and function solely on ego, we merely create and store up more pain
- Sometimes sex is used as a hiding place where we can avoid addressing the real issues that are making us depressed or unhappy. Using sex as an ego boost or an anaesthetic is not a path towards long-term happiness and fulfilment

- If both sexes could begin to trust and understand that no ego damage is caused when we treat ourselves and other humans with due respect, we would all feel a lot freer to experiment. Then, rather than generating more pain, by behaving with awareness we begin to heal
- If we tell each other honestly what we want and how we feel, greater insight and understanding on both sides will arise. Then there will be fewer broken hearts, greater freedom and enjoyment, and a decrease in unwanted pregnancy and rapes
- Very few young teenage men are sufficiently emotionally developed, experienced and equipped to sustain enduring loving relationships. In most cases, their earlier sexual experiences are an essential part of their learning process
- A compassionate, understanding and non-judgemental view from parents, teachers and other role models towards our children is helpful, as we teach them the importance of awareness and treating others with respect at all times
- Our conditioning sets itself up in competition with our hormonal development, which is one reason why so many of us experience conflict and confusion
- The need for self-discovery is just one of the reasons why puberty and adolescence is so often times of enormous confusion
- Many of us arrive in middle age without enough sexual experience. As a result, we find it hard to sustain relationships
- *There are no sort cuts to emotional and sexual maturity, and there is no substitute for experience.* We have to know ourselves and we have to know what we want before we can emotionally prosper and flow
- The major benefit of undertaking self-discovery during our more mature years is that it's much easier to incorporate the ingredient of awareness
- Your bedroom should be a laboratory for discovering the nature of love
- Problems can always be resolved, if both parties are prepared to risk being vulnerable and open to hearing the other person. Otherwise you are left with a power struggle
- The way of the heart requires courage and resolve – it's the only path that can lead you towards greater intimacy, and that is what sets us free

- Boredom in the bedroom is a result of refusing to connect with your creative imagination. If that's you, put some raunchy excitement back into your sex life
- The union between men and woman is a joy to be celebrated and not a situation in which to get hung up in guilt and inhibition
- My appeal is to courageous, receptive individuals who are prepared to lay aside their ego defences to start living according to the dictates of their hearts. Then our relationships will take off into exciting new realms
- Human emotions cannot be controlled, and unless they are given full expression with awareness, dangerously explosive situations can develop
- Giving ourselves the freedom to experiment helps us distinguish between what is real and what is conditioned. That gives us the opportunity to choose what we really want from first-hand experience
- To really let go of our inhibitions during sex so we behave spontaneously from our hearts, we need to be able to trust
- When we feel unworthy, guilty or shameful, it becomes impossible to be true to ourselves and behave with integrity during sex
- If you give vent to your emotions and go deeply into your sexuality with awareness, in a consensual situation, no one will come to any harm
- If you repress or suppress your feelings you could end up with an uncontrollable explosion
- Truly empowered people know that their empowerment comes from within. They do not have to prove themselves at the expense of others
- Knowing our fantasies and recognising them for what they are helps us get reality into perspective, a vital milestone on the road to true empowerment
- Only letting go into who we really are, trusting our hearts, communicating and behaving with awareness will allow feelings of true empowerment and self-esteem to grow
- Repressed anger can lead to violent behaviour, and suppressed fantasies can lead to losing our perspective on what's real

- How can we distinguish between reality and fantasy until we experience the practises about which we are curious, and witness the difference?
- The heart cannot accept a 'distorted reality' for it does not make sense to the heart
- *With anger, better out than in is the golden rule,* but it needs to be put out safely and responsibly. Dumping on another is out of order
- Healing only happens through love
- We can hardly experience sex as joyful when we are out of touch with what we really want, or are too shy to ask for our fantasies to be acted out
- It is our birthright to express and experience our sexuality to the full
- Going deeply into your sexuality can free you from the domination your fantasies may have over you, so you can choose to express them when appropriate and when you want to, not because you are unconsciously driven to
- Explore, act on instinct and discover how to make sex exciting – like it must have been before civilization and religion drowned it in judgements
- Over the centuries we have been fed a stream of distorted, erroneous beliefs that have led many of us into feeling sinful, dirty, perverted, fearful, guilty, ashamed and disgusting, while the reality that we are perfect is overlooked
- Expressing our sexuality is a key ingredient for being happy and fulfilled
- If we surrender to our inhibitions, we risk remaining frustrated for life
- By seizing the initiative and experimenting without recrimination, you re-empower yourself to enjoy sex to the full
- Every time you have sex you discover yourself and your partner just a little bit more, especially if you act with awareness
- Whatever it takes, and with whatever support we need, sexual freedom is a gift available for the taking by every one of us
- Any stand we take against the conditioning that is foisted on us can only be a good thing, for we are making a bid for liberation from our neurosis, guilt, shame and self-limiting beliefs

- Each of us defines the behaviour of the Impeccable Warrior in his or her own terms. The only valid guiding principles are your core values, which are unique to you, and how you feel about each and every issue that arises
- *You don't need anybody to tell you how you should behave*
- *Live every moment of your life to the full.* Go totally into your sexuality and do everything possible to discover what you want
- An active, creative and exciting sex life is a reflection of a fulsome, fulfilling and sustainable relationship

THE FIFTH PILLAR

Your Ongoing Personal Development

If you've read this far you now have virtually all the pieces of the jigsaw, and many powerful tools you can use to get your new life up and running. But your journey doesn't end here. Raising your conscious awareness is a lifelong endeavour and it's essential to keep it growing if you want your new found happiness to endure.

If you think of the new life you have created as a building, this is the fifth and final pillar that will ensure the roof is strongly and evenly supported and stays put.

It's about maintenance, and making sure you stay on track for good.

30

Is This Path Really for Me?

Both success and failure are largely the results of habit
Napoleon Hill

You've spent a lot of time and expended considerable effort in creating the life of your dreams and everything is going swimmingly, when all of a sudden a voice pops into your head asking the deeply unsettling question, 'is this path really for me?'

'Oh no,' you exclaim inwardly to yourself, 'I've gone to all this trouble, been through all those scary changes, and maybe I don't want this after all. Oh my god, am I going to have to start all over again?'

If you are honest with yourself you will acknowledge that with the best will in the world this can happen, especially for those of you who have a habit of self-doubt or wobbly self-belief. If it happens it could imply you might not have been monitoring yourself carefully enough along the way, or that you have avoided looking into the mirror with ruthless honesty. However, don't forget everything we do, say, or pursue as a goal is an experiment, and this may be a legitimate result you could not have known about in advance, so you had to try it.

Most important, don't beat yourself up with harsh self-judgements, and don't be in denial by trying to ignore it, for both of these only create more pain and make it much harder to acknowledge what needs changing. By all means if you feel angry and frustrated, acknowledge those feelings, but don't wallow in self-indulgence or you'll feel worse and it won't help.

Better to take responsibility and face the simple truth that you may need to make more changes or try another experiment. Be careful, however, as there is every likelihood that this could merely be your saboteur on the prowl again, trying to sow seeds of self-doubt about your new-found path, which may suit you down to the ground. Careful investigation is the only answer. I have a simple rule-of-thumb for dealing with situations like these: *when the going gets tough or how you feel seems unclear, go more deeply into self-examination.*

Self-examination

Obviously you will have noticed, I am a great fan of the *go deeply* technique. So far in this book we've had *go deeply into your negativity, go deeply into your resistance, go deeply into your sexuality,* and now we find *go deeply into self-examination.* I knew someone who gave up smoking by using *go deeply into your smoking.* It's a fantastic tool and it can be applied to just about any issue. You can use it to *go deeply into your jealousy, go deeply into your anger, go deeply into your hatred, go deeply into your prejudices, go deeply into your addictions* and of course, *go deeply into your love,* and *go deeply into your happiness.* I've used it many times – it's simple, it's powerful and it works!

So with regard to the issue in hand, how do you go deeper into self-examination? Simply by asking yourself deeply soul-searching questions like, 'Am I still enjoying what I'm doing?' 'If I persevere until I've mastered it, will I enjoy it then?' 'Do I really want to be here?' 'Do I really want to live with this person?' 'Does this feel meaningful and purposeful?' and my old favourite, 'How do I feel about this?'

Again I emphasise, asking yourself what or how you *think* will not do. In all likelihood it will lead to further self doubt. The thinking mind is the terrain of the saboteur and these important questions can only be answered by your heart. For example, you might be doing a high-flying job and earning a fabulous salary with plenty of money to support your family and all of that, but if you are not happy doing it, that's not what I call success. Your friends and family might say you're crazy to even contemplate giving up the job, but they are not living your life for you. Nor will they suffer your frustration, nightmares and lack of fulfillment, and neither will they live day in, day out, with your depression. They obviously don't share your dream and for reasons that seem so reasonable they don't want you to live your dream either. But I do!

We've been over this before but it's worth reiterating because it's vitally important: I'm not suggesting you throw the baby out with the bathwater, or jump from the frying pan into the fire! I'm calling for a better strategy. We're back to *emotional intelligence* now. Maybe it would be reckless to suddenly quit your job with no plan B, for it may result in you losing your house or something equally undesirable. However, slaving away in something you don't love, no matter how lucrative, is not the answer. An effective strategy requires a careful heart/mind balance, but it has to be based on what turns you on, and that's a matter for the heart.

It takes courage to turn away from the golden handcuffs, but only you, in your heart of hearts, know whether you are crazy or sensible in the decisions you make. If you're not particularly enjoying what you are doing right now but you *feel* there's a possibility that you might eventually love it, tune into your heart when making a judgement about whether to quit or persevere. Maybe it's a good idea to try it for a little while longer so that if you do finally give it up, you can feel happy that you traveled the extra mile and left no stone unturned in your experimentation. I repeat, don't *think* about it, ask yourself how you *feel* about it.

Personal development and the art of creating the life you want is a never-ending process, and constant maintenance and vigilance is necessary, even after you have achieved your goal. The behaviour of the Impeccable Warrior is for life, and life simply becomes more and more fascinating as we continue to grow. Therefore I repeat, even when you have achieved the life you want, don't be complacent and *don't forget to keep monitoring yourself.* When you're evaluating your next move, keep an eye on the bigger picture, but focus on your next step.

You may remember, or should I say I sincerely hope you remember, that we talked about the importance of making a written action plan based on one or more goals you want to achieve. The plan is designed to keep you on track and focused on your goal (or goals), and most importantly, to make sure you get all the way to those goals without quitting for whatever reason.

End games

Now it's time to talk about the final part of your plan, which I call the end game. A question coaches often ask their clients when they are setting goals is, 'how will you know when you have achieved your goal?' Sometimes it's obvious, for example if your goal is to get your first novel published you will know you have achieved your goal when you are holding the first printed copy of your book in your hand. Other times it's not so obvious, like when your goal is to build a wonderful relationship or a business you love, or to experience high self-esteem.

Whichever case fits you, it's important to realise *the end is only the beginning*. But the beginning of what? Of a new adventure, of a new path, of a new challenge, of a new learning curve, of a multitude of opportunities for growth and development, yes all of those, but most of all – *of a deeper and deeper journey into you.*

Some people like to be goal junkies, but if there's no meaning and purpose behind those goals it's merely ego gratification, and that's not what I'm talking about at all. What I'm saying is if you've achieved your *heartfelt* goals or feel you're getting near to doing so, you will have begun to get a sense of your amazing human potential. That potential has no limits. Beginning to feel a sense of your amazing, limitless human potential means that at last you've arrived at square one of your real life's journey. Now your life can only get better and better – if you keep going.

If, instead of calling a halt, you carry on doing things to grow more fully into your potential, you will fill your life with meaning, purpose and abundance over and over again, and the possibility arises of feeling fulfilled and at peace.

Now you've got to this stage, getting to like yourself, or being at peace, is simply something that happens with no effort on your part as you flow along your path expressing your creative inner self a little more each day.

But what happens if you stop or become complacent? Think of getting a car moving along a level road from a standing start – a huge amount of energy is required to overcome the car's initial inertia to get it moving, but once the car is rolling along at 30 mph, it takes much less energy to keep it going. If you come to a hill you will have to use more energy by pressing the gas pedal to keep the speed up, but again, with momentum the energy requirement levels off. However, if you stop you might start rolling backwards, and lots more energy will be needed again to move you forward and upward.

OK, enough of metaphors! How in hands-on, practical terms do you keep going? Simply by continuing to travel on your journey of personal development and inner growth. You can set new, more challenging goals or you can actually start to go beyond goals to a higher level of consciousness until your whole life becomes a meditation. It depends on what you feel suited for and what attracts you. Read on and you'll see what I'm getting at.

Whether your goal is already achieved or you are somewhere along your path towards achieving it, the important message to you from this section of the book is about the importance of checking that your chosen path is the right one for you, and keeping going.

Story time

In the next three chapters I am going to recap on some of the more important tools, techniques and practical ideas that we've already discussed for facilitating your ongoing journey in practice. First I'd like to remind you of a very important story about the power of maintaining a positive mental attitude, a fable passed down from generation to generation for almost 3,000 years. It was written, it is believed, by the pen of Aesop, a famous teller of fables. It's the story of *The Tortoise and the Hare* and I'd be very surprised if you don't already know it. What I want to do here is to put the story under the microscope for it has hidden depths that can teach us something of great value.

The Tortoise and the Hare

One day all the animals overhear Hare boasting that he can run faster than anyone else. Tortoise, a very canny fellow who understands and trusts implicitly the values of his own particular qualities and therefore doesn't need to boast, is absolutely fed up with hearing Hare's bragging. Being the sort of chap who absolutely relishes a challenge and loves teaching by example, he throws down a gauntlet to Hare and challenges him to a race.

Hare, posturing and stroking his delicate ego, thinks this is hilarious and falls about laughing, but nevertheless he accepts the challenge. Meanwhile, Fox volunteers to define a course and a finishing line, and offers to adjudicate.

The course is set and the two protagonists set off, Hare bounding away down the lane, Tortoise slowly and painfully creeping at full plod, bristling with determination to keep going. After a while Hare, seeing he is well ahead, stops by the side of the road to feed on some juicy carrots he sees growing nearby and then, his stomach replete, he is overcome by drowsiness and he falls asleep.

Meanwhile, showing his true grit to the maximum while remaining focused on his goal and keeping going in the right direction, Tortoise creeps past him and passes the winning post. Too late Hare awoke with a shock and ran for the finish, but against all the odds Tortoise, exhausted though he was, pipped him to the post!

From this fascinating fable, which incidentally mirrors precisely the story of my life, we learn the importance of finding your true direction, keeping going, never giving up, never taking your eye off the ball, believing in yourself and of the value of dogged determination. Finally we realise there is no shame in being a plodder. On the contrary, you get the job done so you're the person who wins everyone's respect in the end, including your own. You may be exhausted but you made it. Now that the job is over you have rightfully earned your rest and your feeling of fulfilment.

I have seen it time and time again, plodders reach their goals while hasty and less humble folks who are in too much of a hurry fall by the wayside. Readers who are disabled or not so spritely will understand exactly what I'm saying here, for they will have learned this the hard way. Tortoise adopts the behaviour of the Impeccable Warrior, while Hare trips himself up in his own conceit.

In my younger days when I was impatient, headstrong and felt I always knew best, I would often bite off far more than I could chew, and every time I would fall flat on my face and either give up or have to start all over again. It was a very painful and hard won lesson to admit that small steps and plodding, mixed with patience, persistence and determination is the reliable route to success. You may say that's boring, but I can assure you that feeling a sense of success and achievement is far from boring. It thoroughly enjoyable, plain and simple.

There's plenty of room for passion, flare, creativity and all those ingredients we need to spice things up, but that does not detract from my firmly held belief that there are no short cuts to happiness.

Summary

- If you experience self-doubt you might not have been monitoring yourself carefully enough, or maybe you have avoided looking in the mirror with ruthless honesty

- Self-doubt can also be a justifiable result of trying something you now don't feel sure about, but you could not have known that in advance. You had to try it. Therefore, give yourself credit, don't beat yourself up
- If necessary take responsibility and face the truth that you need to make more changes or try another experiment, but remember this could be your saboteur trying to sow seeds of self-doubt
- *When the going gets tough or if how you feel seems unclear, go more deeply into self-examination*
- You can go deeper by asking yourself deeply soul-searching questions
- Asking yourself what you *think* will probably lead to further self-doubt. The thinking mind is the terrain of the saboteur; these important questions can only be answered by your heart
- You don't need to do anything reckless, you need a better strategy and that requires a careful heart/mind balance
- Only you, in your heart of hearts, know whether you are crazy or sensible in the decisions you make
- Tune into your heart when judging whether to quit or persevere
- The behaviour of the Impeccable Warrior is for life
- Life becomes more and more fascinating as we continue to grow
- When you're evaluating your next move, keep an eye on the bigger picture, but focus on your next step
- Remember the importance of making a written action plan based on one or more goals you want to achieve, and use it to keep yourself on track and to make sure you don't quit
- The end is only the beginning of a deeper and deeper journey into your self
- If you've achieved your goals or feel you're getting near to doing so, you will have begun to get a sense of your amazing, limitless human potential
- Beginning to feel this sense of your potential means that at last you've arrived at square one. Now keep going!
- If you carry on doing things to grow more fully into your potential, you will fill your life with meaning, purpose, fulfillment and peace

- When you've achieved what you want you can set new, more challenging goals or start to go beyond goals to a higher level of consciousness until your whole life becomes a meditation
- While you're travelling, it's important to check that the path you are on is the right one for you, *even if you think you have arrived*
- Find your true direction and then keeping going. Never give up, show dogged determination, never take your eye off the ball, believe in yourself, and realise there is no shame in being a plodder. Respect yourself
- Plodders reach their goals while hasty folk fall by the wayside

31

Your Onward Journey

The big picture is now and forever
Dr. Wayne Dyer

No matter how energetically we use our tools, follow our paths, meditate, reach our goals and resolve our issues, and having taken on board all we have discussed so far, it's important to bear in mind that it's very difficult, perhaps impossible, for anyone to operate in a vacuum. What do I mean by that?

Every heart and soul needs nourishment just as much as our bodies do. We humans get that nourishment mainly from interaction with, and support from, other humans, and from doing the things we love. In other words we need close friends and lovers, as well as excellent work colleagues, customers we adore and leisure pursuits we are passionate about. And we need them on a continuous basis.

With the work I do nowadays, writing, coaching, speaking and running workshops about personal development, I am completely besotted with my clients – for two reasons. Not only do they support and facilitate my lifestyle by paying me for my services, they are also my teachers. Every one of them is courageous and pro-active, and grows in my esteem every day. Witnessing their progress gives my life meaning and purpose, I feel fulfilled through helping people with the work I do, and that's what makes it emotionally nourishing.

The amazing thing I discovered after I took up coaching was that once I worked out what my niche or speciality was, I found I only attracted people I wanted to work with, and who want to work with me. That's because I believe 100 per cent in what I do, and those who can see the value and need what I offer are naturally drawn to working with me. I gave up trying to sell years ago, and what a relief that was – I just tell people what I do, allow my enthusiasm to be infectious and sometimes something happens.

It might be useful if I elaborate a little more so you can see where I'm coming from more clearly. You may remember I said, in the context of relationships, our first requisite is a suitable partner. Well exactly the same principle applies in a working relationship between the person offering the service or product and the client or customer. The perceived wisdom in coaching is *coach what you are good at,* which is a great way of looking at finding your niche because it also implies *coach what you are passionate about.*

My target audience, to put it in marketing terms, is a tiny percentage of the population, but by concentrating on what I do, those people who need what I offer seem to find me. This makes for highly nourishing working relationships in which both parties flourish and your work becomes so enjoyable.

I have already talked about my early working life, which was not happy time for me. I mention this again here to emphasise the contrast between how a person feels when he

does meaningless work, toeing the company the line and feeling trapped, as opposed to how he feels when he pursues meaningful work he loves in conjunction with sincere individuals. I hope also, in the context of all I have tried to put across so far, to underline just one more time the importance of raising our awareness and behaving in accord with our true values and beliefs.

Most of the clients I had to put up with when I worked in advertising and public relations were, in my estimation, little more sophisticated than locusts. They would consume anything and everything that came within their orbit while giving back very little of value. They would function only on the level of their personas and they would never share anything of their hearts. They were unscrupulous and unprincipled, they had abandoned any semblance of values and ethics, the work they and I did together was of no use to society whatsoever, and I could find nothing to respect them for. I had allowed myself to be involved with this work and these people and as a result, of course, I could find nothing to respect myself for either.

I used to feel I was dying of emotional malnutrition. Now the exact opposite is true. My cup runneth over and all my work comes from my heart, no hesitation. So what changed? I didn't realise it at the time, but

I underwent a complete revolution of the heart. It was scary at times, but I know if I had not let go of control and allow that to happen, either I would had a nervous breakdown or gone crazy in some way.

I am not exaggerating, nor am I being a drama queen. I simply want to be of service and I mention this story again in the hope of demonstrating that you too can get the emotional nourishment you need in your work. You don't have to put up with situations you hate. With growing awareness you empower yourself to make choices and changes. Be of strong courage!

Reaching the favourable position I describe took a lot of tactical manoeuvring, springing from a strategy spanning many years. I've had a mortgage virtually all of my working life and other financial responsibilities too, so I couldn't just drop everything and do a complete about turn. Some of it happened by serendipity, but my abiding principle was to be guided by my heart to eventually find and follow my true path somehow, and to keep my dream alive.

Now here's an amusing paradox. Your strategy has to be led by your heart. This is why actually it doesn't matter what path you choose or what plans you make, for as long as you keep on travelling with your heart fixed on your dreams, you will go broadly in the right direction and you'll reach your goals sooner or later. *Here's the trick – listen to your heart and use what it tells you to make your plan.* Don't just conjure up a plan in your head, always let your heart dictate your plan. That way you'll be strongly motivated, and happy with whatever results.

You could liken your heart to a GPS satellite navigation system. Even if you go wrong from time to time, if you continually listen to the guidance of your heart it will always get you to where you want to go, even if it has to re-compute your optimum route a million times. It's just that if you can stay on track most of the time, you're more likely to enjoy your journey as well as your arrival.

It's worth noting that an aeroplane flying from London to Tokyo, say, is actually off course at least 90 per cent of the time it's in the air. The pilot or autopilot continually has to make course corrections. When the 'plane comes within reasonable range of its destination airport the course has to be fine tuned enough to land on the correct runway at the right moment in precisely the right spot and at the correct speed. Usually the course deviation averaged over the whole journey is insignificant and unavoidable, so there's probably no point in worrying about it.

What other means can we use to nourish our hearts?

Well, of course, the big one is meditation. It seems contradictory to advocate solitude after saying we need close friends and lovers, but we also need periods of aloneness and silence. Why? Because balance in all things brings inner peace, and silence nourishes your heart because it enables you to get to know and love who you are, and to accept yourself exactly as you are. Aloneness and loneliness are not the same, incidentally, and it's very important to understand the difference.

Just because we've built ourselves a happy life that doesn't mean we don't need to meditate any more. By the time you reach a state of happiness I'm sure you'll thoroughly enjoy and look forward to your moments of meditation and you won't need me to encourage you to keep at it. Suffice to say if you want to remain happy you will find meditation, using the same method I described in the first section of this book, will help you stay on track.

So will keeping your *Success Diary* up-to-date. You might think you've completed the work of reprogramming your unconscious mind to a positive mindset, but it's so easy to slip back into old habits and let that saboteur have his way again. All you need is a slip in your conscious awareness and it can happen. Continuing your *Success Diary* helps you maintain your awareness and continually build it. There's no limit to the reinforcement you can give your positive mindset by keeping your diary going on a regular basis. In fact, maintaining your *Success Diary* will take you to new levels. You'll plumb new depths of understanding and soar to new heights of enjoyment.

Also, don't forget your *Gratitude Diary* and to count your blessings.

Doing affirmations is yet another way to fire your imagination and manifest what you want. Affirmations can be a vital part of your onward journey and you'll be amazed and delighted when you use this powerful technique to direct the power of your mind towards creating what you want. Any time you are wondering exactly how to go about achieving something, even altering your mindset, you can use affirmations as a powerful helper.

The devices, tools or techniques I mention here are some of the big ones, but you can use any or all the tools in this book and mix and match them as you prefer. You'll find some will suit one person, another will suit someone else. By all means try them all and then feel free to cherry-pick the ones you love best and use them imaginatively. What you are doing is finding interesting, enjoyable and stress-free ways of heightening your awareness and honing your focus like a laser.

Don't give up

The ancient Chinese book of wisdom the *I Ching,* thought to have been created in it's original form by Fu Xi, tells us time and time again, 'perseverance furthers', and so it does, as long as you are not barking up the wrong tree.

If you truly believe you're following your heart yet success still evades you, don't give up. Change something and try again. Sometimes success takes a while and sometimes fine tuning your experiment is required. Think Tortoise and Hare. Take small steps in the right direction and *keep going.* Keep checking yourself out, though, by asking yourself, 'Do I really want this?' and 'Do I feel I have the talent to ever become naturally excellent at this?' It sounds obvious but it needs saying because some people give up unnecessarily – if you want to achieve whatever it is with all your heart, you will get there, *but only if you take action and keep going.*

Remember, never listen to critics, especially those that have never done what you wish to pursue. This is really important for if you have a vision in your heart, you and you alone are the expert. So have the courage to believe in yourself 100 per cent. That doesn't mean you are infallible. By all means listen to mentors and teachers who know what they are talking about, *and then make up your own mind* regardless.

That way you stand or fall by your own beliefs, and if you do stumble your integrity will make sure you pick yourself up, dust yourself off, and start all over again.

Finally, if you feel depressed, stop reading newspapers. Be very, very discriminating about what input you allow into your mind and never introduce anything negative.

Become an avid bookworm

When you consider the average price of a paperback book, say between £6 and £12, there is really no excuse for not reading avidly. Books are overflowing with the wisdom and experience their authors have gleaned over many years and wish to share. They are bountiful gifts indeed. If happiness is your goal, books on personal development and popular psychology are your must-read subjects.

Reading for learning can actually be regarded as another powerful tool, for it can give you far deeper understanding and insight into those all-pervading mysteries of life and can help you greatly to increase your awareness. Reading is such an enjoyable thing to do and certainly needs to be a mainstay of anyone's personal development journey. I don't propose to list the many, many authors I could suggest here, especially as it wouldn't be fair on the many brilliant ones I have never read. Rather I would suggest you go to the relevant section of any decent bookstore or library and start browsing. Make sure you allow plenty of time because time will fly once you get there and you won't want to tear yourself away.

The internet is another great resource for learning, and not only by reading. Lots of authors, teachers, mentors and coaches offer online seminars, videos, e-books, e-courses and downloads of one sort or another, and much of the content is free. I have downloaded quite a few seminars onto my iPod so I can listen when travelling.

Just open Google or any other browser you fancy and start surfing, but be aware of the danger and don't get sidetracked or you could waste hours. The internet can be your greatest friend or your saboteur.

Also online you will find many networking groups and blogs. Some are for business, others are for social contact and many are a complete waste of time. However, some are useful and if you find one relevant to what you are interested in, it's a great way to connect with likeminded people from whom you can learn.

Whatever online communications you adopt, don't let it be a hiding place or a substitute for the real thing. Make sure you meet with empathic people in the living flesh and blood in all areas of your life.

Go visit a guru

One great way of connecting personally that I can recommend, especially if you want insight into some of life's deeper questions, is to go and visit a guru.

The Sanskrit word *guru* literally means a teacher or guide, and it's a term usually applied to a teacher of awareness and enlightenment. However, I am taking the liberty here of widening the use of the word to include master teachers of skills, tools and techniques to do with aspects of personal development or business as well. For example Richard Bandler is widely regarded as a guru of NLP (Neuro Linguistic Programming), especially as he jointly invented it with his colleague, John Grinder.

Even the more traditional Eastern spiritual gurus these days don't only inhabit the well known countries of the East, and there are also many Western teachers nowadays, some of whom we have already mentioned. Many of all types live in the West while others visit on a regular basis. They run meditation retreats, courses, seminars and trainings of one sort or another in many places around the globe.

If your goal requires you to train in something skill or knowledge-based, or if you simply want to add to your knowledge, skills and understanding without necessarily doing a full training, the best way is to find the best possible teacher and participate in his or her course, workshop, seminar or event. Watch out for suitable opportunities; sometimes these are free. One powerfully illuminating seminar I attended was entitled *Breakthrough to Success* led by Christopher Howard. It was three intensive and very long twelve hour days, it was absolutely free, and ever since that long weekend what I learned there still helps me very much to this day. Sometimes all you need is one more push or one more lightbulb moment, and that's enough to get started on your path towards achievement.

There are also many spiritually enlightened gurus also visit our major cities, and some country venues and smaller towns, to conduct *Satsang,* or a 'meeting in truth.' In a typical Satsang participants are invited to sit at first for a few minutes of silent meditation in the presence of the master, and then he or she opens the floor to questions.

Typically, someone asks a question and the guru answers. Sometimes he or she takes a long, long time over the answer to let the teaching sink in, or in some cases to let the answer surface from within the questioner. Sometimes the answer is totally unexpected, while at other times you know the questioner already knows the answer but just wants to hear it confirmed by the master.

Quite often you will come away from a Satsang feeling totally frustrated because your questions have merely begotten more questions and there were precious few answers. That is especially true if you are expecting comprehensible intellectual answers based on academic reason, logic or deduction. In the context of Satsang the only answers that matter are to do with truth and love and what's going on in your heart, and they can't be expressed in words.

Other times you will feel a glow of satisfaction because you feel something significant happened in your understanding, or something touched your heart. In an earlier chapter I mentioned a Satsang I attended in London in the presence of Satyananda, and at some point I actually gave up trying to understand, in a cerebral sense, anything that was being said. I found that far more satisfying. Somehow, by osmosis perhaps, I got the point.

When I visited Rajneeshpuram, Osho's ashram in Oregon, at various times between 1982 and 1984, I attended many Satsangs in the presence of the master, but by that time he was sitting in silence and there were no questions, only music and silence.

During earlier discourses Osho explained that the real purpose of Satsang is an excuse for the master and his disciples to sit together in a heart-to-heart communion. He described the relationship between the master and his disciples as 'a love affair' and there was no need for words, especially as the ultimate truth cannot be conveyed in words. Therefore in silence was deemed to be the most honest way of relating.

There are many opportunities for attending Satsang in virtually every major city in the West, and this can be a wonderful extension to your meditation practice. At the very least, it's bound to set you about enquiring more deeply within.

Story time again

Finally, let's examine another famous mythical story that has a significant teaching for us. This one is written by the Roman poet, Ovid, who lived at around the time of Jesus some 2,000 years ago, and it's about maintaining your focus and following a path of balance. It's the story of *Daedalus and Icarus*, or at least part of it.

Daedalus and Icarus

Legend has it that Daedalus was a brilliant architect, inventor and master craftsman who lived in Athens until he was tried for the alleged murder of his apprentice, Talos. After this he was banished from his home town and fled to the island of Crete, where he began work at the court of King Minos and Queen Pasiphae, in the magnificent palace of Knossos.

When the much feared Minotaur was born, Daedalus was commissioned by King Minos to design and build a Labyrinth to contain the monstrous half-man, half-bull. However, Daedalus fell out with the King who became enraged over Daedalus's complicity in helping the visiting hero Theseus to kill the Minotaur, after which Theseus absconded with Ariadne, the king's daughter, who had fallen in love with him.

Minos, enraged at the loss of his daughter, not to mention the killing of the Minotaur, promptly imprisoned Daedalus and his son Icarus in a tower within the Labyrinth.

Now Daedalus, not being the type of person to take this sort of thing lying down, worked out how he could escape from the tower with his son. He also realised that they would have to leave Crete and get away from Minos, before the latter had a chance to wreak his vengeance. However, Minos controlled the sea around Crete, leaving no escape route there. At this point, Daedalus, who had been studying the flight of birds from his window, realised that the only way out was by air.

Being a highly resourceful and imaginative man, Daedalus built wings for himself and Icarus, made of frames covered with feathers and held together with wax. Then they set about learning to fly. Daedalus explained to his son that during their journey to freedom it would be of paramount importance to stay focused, to keep going and to always steer a middle path. He warned Icarus not to fly too close to the sun, as it would melt his wings, and not too close to the sea, as it would dampen them and make it hard to fly.

The moment came and they took off together, successfully flying out of Crete, but Icarus was distracted and lost his focus with disastrous consequences. He grew exhilarated by the thrill of flying, started to lose his awareness and became careless. Flying too close to the sun god Helios, the wax holding together his wings melted from the heat and Icarus fell to his death, drowning in the sea. Daedalus, realising what had happened, lamented his dead son and then continued flying all the way to Sicily.

It's a sad story and it speaks for itself. Balance, the middle way, is what gets you safely to where you want to go.

Summary

- We need close friends and lovers, as well as work colleagues and customers we adore, and leisure pursuits we are passionate about
- When you do what you love, your infectious enthusiasm will be your number one salesman
- You can get lots of much needed emotional nourishment from your work, if you do what you love
- You don't have to put up with situations you hate. If you're involved with people and work that have no meaning or purpose for you, you can't respect yourself and your self-esteem will dwindle
- With your growing awareness you empower yourself to make choices and changes
- Your strategy has to be heart-led, for as long as you keep on travelling with your heart fixed on your dreams, you'll reach your goals sooner or later
- Even if you go wrong from time to time, if you continually listen to the guidance of your heart it will always get you to where you want to go
- We need periods of aloneness and silence, for balance brings inner peace, and silence nourishes your heart because it enables you to get to know and love who you are, and accept yourself exactly as you are
- If you want to remain happy, meditation using the same method I described in the first section of this book will help you stay on track
- It's easy to slip back into old habits and let your saboteur have his way again. All you need is a lapse in your conscious awareness and it can happen
- Continuing your *Success Diary* helps you build and maintain your awareness. It will take you to new depths of understanding and new heights of enjoyment. Also, Don't forget your *Gratitude Diary* and to count your blessing
- If at any time you are wondering exactly how to go about achieving something, even altering your mindset, you can use affirmations as a powerful helper
- Mix and match any of the tools in this book so you cherry-pick the ones you love best and use them imaginatively

- If you truly believe you're following your heart yet success still evades you, don't give up. Change something and try again
- Think Tortoise and Hare. Take small steps in the right direction and *keep going*. Don't forget to keep checking yourself out
- If you want to achieve whatever you want with all your heart, you will get there, *but only if you take action and keep going*
- Listen to mentors and teachers who know what they are talking about, *then make up your own mind* regardless. Never listen to critics who know nothing
- Be very discriminating about what input you allow into your mind and never introduce anything negative
- Become an avid bookworm. If happiness is your goal, books on personal development and popular psychology are your must-read subjects
- Reading is a powerful tool that can give you far deeper understanding and insight into the mysteries of life and can help you greatly to increase your awareness
- The internet is another great resource for learning and connecting, but don't get sidetracked or you could waste hours and then the web will become your saboteur
- Don't fall into the trap of believing that virtual connections are any substitute for personal human contact; for there is no substitute for that
- If your goal requires you to train in something, or if you simply want to add to your knowledge, skills and understanding, find the best possible teacher and do his or her course, workshop, seminar or event. Sometimes these are free
- Sometimes all you need is one more push or one more lightbulb moment to get you galvanised and on-track
- Some spiritually enlightened gurus conduct *Satsang,* a meeting in truth. These can be fascinating and powerfully revealing, and can add great depth to your understanding and acceptance of what's going on inside
- You may feel your questions have merely begotten more questions, especially if you are expecting comprehensible intellectual answers based on academic reason, logic or deduction

- In the context of Satsang, the only answers that matter are to do with truth and love, which can't be expressed in words. At times you may feel something touched your heart
- Osho explains that the real purpose of Satsang is an excuse for the master and his disciples to sit together in a heart to heart communion. It is 'a love affair' with no need for words
- There are many opportunities for attending Satsang in the West, and this can be a wonderful extension to your meditation practice. At the very least, it's bound to set you about enquiring more deeply within
- Balance, the middle way, is what gets you safely to where you want to go

Questions for self-monitoring

- Do I really want this?
- Do I feel I have the talent to ever become naturally excellent at this?

32

A Good Sharing Works Wonders

Love alone is capable of uniting living beings in such a way as to complete and fulfil them, for it alone takes them and joins them by what is deepest in themselves

Pierre Teilhard de Chardin

Imagine being able to walk into a room containing a group of peers you know well and have come to trust over a period of weeks, months, maybe even years. No matter what you are feeling, you sit down and pour out your heart in an atmosphere of love, support and acceptance. What a tremendous feeling of relief you would get if only it were possible to do that on a regular basis.

Even if you are feeling great and well on a path to success, wouldn't it still be excellent to share where you're at and to receive support, feedback and encouragement to give you even more energy to stay on track? Not only would this nourish your heart and soul, encouraging and empowering you, it can also greatly stimulate your creative activity and spark off all kinds of new ideas in your mind.

Happily we live at last in an age of enlightenment and not only is this possible, but it happens every day of every week in cities, towns and villages all over the developed world, in support groups of all kinds. Yet support groups, according to my research, seem to be one of the best kept secrets of modern times, for remarkably few people seem to know about them, and even fewer use them.

Many years ago I regularly attended an ongoing weekly support group for about three and a half years. I quote from the diary I kept at the time.

'It's Monday night, and Monday night is all about sharing. Sometimes it is hard, and it takes a lot of grit, to keep coming back week after week. Often I feel I don't want to be here, showing my vulnerable bits, feeling exposed, fearing attack, letting myself and others see and feel the real me.'

'I know that in reality there is nothing to fear, that's why I keep coming back, for we all love each other in the Monday night group. Well mostly. And even if we can't manage love, we all give each other support and feedback. We are mirrors for each other, no doubt about that.'

The support group I experienced was run by a psychotherapist group leader and was primarily orientated towards healing people's wounded psyches, but support groups are not all like that. They do tend to function on honest relating and sharing, but there are other types too. In my group, sometimes it felt like going back to school, only this school was a place where we could return to square one to relearn how to deal with life and it's myriad challenges, but this time in a truthful, straightforward way. At other times it felt intense, like being in a crucible with all those painful unconscious behaviour patterns being exposed, melted down and crushed, leaving us purified.

Another of my diary entries said, *'I suppose the hard bit about the prospect of another Monday night is that I will become aware of stuff that has been a long time dormant, and I would rather leave that way. The Monday group can sometimes stir things up that are hard to live with.'*

It happened every week. All day Monday I would be full of fear and resistance. In the evening I would drag myself to the group, which I would thoroughly enjoy most weeks, and then, in the cold light of Tuesday, tell myself I had been ridiculous. What was there to fear? Absolutely nothing.

On the contrary, almost every Monday night at going home time I ended up feeling a lot better than I had done before. It is true that some weeks uncomfortable feelings came up that didn't get resolved straight away, and at more than one stage several unpleasant weeks of living and working through them were necessary. However, each time this happened it proved ultimately well worth the effort for, by unearthing these issues and facing them full frontal, they passed with amazing speed and I started to feel better as other, more pleasant feelings arose.

This was in sharp contrast to what used to happen in earlier times when I tried to avoid painful feelings, for inevitably they would hang around and recur from time to time in varying degrees of intensity, and I would never feel free of them.

It sounds dramatic but I don't mean it so. The support groups I'm involved with these days are entirely different and function through support, encouragement, mirroring and feedback rather than on confrontation. However, bottling up feelings is not where it is at in a support group. Being in touch and expressing them spontaneously is.

A support group is designed to do exactly what it says on the tin – provide support. Sharing is what a support group is really all about, so anyone with a little organisational ability and enthusiasm can facilitate one. Formal qualifications are not necessary as long as you are not claiming any professional expertise, just a desire for people to share what is in their hearts. Life experience is far more important.

Types of support groups from which to choose are many and richly diverse, including those which are focused on specific addictions like Alcoholics Anonymous, Gamblers Anonymous, and quit smoking groups. Others focus on bereavement, disability, particular sexual orientations like gay and lesbian groups, and there are those with other specialised remits such as men's groups and women's groups. The group I joined was mixed, and open to any subject of general human interest, which usually translated as peoples' personal issues.

Some four years ago I started a small support group in north London, which I publicised as *'A support group for positive-minded people.'* It was (and still is) for people who are getting over being victims and who want to forge ahead towards success and happiness, and although the attendance is up and down it is still running. Because we meet on alternate Tuesday evenings, it has become known as the *Tuesday Night Group (TNG)*. Though I say so myself, some of the attendees have had a lot of benefit from it, myself included.

Shortly before writing this chapter I started another small fortnightly group, again in north London but this time specifically for writers and aspiring writers, be they professional or amateur, and I was completely blown away by the energy and enthusiasm expressed at our first meetings. We decided to start a website for the group and you can check it out at www.penandinkclub.com

This brings forward an interesting way of extending the helpful influence of such a group for, thanks to modern technology we are now starting to build a writers' community with online as well as offline support, which means members no longer have to be local. But let's not forget, meetings in cyberspace are no substitute for personal contact, they merely add value to, and facilitate, the important business of human heart-to-heart exchanges.

Whatever the focus of support group, the aim is always the same, to share experiences of mutual interest, to provide support and trust and to develop honest exchanges between people. Very often there are rules or structures to encourage continuity, such as a commitment to turn up for a given number of consecutive sessions, after first attending an open evening to sample the flavour of the group.

In his book, *Men are from Mars, Women are from Venus*, John Gray points out that women often want only to talk about their problems whereas men usually want solutions. Though this is a sweeping generalisation and obviously only sometimes true, reading his book did raise for me the idea that there might be benefit to be had from simply discussing or sharing problems and feelings without necessarily reaching an outcome or worrying about whys and wherefores. Of course, the principle can apply to men just as much as it does to women. A support group is an ideal vehicle for facilitating this idea.

I find it hard to believe now, years later, that I had never thought of that myself. It was amazing, and it seemed impossible, that by simply talking about a seemingly insoluble problem I could go away feeling better, even if had had no solution or resolution. But it is possible, and I have done, on many occasions.

Having said that, one of the great strengths of the support groups I have attended and now facilitate was that practical solutions, as well as hands-on support, always seemed to be forthcoming when required – and from right across the so-called gender divide.

For example, in the first group I mentioned, one man who was having problems relating to his teenage son received all sorts of practical suggestions, as well as mirroring and feedback, from both men and women in the group. Many of them were parents, and this helped him improve his relationship with his son significantly.

A woman who was scared and bewildered about trying to buy a house and get a mortgage was given considerable advice and support and eventually carried out the transactions successfully. Another man was given valuable insights to help him find a girlfriend after many years of loneliness. Of course, many relationship breakdowns, divorce proceedings and single parent issues were also thoroughly aired.

There was also considerable social interaction of a supportive nature, for example one woman who was estranged from her parents and her former partner went into hospital to have a baby, and two women from the group attended the birth with her, one of whom subsequently became the child's godmother. Later the baby also joined the group, which behaved like an extended family towards her.

When a group participant had a birthday, someone would arrange a surprise birthday cake for the nearest Monday night when the group was meeting, and often the group would go out the next Saturday night for a meal in a restaurant of the person's choice to help them celebrate their birthday.

Activities like this may seem childish or lacking in gravitas in the context of the serious business of sorting out our real problems, but I do assure you the symbolic value of a birthday celebration is very significant to the individual concerned, even if they don't consciously realise it. This was especially so for those who came from dysfunctional families, suffered from low self-esteem and were not used to being the focus of everyone's love and attention. Such occasions were also valuable vehicles for letting everyone's inner child come out to play.

Sometimes a few group members who had no families would get together over Christmas and maybe New Year, when the group would take a break. Christmas is hyped as a time of celebration, but all to often for many it is a period of intense loneliness, and a time when our pain and sorrow can come up in sharp contrast with what we perceive as everyone else's fun and celebration. Only too often it's a time when many need support more than ever.

Of course, a romance would occur in the group from time to time, and many a lesson was learned from these experiences. At times, because the level of trust and intimacy within the group felt strong, some of the issues arising from these were shared too.

The beauty of a support group is that the ground rules or boundaries can be whatever the participants or facilitator wants them to be. Even though a group needs a leader, he or she doesn't have to be a dictator. The people in the group automatically determine its shape and direction, and as new people join, or someone leaves, the group can, and almost certainly will, often take off in a new direction. The group is made up of individuals who seek to face their truths, so it takes on an organic character of its own that alters as its constituent parts change.

Some groups insist on sharing only, with no feedback allowed. Others allow feedback if requested. Some exclude advice or practical assistance, while others disallow interventions of a therapising nature. *A support group is most emphatically not the same as group therapy.*

Some people feel safer with a narrow, rigid remit, in which case they may benefit from a group with clear guidelines and a strong, directive leader. I have a pet hate for boundaries that are too tight and unnecessarily rigid, I do not appreciate being told how to behave and I want the freedom to decide my own boundaries. The group I joined suited me fine, for we were allowed, or encouraged in fact, to ask for what we wanted and to say what we did not want. In other words to take responsibility for what we got out of the group; it was then up to the other members to decide whether to provide it or not.

Support groups, in my experience, constitute a valuable tool when we are trying to resolve our issues, identify our goals and find out who we are. They can of course be used in concert with one-to-one psycho-therapy sessions, group therapy, meditations and any of the tools mentioned in this book, as well as with reflections from friends and partners, if you feel you need really strong medicine to help you attune to who you are, and to allow the real you to come out and express him or her self. Support groups are yet another powerful tool and, like any other, you can mix and match them with whatever tools you find most helpful to propel you onto your path towards freedom.

I sit here today writing this as someone who now feels, almost all the time, perfectly balanced and integrated as a whole, and much happier and more at ease with myself. Life is sheer delight most of the time, even when the going gets tough, and that's exactly what I wanted to achieve. I speak as someone whose life was a complete disaster in every respect and I needed my tools to be powerful. That's why I'm sharing this with you. The support group is a valuable tool that can help you get your life in order.

The support group is also a microcosm of society in which it is safe to experiment with new roles. I have observed, over a period of time, how very often a participant will evolve a new identity for him or her self through the group. In fact it's not new at all, it's their real self emerging and of course it was there all the time, but it was buried under their multi-layered persona. For example, someone with low self-esteem, after experiencing support from the group, does something to start to make his dreams come true and finds he really does, after a while, start to believe in himself. Of course as his mindset changes so does his behaviour and body language, and he becomes a newly empowered person.

It is beautiful to witness, every so often, someone achieve a breakthrough from sadness and angst into a flowering. Many times I have seen someone emerge from a support group after only a few weeks with a significantly more positive view of him or herself, and of the world as well. It is like a rebirth.

These kinds of life changing benefits can be had by you too! Support groups are an open opportunity begging to be taken up by people who are willing to get involved and take the risk of exposing their vulnerability in a supportive atmosphere. Class, nationality, ethnicity, colour, language and religion are irrelevant – all that is required is a modicum of sensitivity, courage, and an eagerness to participate with an open heart. I do believe everyone is capable of that. Your problems will not necessarily disappear, but support from people who care and understand makes a world of difference as you start to tackle them.

The support group is a place where you can share your pain, happiness, problems, and successes – anything. Here you can get it off your chest and receive support and feedback, or celebration. Sometimes, as we have mentioned, there is a solution that can be found to a problem, but very often your solution, or resolution, lies in merely expressing the feelings that surround your problem, while you experience the empathy of others.

As we have touched on already, many groups exist to address specific needs, and in these gatherings participants are expected to stick to an agenda. These are the groups that have specific objectives, such as helping people overcome addictions. For those who want the outcome badly enough, they are a godsend, for they can and do work for lots of people.

A therapist told me recently that all the programmes which have been successful in helping people quit Class A drug addiction have incorporated a significant element of support and sharing led by facilitators who had been addicts themselves. The organisers of these programmes deemed this support and sharing to be an essential ingredient.

You don't have to be a substance abuser to benefit from support groups. My point is, if sharing helps with dropping addictions – undoubtedly one of the most difficult behaviour modifications a person could ever try to make – then surely it can help with just about any issue.

As we have seen, in many cases, simply acknowledging that there is a problem, or difficult feelings around a situation, can be a major component in the solution. It certainly seems to be essential in kick-starting the healing process into action for most people. Indeed, many find that once the acknowledgement has taken place on a deep level, changes start to happen automatically. In many ways, this phenomenon is working via the support group's fundamental operating system.

Most support groups are ongoing, with meetings held usually once a week, once a fortnight or once a month. In many cases a commitment to attend for at least several weeks is required of participants, though usually newcomers can attend an open evening before making a decision. Some groups will only accept a newcomer during an open evening. This encourages continuity in the build-up of close, trusting relationships between the members; a group rapport which, together with confidentiality, is a vitally important ingredient. It is essential to develop a cocoon-like feeling of safety if people are to open up.

Some support groups actually do not allow feedback, or only if it is specifically requested. The reason for this is that by voicing a problem out loud in the group, the person sharing is acknowledging his or her feelings and taking responsibility for the reality and significance of those feelings, in the knowledge that what they say will not be challenged or manipulated in any way by others in the group. This is deemed to be a major step towards reconciling oneself to, or resolving, the difficulty of accepting the emotions that go with the problem. A well-known example is someone who stands up in an Alcoholics Anonymous meeting and says, 'my name is so and so, and I'm an alcoholic.'

I was curious to discover that it can actually require a good deal more courage to share good news than bad. I recall once sitting in a room in which one person after another shared a catalogue of woe and angst, after which I said, in acute embarrassment, 'actually, I am really happy at the moment.'

'Why's that then?' someone asked, disbelievingly.

I replied, 'I began to notice some of the really good things in my life. I'm in love with a woman who loves me, my son is making his way as a journalist, I'm starting to make money doing a job I adore, I have a beautiful place to live, I have a wonderful boat and I am addicted to sailing her. That's all I ever wanted and it's all worked out at last. I do still have some issues, but I'm beginning to feel I can deal with them now.'

My feeling of embarrassment was very revealing to me. '*Why on earth should I feel uncomfortable to say I was happy,*' I asked myself afterwards? It might be a cultural thing about being English, but it showed me very clearly how easily we can fall unconsciously into the habit of thinking little of ourselves. Perhaps we think we are unworthy and undeserving, and if we start to raise ourselves out of our unhappiness we feel conspicuous and egotistical, as if we might be adversely judged and not loved because we're bragging. It's as if being happy is not cool! What nonsense! What sort of insidious conditioning is that?

It's a tricky phenomenon that when you fear not being well thought of, for then there is an insidious danger of doing yourself down. The group reflected that back to me before anyone even said anything!

When something like this happens, if you have a habit of low self-esteem and you automatically start to think *'nobody loves me,'* you begin to realise the only one who doesn't love you is *you!* This is unconscious self-sabotaging behaviour in the extreme, and it's an easy trap to fall into if you let your awareness lapse.

When I realised I was doing exactly that, I resolved there and then never again to apologise for myself, or to feel badly about myself, or to feel in any way embarrassed or inhibited, as long as I feel I'm doing what is right for me and I am getting what I want out of life. I also realised I had been fantasising wildly, for I had doubted that the others in the group would believe me when I professed to being happy, and if they did, I feared they might feel jealous.

That was when I also learned not to presume I can know how other people feel when I have no evidence. They might not necessarily feel the same way that I might feel under similar circumstances, but to believe they do is merely projecting myself onto others. I realised this because, as it turned out, they were delighted on my behalf, and only too happy to hear some good news for a change.

This was a perfect example of group mirroring, something that enables an individual to see exactly how he or she is behaving, and it's immensely valuable. We must continually watch our unconscious behaviour patterns, once we become aware of them, and use any tool we can find to help ourselves see what we do. For as sure as anything, if we allow our awareness to lapse, our conditioned responses will take over and we will end up sabotaging our new found happiness again.

Something else very significant also happened in that moment, for many of the fears my mind had so brilliantly manufactured suddenly resolved themselves spontaneously. I had gone through a lot of changes in the preceding few months and I really, really wanted them to work. I'd had a strong wake-up message, taken it to heart and run with it. That evening in the group it was taking me a while to get used to my new outlook for I felt really conspicuous. I had taken on a new self-image, but I knew it was more real than the old one. I just had to get used to it. That evening it felt as if I was yelling, 'look at me. I'm daring to be happy. For once I'm sticking my head above the parapet and standing up to be counted on the plus side of life.'

Only afterwards did I realise that making a switch like that is only a change of mindset. Nothing else need change. Therefore anyone can do it anytime, anywhere, at will. I mention this incident because it's another perfect example of what I mean when I say awareness empowers you to make choices. You simply need to acknowledge that your present mindset isn't serving you, and that you *can* change it.

Now I'm not saying that the support group caused all this. I am trying to illustrate with this anecdotal evidence just a few of the ways in which this support group was especially helpful in reinforcing and accelerating the changes I was undergoing. The support and mirroring, not to mention the challenges, given to me by the group helped me to maintain the courage I needed to push through a metamorphosis in myself that was already happening. It was a fundamental grass-roots change that I had already set in motion with the aid of all sorts of tools, including therapy, meditation, other group work, reading, affirmations, many other methods described in this book, and working on my own in various ways. To be thus powerfully supported through the scary process of change was a great gift indeed.

I don't think there's any more I can say about this, except that I am in no doubt that the support group played a vital part in my learning to believe in my potential as a fully functioning, successful, full-blooded, fully paid-up member of the human race; and to begin to make actual that potential in my day-to-day life.

How to find a support group

Word of mouth is the best way to find a great support group, for by definition it comes with the endorsement of someone you know. Failing that you can look in local libraries, colleges, bookshops, community centres and cafes for advertisements for a support group near you, but do be careful with the internet.

Alternative health centres, wholefood shops and vegetarian restaurants are also good places to look, and I have even seen notices in doctor's surgeries. Many countries, counties and cities also have alternative magazines and guides where these events are advertised, and you can find well-known and established organisations in local telephone directories.

Just one final point is to be careful not to confuse a support group with a networking group or organisation, which is not necessarily the same thing at all, whether it's online or offline.

Start your own

Finally, if you can't find the kind of group you want, why not start your own? It could do wonders for your self-esteem. You can start by inviting people you already know and trust, using your own living room as a meeting place. As I mentioned, I've made something of an art form of this, having now started the *Tuesday Night Group* (TNG), a meditation group and a writers' group. You can do the same in your field of interest.

Like the TNG, the meditation group also meets fortnightly, specifically for meditation and then sharing. This group offers people a structure and is especially helpful for those who want to meditate and say they will, but never seem to get round to it. Beginners and experienced meditators alike are welcomed.

The writers' group is very dear to my heart because of my love of writing. It differs from other writers' groups I have attended in that it does not attempt to teach writing, but focuses on helping people find what blocks them, gives them ideas and feedback on what they may have written already or plan to write. It also gives confidence to aspiring writers to find their writer's voice and boost the enjoyment they get from their writing experience.

The world can feel like a scary place when we have to face it alone, and that is what every mature adult has to do. The path of awareness and emerging consciousness can be a rough and rocky one at times, and many are the temptations to give up. Support is, in my view, essential in helping us stay on track, in making sure we do not disappear into a pit of despair at the prospect of the seemingly impossible, endless and potentially overwhelming task of coming to terms and coming alive. So once again I urge you, join a support group, or create your own.

Websites for further information on support groups

www.awareness4life.co.uk
www.dave-robson.co.uk
www.penandinkclub.com

Summary

- No matter what you are feeling, imagine the relief to be able to share it in an atmosphere of love, support and acceptance on a regular basis
- Support and feedback from your fellow humans nourishes your heart and soul, encouraging and empowering you, and stimulating your creative activity
- Support groups differ, but all function on honest relating and sharing so participants can relearn how to deal honestly with aspects of life and it's challenges
- The prospect of telling everyone how you feel can seem scary, but soon you'll realise you have nothing to fear and everything to gain
- By unearthing and facing issues full on, they can pass with amazing speed
- Bottling up feelings is not where it is at in a support group. Getting in touch and expressing them spontaneously is
- A group provides support through sharing and anyone with a little organisational ability and enthusiasm can facilitate one. All you need is a desire for people to share what is in their hearts
- Support groups are many and diverse, including ones that address addiction, sexual orientation, bereavement, disability and illness

- Your group may have a website, but meetings in cyberspace are no substitute for personal contact
- There can be benefits from sharing problems and feelings without necessarily reaching any outcome
- On the other hand, practical solutions, as well as hands-on support, always seem to be forthcoming when required
- In any group the ground rules or boundaries can be whatever the facilitator or participants want them to be
- Even though a group needs a leader or facilitator, that person doesn't have to behave like a dictator
- The people in any support group automatically determine its shape and direction
- Some groups insist on sharing only, with no feedback allowed. Others allow feedback if requested. Some exclude advice or practical assistance, while others disallow interventions of a therapising nature
- A support group is not the same as group therapy
- Some people feel safer with a narrow, rigid remit, in which case they may benefit from a group with clear guidelines and a strong, directive leader
- Support groups are a valuable tool when we are trying to resolve our issues, identify our goals and find out who we are
- The support group is also a microcosm of society in which it is safe to experiment with new roles
- Support groups are an opportunity for people who are willing to get involved and take the risk of exposing their vulnerability in a supportive atmosphere
- All that is required to participate in a support group is a modicum of sensitivity, courage, and an eagerness to participate
- The support group is where people can share pain, happiness, problems, and successes, and to receive support and feedback, or to celebrate
- Often the solution, or resolution, someone seeks lies in merely expressing the feelings that surround the problem, and experiencing the empathy of others

- Some support groups are set up to address specific needs and specific objectives; in these groups, participants are expected to stick to an agenda
- Most support groups are ongoing, with regular meetings; in most cases a commitment is required
- Group rapport and confidentiality between members are essential in developing a feeling of safety, so you feel encouraged to open up
- Beware, for when you fear not being well thought of, there is a danger of doing yourself down. A support group can reflect that back
- In many cases, if you let your awareness lapse and say to yourself *'nobody loves me,'* you begin to realise the only one who doesn't love you is *you!*
- There is never any need to apologise for yourself as long as you feel you're doing what is right for you and getting what you want out of life
- It's presumptuous to believe you can know how other people feel when you have no evidence
- We must make ourselves aware of our unconscious behaviour patterns or our conditioned responses will take over and we'll sabotage our happiness again
- If you want to switch to being positive and creative, all you need do is to change your mindset. Nothing else need change
- Word of mouth is the best way to find a support group, but there are many places such as shop windows and noticeboards where some of them advertise
- If you can't find the group you want, start your own. You can start by inviting people you already know and trust, maybe meeting in your own living room
- Information about the *Tuesday Night Group (TNG)*, the meditation group and the Pen and Ink Club is on all three websites listed above
- The path of awareness and emerging consciousness can be rough and rocky and support is essential. To get maximum support on your journey of self-discovery, join a support group or create your own

33

Ongoing Support

Love doesn't just sit there, like a stone; it has to be made, like bread, remade all the time, made new

Ursula K. LeGuin

This chapter contains some ideas other than support groups to make sure you keep going and feel supported all the way. This is important because it is all too easy to stumble or feel disheartened if you feel you're all alone. Do yourself a favour, don't make the retraining of your psyche more difficult than it needs to be, and don't fall back into your old, negative sabotaging ways. Instead, get the support you need.

Personal development and the quest for happiness is a never-ending journey and as long as you feel supported you can thoroughly enjoy your travelling. Imagine you are on an infinite railway journey through an endlessly fascinating and ever-changing panoramic landscape. At times there will be stations to stop at for a short while, but soon the guard will blow his whistle and it'll be time to jump back on board.

You could get off the train forever at any of the stops, and you could even tramp slowly back to where you came from on foot. However, this train cannot go backwards and there's no train going in the opposite direction. The journey, of course, is always voluntary, but the committed traveller will make sure he never misses the train when it resumes its journey, for he relishes the next adventure and the non-stop stream of challenges that will engage him. Come what may he feels stronger after each encounter, and a little more liberated each time he undergoes a new experience. Eventually the whole world will be his comfort zone. He feels fully alive.

Some 2,000 years ago the Roman scholar and scientist Pliny the Elder accurately observed 'the only certainty is that nothing is certain,' and some 1,800 years later the author Robert Louis Stephenson asserted, 'it's better to travel hopefully than to arrive.' I used to disagree in the belief that an arrival is a great relief, and at least as enjoyable as any journey, but one day I saw that every arrival is just another station, a brief resting place and a prelude to a new departure.

Many of the people I meet want to control outcomes at whatever cost because change is unknown and therefore too scary to contemplate; they cannot fully enjoy their journeys because inevitably they are in conflict. They are anxious they might end up in the 'wrong' place; or be on the 'wrong' journey; or something 'disastrous' might happen during the journey; or they might 'regret' giving up whatever they were doing. Any or all of the above simply ensure they are unable to relax and relish their journey.

That's because they are making value judgements about the journey and the destination, and resisting both. They haven't realised there is no right or wrong journey; there is only your journey that unfolds as it will. They fear allowing their heart to direct their travels and letting themselves to go with the flow.

No-one who has the courage to let go and follow their heart can foresee their destination or what might happen on the way, which is why those who allow themselves to accept and embrace uncertainty can enjoy the fascination of watching their life's journey unfold day by day.

A wise sage once said there is no path to enlightenment or anywhere else, there is only the path you forge for yourself by walking along it. As you discover your true self at deeper and deeper levels, your passions, talents and callings begin to emerge and your journey towards fulfilment takes shape. This way your goals become self-evident and there is little or no stress or anxiety. This is the opposite of trying to figure out with your mind what you should achieve and fixating on achieving that.

So where is this philosophical thread taking us? I promised you concrete tools but now I'm philosophising! Well, this is how it is: you might say that the final stop of your journey is a station called *Happiness,* but actually that's the starting place for a brand new journey, a venture deep, deep, deep into a land called *Happiness.* The tools we will discuss in this chapter are designed to support you on your pilgrimage further into the territory of *Happiness.* They will help you to continue dealing effectively with your fears, issues, self-limiting beliefs and other manifestations of your saboteur which are bound to resurface occasionally, and to make sure they cannot stop you or get you re-entangled in unhappiness.

Everyone encounters difficulties. It is how we deal with them that makes the difference. Since everything about your journey through happiness is about learning to live more consciously, let's start with meditation.

Meditation

Meditation truly knows no limits. The reason it's included here in a chapter about ongoing support when we've already discussed it at length several times before is because meditation never lies, it never lets you down and it's always your best friend. It will give you ongoing support through hard times and easy times as long as do it on a regular basis. Think of it as a free gift from heaven, and I don't want to hear any excuses for not doing it regularly!

When a client says to me, 'oh yes, yes, I must meditate …' I immediately hear the subtext of what the person is really saying, which is '… but I'm not going to' (for 100 brilliant reasons, all of which are excuses).

Of course I can't leave that unchallenged, so I ask, 'what do you mean, must? Is someone holding a gun to your head? I don't want you to meditate just to please me, and I don't want you to meditate because you'll feel guilty if you don't. If you meditate, you benefit, if you don't meditate you're the loser, not me. I'll benefit from my meditation whether you meditate or not.'

Let's recap on this point about excuses for not meditating: If you believe you haven't got time, I'll tell you 'yes you have because it will save you time in the long run;' if you tell me you 'can't afford it' I will remind you it costs nothing; and if you say 'I don't know how to do it' I will reiterate, 'yes you do, because there is nothing to do and nothing to know.' Meditation is about non-doing and everyone can do that, or more correctly, everyone can *allow* that. It's really not as scary as you might think.

Allow me to repeat for one last time, unlike everything else we do, meditation requires *no* effort, not *more* effort. No skill is needed, no brilliant performance is expected, you need not have had any education. The only necessary ingredient is a willingness to let go and be a witness. Therefore, once you have decided you will, anyone can do it.

Any time you are in a quandary, when you feel confused or in conflict, or when you simply cannot hear your inner voice, the voice of your heart, above the din and clamour of your battling mind, you can turn to meditation to help you step outside the war and get a clearer perspective.

If you find you continue avoiding despite your best intentions, get support from your fellow humans on your meditation journey by joining a meditation or Satsang group. If you know you are going to meet up with a bunch of like-minded people all intent on meditating, you are bound to feel more motivated. Everywhere I look near where I live in north London I see notices on boards in cafes, wholefood shops and in newsagents' windows for meditation groups of all kinds, so they are not hard to find. The reason I started my fortnightly meditation group was solely to make it easier for people who struggle to meditate alone, to provide a structure you don't even have to think about and thus to finally remove all possible excuses. Within two minutes I can explain the procedure to anyone who has never meditated before.

After the group meditation we have a chat and a 'cuppa' so the more experienced people present can answer any queries novices may have. All participants can share their experiences, so no one need go away feeling they've been left stranded, high and dry. You can find details on any of the websites listed at the end of this chapter.

If you are having trouble connecting with your feelings, one truly amazing website well worth checking out is: www.mitendevapremal.com. This couple, Miten and Deva Premal, both Sannyasins of Osho, perform meditative sacred music that creates an atmosphere of absolute magic. After one of their live appearances one audience member said, 'they are nourishing and nurturing the world with their mantra,' and I heartily agree. Another person said, 'I'm lost for words …' and another added, 'the music put me in touch with my heart.'

That's the whole point of meditation, and also of sacred music. To put you in touch with your heart. It's great news if you are literally lost for words, for it means at last the voice of your heart has moved into the foreground and your thinking mind, at least for a moment, has given up the war. So although you might have tears streaming down your face, even though you might be feeling intense pain, you are at peace. That's how your healing journey can begin.

Get what you need

Here is another suggestion for ongoing support – make it your business to get what you need.

That's a polite way of saying instead of sitting around moaning about your misfortunes and being forever a helpless victim, take responsibility for fashioning your own good fortune – not just today, but every day. Getting what you need and want is nobody else's business but yours.

For example, if your bones and muscles are aching from a period of intense physical work, get a massage or go and sit in a hot tub. Even better, if you are in a relationship, ask your lover to massage you. If you have physical pain, see a chiropractor or an osteopath, and if you get a toothache, go to the dentist. It's true we have said you are not your body, but that doesn't mean your body doesn't need looking after. The mystics all tell us your body is your temple and must be treated with respect for it gives the real you shelter and somewhere to live on this Earth, in this life, in this form. Therefore it behoves you to keep it clean, healthy, fit and well nourished.

Some people take a stoical approach to physical suffering, as if pain is 'character building' or 'good for the soul.' What nonsense! Suffering is suffering, plain and simple, and in most cases it's unnecessary, so where's the virtue in that? Character building just means it helps you strengthen your persona, but that merely takes you further away from your heart so it's counterproductive in the extreme. Making a virtue out of suffering reminds me of the monks of old with their sackcloth and ashes. It's as fruitless as believing poverty makes you a 'better person.'

Another example of getting what you need is giving yourself a day off after a period of intense work. Sometimes I even give myself a day off when I've just returned home from a holiday because I am fatigued from travelling and manoeuvring heavy luggage.

Too many people I know believe it's a great idea to become workaholics, but I'm afraid I learned years ago it doesn't earn you any extra brownie points. If you work for someone else you are merely inviting your employers to exploit you, and if you are self-employed or in charge of a large business, you could ask yourself what you are hiding from. If you get flu, or even just a cold, stay in bed with a hot toddy liberally laced with honey. What are you trying to prove or who are trying to impress by struggling into work? *No-one ever achieved happiness through struggling.*

There are many excellent employers and any one of them worth their salt will be relieved and delighted you elected to stay home and desist from sharing your germs. This is real life and you are responsible for taking care of yours.

Even if you are trying hard to climb the slippery pole or build your brand new business, overworking doesn't help. Instead it results in dangerous stress levels and soon you'll forget to enjoy your work.

One of my clients quit his job and started his own charity, which suddenly took off. Before he knew it, he was working eighteen hours a day and staving off exhaustion, and he wasn't even getting paid. This was a charity and he pursued his work out of passion. One day he was driving somewhere when he suddenly blacked out behind the wheel. His car veered off the road into some railings and came to an abrupt halt.

Luckily for him he came round about twenty seconds later, shocked, stunned and only slightly injured. Fortunately no other cars or pedestrians were hit, so although his car was written off and there was a row of bent railings, he got away with it. The hospital pronounced him fit to go home and after a day or two he got over the shock, returned to work and got a new car. He was chastened after his wake-up call, realising he was very lucky no one had been killed or seriously injured.

Now guess what happened? While he was recovering and away from his beloved work for two or three days, the world kept on turning, the sun came up in the morning and set in the evening, people got up, went to bed, made love, had arguments and made friends again. Even though my client wasn't there to keep the wheels turning!

Some people suffer from a strong work ethic that drives them on and on (and I do mean *suffer*), so much so that they feel guilty when they have time off, even if they have legitimately earned it. That's powerful negative conditioning. If that's you, stop to think about it for a moment and ask yourself, 'who says I'm not worthy if I take time off?' Also ask yourself, 'where did I get this idea that I must work hard to please everybody, even at the expense of my health and the toll it takes on my relationships?' and 'how did I get the idea that time off isn't a worthy use of my time?'

Let me give you a hint. Think saboteur, then try and remember who fed the message into your unconscious, 'I must work harder.' It's certainly not coming from your real self.

Another idea you can combine with taking a day off is to give yourself a treat from time to time, especially if you've just achieved another stage towards your goal.

Let's say you've spent some weeks focusing intently on achieving the first step of a long-term goal and today you make it – why not, if it's a hot sunny day tomorrow, take a day off. Go for a stroll in the park *and* treat yourself to an ice cream. Maybe one of those yummy vanilla whirly cones with a flaky chocolate thing stuck into it! Mmmm. Then you will realise you don't have to work hard to reach paradise, you're already there.

Nearest and dearest

When you continually support yourself like this, and get other support you need at regular intervals, you will indeed find your journey enjoyable. Another important thing you can do to facilitate a joyful journey is to tell your nearest and dearest what you need from them and what they can do to support you on your journey.

Let's take a simple example. Your goal is to lose some weight. You have, of course, written it down as a SMART goal expressed in positive terms, such as 'I enjoy being twelve stone.' You ask your partner please not to buy any biscuits and to make sure there are no cakes or sweet things in the house if these are not within your diet, so you won't be tempted. Should your partner agree then he or she is supporting you.

Similarly, if you are a recovering alcoholic you might empty your home of alcohol and ask the people you live with to make sure none is brought in by them, and if you have dinner guests you could ask them to bring fruit juice and mineral water instead of wine. Needless to say it's up to you not to bring in any alcohol yourself.

Explaining to your friends, family, colleagues and even your customers what you need from them to help you reach your goals can empower them enormously to be supportive. Most of them, given that they are intelligent, sensitive, understanding, and that they love you (otherwise why would you want to know or work with them?), will be delighted and maybe even honoured to help.

Sometime old habits die hard, however. I must have told my ninety-six year-old mum five hundred times that I'm watching my weight, yet she still says to me in one breath, 'it wouldn't do you any harm to lose a little weight, you know dear. I think you should,' and then literally in the next breath she says, 'go on, have a piece of cake!'

In her typically motherly way she likes to show her love through food and hospitality, but in a case like this it's not very helpful. Of course she means well, for offering food is one of her ways of showing love, but our awareness tells us we don't at the moment live in times of adversity and food shortage like we did when I was born, shortly after World War II – indeed at present we live in a time of glut and obesity and most of us in the West eat far too much of the wrong things.

I remind myself at such times of great temptation that I can't have it both ways and it's better to make a conscious choice. Occasionally that choice is to have the piece of cake and be done with it, but most often I settle for a cup of tea or coffee (without sugar) instead. On extreme occasions I realise the only way I can deftly avoid the cake is to make my hasty getaway before temptation sabotages my positive mindset!

Most important – if you do realise you sabotaged yourself, that is, you made an *unconscious* decision or one you know is self-sabotaging, don't beat yourself up. Acknowledge what happened and resolve that next time you'll be sufficiently aware to make a *conscious* and supportive choice.

As it happens I do have a strategy for losing weight which allows for eating the *occasional* biscuit or piece of cake, but that's another story …

Wheel of Life revisited

Although the *Wheel of Life*, which we discussed in Chapter 6, is essentially a diagnostic tool designed to help you see where you are at the time of doing the exercise, it can also be used in a support role to help you monitor your progress, detect trends, and to stay on track.

To be able to do this, when you first do the exercise you must remember to write the date on it. Then months later you can do it once more, making sure you write the current date on it again and compare the two. You can repeat the exercise at, say, three monthly intervals, and you will be able to see from your dated comparisons how you are progressing (or not). You can also see what's changed and what needs working on next.

A useful way to approach this is to devote a whole Wheel to one long term-goal which has many aspects, and you assign to each of those aspects its own segment of the Wheel. In the beginning one of those aspects may have stood out as needing urgent action, but as you achieve your first stage or sub-goal, your priority for continuing the next phase of your strategy might shift to another segment or aspect. In which case your new *Wheel of Life* exercise will help you spot the necessary change so you can amend your action plan accordingly.

Another way you can use this tool started with the general *Wheel of Life* exercise you did way back at the beginning of Chapter 6, which reflected the various different facets of your life. Your first exercise, which of course you dated, might have shown, for example, that your business life and finances scored low and needed working on, while your relationship scored ten out of ten. So between then and now you spent some months building your business and your bank account grew, but now you do another updated *Wheel of Life,* which you also remember to date, and you spot that your relationship has slipped to eight out of ten. Thanks to this latest exercise, you have alerted yourself to the situation before things slip out of control and if you're not happy about it you now realise you're going to have to switch more attention to maintaining the health of your relationship.

In this way, you can use the Wheel to help you to awaken your awareness and find a good balance between your relationship, your business and your income.

Doing a sedentary job is another example. Maybe you've had to focus on office work for a few months but now you do the *Wheel of Life* again and it brings to your attention that you're not as fit and healthy as you would like. That will help you realise the need to go out, get some fresh air and exercise and maybe go to the gym more often.

Getting the various elements of your life all functioning as you would like is a delicate balancing act and the *Wheel of Life* can help you fine-tune that balance. Don't be afraid to use it at regular intervals but also at any time you feel the need, especially every time you reach a new stage in your strategy or action plan, or any time you feel unclear about what you are doing or what to do next.

You can download free blank forms for your *Wheel of Life* exercises from www.thefivepillarsofhappiness.com

Success Diary

As you proceed towards your goals or make progress with resolving your issues, don't forget to continue to regularly update your *Success Diary*. Don't wait for a major breakthrough before you do it, use your Diary to celebrate your transformation into a successful, can-do person at every step of the way, every day. It will help you very much to implant your new mindset so it can take root.

Also remember your *Gratitude Diary* and counting your blessings, especially if your history is one of depression or feeling negative. You'll be amazed at how it can help you see the positive side in everyday life, especially when your path seems particularly challenging.

Mix and match

This book contains a huge bagful of powerful tools and you can use any or all of them any time you like. In this chapter I've recapped some of the more important ones, but it's a very good idea to re-read the parts of this book that describe the tools that struck you as potentially most useful. You'll find them all mentioned in the chapter summaries.

Imagine you have a pallet of colours. Be imaginative and creative in how you mix and match the tools you need to colour your life, and master their use. Then you can trust them to help you achieve the results you want.

Websites for ongoing support

www.thefivepillarsofhappiness.com
www.awareness4life.co.uk
www.dave-robson.co.uk
www.mitendevapremal.com

Summary

- Personal development and the quest for happiness is a never-ending journey. As long as you feel supported you can enjoy every step along the way

- The committed traveller relishes the next adventure in his or her non-stop stream of challenges. You will feel stronger and more liberated after each encounter. Eventually the whole world will be your comfort zone. You feel fully alive
- The train cannot go backwards and there's no train going in the opposite direction. Every arrival is just another station, a brief resting place and a prelude to a new departure
- If you are in conflict you cannot enjoy your journey
- If because of your fear you make value judgements or resist your journey or destination, you haven't realised there is no right or wrong journey
- When you start to feel happy, that's the starting place for a brand new journey, a venture deeply into the land called *Happiness*
- *Everyone encounters difficulties. It's how you deal with them that makes the difference*
- Meditation knows no limits. It never lies and it will always support you, so there's no excuse for not doing it on a regular basis
- Meditation requires *no* effort, not *more* effort. No skill is needed, no brilliant performance is expected, and you need not have had any education
- You need only one thing to meditate – a willingness to let go and be a witness
- The whole point of meditation is to put you in touch with your heart
- If you are so touched you are lost for words, it means the voice of your heart has moved into the foreground and your thinking mind has given up the war, for the moment, at least
- Even though you might be feeling intense pain, when you are at peace your healing journey can begin
- Take responsibility for creating your own good fortune – not just today, but every day
- Getting what you need and want is nobody else's business but yours
- 'Character building' just means helping to strengthen your persona, but that merely takes you further away from your heart, so it's unhelpful
- Making a virtue out of suffering is as fruitless as believing poverty makes you a 'better person'

- Give yourself a day off after a period of intense work
- Being a workaholic doesn't earn you extra brownie points. Ask yourself what you are hiding from
- *No-one ever achieved happiness through struggling*
- Even if you are trying to progress at work or build a new business, overworking doesn't help, instead it results in dangerous stress levels
- Many suffer from a strong work ethic, a powerful conditioning that drives them and they feel guilty when they have time off, even if it is legitimate
- Try and remember who fed the message into your unconscious, *'you must work harder.'* It's certainly not coming from your real self
- Give yourself a treat from time to time, especially if you've just achieved another stage towards your goal
- Tell your nearest and dearest what you need from them and what they can do to support you on your journey
- Explaining to your friends, family, colleagues and customers what you need from them to help you reach your goals can empower them to be supportive
- If you do realise you have sabotaged yourself, don't beat yourself up
- The *Wheel of Life* can also be used in a support role to help you monitor progress, detect shifting trends, and to stay on track
- The *Wheel of Life* can help you fine tune the balance between the various elements of your life so you can get them all functioning as you would like
- Use it regularly and any time you feel the need, especially when you reach a new stage in your action plan, or when you feel unclear about what to do next
- This book contains a many powerful tools that you can use any time you like. Use them imaginatively; they will help you achieve the results you want

THE ROOF

Happiness – Putting on the Roof

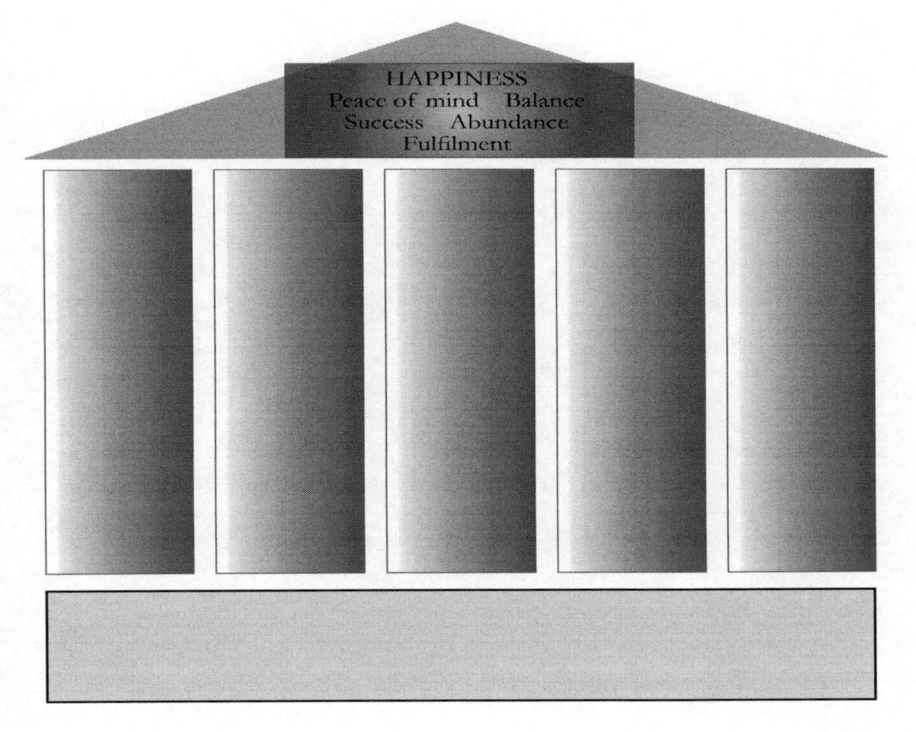

At last our foundation is built and our five pillars are completed. The new building that is you and your new life is strong and sturdy and we can now put the roof on in the knowledge that it will be firmly and sustainably supported.

You have so lovingly engineered the supporting structure and built it so skilfully with limitless care and attention that the roof will probably fit easily, with only a little fine tuning. This final section is about that all-important fine tuning, sanding and polishing, essential ongoing tasks to ensure a harmonious, well fitting result.

34

What Does Happiness Mean to You?

Little by little, as you practice 'trusting your gut,' you will be led to many wonderful places
Susan Jeffers

Finally we arrive at the $64,000 question, or what you might call *'the proof of the pudding'* question.

Obviously now that you've done all this work on yourself and made all those changes, coming way out of your comfort zone on numerous occasions to do so, if you're still not happy, then all your efforts 'don't amount to a hill of beans,' as they say in America!

If you have come this far, that possibility seems very unlikely, or you would have given up a long time ago and tossed this book into the bin. But almost certainly a little fine tuning will be required, probably on a regular basis. For the sake of thoroughness, if for no other reason, there are some important questions for you to ask yourself while doing that fine tuning. The world and it's events are forever changing and it's as well to continue checking out everything within yourself to asses your evolving needs as time goes by. Then you leave no stone unturned and you'll have a satisfying feeling of completion.

As the saying goes, one man's meat is another man's poison, which is why the first question, which I hope you have been asking yourself all along, is so important: *What does happiness mean to you?*

When I was growing up it seemed to be assumed that a good career, a family with 2.4 children, a nice car in the drive, a house, a reasonable income and at least one summer holiday a year were the required ingredients for happiness. As a lad I couldn't help noticing that not everybody who had ticked all these boxes was happy.

Even as I was going through school I had a feeling that my powerful innate sense of curiosity was going to get me into trouble, and indeed it did cause me to ask searching questions of myself, my teachers, my parents and of my friends. I could never understand why I should be interested in things that bored me, or be satisfied with half-truths and compromise. Even at that tender age I was looking for meaning and purpose. The result was a very long road towards self-discovery, but in the end I did get a satisfactory answer to my question.

As we know, if you are looking for happiness the search has to be within, not on the outside. We all have to live in the material world as well as the spiritual one, and of course it's nice to have a car, a house, a job, and so on. However, *you cannot depend on anything outside yourself to make you happy.*

Not such an original revelation, you might think, but it's crucial. You might know in theory that the answer lies within, but you still have to find it. That's what the work in this book has been about. Finding and connecting with your inner being and discovering who you are.

Every one of us who is in search of happiness must answer the question for ourselves and never adopt someone else's answer to fit our own take on life. This book aims to accompany and support you on your journey sufficiently to enable you to find your answer but, much as I wish I could, I can't answer it for you. For that reason please don't take my slant on this as the definitive truth. What you've been reading is my perception and my experience and I share it with you in the hope of inspiring you to search within yourself for your own answers.

It's essential you start to believe in yourself and trust your instincts, your gut feelings and your intuition, or you will be swayed off track by others, like the man in the pub who insists that happiness can't possibly be how you say it is, it's got to be like he says it is. Then you discover he suffers from depression and hasn't experienced a genuinely happy moment for years.

What makes you happy is entirely unique to you, so if you want happiness to become your default setting you must be prepared to be a true individual, no matter how much we are all part of the whole.

I could answer the question for myself by saying, for example, 'going sailing makes me happy,' which, though true most of the time, misses the point entirely. *Happiness is a state of heart and mind* and there are many things that can happen to produce that state of heart and mind. In my case sailing is only one of them, and in any case that doesn't answer the question of why sailing can sometimes be profoundly unenjoyable (when you are caught in a gale, for example). *What really matters in producing the required state of mind on a continual basis is knowing who you are deep down in your heart, and accepting that unconditionally.*

The five qualities of happiness

Now finally let's put together the final pieces of the puzzle of how we achieve enduring happiness. When I sat down to analyse it, I found five main qualities required for a person, or to be more accurate for me, to feel 100 per cent happy deep down inside. They are, in no particular order:

- Peace of mind
- Balance
- Abundance
- Success
- Fulfilment

Each one of these qualities can be further subdivided because they embody lots of other qualities. But before we consider each of the five, let's take a look at one other quality – freedom.

Where I live I constantly receive requests from a multitude of charities looking for financial support, and I feel rather than support each one a tiny amount it would be best to choose only one to support, and stick to it. So I considered Greenpeace, Friends of the Earth, Oxfam, Great Ormond Street Hospital for Children, the RSPCA, Cancer Research and lots of others that beat a path to my front door and staked out my local high street. In the end, after much deliberation, I chose Amnesty International, on the basis that *a person's freedom is the most important thing of all, even above food and shelter,* and being tortured is the most heinous situation any person can find himself or herself in that I can think of. I made my decision because in my opinion Amnesty's work in campaigning for liberty, justice and the abolition of torture is so important I wanted to support it above all else. That's how important freedom is. If you don't have your freedom, you don't even get to first base.

So why then is freedom not listed among my five qualities? Because I realised that freedom, especially after reading Victor Frankl's book, *Man's Search for Meaning*, is also a state of heart and mind and when you embody the five qualities you will feel free. Conversely, you will only ever embrace the five qualities if you have already made the decision to set yourself free.

Now before we get lost in semantics, let's take a closer look at the five qualities:

Peace of mind

The behaviour of the Impeccable Warrior is crucial for peace of mind. That's because whatever happens, the Impeccable Warrior, whose behaviour is always aligned with his core beliefs and values, never has any reason to reproach himself, *no matter what might befall.* His mantra is *to thine own self be true.* When you live your life like that you can simply relax, chill out, love and accept yourself, the world around you and all that it contains, and step out of the war.

If you suffer from inner conflict and anxiety I would suggest you take this to heart and find the courage to be true to yourself. I can attest from my own experience, *peace of mind is a blessed relief.*

Balance

When we talk about balance we are talking about the middle way and we're also back to the subject of developing a suitable heart/mind balance.

Remember, we all encounter difficulties and challenges from time to time, and its how we deal with them that matters. Taking a balanced view means taking a step back to get the bigger picture within your frame of vision; a proper perspective, so you don't inadvertently sabotage yourself by reacting in an unconscious knee-jerk manner.

You may remember my example of the woman who wouldn't throw anything away because 'it might come in handy' or 'it's got sentimental value,' although her partner couldn't stand living in what he considered to be a mess. Despite their love for each other, this situation set them up in constant conflict.

It was only after each partner accepted his and her own feelings, and each others, that they realised the importance of finding a middle way, and the solution they came to was to put lots of her possessions into the loft, where it was invisible but still accessible if need be. This gave them both peace of mind and their relationship blossomed once more. They were able to take a step back to see the bigger picture and get a more balanced view. Both agreed their relationship, not the clutter issue, *was* the bigger picture and was more important.

Next time your partner infuriates you by leaving the lid off the toothpaste, stop before you react blindly and ask yourself, 'is it really worth making an issue out of this?' 'Am I taking a balanced view?' Maybe a better solution would be to tell the other person how angry or upset you feel, without blaming or dumping your anger.

Abundance

If you feel you lack abundance, try counting your blessings. When you feel a profound gratitude for everything you are, everything you have, everything you are capable of and everything that has ever happened to you, you can't help being blown away by feelings of awe and wonder – about your miraculous self and about every living being on this planet, including the planet itself. Somehow we have been chosen for the privilege of living on this verdant orb spinning in an infinite Universe, and it provides everything we need to sustain life. How truly amazing is that?

No matter how poverty stricken you might be, you are a miracle on legs living in a miraculous environment. When you look at the awe-some grandeur of the bigger picture your well of abundance overflows just because of being alive.

Be careful not to confuse abundance with wealth. Many people I know feel abundant in every way except financially, but if improving your financial status is one of your goals, celebrating your abundance is a great place to start. It will give you the necessary positive mindset and, bearing in mind we manifest in the material world more of whatever is our dominant thought, it's a surefire way to ensure your thoughts are suitably orientated to create the wealth you desire.

I hope I am beginning to clarify what I mean when I say that happiness is a state of heart and mind. There's not one person on this Earth who cannot celebrate his or her abundance, whatever your situation, *if you choose to look at it like that.* It's the classic 'is the glass half empty or half full' question. The answer depends on your point of view.

It is my ardent belief, if you realise and focus on what an incredible, miraculous existence we have all been given, you will see that your cup is neither half empty nor half full – your cup runneth over!

Success

We have already discussed at length the need to figure out what success means to you, and just as with happiness, your definition will be unique to you. All I want to emphasise here is that success, just like everything else, is also something to be kept in balance. For example, if your goal is to make money and you are working long hours doing a job you hate, you can't possibly be happy even if you achieve your goal. Hence the slogan on my website, *do what you love, love what you do.* Keeping your *Success Diary* and meditating regularly will give you deep insight into how you are feeling in this regard.

Similarly, if you work such long hours that eventually your wife and children leave you, that's not going to bring you much joy either. Every one of your goals needs to be kept in balance.

It's worth taking a long, hard look at this issue on a regular basis, and the *Wheel of Life* can help you to check what elements of your life are in or out of balance. Achievement that doesn't make you happy is not what I call success. If that's happening to you, something needs to change and fast. If you achieve goals that align with your true self, mean something to you and enable you to keep all the elements in your life in balance, now that's what I call success!

From all this we see that the happy person constantly doing his fine tuning has to master the subtle arts of metaphorically doing jigsaws, juggling and tightrope walking. The line between happiness and misery is a fine one indeed, and awareness, especially self-awareness, is what stops you falling or straying. If you want to see what I mean, go to the circus next time one comes to town and watch how focused the jugglers, the tightrope walkers, and the trapeze artists are. The success of their acts, and their good health and longevity, depend entirely on 100 per cent awareness at every moment.

Fulfilment

This is the big one; the state of being that makes your whole journey worthwhile. When you seek deep within yourself, connect with your heart and start to act in accordance with its guidance, no matter what fears or difficulties arise, the possibility of fulfilment comes onto your radar.

As we have seen, we are each a bottomless reservoir of possibilities and to actualise the ones that matter to you is what I mean by fulfilment. It's exactly like a company that *fulfils* an order. Someone orders a product from your company and the company, wanting to supply the stated need, *fulfils* the order. The customer is *satisfie*d or *contented.* In your case you are fulfilling an order that comes from your heart and as a result you feel satisfied and contented. Your deepest desire is fulfilled.

The beauty of the fulfilment experience is that you get a feeling you are doing, being and feeling, what you were put on this planet to do, be and feel. You are developing the gifts, talents, aptitudes, interests, vocation and passions you were born to express, hence your life develops meaning and purpose.

Freedom

Finally, when your life takes on meaning and purpose, you feel free. As Nelson Mandela and Victor Frankl show us, you can imprison a person's body under the most appalling conditions, but you can never keep captive a person's heart, mind, soul and creative imagination.

The happiness equation

Here's a simple formula to express the above principles in a more graphic format:

Peace of mind Balance Abundance Success Fulfilment	}	=	Freedom	=	Happiness

Summary

- If happiness is your goal then to find out if you have finally achieved it, or whether further adjustments are necessary, ask yourself, 'what does happiness mean to me?'
- If you are looking for happiness, the search has to be within, for *you cannot depend on anything on the outside of yourself to make you happy*
- Every one of us who is in search of happiness must answer the question for themselves and never adopt someone else's answer

- It's essential you start to believe in yourself and trust your instincts, your gut feelings and your intuition, or others will sway you off track
- What makes you happy is unique to you, so if you want happiness to become your default setting you must be prepared to be a true individual
- *Happiness is a state of heart and mind*
- *What really matters is knowing who you are deep down in your heart, and accepting that unconditionally*
- My five main qualities required for happiness are: peace of mind, balance, abundance, success and fulfilment
- *A person's freedom is the most important thing of all, even above food and shelter*
- Freedom is also a state of heart and mind. When you embody the five qualities you will feel free
- Conversely, you will only ever embrace the five qualities if you have already made the decision to set yourself free
- The behaviour of the Impeccable Warrior is crucial for peace of mind. If you suffer from inner conflict and anxiety take this to heart, for *peace of mind is a blessed relief*
- Taking a balanced view means taking a step back to get the bigger picture within your frame of vision, a proper perspective
- Sticking to extreme behaviour at all costs is obsessive. Unconscious behaviour wipes out all possibilities of making conscious choices

  If you feel you lack abundance, try counting your blessings
- We have the privilege of living on this verdant orb spinning in an infinite Universe; it provides everything we need to sustain life. How amazing is that?
- Be careful not to confuse abundance with wealth
- If improving your financial status is one of your goals, celebrating your abundance is a great place to start. It's a surefire way to ensure your thoughts are suitably orientated towards creating the wealth you desire
- There's not one person on this Earth who cannot celebrate his or her abundance, whatever your situation, *if you choose to look at it like that*
- Success, just like everything else, also needs to be kept in balance. Keeping your *Success Diary* and meditating regularly will give you deep insight

- Achievement that doesn't make you happy is not what I call success. If that's happening to you, something needs to change and fast
- If you achieve goals that align with your true self, mean something to you and enable you to keep your life in balance; now that's what I call success!
- The line between happiness and misery is a fine one indeed, and awareness, especially self-awareness, is what stops you falling or straying
- When you seek deeply within, connect with your heart and act in accordance with its guidance, the possibility of fulfilment comes onto your radar
- We each have within ourselves a bottomless reservoir of possibilities and to actualise the ones that matter to you is what I mean by fulfilment
- Experiencing fulfilment makes you feel you are doing, being and feeling what you were put on this planet to do, be and feel. You are developing the gifts, talents, aptitudes, interests, vocations and passions you were born to express, hence your life develops meaning and purpose
- When your life takes on meaning and purpose, you feel free
- You can imprison a person's body under the most appalling conditions but you can never keep captive a person's heart, mind, soul and creative imagination

35

Wheel of Life Last Visit, and Final Questions

Work like you don't need money, love like you've never been hurt – and dance like no one's watching!

Daniel Wagner

Wheel of Life

As we have seen many times now, the *Wheel of Life* helps you not only to diagnose where you need to put your attention in sorting out your life, but also to conduct self-monitoring. It's also very useful in this fine tuning process to make sure that once you've arrived at the doors of happiness, you go deep inside and continue to partake fully in the happiness experience.

At the risk of repeating myself too much, I cannot escape the feeling I would not be fully discharging my duty as an Impeccable Warrior if I did not bring you back for one last look at some of the details of the process, just to make sure you wring out the absolute maximum benefit from your *Wheel of Life*.

Remember, it's important to put the date, as well as your name, at the top of the form every time you do this exercise. You might ask why I'm being so fussy about tiny details such as the importance of putting your name on the form, since you are going to keep the completed forms in your room or somewhere private, and it'll be obvious to you who they belong to.

It matters because it gives you a subtle and very helpful psychological edge, which is important because all the work in this book is about changing your mindset and tuning into your heart. Subliminally, when you write your name on your Wheel, you take ownership of the information you enter, and assume responsibility for what is revealed and what changes you want to make.

The date is important too, so you can compare your results with previous results to see exactly how much progress you have made since you compiled earlier Wheels, as well as assessing what needs changing, tweaking or adjusting.

At this stage it's also a good idea to re-personalise your Wheel by deciding if any new segments need to be added to your form, or indeed if any need to be deleted. For example, if you have just completed your divorce, you might want to delete a segment you might have labelled *'my marriage'* and replace it with *'new relationship,'* or *'seeing the kids.'*

Similarly, if you have been made redundant, you might want to remove *'job,' 'employment'* or *'work'* and replace it with *'job hunting,' 'new job'* or *'new career.'* As we noted in Chapter 6, it's for you to decide how many segments and what labels are included in your own personal *Wheel of Life*.

Don't forget you can also draw up specialised *Wheels of Life* where one aspect of your life, say *'health and fitness,'* is subdivided into eight, ten or twelve segments for deeper scrutiny. This really puts the issue under the microscope and facilitates an in-depth view of how happy or otherwise you are with it.

The comparison with earlier *Wheels of Life* is important because it's obviously a good idea to make sure you are making overall progress. You may remember in the chapter about setting SMART goals we remarked that goals should be measurable, meaning you need to know when you have achieved your goal, or if you are moving towards it. Repeating the *Wheel of Life* exercise will help you evaluate that.

It could happen that you discover you're actually moving away from your goal, or not moving at all, in which case immediate further investigation is called for, or perhaps further or different action. Are you doing the 'wrong' things, are you doing nothing, has your goal changed, are you feeling de-motivated, why didn't you notice you were slipping backwards? These are just some of the many questions you should be asking yourself in such a situation.

Final questions

Continually raising your awareness has to a lifelong habit now and as part of your fine tuning, here are some key questions you can ask yourself at this stage and at regular intervals in the future.

Am I sure I'm coming from my heart?

Remember, if happiness and fulfilment are your goals, there is only one path and that's the way of the heart. Achieving goals is easy – that's not the issue. Achieving *meaningful* goals that come from your heart is the issue. Funnily enough it's even easier to achieve heartfelt goals, if you have the courage and patience to first enquire deeply within to make sure of what they are.

Achievements designed to please someone else simply won't cut it. Maybe they were a result of someone else's idea; or because you couldn't be bothered to listen to your heart; or your courage failed you; or because it was convenient; or because you could do it without leaving your comfort zone; or because you settled for a compromise; or because you still don't believe you can do what you really want to do; or for any other reason whatsoever. You might feel happy for a while but not on a deep level, and you'll never feel fulfilled. *Only goals that come from your heart will give you a profound sense of meaning and purpose.*

If you want to listen to the voice of your heart but you're having trouble getting tuned in, be still and silent for a while, and just witness. If your mind is turbulent, don't try to stop it or judge it. Just wait patiently and watch the turbulence. Eventually it will pass. Watching and listening in silence. Nothing else is needed.

Do I feel fully alive?

If by now you don't feel fully alive, at least most of the time, you're probably on the wrong track, because when you do what you love and love what you do, exciting things happen all the time.

I'm not talking about the kind of temporary thrills you might get on a roller coaster at a theme park, I'm talking about the joy of aliveness that comes when you create something that has meaning for you, and the rush that comes when you move nearer to a heartfelt goal.

Decide what your passion is, and your talent or gift, and find the courage to go for it. Don't let anything stop you, including yourself in the disguise of your saboteur.

Am I in my maximum creative flow?

Ask yourself how you feel about what you are doing now. Is everything a major effort, do you find it hard to get people to co-operate with you, do you feel you're banging your head against a brick wall, are you continually broke? Or are things flowing easily, does the path you are on feel relatively effortless, are magnificent and exciting opportunities opening up to you regularly, do you feel abundant?

If the answer to the last four questions is 'yes', all well and good, but if you are struggling that suggests a need to carry out further deep introspection.

If you are fighting an uphill battle it could be that you are on the wrong path – that your goal is not really heartfelt. You could try asking yourself, *'am I being honest with myself?'* which might shed some light on the matter for you.

Alternatively, it could be the right goal but the way you are going about it is not quite right. Maybe it's your attitude or self-limiting beliefs that are holding you up. For example, let's say your goal is to save enough money for a deposit to buy a house, but deep inside you have an unconscious belief that estate agents are rogues, banks and building societies are out to get you and any person who wants to sell their house is not to be trusted. In such a situation, even though you might want that house from deep in your heart – you don't need me to state the obvious but I'm going to anyway – you're going to have really, really hard time going against your flow!

Part of the art of getting into your *maximum creative flow* is to notice when your thinking is negative so you can put a positive thought into your mind instead.

Finally, don't forget the start of any new ambitious project, for example starting a business, is bound to be abnormally labour intensive, but that need not mean you can't flow. If you are doing what's right for you it is still possible to flow, even if you have to work hard in the initial stages.

Am I living effortlessly?

This is a very subtle matter and it's about non-doing. Let me put it this way – if you are making undue effort to achieve something or to get somewhere, you are not in your *maximum creative flow.* If you are not in your flow, then almost certainly you are not coming from your heart. If you insist on continuing your struggle in spite of making little progress, you are almost certainly coming from your ego. If you travel the path of placating your ego, you will never experience true and lasting fulfilment.

Let's unravel some of that: take the example of *I want to learn sailing.* Obviously in the early stages I am going to be making an enormous effort to acquire knowledge and master practical skills. I have to understand the workings of the tides, I have to learn coastal navigation, I have to absorb the rules and laws of the sea, I have to master boat handling, sail-setting, provisioning, first aid, safety, how the instruments work, and even how to make the coffee (believe me there's nothing more unpleasant than a stroppy skipper who didn't get his strong, hot cup of coffee when he goes on watch early in the morning), and so on.

Daunting as it may seem, the journey up that steep and complicated learning curve was an enjoyable and fascinating one for me because I have always wanted to sail for as long as I can remember, with a burning passion. The only way I could cope was to accept the requirement for intense work and learning in the early stages, and then to keep my eyes fixed firmly on the bigger picture while at the same time allowing my inner tortoise its full expression. In other words I took it step-by-step.

Of course I had many dark moments and there were many times when I wanted to give up. Under such circumstances, only the passion in your heart will make you persevere. It may not sound like living effortlessly, but eventually the flow starts to build and then everything you do comes naturally. Something coming from my heart drives me to want to go to sea. I don't know what it is or where it comes from, and I don't need to know. I just need to do it.

If you are doing something for which you have a gift, once you have learned how the game works and mastered the basics, raising your standards higher and higher becomes a joy rather than feeling like hard work. That's what I'm getting at when I talk about effortless living, or indeed, effortless achieving.

Do I feel fulfilled?

This is *the* definitive question and really it needs a 'yes' or 'no' answer.

Feeling moderately fulfilled, or somewhat fulfilled, even if that were possible, is absolutely not what we are aiming for. So be brutally honest with yourself. A miss is as good as a mile, so the saying goes, and we want the full monty, to gloriously mix our metaphors. Truth is, it may be necessary to try again to find your true path in your quest for happiness.

No matter, look at the skills you've learned and the tools you've acquired, appreciate the insight and understanding you have developed if you have partnered with me on this journey so far. Look how far you have come.

It may be only a matter of fine tuning, but even if you have to go right back to the drawing board and have another go, you're going to be in a far stronger position now. You will have a better grasp of the rules of the game (and no matter how seriously you might regard this, it is essentially a game) and there's no reason why you shouldn't play all out and enjoy the journey. Trust me, the guy who pointed out 'Rome wasn't built in a day' knew exactly what he was talking about. As they say in the field of property investment, 'you've got to be in it for the long-term.' I reckon I must have restarted my life at least six times before I could honestly answer 'yes, I feel utterly fulfilled' to this question.

If you do get a 'yes' answer, that doesn't mean you can sit on your laurels and expect everything to remain hunky-dory without any input from you. It's your responsibility to maintain your awareness as highly as possible, and to make sure you remain tuned in to your heart even after you have achieved your goals.

Hand on heart, am I happy right now?

Not tomorrow, not yesterday, but right now!

There's one final ingredient to consider and that's *this moment.* If you're saying 'today is rubbish but it'll be alright tomorrow because so and so will happen,' or 'yesterday was fun because such and such a thing happened but it didn't last,' you are missing the point. The point is we are aiming for our happiness to be ongoing, not just intermittent.

If you live your life fantasising about the future or worrying about the past, you are storing up trouble for yourself, for reasons we have already discussed at length. Now you know what I'm going to say. If the answer to the happiness question is in the affirmative, celebrate your joy and don't forget your maintenance. But if you're not happy you need to take a view and ask yourself what issues still need addressing, or addressing again. You can start again by meditating in silence some more, while simply being a witness.

Do not despair, you can start again as many times as you like.

Your amazing staying power

To conclude this section I want to congratulate you on your sterling work and amazing staying power in accompanying me on this journey of building your five pillars of happiness. I know the contents of this book require time, patience and courage to take on board, and that's why all the people I work with and all my readers are so courageous.

I'd love to wrap up this part of the book with one final quote from someone unknown to leave you feeling inspired: 'the happiest people don't *have* the best of everything; they *make* the best of everything.'

Please don't hide your light under a bushel, don't do yourself down. Reach out and grasp your magnificence, decide what you want and go for it with no-holds-barred. Allow this book to support you on your journey. That's what it's designed to do. And please, if you require further support, don't hesitate to use the resources you will find on the following websites:

www.thefivepillarsofhapppiness.com
www.daverobsoncoaching.com
www.dave-robson.co.uk

Summary

- When you write your name on your *Wheel of Life*, you take ownership of the information you enter, and assume responsibility for what is revealed and what changes you want to make
- The *Wheel of Life* is a valuable tool for diagnosing where to put your attention in sorting out your life, for self-monitoring and in the fine tuning process
- Put your name and the date on your Wheel every time you do this exercise
- Decide if any new segments need to be added to your current Wheel, or if any need to be deleted

- You can also draw up specialised *Wheels of Life* where one aspect of your life is subdivided into eight, ten or twelve segments for deeper scrutiny
- The *Wheel of Life* will help you evaluate your progress
- You could discover you're actually moving away from your goal, or not moving at all, in which case immediate further investigation is called for
- Continually raising your awareness has to a lifelong habit by now
- It's easy to achieve meaningful, heartfelt goals if you have the courage and patience to first enquire deeply within to know what they are
- Achievements designed to please someone else simply won't cut it
- *Only goals that come from your heart will give you a profound sense of meaning and purpose*
- If you want to listen to the voice of your heart but you're having trouble getting tuned in, be still and silent for a while, and just witness
- If by now you don't feel fully alive you're probably on the wrong track
- The joy of aliveness comes when you create something that has meaning for you, and when you move nearer to a heartfelt goal
- Decide what your passion is, and your talent or gift, and find the courage to go for it. Don't let anything stop you, including yourself!
- If things are going really well for you, all well and good, but if you are struggling that suggests a need to carry out further deep introspection
- If the going feels tough perhaps you are on the wrong path – maybe your goal is not really heartfelt. Ask yourself, 'am I being honest with myself?'
- Alternatively, it could be the right goal but your attitude or a self-limiting belief is causing your problem
- Part of getting into your *maximum creative flow* is to notice when your thinking is negative so you can put a positive thought into your mind instead
- Effortless living is a very subtle matter and it's about non-doing
- If you travel the path of placating your ego, you will never experience true and lasting fulfilment

- When you pursue heartfelt goals, your heart will keep you motivated until you feel equal to the challenge and then get on top of it. Then you can relax, go with the flow and enjoy feeling fulfilled
- If you are doing something for which you have a gift, once you have learned the basics, raising your standard becomes a joy rather than hard work
- Feeling moderately fulfilled, or somewhat fulfilled, even if that were possible, is absolutely not what we are aiming for, so be brutally honest with yourself
- It may be only a matter of fine tuning, but even if you have to have another go, there's no reason why you shouldn't play all out and enjoy the journey as you try again in a different way
- If you do get a 'yes' answer to feeling fulfilled, that doesn't mean you can expect everything to remain hunky-dory without any input from you
- It's your responsibility to maintain your awareness, and to make sure you remain tuned in to your heart even after you have achieved your goals
- If you live your life fantasising about the future or worrying about the past, you are storing up trouble for yourself
- If you're not happy you need to take a view and ask yourself what issues still need addressing, or addressing again
- You can start again by meditating in silence while simply witnessing
- Don't do yourself down. Reach out and grasp your magnificence, decide what you want and go for it with no-holds-barred
- Allow this book to support you on your journey. That's what it's designed to do
- Make full use of the resources you will find on our websites, listed above. You can download and print blank *Wheel of Life* forms from this book's website, www.thefivepillarsofhappiness.com

Final questions

- Am I sure I'm coming from my heart?
- Do I feel fully alive?
- Am I living effortlessly?

- Am I in my *maximum creative flow*?
- Do I feel fulfilled?
- Hand on heart, am I happy right now?
- Am I being honest with myself?

PART THREE

Beyond Goals

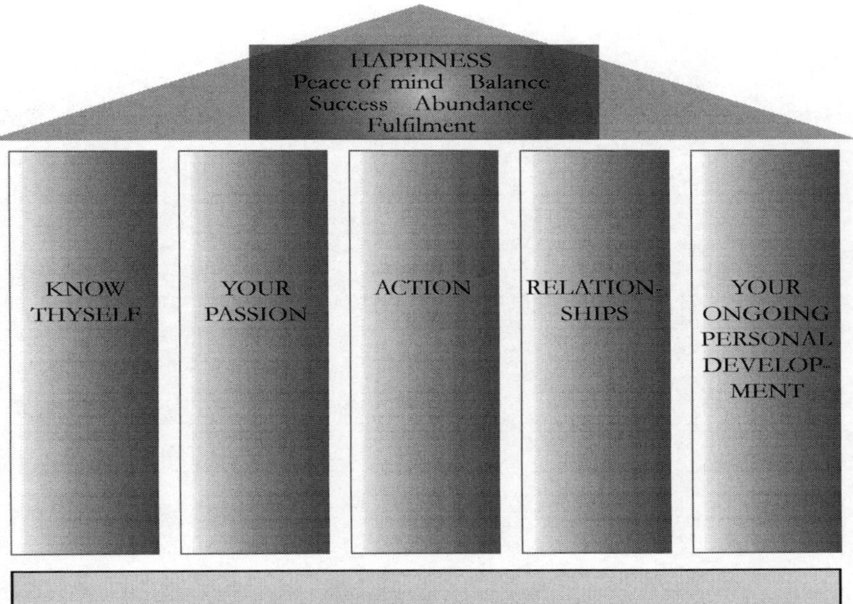

For those of you who want to take the ultimate step beyond happiness, beyond pain and beyond our normal perceptions to a state of continual consciousness and acceptance in which the diamond which is the original you is liberated to shine forth, this last chapter is for you.

Here I want to share a few of the more notable experiences I have encountered in the presence of various enlightened masters, teachers of conscious awakening and other key people in my life, as well as some lightbulb moments I've had along the way. Some I have mentioned already, others I have not. I hope you'll find this an interesting postscript and that it will further inspire you to take up your true path.

36

Shine Like a Diamond

Witness that you are not the body. Witness that you are not the mind. Witness that you are only a witness. As the witnessing deepens, you start becoming drunk with the divine. That is what is called ecstasy

Osho

The iron fist in the velvet glove

When I came home from America in 1982 after the First Annual World Celebration at Rajneeshpuram, Osho's erstwhile ashram in Oregon, most of my 'friends' told me I'd been brainwashed. The celebration was a festive gathering of Osho's Sannyasins (disciples) and friends from all over the globe.

I told them I hoped I had indeed been brainwashed because I'd been so depressed and in despair before I went, I felt my brain was urgently in need of washing. At the time I wished I could be reborn and start my life again, and in effect taking Sannyas (becoming a disciple), which what I did during the festival, enabled me to do exactly that, in a symbolic sense.

Then they said Osho was after my money and that was all he wanted, to which I replied he'd come to the wrong person in that case because I was stony broke and any cash I managed to lay my hands on would soon end up in the vaults of the bank to whom I was indebted. You see, I had nothing to fear and I knew it, because I had nothing to lose and all to gain. My life couldn't possibly have got any worse.

Perhaps my so-called friends and acquaintances found it strange that I should get involved with a guru because they knew how completely disinterested in religion I was (and still am). Their mistake was to assume this was a religious-based ideology, which it most certainly wasn't. That was the whole point. Nor were we expected to idol-worship the guru or put him on a pedestal, otherwise I would have run a mile. It was a simple relationship between the master and his disciples, *'a love affair'* in which all parties treated each other with respect and acceptance.

I was very clear in that *I was interested only in the teachings,* not the hierarchy or politics of Osho's organisation. I wanted the kinship of fellow spiritual soul searchers, I wanted wisdom and guidance from somebody who knew what he was talking about, I wanted to understand why I had made such a mess of my life and to find out how to put it right. I did not want to be told what to do, to be controlled or manipulated, to let someone else do my thinking for me or to tell me how I should behave. Most of all I didn't want dogma.

You may remember how, in earlier chapters, I described my early 'careers' in the dog-eat-dog worlds of advertising and public relations. Imagine then how I felt when finding myself catapulted from the abject misery of a failing marriage and a working life I despised into an environment in which I felt unconditionally loved and accepted, no questions asked, from the moment I stepped through the front gateway. That's what happened when I arrived for the first time at Rajneeshpuram, deep in the Oregon countryside.

It was then that I actually experienced that the only thing that matters in life, that counts for value in this world and that heals, is unconditional love and acceptance. Everything else is just a part of the game of life and not to be taken too seriously. In the Hindu tradition, the ups and downs of life are known as *'god's leela'* (god's play).

One of Osho's most important teachings was that each person must take responsibility for himself, his feelings, thoughts and behaviour, and everything he manifests in his life. The wholly integrated person never idolises or venerates any authority figures – rather he meets them on equal terms because he believes wholeheartedly in his own validity. 'Don't look at my finger, look where I'm pointing!' Osho used to say.

I tried to explain to my friends back home that Osho wasn't saying anything new that I didn't know already, and that's why it was obvious to me he spoke the truth. His wisdom and guidance gave me the confidence, at a very wobbly time in my life, to believe in myself and what I already knew to be true, and to begin to make sense of it all.

Osho certainly lived up to his avowed intention of turning my life upside down and shaking me to the roots. I'm so grateful, for that's exactly what I needed, a complete re-evaluation of my life and a total re-invention of myself.

Any enlightened master worth his or her salt will take any and every opportunity to give you the most powerful wake-up call he can, and to that extent Osho was well capable of administering the metaphorical *Zen Stick* with force and alacrity. That was why I called him the 'iron fist in the velvet glove'.

I realise this sort of thing is not everyone's cup of tea and if you're not up for it, best keep well away. For me, it was a case of *feel the fear and do it anyway.* Although I was terrified, I actually wanted my life to be turned upside down. The moment I got involved with Osho I knew somehow that my life, as it was then, would be radically shaken up but I had no idea how. I knew I would have to rebuild it differently, but again I had no idea how.

I needed a root and branch transformation and that's exactly what I got. Some gifts are pretty hard to take, but this one opened a door towards happiness, fulfilment, achievement, peace, balance and abundance for me. Sometimes I feel a little sad I no longer feel much kinship with most of those people I used to know before I met Osho, for I had to leave them behind together with my own turmoil and confusion.

For more information visit: www.osho.com

The freedom this moment gives you

Around the time I got involved with Osho was also the time I took up sailing, which as I have said is an activity that has become like another form of meditation to me. That's because sailing helps me to be in the moment.

Learning to sail has literally been, and still is, a voyage of self-discovery, a process that has really shown me what I'm made of deep inside. It is an activity that has caused me to believe deeply in myself and to have utter faith in my abilities to achieve anything if my heart is set on it. Sailing allows me a channel for my creative streak, but most important, when I go sailing I am totally in the moment for almost all of the time, and that translates as nothing short of an experience of true, blissful real life. That's why I think of it as a meditation.

When I talk about being in the moment, I'm talking about what Eckhart Tolle calls *the power of now.* I had never realised, until I read Tolle that only the present moment is real, because the past and future don't exist. The importance of understanding this cannot be overstated, because if you say, for example, 'I had a very unhappy childhood,' you will now realise it's no longer your reality. It exists only as a memory and a memory is a thought and a thought is a construct of your mind. Therefore you can acknowledge that it was real once but is no longer so, and you can let it go.

To put it another way, if you decide, as an adult, to hang onto the suffering you experienced as a child, you punish yourself with a memory of something that is no longer real. Once you realise and acknowledge it's no longer real, you can let it go. This is the massive importance of Tolle's teaching: *you can end your suffering right now.*

When you live in the now, as Tolle points out, you will notice that all you so-called 'problems' disappear, which indicates they were also mere constructs of your mind, and therefore not real. That's why living in the now is the ultimate liberation. You are no longer bothered by mental constructs of the past.

Sailing can do that for you, but it doesn't have to be sailing, it could be hiking, mountaineering, karate, badminton, rugby, music, genealogy, basket weaving, reading, writing, or simply sitting in silence – anything you care to mention as long as it's something you love doing that absorbs you whole attention. If you know of a multi-dimensional sport or recreational activity that strongly appeals to you, I urge you to pursue it as actively as possible as part of your personal development programme. Find the best possible teachers and tackle the challenges that are presented to you. If you do that and eventually master the knowledge and skills required, you'll feel like a million dollars!

Katy and goodbye to co-dependency

Katy (not her real name) was the woman who taught me about co-dependency, one of the most important insights any of us can have into the happy and successful conduct of intimate relationships. Until she told me about it, I had never heard of co-dependency, scary considering what an important matter it is.

Co-dependency is a pattern of behaviour in which one or both partners in a relationship feel psychologically or emotionally dependent on the other for their emotional and sometimes physical survival. It is a potentially devastating state of affairs, for if one partner moves on, dies or is unfaithful, the other is distraught, perhaps even emotionally crippled, and in extreme cases unable to cope.

Without going into too much detail, this is a manifestation in adult life of the existential terror a baby suffers when he or she unconsciously fears that whatever is needed for his or her survival will not be supplied by the mother and/or father, and therefore his or her very existence feels threatened. The book Katy gave me to read, which I mentioned earlier in Chapter 26, explains this in detail. It was *Women Who Love Too Much*, by Robin Norwood. I shall be forever grateful to Katy and Robin Norwood for the gift of understanding this crucial matter.

It's important because if two adults want to relate successfully, each must take responsibility for his or her own wellbeing – depending on the other simply won't work. The behaviour of the Impeccable Warrior is also impossible if you are being unconsciously driven by co-dependency. By the same token the co-dependent person can never feel free to be 100 per cent who he or she is. You can never live comfortably with yourself, and neither can anyone else live comfortably with you, unless they want to be co-dependent too.

Don't let co-dependency ruin your life. If you suspect it might be one of your patterns, read Robin Norwood's book. It might help you get over it.

Brandon Bays and a voyage of self-discovery

Luckily for me I've been an avid bookworm since the age of eleven, and as an indirect result of that it was in the mid 1990s that I discovered the remarkable Brandon Bays. She and her work came to my attention though her then newly published book, *The Journey*.

I've mentioned Brandon and her work earlier in this book and I don't propose to repeat myself. I just want to share one or two experiences of doing her *Journey Intensive* weekend workshop in London a year or two after reading the book. It may well prove helpful to some of you, especially if you like teachers who walk their walk and talk their talk, as the saying goes.

Brandon Bays has certainly done that. In 1992, when working as a trainer with personal development guru Anthony Robbins, Brandon discovered she had a tumour the size of a football in her stomach.

While she was teaching herself how to heal from this (she wanted to avoid surgery and drugs at all costs), was hit with every type of challenge you could imagine. First her daughter told her she didn't want anything more to do with her, then her husband left her for another woman, the Internal Revenue Service in America started pursuing her for alleged unpaid taxes, and finally her house in Malibu was burnt to the ground. It was uninsured.

When Brandon described this series of events as 'a gift from god' I remember thinking either she's barking mad or she has something immensely valuable to share. When I discovered she had translated her *Journeywork* into a weekend workshop format to be conducted by the woman herself, and that she was bringing it to London, I jumped at the chance to find out.

Suffice to say that by halfway through the Sunday I experienced a tremendous emotional release that was worth its weight in gold. When it happened it didn't seem like such an Earth shattering event. The effect was quite subtle really, it gradually grew on me. It was only after a couple of hours and on into the next few days that the enormous significance of what had happened revealed itself to me. I had certainly let go of some huge emotional baggage and I felt liberated and as light as a feather.

What came as a major surprise was that when it happened that Sunday afternoon, I couldn't stop laughing. I was reminded of the laughing Buddha, who fell about in mirth when he became enlightened. What was I laughing about? I certainly hadn't become enlightened. Well, certainly tears of happiness burned their way down my cheeks from the sheer joy of the release, but really I was laughing at what seemed to be the absurdity of it all. What I mean is, most of us spend our lives tying ourselves up in knots and getting stuck in all kinds of dysfunctionality and misery because of our fears, resistance, egotistical hopes, denial, and all our other unconscious behaviour that makes us anxious, stressed and in turmoil. When I finally let go of that resistance, my former behaviour of the sort described above seemed to me nothing other than absurd. This was *'god's leela'* (god's play) in action and I could see how we merely play a game as we pass through life. Yet we get so hung up about it all! We take ourselves so damn seriously! How futile is that?

Life certainly seemed like a cosmic joke all of sudden, and I understood Osho's phrase, *'drunk with the divine.'* It was an euphoric feeling indeed, but best of all, *where was god?* He was nowhere, he was not necessary because I realised I contained the entire world and everything I needed within myself, just as we all do. Without meaning to sound arrogant, I felt vindicated absolutely in my belief that we already have everything we need to be happy and fulfilled and the place to look is not out there in the material world, nor in the heavens in search of god, *but within.*

You are complete – you don't need anything or anyone else, and you don't need to invent god. Now ain't that a miracle, and a mystery indeed?

For more information visit: www.thejourney.com

'I don't care about your story ...'

As I mentioned in the fifth pillar, the section about ongoing support, there is now a sizeable number of enlightened or spiritually awakened teachers or guides who share their energy via *Satsangs,* meetings and retreats in many countries and continents, and many of whom write books. If you want to hear them speak in the quiet of your own home, you can find most of them in video format on YouTube and virtually all have websites. Such people can contribute something of immense value to your life, and their material is out there just waiting for you.

However, there's no substitute for a personal encounter, so I thought it might be interesting to recount a few experiences I've had in the presence of three such people, starting with Catherine Ingram. By the way, you can check the websites you'll find listed in this chapter to see when your preferred awakened teacher is visiting a city or a country retreat near you, or to order whatever material they offer. When one of these beings is going to be somewhere near you, I strongly recommend you get yourself down there.

It's hard not to fall in love with Catherine Ingram, and anyway, why resist? She is a delightful, down-to-Earth sincere woman and she's absolutely radiant. You can always tell a genuine and sincerely awakened teacher because they simply radiate.

Catherine was a Buddhist for some twenty years until finally, feeling she could not continue, she gave up her practice. Somehow after about two years she came upon the Guru Poonjaji and he became her teacher. Just by being in his intense awakened presence, Catherine also awakened. Interestingly, reports say he didn't teach her anything, he simply told her she was already free.

Although she has been holding what she calls *'Dharma Dialogues'* and retreats around the world since her awakening some years ago, her most significant teaching is now distilled into her book *Passionate Presence.* It's about the seven qualities of awakened awareness, which Catherine tells us are *silence, tenderness, embodiment, genuineness, wonder, discernment* and *delight.*

Catherine also explains we all have these qualities within ourselves already, so there is nothing we need to achieve. It's more a matter of letting go, relaxing, and easing our way into our own very alive, passionate and loving presence. I myself have noticed, having been to many Satsangs, if you ask a lot of questions you might get a few unsatisfactory answers, but if you sit in silence for long enough, eventually all your questions will disappear.

I already alluded to this teaching of Catherine's but it's worth mentioning again briefly, it was during one such meeting with her that she helped me realise your life story is irrelevant, because it's not who you are. For example you might describe yourself as someone from a broken home who was adopted or fostered, who got into petty crime, who spent time in jail, who got married and also ended up divorced, and so on. Every person has a story and more often than not it's a hard luck story, but that story does not define who you are or what you can be. *It certainly can't stop you from shining like a diamond* if you get it into your head, or more importantly your heart, to rediscover and rekindle your inner light.

The world is littered with examples of people who had the vision to break away from their stories to fulfil themselves. Only recently I saw Sir Alan Sugar on the television. He grew up in a deprived neighbourhood in London's East End with hardly two pennies to rub together, he started selling in his local market from a barrow, discovered an innate talent for selling and business and eventually grew a multi-million pound business empire. The Beatles, another example, grew up in a working class Liverpool environment and went on to become arguably the most successful band the world has ever known. There is a very long and growing list of people who have transcended a difficult story to excel at giving their gift.

I emphasise this because I want to give you one last shot of inspiration to find the courage to be happy by actualising your amazing potential and living a life of meaning and purpose, whatever your background. Please don't let your story be an excuse for giving up or feeling powerless, hopeless and helpless.

For more information visit: www.catherineingram.com

Frustration then understanding – Satsang with Tony Parsons

Tony Parsons, also mentioned earlier as another awakened teacher who holds Satsangs and retreats in various parts of the UK, has a wicked yet compassionate sense of humour and if anyone can encourage you not to take yourself too seriously, he can. If you want a flavour of what he's talking about you can read his book, *The Open Secret*, and check his website too.

If, like me, you have a tendency to try to follow conversations and make sense of them on an intellectual level, you will probably find that attending a Satsang with Tony is an infuriating and frustrating experience. Yet it's fascinating at the same time, and that's what stopped me walking out in a state of high dudgeon the first time I went to one of his meetings.

Then something happened the second time (yes, amazingly there was a second time. I must have been strongly thirsting for something). After a while of listening and following, I simply gave up and just allowed his presence and that of the other people at the meeting to wash over me, and that felt better. I felt much relieved when I finally realised I didn't have to 'understand' anything, or rather whether I understood or not didn't matter. Tony Parsons is possibly unique in that he offers the seeker absolutely nothing at all.

If you are wondering what on Earth I'm talking about, allow me to quote a few short extracts I found recently on Tony's website and maybe you'll see what I mean:

> *'There's no such thing as an enlightened person. It's a complete misconception. But the difficulty is that being seekers, the energy of seeking pushes us into being attracted to the idea that somebody else has found something that we can find, because we grow up believing that effort brings results. So, if effort brings results, and we've heard of something called enlightenment or liberation, we can make the effort and then we can become liberated or enlightened ... like this guy up the road we've heard about, or that woman that's giving Satsangs. They have got something that I want. If I go there I will learn how to get it.'*

Again, it's the story of the Buddha sitting under his Bhodi tree. There is nothing for us to find for nothing has ever been lost. We already have the treasure we seek, in fact we *are* the treasure. Therefore all effort is futile. When the Buddha gave up his search and sat under the tree in deep meditation, he realised he was enlightened and always had been, just as we all are but most of us don't realise it.

This is an important teaching because it empowers us to relax, chill out and enjoy this wonderful existence we call life – if only we will take it in board!

When you visit this kind of a teacher, even if you haven't a clue what he or she is on about, something can sink in. Something obviously sunk in when I went to Tony Parsons' Satsang because that was when I started to give myself full permission to pursue the things I loved doing the most without fretting or feeling guilty because I 'should' be doing something 'more worthy or meaningful.'

I actually began to stop judging or censuring myself and strangely I began to notice feelings of satisfaction and fulfilment coming up rather than the guilt I had anticipated, but not because I was seeking the 'noble goal of enlightenment.' I realised it was because *I was doing things I loved doing just because I love doing them.* A subtle difference but the effect was revolutionary and very liberating.

Consider this parting shot, once again from Tony's website:

> *'This is not a message about you or me or anyone getting anything. This is about the realisation that there's nothing to get … that what has been sought has never been lost.'*

> *'The very intention to seek for a mythical treasure within life inevitably obscures the reality that life is already the treasure.'*

For more information visit: www.theopensecret.com

Had any really good failures lately?

I have already discussed Satyananda's suggestion that we allow ourselves to fail with grace, dignity and acceptance. I wanted to give Satyananda one more mention here because if one of your goals is inner peace, I believe it will be very much in your interests to pay attention to this man's teaching. Just to recap, Satyananda is the amiable and amusing awakened teacher from Uruguay whose Satsang I visited in London around 2008. At the time of writing, he spends his time giving Satsangs and retreats in Bristol and Cornwall, and other places too. You can find his schedule on his website.

Since my bemusing encounter with Satyananda I have thought deeply about this notion of allowing oneself to fail and I've experimented with it at length, until eventually this very liberating realisation came over me. *If you do what you love, the concept of failure simply does not arise because you are not trying to achieve anything in the conventional sense, you are merely expressing yourself and conducting your life as if it was an experiment.*

For example, you set up a business in a field you feel passionate about, but it doesn't work. So you relaunch your enterprise using a different business model to see what happens. You may do this many times, experimenting until you find a formula that works for you. Instead of seeing that as a series of failures leading ultimately to success, you could take the view that you were simply experimenting and learning until you learned what you needed to know. This is a very empowering and motivational way of looking at it.

However, if you aim for success in something that doesn't really come from your heart, or if you are being a control freak or a perfectionist, insisting on 'success' the first time you try, you may well set yourself up for 'failure,' or at least the possibility of 'failure.' You will also introduce a lot of stress into your life.

What exactly does that mean? I hope you will indulge me if I explain by briefly visiting another Mozart example, because it illustrates the point so perfectly.

The story of Mozart and Salieri as depicted in the movie *Amadeus* offers an important teaching, and whether it be founded on truth or not is of no importance in this context. The teaching is all that matters.

Antonio Salieri was the Court Composer to Emperor Joseph II of Austria, and later the Royal and Imperial Kapellmeister, and he held various other top musical posts as his career progressed. Salieri was well respected among the eighteenth century musical elite of Vienna and achieved elevated social standing. He was a teacher to many famous composers, including Ludwig van Beethoven, Franz Liszt, Franz Schubert and others.

By all accounts he was very good at what he did and I daresay he would have continued to work happily in his various musical roles *if only he had concentrated on the path he was talented for*. Instead, he took his eye off the ball, allowing himself to become sidetracked, when a young upstart came to town, one Wolfgang Amadeus Mozart, a young, precocious and irrepressible musical genius. Salieri became jealous of the young man's undoubted musical gifts and he also started feeling insecure about his own position, trying to outshine Mozart and show him up to be an idiot.

You probably know the unfortunate outcome. There could only ever be one Mozart, and trying to outdo him or even imitate him was obviously going to be a complete hiding to nothing for Salieri. It was inevitable it would end in tears. In the end the deceit he played on Mozart sent the young composer crazy. He fell ill and died, while Salieri, full of remorse, tried to end his own life and was taken to a sanatorium.

Here's the point: there could also only ever be one Salieri. If only Salieri had realised he, like every one of us, was a perfectly valid person in his own right and that he, like every one of us, had his own valuable and unique gift to contribute, he could have got over his disappointment and realised it was unnecessary and fruitless to try to imitate someone else, or to bring him down – before it was too late. As it was, sadly Salieri referred to himself at the end of the film as 'the patron saint of mediocrity.'

Let's now relate this tale to the teachings of Satyananda. If Salieri had allowed himself to 'fail' at being Mozart, which was inevitable, he could have cleared the way for himself to be successful at being Salieri, also inevitable if he had stuck to it. His insistence on clinging obsessively to this futile vanity of trying to outshine Mozart or knock him off his perch, fuelled unconsciously by his strongly conditioned ego, led him instead to insanity.

Satyananda speaks of inner peace and according to his website, he offers his life in the service of peace. Many people, myself included, are inspired to cultivate his liberating insight in their own lives. You can be one of them.

For more information visit: www.satyananda.org

Unconditional love and acceptance – very nice!

It seems only right that the last words should be about my beloved partner Rachella, and our relationship. After all, the lessons I learn from her are ongoing.

Shortly before I met Rachella in 1995 I had finally reached the point where I understood the value of a suitable partner, and I started the 'wish list' exercise for getting clear about what I wanted in a relationship. Apart from wanting a sailing companion, as I have already mentioned, I wanted someone I could talk to about the major life issues I raise in this chapter and throughout this book, someone who would be a great mirror and someone who would help me grow in every way. And what did I get? A psychotherapist!

At the time we met, Rachella was doing a full-time 'day job' for a well known multinational company, and in her spare time she was studying to be a psychotherapist and seeing a few clients. Though she enjoyed her job and she was good at it, to me it was obvious where her passions and her talents lay. When the time came for her to retire from her career, she went full-time into being a psychotherapist.

The flowering of her creative side since that time has been a joy to behold. First she finished the thesis that had been hanging over her head for years and received a distinction; then, fully qualified as a Psychosynthesis Psychotherapist, she started writing a novel which I'm sure will be finished soon; after that she started painting again on holiday in Scotland; then she resumed her life-long passion for photography; then she went to Canada to do a training in Couples Counselling, finally when she came home she created her new website for Couples Counselling. At the same time she started attracting new psychotherapy clients like a magnet.

There's no doubt Rachella experiences deep fulfilment from helping her clients, who absolutely adore her, I'm sure. Having to retire gave her the spur she needed to take the risk of changing horses. Now she does what she loves and loves what she does and because of that new doors open for her every day.

The effect on me of witnessing this phenomenal change in her was to give me increased confidence in my *'do what you love …'* theory, and in my ability to do good work in reflecting back what I see in my clients as their passions begin to reveal themselves.

There have been many other benefits and things to learn or understand too, and this experience has proven to me that when you find your suitable partner, all kinds of doors open as time goes by, and literally there's never a dull moment. I'm not going to go into personal details save to say since those early days when I set about confronting my issues one at a time, I've had really strong lessons in acceptance, boundaries, facing reality, synergy, intimacy, the meaning of love, generosity, abundance, sincerity, meaning, purpose and having fun - to name but a few.

With reference to relationships, it has become abundantly clear to me that the behaviour of the Impeccable Warrior, in other words always being true to yourself within your relationship, is of paramount importance, even when it's hard or scary or there's a price to pay. That means sticking to your true path. When you are both true to yourselves not only does accepting each other have real meaning, but you are also able to more easily accept yourself.

If you are still wondering if it's possible for you to have a sustainable, joyful relationship with a partner, let me reiterate one more time my three golden rules that make it possible:

- find a suitable partner
- stick to the behaviour of the Impeccable Warrior
- from time to time stop, be still and silent, and be guided by your heart

Refer back to the Fourth Pillar, the section devoted to relationships, to remind yourself about finding out who is a suitable partner for you. This will get you off to a good start, and one that stands a chance of having a future. The second rule will keep you on track, even through the hard times.

Listening to your heart, which of course is part and parcel of Impeccable Warrior behaviour, enables you to know whether you are happy or whether you need to make adjustments, speak your mind, clear the air, resolve issues or whatever. Ask yourself, *'how do I feel about this.'*

Finally…

Finally, if you want to shine like the diamond you already are, I invite you to consider the insightful comment made by Paul McCartney at the end of the famous 1969 Beatles album, *Abbey Road*:

> *'And in the end, the love you take*
> *is equal to the love … YOU MAKE …!'*

It's just another way of saying *do what you love, love what you do.*

Resources

For more resources, comment and insight into the material covered in this book, please feel free to visit the following websites:

www.thefivepillarsofhappiness.com
www.daverobsoncoaching.com
www.dave-robson.co.uk

You can also subscribe to my monthly e-newsletter, *Namaste*, absolutely free by dropping an e-mail stating *Namaste* in the subject line, with your name and e-mail address to: info@daverobsoncoaching.com

Summary

- Osho offered a simple relationship between the master and his disciples, *'a love affair,'* in which both parties treated each other with respect and acceptance
- At Rajneeshpuram I entered an environment in which I felt unconditionally loved and accepted, with no questions asked
- The only thing that matters in life, the only thing that counts for value in this world, and the only thing that heals, is unconditional love and acceptance
- Osho taught that each person must take responsibility for himself, his feelings, thoughts and behaviour, and everything he manifests in his life
- Being around an enlightened master is a dangerous place to be because his intention is to turn your life upside down and shake you to the roots
- My experience with Osho opened doors to happiness, fulfilment, achievement, peace, balance and abundance. I began to leave behind my turmoil and confusion
- The past exists only as a memory, a memory is a thought and a thought is a construct of your mind. Acknowledge it was real once but is no longer, and you can let it go
- *You can end your suffering right now*
- When you live in the now, all you so-called 'problems' disappear, which indicates they were constructs of your mind, and therefore not real

- If you know of a sport or recreational activity that strongly appeals to you, find the best possible teachers and tackle the challenges it presents
- Co-dependency is a potentially devastating state of affairs. If one partner moves on, dies or is unfaithful, the other is distraught, perhaps even emotionally crippled, and in extreme cases unable to cope
- Co-dependency is a manifestation in adult life of the existential terror babies unconsciously suffer when they fear that their mother or father will not supply their needs for survival. Your very existence feels threatened
- If two adults want to relate successfully, each must take responsibility for his or her own wellbeing – depending on the other simply won't work
- The behaviour of the Impeccable Warrior is impossible if you are being unconsciously driven by co-dependency
- The co-dependent person can never feel free to be 100 per cent who he or she is. They can never live comfortably with themselves; neither can anyone else live comfortably with them, unless they are co-dependent too
- The sheer joy of the release I experienced during *The Journey* weekend workshop made me laugh at the absurdity of it all
- We merely play a game as we pass through life. Yet we get so hung up about it all! We take ourselves so damn seriously! How futile is that?
- We already have everything we need to be happy and fulfilled. The place to look is not in the material world, nor in a search for god, *but within*
- *You are complete – you don't need anything or anyone else, and you don't need to invent god*
- Guru Poonjaji, Catherine Ingram's teacher, reportedly didn't teach her anything, he simply told her she was already free
- There is nothing we need to achieve. It's more a matter of letting go, relaxing, and easing our way into our own very alive, passionate and loving presence
- If you ask a lot of questions you might get a few unsatisfactory answers, but if you sit in silence, eventually all your questions will disappear

- Every person has a story and more often than not it's a hard luck story, but that story does not define who you are or what you can be
- *Your story can't stop you from shining like a diamond* if you get it into your head, or perhaps your heart, to rediscover and rekindle your inner light
- Tony Parsons is possibly unique in that he offers the seeker absolutely nothing at all. That's because there's nothing to 'get'
- There is nothing for us to find for nothing has ever been lost. We already have the treasure we seek, in fact we *are* the treasure. Therefore all effort is futile
- When I stopped judging myself for doing what I love, I experienced feelings of satisfaction and fulfilment rather than guilt. It was because *I was doing things I loved doing – just because I love doing them.* The effect was liberating
- If one of your goals is inner peace, pay attention to Satyananda's teachings
- If you do what you love, the concept of failure does not arise because you are not trying to achieve anything; you are merely expressing yourself and conducting your life as if it was an experiment
- If you realise that the goal you have been aiming at comes from your ego and not from your heart, best to let it go immediately even if you succeed
- If Salieri had allowed himself to fail at being Mozart, he would have cleared they way for himself to be fulfilled in being Salieri
- Rachella took the risk of changing horses. Now she does what she loves and loves what she does and because of that, new doors open for her every day
- Finding a suitable partner has given me strong lessons in acceptance, boundaries, facing reality, synergy, intimacy, the meaning of love, generosity, abundance, sincerity, meaning, purpose, and having fun
- Being true to yourself within any relationship is of paramount importance, even when it's hard or scary or there's a price to pay
- When both partners are true to themselves not only does accepting each other have real meaning, but you are also more easily able to accept *yourself*

- My three golden rules that make it possible to have a sustainable, joyful relationship with your partner:
    1) find a suitable partner
    2) stick to the behaviour of the Impeccable Warrior
    3) from time to time stop, be still and silent, and be guided by your heart

Further support and resources are available. Please feel free to visit:

www.thefivepillarsofhappiness.com
www.daverobsoncoaching.com
www.dave-robson.co.uk

Bibliography and list of Useful Websites

A list, organised as far as possible in chapter order, of the authors, books and websites mentioned in the text

Chapter	Author	Book Title & Website
Chapter 1	Dr Phil McGraw	*Life Strategies* *www.drphil.com*
	Osho	The Orange Book (and many other books) www.osho.com & www.osho.co.uk
Chapter 2	Catherine Ingram	*Passionate Presence* www.catherineingram.com
	Prem Rawat	www.man-of-peace.com
	Susan Jeffers	*Feel the Fear and Do It Anyway* www.susanjeffers.com
Chapter 3	William Shakespeare	*Hamlet*
	Carlos Castaneda	*The Teachings of Don Juan, a Yaqui Way of Knowledge*
Chapter 4	Brandon Bays	*The Journey* www.thejourney.com
	James Allen	*As A Man Thinketh*
	Robert Kiyosaki	*Rich Dad, Poor Dad* www.richdad.com
	Ingrid Bacci	*The Joy Of Effortless Living* www.ingridbacci.com
Chapter 5	Bill Harris, Centrepointe Institute	www.centrepointe.com
Chapter 8	Satyananda	www.satyananda.org
Chapter 9	Dr. John Demartini	www.drdematini.com
Chapter 12	Christopher Howard	www.chrishoward.com

Chapter	Author	Book Title & Website
Chapter 14	Aum Meditation	www.aumeditation.icom43.net
	Osho Humaniversity	www.humaniversity.nl
	Osho Leela	www.osholeela.co.uk
Chapter 15	Dr. Wayne Dyer	*You'll See It When You Believe It* www.drwaynedyer.com
Chapter 16	Eckhart Tolle	*The Power of Now* www.eckharttolle.com
Chapter 17	Brian Mayne	*Goal Mapping* www.liftinternational.com
Chapter 20	Paul McKenna	*I Can Make You Thin* www.paulmckenna.com
	Leslie Kenton	*Raw Energy Food Combining Diet* www.lesliekenton.com
	Deepak Chopra	*Perfect Weight* www.chopra.com
	Stephen Covey	*The Seven Habits of Highly Effective People* www.stephencovey.com
Chapter 21	Richard Branson	*Losing my Virginity. The Autobiography* www.virgin.com
Chapter 24	John C. Maxwell	*Developing The Leader Within You* www.johnmaxwell.com
Chapter 25	Napoleon Hill	*Think and Grow Rich* www.naphill.org
Chapter 26	Robin Norwood	*Women Who Love Too Much*
Chapter 27	John Gray	*Men are from Mars, Women are from Venus* www.marsvenus.com
Chapter 28	Jack Kornfield	*A Path With Heart* www.jackkornfield.org
	M. Scott Peck	*The Road Less Travelled* www.mscottpeck.com
Chapter 29	Mallanaga Vatsyayana	*The Kama Sutra*
Chapter 30	Aesop	*The Tortoise and the Hare*

Chapter	Author	Book Title & Website
Chapter 31	Fu Xi (Originator)	*I Ching (Book of Changes)*
	Ovid	*Daedalus and Icarus* (from Metamorphoses Book VIII)
Chapter 33	Miten and Deva Premal	*Dakshina* (CD of meditation music) www.mitendevapremal.com
Chapter 34	Victor Frankl	*Man's Search For Meaning*
Chapter 36	Tony Parsons	*The Open Secret* www.theopensecret.com
	The Beatles	*Abbey Road* www.thebeatles.com

Further information and resources on the work highlighted in The Five Pillars of Happiness can be found on the following websites:

Dave Robson's web site details:

www.thefivepillarsofhappiness.com
www.daverobsoncoaching.co.uk
www.dave-robson.co.uk
www.penandinkclub.com

Additionally, Dave's Blog and Twitter details are:

http://lifeloveandlaundry.wordpress.com
http://twitter.com/DaveRobson